Bills of Rights Before the Bill of Rights

"Scholars of American constitutionalism and political thought have long needed and will benefit a great deal from this comprehensive analysis of the original state bills of rights. In *Bills of Rights Before the Bill of Rights*, Galie, Bopst, and Kirschner show that founding-era state constitutions and declarations of rights are worthy of attention not merely as precursors to the federal bill of rights but because they embody a coherent and distinctive tradition of rights protection and governance that differs in key respects from the understanding that took hold at the federal level."

—John Dinan, *Professor of Political Science, Wake Forest University, and author of* The American Constitutional Tradition

"A long tradition in constitutional law dismisses the earliest state bills of rights as amateurish documents, haphazardly drafted during the chaos of the American Revolution. This invaluable book teaches us otherwise. Through a meticulous excavation of the philosophical, religious, and legal thought of the age, the authors reconstruct a now lost set of understandings and practices that allow them to decode these documents, revealing a fascinating, internally coherent narrative of robust popular sovereignty that deserves an important place in the American constitutional family tree."

—James Gardner, *SUNY Distinguished Professor, University of Buffalo School of Law, and author of* Interpreting State Constitutions: A Jurisprudence of Function in a Federal System

"Brilliant analysis...a very impressive work of scholarship and an important contribution to our understanding of state constitutions within our federal constitutional structure of dual sovereignty."

—Randy Holland, *Associate Justice, Delaware Supreme Court (1986–2017), and author of* The Delaware State Constitution

"*Bills of Rights Before the Bill of Rights* shows that a rich discourse of rights talk preceded the adoption of the Federal Constitution and found expression in the declarations of rights of early state constitutions. It is a major contribution to our understanding of rights in the American context."

—G. Alan Tarr, *Professor Emeritus of Political Science and former director of the Center for State Constitutional Studies, Rutgers University, and author of* Understanding State Constitutions

Peter J. Galie · Christopher Bopst · Bethany Kirschner

Bills of Rights Before the Bill of Rights

Early State Constitutions and the American Tradition of Rights, 1776–1790

palgrave
macmillan

Peter J. Galie
Department of Political Science
Canisius College
Buffalo, NY, USA

Christopher Bopst
Wilder & Linneball, LLP
Buffalo, NY, USA

Bethany Kirschner
Woehrle Dahlberg Jones Yao, PLLC
Fredericksburg, VA, USA

ISBN 978-3-030-44300-9 ISBN 978-3-030-44301-6 (eBook)
https://doi.org/10.1007/978-3-030-44301-6

This Palgrave Macmillan imprint is published by the registered company Springer Nature Switzerland AG
The registered company address is: Gewerbestrasse 11, 6330 Cham, Switzerland

Preface

Celebratory treatment has been the hallmark of America's heritage of rights. Even historians have been caught in the celebration of the founding with hagiography masquerading as history, although dissenting voices have accompanied that dominant chord. This dissenting tradition focused on class conflict and economic inequality. More recently, racism and ethnic cleansing have been added to the indictment.[1] For these historians, the beneficiaries of the Revolutionary War were white Europeans of high and moderate incomes; left out were slaves, Indians, indentured servants, women, poor whites, and Loyalists (their property confiscated, they were terrorized, killed, and driven out).

[1] In 2019, the *New York Times Magazine*'s "1619 Project" asserted that protecting the institution of slavery was a central motivation for declaring independence and fighting the Revolutionary War, making the ideals proclaimed in the Declaration of Independence a smoke screen for perpetuating racial inequality. Nikole Hannah-Jones, "Our Democracy's Founding Ideals Were False When They Were Written. Black Americans Have Fought to Make Them True," *New York Times Magazine*, August 14, 2019, Online at: https://www.nytimes.com/interactive/2019/08/14/magazine/black-history-american-democracy.html.

Our "foundation myth" explains, in part, the "take no prisoners" character of the more radical "race, class, and gender" historians.[2] Such critiques, however informative and cogent, judge past events from a contemporary understanding of the political community: one that is inclusive, diverse, and tolerant of a wide variety of lifestyles. It is this understanding that informs the work and the judgments of the neo-Progressive historians. Combining a contemporary understanding of rights with a contemporary understanding of a political community seals the deal. A less "presentist" perspective would have us ask a different set of questions: What were the founders attempting to accomplish? What was their understanding of the community in which these rights would function? What were the constraints or obstacles they faced? In addition to the presentism, there is the perfectionist assumption that the failure to conform reality to the rhetoric of the declarations of rights, *tout suite*, demonstrates hypocrisy and duplicity. What such perfectionism fails to understand, as Michal Jan Rozbicki points out, is that:

> liberty exists in society at the factual and the symbolic levels simultaneously, and that the two are neither separate nor mutually exclusive.... symbolic manifestations of freedom as a rule *preceded* the factual ones—until the culture changed sufficiently to make turning them into practice and law imaginable.[3]

It is not the rhetoric of the declarations of rights; it is the uses to which that rhetoric is put that defines their real meaning. Noting the distortion introduced into the meaning of liberty by importing an anachronistic understanding, Rozbicki writes: "The issue before us...should be less whether liberty was verbally defined in this or that way, or whether it derived from this or that philosopher, but what exactly was being communicated by the language of liberty in the Revolutionary era about

[2] See, e.g., Alan Taylor, *American Revolutions: A Continental History, 1750–1804* (New York: W. W. Norton & Co., 2016); Kathleen DuVal, *Independence Lost: Lives on the Edge of the American Revolution*, reprint ed. (New York: Random House, 2016); and Robert G. Parkinson, *The Common Cause: Creating Race and Nation in the American Revolution* (Chapel Hill: University of North Carolina Press, 2016).

[3] *Culture and Liberty in the Age of the American Revolution* (Charlottesville: University of Virginia Press, 2011), 3, 9. Rozbicki offers a sophisticated critique of the presentist and perfectionist assumptions that undergird much of the new progressive social history.

actual relations within American society."[4] Bernard Bailyn noted the extent to which colonists at all levels believed that "a proper social organization was hierarchical, with … articulated levels of superiority and inferiority, respected both in principle and practice."[5] Jack P. Greene's essay "All Men are Created Equal"[6] claims that social and political change during the Revolution was limited not just by the strong commitment to property rights among colonists, but also by the "deep and abiding commitment of the Revolutionary generation to political inequality."[7] His analysis suggests that a radical implementation of the "all men are created equal" clause would have precipitated a social upheaval not unlike that created by the French Revolution. Others have noted and contrasted the limited political character of the American Revolution with the root and branch character of the French Revolution.[8] The complaint seems to be that the Revolutionaries were insufficiently revolutionary!

Moreover, very few colonists believed that signing onto the equality clause committed them to cleanse the common law of those hierarchies. To understand equality, we need to ask: What did the language of equality in the Revolutionary Era communicate about actual relations within American society? If liberty was invented by a ruling class to provide elites with a privileged position as enlightened leaders, it is difficult to claim that it was offered or invented as egalitarian liberty. Theirs was "a pre-egalitarian, elite-made, inequality-premised liberty."[9] Modern freedom was neither invented nor prevented by the founders, who had a stake in selective liberty. Ironically, it was this stake that led them to promote, cultivate, and legitimate liberty as natural, setting off a process in which wider equality of rights was thinkable. Once unleashed, the idea that all

[4] Rozbicki, *Culture and Liberty*, 18.

[5] "The Central Themes of the American Revolution: An Interpretation," in *Essays on the American Revolution*, ed. Stephen G. Kurtz and James H. Hutson (Chapel Hill: University of North Carolina Press, 1973), 21.

[6] "All Men Are Created Equal: Some Reflections on the Character of the American Revolution," in Greene, *Imperatives, Behaviors, and Identities: Essays in Early American Cultural History* (Charlottesville: University of Virginia Press, 1992).

[7] Green, "All Men Are Created Equal," 238.

[8] See, e.g., Martin Diamond, "The Revolution of Sober Expectations," in *The American Revolution: Three Views* (New York: American Brands Inc., 1975), 57–85.

[9] Rozbicki, *Culture and Liberty*, 229.

men were created equal could not be put back in the bottle, as competition among elites gave rise to an expanded and more active electorate.

The language of the Declaration of Independence opened new possibilities and offered a more expansive understanding of equality, but it did not *give* anyone equality. It invited the members of the newly independent states to "claim it, invited them, not to know their place and keep it, but to seek and demand a better place."[10] The process of refining and cleansing the common law of its hierarchical elements, however, could not happen overnight. The gap between the Declaration and the economic and social realities of the colonial world could not be eliminated with the flourish of a pen; it could only be closed by political struggles invited by the declarations of rights. These struggles are a large part of this nation's history. The history of this discontinuous aggrandizement has been well told recently by Jill Lepore:

> Some American history books fail to criticize the United States; others do nothing but.... Between reverence and worship, on the one side, and irreverence and contempt, on the other, lies an uneasy path....[11]

The Declaration of Independence and the declarations of rights in the state constitutions that rejected monarchy are part of a long and ongoing dissolution of the various hierarchies embedded in the common law. Richard B. Morris captured the character of this evolution in his felicitous phrase: "a cautiously transforming egalitarianism."[12] We hope the reader will approach our work as an "uneasy path," and, like Ralph Ellison's *Invisible Man*, "become acquainted with ambivalence."[13]

This project has had a long gestation period. It began with a promise from Peter Galie to Bethany Kirschner, currently a practicing lawyer in

[10] Edmund S. Morgan, "Conflict and Consensus in the American Revolution," in Kurtz and Hutson, *Essays on the American Revolution*, 307.

[11] *These Truths: A History of the United States* (New York: W.W. Norton & Co., 2018), xix. Such an approach is exemplified in Colin G. Calloway's *The Scratch of a Pen: 1763 and the Transformation of North America* (New York: Oxford University Press, 2006).

[12] Morris, *The Forging of the Union, 1781–1789* (New York: Harper & Row, 1987), chapter 7. Ira Berlin expresses a similar understanding, describing the demise of slavery as "a near-century-long process in the United States...." *The Long Emancipation: The Demise of Slavery in the United States* (Cambridge, MA: Harvard University Press, 2015), 12.

[13] (New York: Vintage Books, Random House, 1952), 10.

Fredericksburg, Virginia, that he would not let her Canisius College senior honors thesis on early bills of rights gather dust on a library shelf. It was given added impetus by Peter's twenty-five years of collaboration with Christopher Bopst, another former student and a practicing lawyer in Buffalo, New York. During that quarter-century, Peter and Chris have collaborated in creating a body of scholarship on the New York Constitution and its history that has informed this work. In many ways, this project is an extension of their work to other states. Others who have made measurable contributions to this work include G. Alan Tarr, the leading scholar on subnational constitutions. The authors have benefitted from his advice while he was editor of the Oxford Commentaries on the State Constitutions of the United States series and from interactions with him on panels and conferences. Gerald Benjamin has provided similar support. Over a quarter century Jerry and Peter, and more recently, Jerry, Peter, and Chris have collaborated on several publications, served on panels, and spent countless hours campaigning for a New York state constitutional convention in 1997 and 2017. Alan's and Jerry's support, scholarly advice, and friendship have increased the quality and quantity of our research. We would note our special thanks to James Gardner and John Dinan, who, along with Jerry, offered their comments and criticisms at a round table as part of the 2019 meeting of the New York State Political Science Association. Those suggestions led us to rethink and reorganize our materials. The changes have enhanced our presentation and made it more reader-friendly. Jim and John, along with Randy Holland, former Associate Justice of the Delaware Supreme Court, provided additional comments on the final manuscript. A special note of thanks goes to Robert Klump, Pre-Law Director at Canisius College, friend, and colleague, for his careful review of our introductory chapters. The sometimes frustrating task of tracking down and retrieving arcane materials was lightened and enlightened by the professional staffs at the Canisius College Library, the University of Richmond Law Library, and the Montpelier Branch Library in Montpelier, Virginia.

Chris would like to thank his current firm, Wilder & Linneball, LLP, and his previous employer, Sam-Son Logistics, for their support and encouragement during the writing of this book. Bethany would like to thank her firm, Woehrle Dahlberg Jones Yao PLLC, for their helpfulness and interest.

Finally, we would also like to thank our families, who have endured the numerous sacrifices of time and attention necessary for this book to become a reality.

Buffalo, USA — Peter J. Galie
Buffalo, USA — Christopher Bopst
Fredericksburg, USA — Bethany Kirschner

Contents

List of Tables

Framing

Introduction

The attention we have lavished on the national Constitution is nothing short of extraordinary. It has been the subject of high praise and extensive analysis.[1] The closest thing our secular republic has to sacred scripture, the Constitution is treated with reverence, enshrined in a massive, bronze-framed, bulletproof, moisture-controlled, and vacuum-sealed container in the Rotunda of the National Archives Building in Washington, DC, and lowered into a multi-ton bombproof vault by night.[2]

The devotion shown to the national Constitution has overshadowed a rich and vibrant constitutional history that occurred at the state level well before that document was drafted. Over a century ago, William C. Morey lamented this fact:

[1] Gaspare J. Saladino compiled a fifty-four page, single-spaced bibliographic essay, "The Bill of Rights: A Bibliographic Essay," in *The Bill of Rights and the States: The Colonial and Revolutionary Origins of American Liberties*, ed. Patrick T. Conley and John P. Kaminski (Madison, WI: Madison House, 1992), 461–514. Saladino suggests the scope of the literature on the Bill of Rights when he writes: "it is not possible to list all worthwhile studies within the confines of a single article." Ibid., 461. Publications continue. Leonard W. Levy, *Origins of the Bill of Rights* (New Haven, CT: Yale University Press, 1999); Carol Berkin, *The Bill of Rights: The Fight to Secure America's Liberties* (New York: Simon & Schuster, 2015); Barry Alan Shain, ed., *The Nature of Rights at the American Founding and Beyond* (Charlottesville: University of Virginia Press, 2007).

[2] Gerard N. Magliocca ends his monograph, *The Heart of the Constitution: How the Bill of Rights Became the Bill of Rights* (New York: Oxford University Press, 2018), with an epilogue: "A Sacred Relic".

P. J. Galie et al., *Bills of Rights Before the Bill of Rights*,
https://doi.org/10.1007/978-3-030-44301-6_1

> The exalted place which Americans have been accustomed to assign to the Federal Constitution...has tended somewhat to obscure the great significance which our State constitutions possess, not only as integral elements of our federal system, but especially as factors in the growth of American constitutional law. When the average American thinks of the constitutional law of his country his mind naturally reverts to the written document drawn up by the convention of 1787... He is inclined to forget that when our Fathers met together in Philadelphia to 'form a more perfect union,' they had already before their eyes the written constitutions of thirteen independent States. He would be inclined to question the statement that the most eventful constitution-making epoch in our history was not the year 1787, but an antecedent period extending from 1776 to 1780.[3]

A similar overshadowing of state declarations of independence occurred after the adoption of the Declaration of Independence.[4]

Nowhere is the distinctiveness between the dual and distinct constitutional traditions of this country more evident than in the area of rights.[5] The first ten amendments to the U.S. Constitution, the Bill of Rights, has taken on a life of its own—for some, it *is* the Constitution. Gerard Magliocca chose the title *The Heart of the Constitution* for his monograph on the Bill of Rights. So successful was this instrument as a symbol of our commitment to individual liberty that it soon eclipsed the multifaceted, rich tradition of constitutionalism and rights that preceded its adoption. Rights in America have been identified almost exclusively with the tradition that derives from the national Bill of Rights, limiting our understanding of rights to those explicit or implicit in that document.

[3] "The First State Constitutions," *Annals of the American Academy of Political and Social Science* 4 (September 1893): 201. Echoing this judgment more than a century later, Sanford Levinson wrote: "And, as a matter of fact, early state constitutions especially were far more attentive to bills of rights-- something notably lacking in the 1787 Constitution..." "America's 'Other Constitutions': The Importance of State Constitutions for Our Law and Politics," *Tulsa Law Review* 45, no. 4 (Summer 2010): 818.

[4] Pauline Maier unearthed at least ninety different declarations of independence that Americans in their colonies (later states) and localities adopted between April and July of 1776. *American Scripture: Making the Declaration of Independence* (New York: Knopf, 1997), 47–96 ("The 'Other' Declarations of Independence").

[5] G. Alan Tarr has explored this distinctiveness in *Understanding State Constitutions* (Princeton, NJ: Princeton University Press, 1998).

Between 1987 and 1991, this country celebrated the bicentennials of the Constitution and the Bill of Rights. The celebrations included publications, conferences, public gatherings, and television specials in which participants examined and reassessed our founding documents.[6] One byproduct of this flurry of activity was to bring into focus the rights found in the state constitutions adopted over the fifteen-odd years immediately preceding the ratification of the national Constitution. These rights, long submerged by the success of the national Constitution, are the subject of this volume.

From the "First Ten Amendments" to the "Bill of Rights"

The apotheosis of our rights tradition was reached, so the story goes, with the 1791 addition of ten amendments[7] to the national Constitution adopted in 1787.[8] Though it would come to be seen as "the high temple of our constitutional order- America's Parthenon,"[9] the national Bill of Rights had modest beginnings. Initially, the document had as its primary

[6] Among these are Jon Kukla, ed., *The Bill of Rights: A Lively Heritage* (Richmond: Virginia State Library and Archives, 1987); Michael J. Lacey and Knud Haakonssen, eds., *A Culture of Rights: The Bill of Rights in Philosophy, Politics, and Law—1791 and 1991* (Cambridge: Woodrow Wilson International Center for Scholars and Cambridge University Press, 1991); Conley and Kaminski, *Bill of Rights*; Helen E. Veit, Kenneth R. Bowling, and Charlene Bangs Bickford, eds., *Creating the Bill of Rights: The Documentary Record from the First Federal Congress* (Baltimore: John Hopkins University Press, 1991); Gary C. Bryner and A. Don Sorensen, eds., *The Bill of Rights: A Bicentennial Assessment* (Albany: State University of New York Press, 1994);William E. Nelson and Robert C. Palmer, *Liberty and Community: Constitution and Rights in the Early American Republic* (New York: Oceana, 1987).

[7] On September 25, 1789, the first Congress passed twelve articles of amendment to the Constitution. Articles three through twelve were ratified by the requisite number of states on December 15, 1791, and later became known as the "Bill of Rights".

[8] The Constitution was ratified by the thirteen existing states between December 7, 1787 (Delaware) and May 29, 1790 (Rhode Island), with all but two ratifying it during the first eight months of that period.

[9] Akhil Reed Amar, *The Bill of Rights: Creation and Reconstruction* (New Haven, CT: Yale University Press, 1998), xi.

goal the protection of federalism (states' rights) and majoritarian or community rights.[10] A. E. Dick Howard notes that "[f]or the first century and a half after the Bill of Rights was added to the Constitution, those Amendments saw surprisingly little judicial use."[11] This point is punctuated by Akhil Reed Amar: "[B]efore the adoption of the Fourteenth Amendment, the Supreme Court never—not once—referred to the 1791 decalogue as 'the' or 'a' bill of rights."[12]

What explains this remarkable shift? The answer takes us back to James Madison's campaign for a seat in the newly established House of Representatives. Though ambivalent about adding a bill of rights, thinking it would not serve the "national object," Madison nevertheless fulfilled a campaign promise: In June 1789, he recommended to Congress nine amendments. The fourth of these amendments included much of what ultimately became the U.S. Bill of Rights. Madison proposed, unsuccessfully, that these amendments be woven seamlessly into the text of the Constitution so that they would not be understood or seen as a separate "Bill of Rights."[13] Had Madison's argument prevailed, there would have been prefixed to the Constitution the following declaration:

> ...that all power is originally vested in, and consequently derived, from the people.
>
> That Government is instituted and ought to be exercised for the benefit of the people; which consists in the enjoyment of life and liberty, with the right of acquiring and using property, and generally of pursuing and obtaining happiness and safety.
>
> That the people have an indubitable, unalienable, and indefeasible right to reform or change their Government, whenever it be found adverse or inadequate to the purposes of its institution.[14]

[10] Ibid., xii–xv. The history of this transformation is found in Magliocca, *Heart of the Constitution*. Pauline Maier compared the bills or declarations of rights in the states to the national Bill of Rights and concluded: "the federal Bill of Rights was a sorry specimen, a lean summary of restrictions on the federal government, tacked onto the end of the Constitution like the afterthought it was, with no assertion of fundamental revolutionary principles." *American Scripture*, 194.

[11] Foreword to Veit, Bowling, and Bickford, *Creating the Bill of Rights*, vii.

[12] Amar, *Bill of Rights*, 284.

[13] Roger Sherman of Connecticut convinced the House to append the proposals to the document as amendments. Veit, Bowling, and Bickford, *Creating the Bill of Rights*, xv.

[14] Veit, Bowling, and Bickford, *Creating the Bill of Rights*, 11–12.

The prefix, which he referred to as a "bill of rights" in his speech to Congress, reads more like the Declaration of Independence; yet we do not think of the Declaration as a bill of rights.[15]

Subsequently, the House formed a select committee to consider amendments to the Constitution. The committee, chaired by John Vining (Del.), included among its members Madison and Roger Sherman (Ct.). A draft bill of eleven rights was generated and recorded by Sherman.[16] The committee's initial draft echoed language found in various state declarations of rights and provided striking examples of the tradition of rights embodied in the state constitutions. There were specific references to "natural rights," the "inherent and unalienable right to change or amend their political Constitution," explicit commitments to the separation of powers, and protection for speech spoken "with Decency." None of these items made it into the committee's final report[17] or the twelve amendments ultimately adopted by Congress on September 25, 1789.

Madison may have proposed a bill of rights as a tactic to win ratification of the Constitution without calling another convention, but his remarks accompanying the proposal harken back to the aspirational and hortatory language found in the declarations of rights that prefaced most of the state constitutions and proclaimed the constitutional principles, fundamental rights, and civic morality of these new republics. Madison thought that a bill of rights, over time, could "act[ ] as a kind of republican schoolmaster,

[15] Compare George Mason's draft of the Virginia Declaration of Rights (1776). Mason was taken to task for the Virginia declaration's failure to include the broader range of civil rights later found in the 1791 Bill of Rights. But this judgment mistakes Mason's purposes for the Virginia declaration, which were to define the duties of the republican citizens of Virginia and to describe the nature of the political and constitutional principles that defined them as a community. Jack Rakove, *Revolutionaries: A New History of the Invention of America* (Boston: Houghton Mifflin Harcourt, 2010), 173. A comparison of Sections 2 and 3 of the Virginia declaration with the prefix Madison recommended cements the connection.

[16] The draft bill of rights is reproduced in Scott D. Gerber, "Roger Sherman and the Bill of Rights," *Polity* 28, no. 4 (Summer 1996): 532–533. Gerber also describes the uncertainty behind the provenance of that document. Ibid., 521–531. Richard Labunski, *James Madison and the Struggle for the Bill of Rights* (New York: Oxford University Press, 2006), offers a clear and illuminating examination of the adoption of the first ten amendments from Madison's initial proposals to ratification.

[17] The final proposals of the committee can be found at House of Representatives, Report of the Select Committee on Amendments, July 28, 1789, accessed January 1, 2019, http://teachingamericanhistory.org/library/document/report-of-the-house-select-committee/.

serving as a civic lexicon by which the people teach themselves the grammar and meaning of freedom."[18] Resort to this language was the tribute Federalists paid to the tradition they were in the process of replacing.

The Study of Rights in the First State Constitutions

This well-known history of the U.S. Bill of Rights stands in stark contrast to the relatively unknown tradition of rights in the early American states. No comprehensive analysis of the history and character of early state declarations of rights exists. When historians did focus on these declarations, they were likely to view them as preludes to the adoption of the national Bill of Rights.[19] When examined on their own terms, these declarations were described as having neither pattern nor coherence. This is the view of Oscar and Lillian Handlin, who write of the "important omissions" that "revealed the erratic nature of the enumerations" at the founding.[20] With

[18] Colleen A. Sheehan, *James Madison and the Spirit of Republican Self-Government* (New York: Cambridge University Press, 2009), 108. Although the terms "declaration" and "bill" have come to be used synonymously when applied to rights, early states (except for New Hampshire) followed the usage of the English Declaration of Rights of 1689. That declaration had some of the characteristics of a petition, a proclamation in solemn, emphatic terms, and a declaration and assertion of a new policy: the rights of the people. Thoughtful and informative examination of the term "declaration" can be found in Lois G. Schwoerer, *The Declaration of Rights, 1689* (Baltimore: John Hopkins University Press, 1981), 14–19, and Maier, *American Scripture*, 50–55. A subsequent statute, "An Act Declaring the Rights and Liberties of the Subject and Settling the Succession of the Crown," 1688 c.2 (1 William and Mary Sess 2), gave legal authority to the declaration, changing it to a "bill".

[19] One of the earliest studies devoted to the origins of the U.S. Bill of Rights, Robert Allen Rutland's *The Birth of the Bill of Rights, 1776–1791* (New York: Collier Books, 1962) provided a brief overview of developments in the states with rights provisions treated as a prelude to what would come at the national level. Bernard Schwartz's *The Bill of Rights: A Documentary History*, 2 vols. (New York: Chelsea House Publishers, 1971) examines the state bills of rights and other rights documents as way stations to a final destination: The Bill of Rights. Neil H. Cogan, ed., *The Complete Bill of Rights: The Drafts, Debates, Sources, and Origins*, 2nd ed. (New York: Oxford University Press, 2015) is a thorough (1300 pages) if not complete collection of materials organized by amendment.

[20] *Liberty in America: 1600 to the Present*, vol. 2, *Liberty in Expansion, 1760–1850* (New York: Harper & Row, 1989), 337. For a similar understanding, see Jackson Turner Main, *The Sovereign States, 1775–1783* (New York: New Viewpoints, 1973), 210.

more balance, Gordon S. Wood described these rights provisions as "a jarring but exciting combination of ringing declarations of universal principles with a motley collection of common law procedures."[21] Leonard W. Levy presents the extreme version of this understanding:

> ...the phrasing of various rights and the inclusion or omission of particular ones in any given state constitution seems careless...inexplicable except in terms of shoddy craftsmanship...baffling... incredibly haphazard.
>
> ....
>
> [T]he first American bills of rights...were imitative, deficient, and irrationally selective.... Americans tended simply to draw up a random catalog of rights....[a] task...executed in a disordered fashion that verged on ineptness.[22]

His conclusions rested on the assumption that the state declarations of rights, like the U.S. Bill of Rights, were intended to be or should have been comprehensive lists of rights. He did not consider the possibility that the declarations of rights in state constitutions derived from a different tradition, operated in a different context, and served different purposes than the national Bill of Rights.[23] The judgments of Levy and other critics of these early rights provisions are open to the same criticism Quentin Skinner leveled at Whig intellectual historians who imputed "incoherence or irrationality where we have merely failed to identify some local canon of rational acceptability."[24]

[21] *The Creation of the American Republic, 1776–1787* (Chapel Hill: University of North Carolina Press, 1969), 271.

[22] Levy, *Origins of the Bill of Rights*, 11, 186. In his study of the free press in early America, Levy refers to the clauses protecting that right as "flabby" and "namby-pamby." *Emergence of a Free Press* (New York: Oxford University Press, 1985), 184, 324. Levy's harsh judgments about early state declarations are made in the absence of any indication that he consulted any of the works produced during the bicentennial of the Bill of Rights that focused on that document and its antecedents. None are cited, let alone addressed.

[23] Richard A. Primus argues that while the English constitutional tradition provided and guided the discourse on rights in the American colonies, the particular rights asserted were shaped by the specific adversities incident to British rule. *The American Language of Rights* (Cambridge: Cambridge University Press, 1999), 90.

[24] Ibid., 93, citing James Tully, ed., *Meaning and Context: Quentin Skinner and His Critics* (Cambridge: Polity Press, 1988), 244.

Revisionist attention to these first state constitutions sprung up in the wake of Gordon Wood's *The Creation of the American Republic, 1776–1787*, a seminal work that ushered in a re-evaluation of the American Founding that is still in progress. Wood claimed it was not Locke who gave us our bearings; it was the classical republican/radical Whig tradition that provided the political theory that gave birth to the American political tradition. Building on Wood's research, Donald S. Lutz advanced the case for seeing the early constitutions as manifestations of the Whig political tradition rather than the Federalist theory embodied in the national document. Lutz suggested that the national Constitution represented a significant departure from the political tradition that characterized the English colonies in North America.[25] He noted that the declarations of rights in early state constitutions preceded the frames of government. Delegates believed that natural or inalienable rights did not originate with governments: Governments were established to recognize and guarantee those rights.

In the late 1980s, other scholars began working from the hypothesis that state bills of rights were embedded in a different understanding of community and functioned differently than their counterpart at the national level.[26] Marc W. Kruman saw coherency in the rights provisions, claiming that these declarations of rights "were much more broadly conceived, internally coherent, and intimately interwoven with the plans of government than historians have allowed."[27] Others, including William E. Nelson and Robert C. Palmer,[28] Willi Paul Adams,[29] Jack

[25] *Popular Consent and Popular Control: Whig Political Theory in the Early State Constitutions* (Baton Rouge: Louisiana State University Press, 1980), 221.

[26] Ibid., xv.

[27] *Between Authority and Liberty: State Constitution Making in Revolutionary America* (Chapel Hill: University of North Carolina Press, 1997), 38.

[28] Nelson and Palmer, *Liberty and Community.*

[29] *The First American Constitutions: Republican Ideology and the Making of the State Constitutions in the Revolutionary Era* (Lanham, MD: Rowman & Littlefield, 2001).

N. Rakove,[30] John J. Dinan,[31] and Lee Ward[32] undertook explorations of this rights tradition on its own terms.

What Remains to Be Done

The year 1776 marked the beginning of a new epoch in the world's understanding of constitutions as founding documents.[33] Between 1776 and 1790, eleven of the former American colonies and the independent republic of Vermont adopted constitutions, in some cases more than one. Eight of these republics had separate declarations of rights as part of their constitutions (Table 1).

These constitutions were not treated simply as "working description[s] of ... government[s], but as...single authoritative document[s], written at...known moment[s] of historical time, under rules that made [them]

[30] "Parchment Barriers and the Politics of Rights," in Lacey and Haakonssen, *Culture of Rights*, 98–143; *Original Meanings: Politics and Ideas in the Making of the Constitution* (New York: Vintage Books, 1997), 288–338; *Declaring Rights: A Brief History with Documents* (New York: Palgrave Macmillan, 1998).

[31] *Keeping the People's Liberties: Legislators, Citizens, and Judges as Guardians of Rights* (Lawrence: University Press of Kansas, 1998). See also Vincent Phillip Munoz, "Church and State in the Founding-Era State Constitutions," *American Political Thought: A Journal of Ideas, Institutions, and Culture* 4 (Winter 2015): 1–38.

[32] *The Politics of Liberty in England and Revolutionary America* (Cambridge: Cambridge University Press, 2004).

[33] John Jay noted the worldwide historical significance of these events just after the adoption of New York's first constitution in 1777, an event in which he played a major role:

> The Americans are the first people whom Heaven has favoured with an opportunity of deliberating upon, and choosing the forms of government under which they should live. All other constitutions have derived their existence from violence or accidental circumstances...

Charge to the Grand Jury of Ulster County, September 9, 1777, *The Correspondence and Public Papers of John Jay*, ed. Henry P. Johnston (New York: G.P. Putnam's Sons, 1890), 1:161, http://oll.libertyfund.org/titles/jay-the-correspondence-and-public-papers-of-john-jay-vol-1-1763-1781. Readers of Jay's remarks, unaware of the date on which they were made, might be forgiven if they assumed he was referring to the Constitution of 1787, an assumption that continues to be made even by reputable scholars: "The US Constitution of 1787 became the world's first modern written constitution." Martin Loughlin, *The British Constitution: A Very Short Introduction* (Oxford: Oxford University Press, 2013), 9–10.

Table 1 State constitutions adopted, 1776–1790

State	*Drafting body*	*Approving body*	*Separate declaration of rights*	*Date declaration of rights adopted by convention*	*Date constitution adopted by convention*
Delaware (1776)	Elected Convention	Drafting Body	Y	September 11, 1776	September 21, 1776
Georgia (1777)	Elected Convention	Drafting Body	N	N/A	February 5, 1777
Georgia (1789)	Elected Convention	Elected Ratifying Convention	N	N/A	May 6, 1789
Maryland (1776)	Ninth Provincial Convention	Drafting Body	Y	November 3, 1776	November 8, 1776
Massachusetts (1780)	Elected Convention	People at town meetings	Y	March 2, 1780	March 2, 1780
New Hampshire (1776)	Fifth Provincial Congress	Drafting Body	N	N/A	January 5, 1776
New Hampshire (1784)	Elected Convention	People at town meetings	Y	August 21, 1782	June 3, 1783[a]
New Jersey (1776)	Provincial Congress	Drafting Body	N	N/A	July 2, 1776
New York (1777)	Fourth Provincial Congress	Drafting Body	N	N/A	April 20, 1777
North Carolina (1776)	Fifth Provincial Congress	Drafting Body	Y	December 17, 1776	December 18, 1776
Pennsylvania (1776)	Elected Convention	Drafting Body	Y	August 16, 1776	September 28, 1776
Pennsylvania (1790)	Elected Convention	Drafting Body	N[b]	N/A	September 2, 1790
South Carolina (1776)	Provincial Congress	Drafting Body	N	N/A	March 26, 1776
South Carolina (1778)	General Assembly	Drafting Body	N	N/A	March 19, 1778

(continued)

Table 1 (continued)

State	*Drafting body*	*Approving body*	*Separate declaration of rights*	*Date declaration of rights adopted by convention*	*Date constitution adopted by convention*
South Carolina (1790)	Elected Convention	Drafting Body	N[c]	N/A	June 3, 1790
Vermont (1777)	Elected Convention	People at town meetings	Y	July 8, 1777	July 8,1777
Vermont (1786)	Elected Convention	Elected Ratifying Convention	Y	July 4, 1786	July 4, 1786
Virginia (1776)	Fifth Virginia Convention	Drafting Body	Y	June 12, 1776	June 29, 1776

Note Connecticut and Rhode Island did not adopt state constitutions during the period under consideration

[a]The 1784 New Hampshire Constitution submitted by the convention in 1782 received approval of all but the executive department article

[b]The 1790 Pennsylvania Constitution relocated most of its rights provisions to Article IX. This constitution did not denominate Article IX as a Declaration of Rights or otherwise separate it from the frame

[c]The 1790 South Carolina Constitution placed most of its rights provisions in Article IX. This constitution did not denominate Article IX as a Declaration of Rights or otherwise separate it from the frame

legally superior to all the other acts that the government[s] [they] created would subsequently adopt."[34] The efflorescence of rights that accompanied the establishment of the fourteen constitutional republics was unprecedented in human history.[35] Yet there is no one-volume work that brings these materials together in a systematic fashion, and in a context that corrects the long-standing but misleading image of state bills of rights as simply dress rehearsals for the national Bill of Rights. Surely justification exists for examining the tradition of rights at the state level between

[34] Rakove, *Revolutionaries*, 159.

[35] Donald S. Lutz, in "The State Constitutional Pedigree of the U.S. Bill of Rights," *Publius: The Journal of Federalism* 22, no. 2 (Spring 1992): 19–45, concluded that the state bills of rights adopted between 1776 and 1789 were, by far, the source of the largest number of provisions found in the national Bill of Rights.

the time of the American Revolution and the adoption of the U.S. Bill of Rights on its own terms as part of this country's heritage of rights.

We believe there is a coherence in the declarations that has yet to be fully explored. The declarations included the constitutional principles on which the regimes were founded; the fundamental rights on which they believed all others freedoms depended; and provisions that tracked the grievances found in the Stamp Act Congress's 1765 "Declaration of Rights and Grievances," the "Declaration and Resolves on Colonial Rights" adopted by the Continental Congress in 1774, and the Declaration of Independence.[36] Colonial complaints were based on the argument that the Crown and Parliament had violated the rights of colonists guaranteed under the English Constitution and specified in documents such as the Petition of Right and the English Bill of Rights. Spelling out the protections against these past abuses offered retrospective condemnation while making clear that such behavior, whatever its legal status under English common law, would be no part of the new republican order. Distancing from parts of the common law thought inconsistent with the new order was also reflected in provisions that softened or eliminated some of the harsh consequences of that body of law.[37]

Our Goal

This work will enable students, scholars, and citizens to discover the first attempts in human history to found rights-based constitutional republics by debate and deliberation. In addition to presenting a thematic overview of the rights tradition in the colonies, this documentary history will provide the rights provisions, with commentary, found in these first state declarations and constitutions.

The following two chapters will describe the sources of rights in the colonies and provide a comparative analysis and a summative assessment of the rights tradition in the states. We present the evidence for our thesis that these declarations contained a coherent political philosophy that

[36] These documents are available in Barry Alan Shain, ed., *The Declaration of Independence in Historical Context: American State Papers, Petitions, Proclamations, and Letters of the Delegates to the First National Congress* (Indianapolis: Liberty Fund, 2014). Remarkably, none of the grievances listed rely on natural rights for their vindication.

[37] See Table 5, p. 85, for examples of provisions eliminating the punishment for suicide, limiting sanguinary punishments, and removing imprisonment for debt.

differed in significant ways from the tradition represented by the national Bill of Rights adopted in 1791.

The chapters in the following three parts examine the rights protected in each of the fourteen states following the Declaration of Independence. We begin with the eight states whose constitutions were prefaced by declarations of rights, and present them, with one exception, in the order in which the declarations were adopted.[38] Following those eight states, we explore rights found in the state constitutions lacking an accompanying declaration of rights—South Carolina, New Jersey, Georgia, and New York.[39] Finally, we study the rights traditions in Connecticut and Rhode Island, two states that retained their colonial charters—with some symbolic modifications—as their constitutions. If a state adopted more than one declaration or constitution during the relevant period, the rights from both documents will be examined.

Each rights provision, whether in a declaration or a frame of government, is annotated, providing its meaning, provenance, and purpose. Given the consensus on the character of the regimes, aptly named "natural rights republics,"[40] the acceptance of a common set of rights derived from that regime choice, the common grievances of the colonies, and the acceptance of English common law constitutionalism, the extensive repetition of rights found in these declarations and frames or forms of government is not surprising. In such cases, we have confined our annotations and comments to the declaration or constitution in which the right first appeared. When the right appears in subsequent declarations, the reader is referred to the commentary accompanying its first treatment. Where there are substantive changes—additions or subtractions—in the expression of

[38] In one case, such sequencing would be misleading. The bordering states of Delaware and Maryland adopted their declarations in that order. Maryland's first draft of its declaration, however, was completed the first day the Delaware convention met; that draft was made available to the Delaware convention, and the declarations are too similar for any conclusion other than that Maryland's declaration was the model for Delaware's. So we treat Maryland first. See Dan Freidman, "Tracing the Lineage: Textual and Conceptual Similarities in the Revolutionary-Era State Declarations of Rights of Virginia, Maryland, and Delaware," *Rutgers Law Journal* 33, no. 4 (Summer 2002): 942–945.

[39] In some cases, e.g., New York, a statutory bill of rights was adopted. See pp. 342–345.

[40] Here we follow Michael P. Zuckert, *The Natural Rights Republic: Studies in the Foundation of the American Political Tradition* (Notre Dame, IN: University of Notre Dame Press, 1996).

the right, we provide comments on the significance of those changes. We explore how the rights in each of the state constitutions relate to rights found in other state constitutions and note the presence of rights unique to each state.

In addition to the relevant texts involving rights, each chapter contains an introduction designed to complement and supplement the broader framework provided in the introductory chapters. These introductions provide a brief review of the state's colonial history, focusing on previous charters or legislation related to rights protections that help explain the constitutional provisions. Finally, the English common law, widespread in the colonies and then in the new states by way of incorporation provisions in their state constitutions, provided additional rights protections. In states where the development of the common law was extensive, such as Connecticut, we have assessed the impact of that development. We have provided extensive notes throughout the work that include suggestions for further reading. Where available and reliable, we have provided online sources for the material.

A Note to the Reader

Our source for almost all the declarations of rights and relevant rights provisions in state constitutions we have reproduced in this book is Francis Newton Thorpe's seven-volume *The Federal and State Constitutions.*[41] The only declaration or constitution not taken from Thorpe is Delaware's Declaration of Rights, which at the time of his compilation, was not thought to be part of the constitution.[42] His work will be cited as "Thorpe, *Constitutions*," followed by the appropriate volume and page number.

[41] Francis Newton Thorpe, ed., *The Federal and State Constitutions, Colonial Charters, and Other Organic Laws of the States, Territories, and Colonies Now or Heretofore Forming the United States of America*, 7 vols. (Washington: Government Printing Office, 1909), https://oll.libertyfund.org/titles/thorpe-the-federal-and-state-constitutions-7-vols.

[42] The Delaware Declaration of Rights of 1776 replicated in this book is taken from Philip B. Kurland and Ralph Lerner, *The Founders' Constitution* (Chicago: University of Chicago Press, 1986), vol. 5, doc. 4, http://press-pubs.uchicago.edu/founders/documents/bill_of_rightss4.html, which in turn relies upon Richard L. Perry and John C. Cooper, eds., *Sources of Our Liberties: Documentary Origins of Individual Liberties in the United States Constitution and Bill of Rights* (Chicago: American Bar Foundation, 1959), 338–340.

Seventeenth- and eighteenth-century spelling, punctuation, capitalization, and even calendar dates are not consistent with modern usage. Where the differences are not likely to affect the reader's understanding, we have left them untouched; where they might obscure, we have modernized the text or used brackets to signal changes.

Before 1752, England and her colonies used the Old Style, or Julian, calendar. Using that calendar, the new year began on the Western Christian Feast of the Annunciation (March 25), also called "Lady Day." Events that occurred before March 25 of a particular year preceding the transition are noted with both the Julian and Gregorian years (e.g., 1710/1711). Colonists used the term "English Constitution" both before and after the 1707 union between England and Scotland, and we follow that usage. Any reference to Magna Carta is to the 1215 version of that charter, unless otherwise noted.

Rights in Colonial America: 1620–1776

By the last half of the eighteenth century, the founding generation came to see its rebellion as a rights-driven rejection of the British Empire and its colonial officials. The pamphlets, sermons, and newspaper articles produced during that period fill volumes, and much of the discourse carried on in those writings was in the language of rights. In the words of Donald S. Lutz, "rights are, in a sense, part of the preface to American political theory."[1] Being universally applauded and embraced is not to say these rights were clearly understood. Robert A. Ferguson captures the mutable and expansive range of meanings encompassed by the words "liberties" and "rights":

> Liberty could signify an exact or identifiable right, a loose encomium, a term of worship, membership in the British Empire, a personal possession, or the simple enjoyment of property. It also appeared as a badge of virtue, a distinction between peoples, a divine guarantee, a natural law, ... a political goal, participation in government, an affirmation of security....[2]

[1] *A Preface to American Political Theory* (Lawrence: University Press of Kansas, 1992), 49–50.

[2] "The Dialectic of Liberty: Law and Religion in Revolutionary America," in *Liberty and American Experience in the Eighteenth Century*, ed. David Womersley (Indianapolis: Liberty Fund, 2006), 103–104.

P. J. Galie et al., *Bills of Rights Before the Bill of Rights*,
https://doi.org/10.1007/978-3-030-44301-6_2

Complaints were regularly voiced by public figures and leaders in the colonies and in England that the incessant talk about and assertion of rights were bereft of an understanding of the nature of rights or their sources. During that time, "the public's penchant for asserting its rights outran its ability to analyze them and to reach a consensus about their scope and meaning."[3] Others have noted the vague character of this discourse: "By 1763 Americans had made imprecision in the area of rights and liberty a positive virtue."[4]

This condition was exacerbated by the fact that the language used in the public square to express the colonists' understanding of rights changed over the nearly two centuries between the establishment of the colonies and the ratification of the Bill of Rights. The language of "liberties, immunities, and privileges" gradually evolved into the language of "rights."[5] Adding to the difficulty is the fact that the colonists derived their claims to liberties and rights from a variety of sources and attributed rights to a variety of entities: individuals, corporations, communities, states, institutions, and the people as a whole.[6]

If the public understanding of the nature and origins of rights did not rise much above the level of slogans and rallying cries, the intricate parsing of these notions at the philosophical and theological levels indicated a lack of clarity and consensus on these terms and what they meant for the political order. As James Wilson lamented in 1787: "All the political

[3] James H. Hutson, "The Bill of Rights and the American Revolutionary Experience," in *A Culture of Rights: The Bill of Rights in Philosophy, Politics, and Law—1791 and 1991*, ed. Michael J. Lacey and Knud Haakonssen (Cambridge: Woodrow Wilson International Center for Scholars and Cambridge University Press, 1991), 63.

[4] Lawrence H. Leder, *Liberty and Authority: Early American Political Ideology, 1689–1763* (Chicago: Quadrangle Books, 1968), 130. Michael G. Kammen notes that "[b]etween about 1600 and 1750, discussions of liberty in Great Britain and her colonies were spasmodic, unsystematic, sometimes reductive and even inconsistent." *Spheres of Liberty: Changing Perceptions of Liberty in American Culture* (Jackson: University Press of Mississippi, 2001), 19.

[5] This transformation is described in James H. Hutson, "The Emergence of the Modern Concept of a Right in America: The Contribution of Michel Villey," in *The Nature of Rights at the American Founding and Beyond*, ed. Barry Alan Shain (Charlottesville: University of Virginia Press, 2007), 38–41.

[6] Richard A. Primus, *The American Language of Rights* (Cambridge: Cambridge University Press, 1999), 85.

writers ... have treated on this subject, but in no one of these books, nor in the aggregate of them all, can you find a complete enumeration of rights...."[7]

The English Petition of Right (1628), the Declaration of Rights of 1689,[8] and their homegrown colonial equivalents, the 1765 Declaration of Rights and Grievances of the Stamp Act Congress and the 1774 Declaration and Resolves on Colonial Rights of the First Continental Congress,[9] were lists of grievances accompanied by assertions or reaffirmations of rights claimed to have been established under the English Constitution and common law. None of these documents contained any rights that were natural or inalienable: They were meant to address the stated grievances. Even the Declaration of Independence, which begins with a ringing statement of natural rights and constitutional principles, was in substance a list of 27 grievances derived not from natural rights but largely from the English Constitution.

The early state declarations of rights adopted a natural rights philosophy derived from the 1776 Declaration that provided the fundamental principles on which the new regimes would be founded. The Reformed

[7] Remarks in the Pennsylvania Convention to Ratify the Constitution of the United States, December 4, 1787, in *Collected Works of James Wilson*, ed. Kermit L. Hall and Mark David Hall (Indianapolis: Liberty Fund, 2007), 1:211. Rights consciousness is at least as pervasive today as it was in the eighteenth century. Ignorance or misunderstanding of rights is a complaint that continues to be heard.

See, e.g., Mary Ann Glendon, *Rights Talk: The Impoverishment of Political Discourse* (New York: The Free Press, 1991); Richard E. Morgan, *Disabling America: The "Rights Industry" in Our Time* (New York: Basic Books, 1984). Criticism of the expansive nature of rights comes from both the left and the right. See Richard Rorty, "Fraternity Reigns: The Case for a Society Based Not on Rights but on Unselfishness," *New York Times Magazine*, September 29, 1996, 155–158; George F. Will, "Our Expanding Menu of Rights," *Newsweek*, December 14, 1992, 90.

[8] Lois G. Schwoerer, *The Declaration of Rights, 1689* (Baltimore: John Hopkins University Press, 1981), 14–19.

[9] A convenient source for these documents is Barry Alan Shain, ed., *The Declaration of Independence in Historical Context: American State Papers, Petitions, Proclamations, and Letters of the Delegates to the First National Congresses* (New Haven, CT: Yale University Press, 2014), 88–89, 211–214. See Table 5, pp. 84–85, where we note provisions in the state declarations of rights that address the grievances found in these two documents, as well as those listed in the Declaration of Independence. See p. 83, footnote 116 for colonists' use of the phrase, "immutable laws of nature".

Protestant tradition would be the primary source for the liberty of conscience, and the English Constitution and common law would be the source of the other enumerated rights included in the first constitutions.

Viewed through this prism, a clearer and more coherent pattern of rights selection emerges, rather than the motley described by earlier scholars.[10] These scholars began their analysis not with the tradition of petitions, bills, and declarations of rights on which the colonists relied, but with an understanding of what a bill of rights should contain, no doubt having the national Bill of Rights in mind. But in 1776, such a model did not exist!

The Sources of Rights

In this section, we focus on four major sources from which rights made their way into the first state constitutions: English constitutional history and common law, colonial charters and statutes, natural law/rights, and religion/theology.[11]

The English Constitution and the Common Law[12]

The language of the colonial charters, covenants, agreements, and general laws from the earliest settlements to the American Revolution demonstrates a commitment to embrace English law and the rights and

[10] See pp. 8–11, for a description of how scholars viewed these declarations.

[11] Primus provides six grounds for the rights claimed by the colonists: nature, history, the common law, contract, right reason, and God. *American Language of Rights*, 19–21. Lutz has a similar list: right as privilege, right as duty, right as promise or contract, civil right, common law right, and natural right. *Preface*, 83. John Phillip Reid claims that by 1776 no fewer than ten authorities or grounds for rights claims were being asserted by the colonists. "The Authority of Rights at the American Founding," in Shain, *Nature of Rights*, 69. We have collapsed these into four categories.

[12] Morris L. Cohen found six distinct meanings associated with the term "common law." "The Common Law in the American Legal System: The Challenge of Conceptual Research," *Law Library Journal* 81, no. 1 (Winter 1989): 17–18. In this work, the term "common law constitution" will refer to the statutes viewed as fundamental to the English Constitution, see text accompanying footnote 16, as well as the law developed by the king's ordinary bench. The connection is profound: Chapter 39 of Magna Carta, coupled with the directive in chapter 45 of that document, constituted an authorization for judges to apply the law of the realm, not the king's law, canon law, or local law.

liberties of Englishmen.[13] Magna Carta played an essential role in America's constitutional development, and the colonies would model their founding documents on the compact between King John and his barons. The Massachusetts Body of Liberties (1641), New York's Charter of Liberties and Privileges (1683), and the Pennsylvania Charter of Privileges (1701), among others, are prime examples of early laws containing provisions repeating or resembling those found in Magna Carta. Of greatest significance is Magna Carta's Chapter 39, the "law of the land" clause, which provides that no freeman shall suffer loss of life or liberty "except by lawful judgment of his peers or by the law of the land."[14] This language would later be replaced by "due process of law."[15]

Colonists frequently used Magna Carta as shorthand for all the documents constituting the English Constitution, which included, among others, the Petition of Right of 1628, the Habeas Corpus Act of 1679, and the English Bill of Rights of 1689.[16] Moreover, the Magna Carta they claimed as a birthright was not the Magna Carta of the thirteenth century

[13] George Dargo, *Roots of the Republic: A New Perspective on Early American Constitutionalism* (New York: Praeger, 1974), 57–58; Jack P. Greene, *The Constitutional Origins of the American Revolution* (New York: Cambridge University Press, 2011), 8–9.

[14] The New York Charter of Liberties and Privileges (1683) provided:

> THAT Noe freeman shall be taken and imprisoned or be disseized of his ffreehold or Libertye or ffree Customes or be outlawed or Exiled or any other wayes destroyed nor shall be passed upon adjudged or condemned But by the Lawfull Judgment of his peers and by the Law of this province. Justice nor Right shall be neither sold denyed or deferred to any man within this province.

Donald S. Lutz, ed., *Colonial Origins of the American Constitution: A Documentary History* (Indianapolis: Liberty Fund, 1998), 258, https://oll.libertyfund.org/pages/1683-charter-of-liberties-and-privileges-new-york.

[15] An early exploration of this influence is found in H. D. Hazeltine, "The Influence of Magna Carta on American Constitutional Development," *Columbia Law Review* 17, no. 1 (January 1917): 1–33. A collection of essays assembled to commemorate the 800th anniversary of Magna Carta included essays by A. E. Dick Howard, G. Alan Tarr, William C. Koch Jr., Thomas J. McSweeney, and Justin Wert exploring the impact chapters in that document had on colonial American charters and early American state constitutions. Randy J. Holland, ed., *Magna Carta: Muse and Mentor* (Washington: Thomson Reuters/Library of Congress, 2014).

[16] These documents are available in Richard L. Perry and John C. Cooper, eds., *Sources of Our Liberties: Documentary Origins of Individual Liberties in the United States Constitution and Bill of Rights* (Chicago: American Bar Foundation, 1959).

which affirmed feudal law and privilege; it was the Magna Carta viewed through the lenses of seventeenth-century English jurist Edward Coke, who translated Magna Carta into an affirmation of the common law and a limit on the Crown and Parliament.[17] Seventeenth-century common law practitioners in England and eighteenth-century American colonists conflated statutory law and judge-made law, contending that all law in England could properly be termed common law, that the common law preceded the coming of the Norman kings in 1066, and that Magna Carta was an attempt to return to the earlier common law and limit the prerogative powers of the king.[18]

One of the earliest colonial charters, the Virginia Charter of 1606, contained a guarantee that colonists shall "HAVE and enjoy all Liberties, Franchises, and Immunities…."[19] That phrase would be repeated in other charters. The words appear to constitute an assurance that English colonists carried with them the protections and privileges of the common law they would have had in their home country. The claim that the English Constitution guaranteed colonists the rights of Englishmen was

Historians are divided as to the grounds on which the colonists relied on natural rights in their dispute with Britain. Rejecting the natural rights origin are Jack P. Greene, *Constitutional Origins*, xii–xiv, and John Phillip Reid, "Authority of Rights," 82–86. Reid and Greene claim that the colonists rarely made an appeal to natural rights without that claim being accompanied by an appeal to the English Constitution, common law, immemorial usage, or custom. Reid argues that "nature as one authority for the validity of rights is quite different from saying that nature defined rights or determined which rights were enjoyed by British subjects or provided for the enforcement of rights." Reid, "Authority of Rights," 92, 97. Michael Zuckert suggests that the path to the Revolution was created by an amalgam of constitutional principles and natural rights. Americans read the English Constitution through "natural rights/social contract colored glasses…." "Natural Rights and Imperial Constitutionalism: The American Revolution and the Development of the American Amalgam," *Social Philosophy and Policy* 22, no. 1 (Winter 2005): 31. Greene appears to accept the amalgam approach when he writes: "natural rights theory had never been more than complementary to their principal argument which rested on law." *Constitutional Origins*, 185. Primus sees natural rights as just one of many sources colonists employed, suggesting no pride of place for that tradition. *American Language of Rights*, 88–90.

[17] Herbert Butterfield, *The Englishman and His History* (Hamden, CT: Archon Books, 1970), 69ff.

[18] See J. G. A. Pocock, *Virtue, Commerce, and History: Essays on Political Thought and History, Chiefly in the Eighteenth Century* (Cambridge: Cambridge University Press, 1985), 94ff.

[19] The First Charter of Virginia (1606), in Thorpe, *Constitutions*, 7:3788.

made repeatedly in petitions, speeches, and publications. In its petition to the king, the Stamp Act Congress spoke of "securing the inherent Rights and Liberties of your Subjects here, upon the Principles of the *English* Constitution."[20]

By 1776, English common law, in one form or another, was being used for legal proceedings in all the colonies.[21] Although looked upon by colonists as a "'repository of liberty' and 'the primary guarantor of English liberties,'"[22] the common law functioned differently in England than in the colonies, and differences existed from colony to colony. As William E. Nelson, in his comprehensive four-volume study, *The Common Law in Colonial America*, concluded: "American colonists ended up receiving only so much of the common law as was appropriate to their needs and circumstances."[23]

The colonists did not incorporate or enforce all the requirements of the common law, refusing to accept parts they thought irrelevant to their circumstances or inconsistent with their beliefs and practices. Provisions dealing with feudal structures and the establishment of the Anglican Church were ignored or superseded. Colonial governments granted protections not available under the English Constitution or the common law. Noteworthy in this respect were the colonists' view that the

[20] Petition to the King, October 21, 1765, in Shain, *Declaration of Independence*, 90 (emphasis in original). From the founding of the Virginia colony, there was dispute as to whether the protections afforded by the common law extended to the colonies. *Calvin's Case*, 7 Co. Rep. 1a, 77 Eng. Rep. 377 (C.P. 1608), laid down criteria for determining when and under what conditions the common law applied to lands acquired by conquest or by title of descent. English authorities maintained that America had been conquered from infidels and thus were the personal holdings of the king and were subject to the royal prerogative. William Blackstone, citing *Calvin's Case*, concluded that protections of the common law of England had "no allowance of authority" in the colonies. *Commentaries on the Laws of England in Four Books* (1753; reprint, Philadelphia: J.B. Lippincott Co., 1893), 1:107, https://oll.libertyfund.org/titles/blackstone-commentaries-on-the-laws-of-england-in-four-books-vol-1.

See discussion of these questions in Dargo, *Roots of the Republic*, 53–57.

[21] Lutz, *Preface*, 62.

[22] William E. Nelson, *The Common Law in Colonial America*, vol. 4, *Law and the Constitution on the Eve of Independence, 1735–1776* (New York: Oxford University Press, 2018), 9, quoting Daniel J. Hulsebosch, *Constituting Empire: New York and the Transformation of Constitutionalism in the Atlantic World, 1664–1830* (Chapel Hill: University of North Carolina Press, 2005), 35, 42. See also generally Nelson, *Law and the Constitution*, 7–10.

[23] Nelson, *Common Law*, vol. 1, *The Chesapeake and New England, 1607–1660* (New York: Oxford University Press, 2008), 3.

temporal and spiritual realms should be separate and the gradual recognition of the sacred right of conscience.[24] Colonists extended criminal procedure rights beyond those afforded under the common law. The common law, e.g., did not allow the benefit of counsel in felony cases; a number of colonies provided that right. Grand juries in the colonies exercised more autonomy and independence than their English counterparts, and that institution came to be seen as a defense of individual liberty.[25] Colonial legislatures reduced the number of felonies carrying the death penalty, and abandoned that punishment for any form of theft.[26] Freedom of the press was the rule in practice if not in law, where neither the limits of the common law nor efforts by local authorities proved sufficient to staunch the active and spirited assertion of press freedom.[27] Of greatest significance, however, was the expansion of the franchise in the colonies.[28]

Although English common law formed part of the background to the early American tradition of rights, in America the common law was "exposed to the powerful air of equality and independence that transformed it into a profoundly different American version."[29] Among the factors creating this "air of equality and independence" were:

[24] Leder, *Liberty and Authority*, 77.

[25] Dargo, *Roots of the Republic*, 70.

[26] Bradley Chapin, *Criminal Justice in Colonial America, 1606–1660* (Athens: University of Georgia Press, 1983). However, the General Laws and Liberties of New Hampshire (1679/1680) and the Massachusetts Body of Liberties (1641) made capital offenses the crimes listed as such in the Old Testament. Lutz, *Colonial Origins*, 6–8, 83–84.

[27] Most prominent in this regard is the case of John Peter Zenger in New York, who was acquitted on charges of seditious libel. Though it established no new law, the case gave impetus to similar results in other colonies, and by the 1760s prosecutions for seditious libel were rare and usually unsuccessful—though criticism of the government was not. For further analysis, see Roger P. Mellen, *The Origins of a Free Press in Prerevolutionary Virginia: Creating a Culture of Political Dissent* (Lewiston, NY: Edwin Mellen Press, 2009).

[28] Alan Tully, "The Political Development of the Colonies After the Glorious Revolution," in *A Companion to the American Revolution*, ed. Jack P. Greene and J. R. Pole (Malden, MA: Blackwell Publishers, 2000), 32. For the colonies collectively, Bernard Bailyn writes: "fifty to seventy-five per cent of the adult male white population was entitled to vote…." *The Origins of American Politics* (New York: Vintage Books, 1970), 87, and the studies cited therein. Forrest McDonald explores other instances where American practice deviated from the common law. *Novus Ordo Seclorum: The Intellectual Origins of the Constitution* (Lawrence: University Press of Kansas, 1985), 29–36.

[29] Lutz, *Preface*, 71.

- the presence of vast amounts of land unencumbered by feudal entanglements;
- an intrepid group of reformed or dissenting Protestants on an errand into the wilderness, who formed communities ("visible saints") under a covenant theology with leadership contingent on the authenticity of an inward experience;
- a geographic separation of 3000 miles from the metropolitan government; and
- existential threats to settlements created by their isolation and, in some cases, desperate circumstances that put a premium on cooperation.

Americans created and expected a set of rights characterized by a "breadth, detail, equality, fairness, and effectiveness in limiting all branches of government that distinguished it from English common law."[30]

Colonial Charters: From Covenant to Constitution

The founding documents of the colonies written in England—charters, letters of patent, and instructions—provided colonists with authority "to design their own political institutions and practice self-government, and most of those charters that did not so provide explicitly at least permitted the colonists to fill in the blanks themselves."[31] By the end of the seventeenth century, representative assemblies, deriving their authority from the charters, had become a fixed feature of colonial administration.[32] By the time of the Revolution, these charters "had become defensive bulwarks against the misuse of power."[33] They accustomed the colonists to running their own local governments within the framework of a document that legitimized and limited their political activity.[34] Along with

[30] Ibid., 70.

[31] Donald S. Lutz, "Introductory Essay," in Lutz, *Colonial Origins*, xxi.

[32] Michael Kammen, *Deputyes & Libertyes: The Origins of Representative Government in Colonial America* (New York: Alfred A. Knopf, 1969), 189.

[33] Bernard Bailyn, *The Ideological Origins of the American Revolution* (Cambridge, MA: Belknap Press of Harvard University Press, 1967), 192.

[34] Donald S. Lutz, *The Origins of American Constitutionalism* (Baton Rouge: Louisiana State University Press, 1988), 37.

charters of liberties and declarations of rights adopted in the colonies between 1620 and 1775, they provided the basis and immediate sources for the rights provisions enacted by the newly independent states. Lutz notes that a "high degree of overlap occurs between a state's bill of rights and the documents written during its respective colonial experience."[35] These documents had become, in the words of Gordon S. Wood, "so many miniature magna cartas."[36]

Noteworthy is the fact that the word "right" rarely appeared in the earliest colonial documents. More common were phrases like "liberties, franchises and immunities,"[37] "liberties and privileges,"[38] and "liberties, immunities, and privileges."[39] Occasionally the word "right" appeared in phrases, such as "lawful right and liberty,"[40] "civil rights and liberties,"[41] and "rights, liberties, immunities, privileges, and free customs."[42]

The pedigree of this language predates Magna Carta. Monarchs seeking monetary or political gain would grant privileges, immunities, or liberties to individuals (e.g., to cultivate land within the king's forest); to discrete groups (e.g., liberty of widows from forced marriage); or to corporate entities (e.g., London). Magna Carta contains numerous provisions that guaranteed these privileges and liberties as a matter of right.[43]

By the opening of the eighteenth century, the word "right" began appearing with more regularity, and by the end of that century it had largely replaced the archaic English language of franchises, liberties,

[35] Lutz, *Preface*, 68.

[36] "The Origins of Vested Rights in the Early Republic," *Virginia Law Review* 85, no. 7 (October 1999): 1427. A convenient collection of these documents can be found in Lutz, *Colonial Origins* and Perry and Cooper, *Sources of Our Liberties*.

[37] First Charter of Virginia, 3788.

[38] The Oath of a Freeman (1634), in Lutz, *Colonial Origins*, 52; [New York] Charter of Liberties and Privileges, 256–262.

[39] [Massachusetts Body of Liberties] (1641), in Lutz, *Colonial Origins*, 71.

[40] [Rhode Island] Acts and Orders of 1647, in Lutz, *Colonial Origins*, 185.

[41] The Laws and Liberties of Massachusetts (1647), in Lutz, *Colonial Origins*, 113.

[42] [Maryland] An Act for the Liberties of the People (1638), in Lutz, *Colonial Origins*, 308.

[43] J. C. Holt, *Magna Carta*, 3rd ed. (Cambridge: Cambridge University Press, 2015), 69–87.

immunities, and privileges.[44] The initial assertions of specific rights were meant to curb an arbitrary and unresponsive Crown.[45] Generalized search warrants were the occasion for demanding a right to be free from unreasonable searches and seizures; the imposition of taxes by a Parliament to which colonists could not elect members provoked the claim of "no taxation without representation." Trial by a jury of one's peers was asserted in the face of British attempts to have cases decided in juryless vice admiralty courts.[46]

Charters were valued as evidence of rights, though the security they provided was tenuous at best. As grants of power to corporations, they were subject to revision or revocation at any time.[47] Nevertheless, to the

[44] James H. Hutson plots this displacement in "Emergence of the Modern Concept of a Right in America," 38–41. The phrase "privileges and immunities" did survive, but not in the state or national bills of rights. It appears in the Articles of Confederation (Art. IV), in Article IV, section 2 of the U.S. Constitution, and in section 1 of the Fourteenth Amendment ("privileges or immunities"). A grant of these privileges, immunities, and franchises was "[a] right, advantage or immunity granted to or enjoyed by a person, or a body or class of persons, beyond the common advantages of others." *Oxford English Dictionary*, 2nd ed. (Oxford: Oxford University Press, 1989), 12:522. The significance of the difference between "liberties" and "liberty" is pointed up by Friedrich Hayek: "...[W]hile the uses of liberty are many, liberty is one. Liberties appear only when liberty is lacking: they are the special privileges and exemptions that groups and individuals may acquire while the rest are more or less unfree." F. A. Hayek, *The Constitution of Liberty* (Chicago: University of Chicago Press, 1960), 19. Charles M. Andrews argues that such phraseology had "nothing to do with civil liberty, self-government, or democracy; they were strictly legal, tenurial, and financial in their applications." *The Colonial Period of American History* (New Haven, CT: Yale University Press, 1934), 1:86 n. 1; A. E. Dick Howard, while acknowledging the force of Andrews's objection, notes that some provisions went beyond Andrews's limiting categories, e.g., trial by jury and due process of law. *The Road from Runnymede: Magna Carta and Constitutionalism in America* (Charlottesville: University of Virginia Press, 1968), 24. Nonetheless, the difference between "liberties, immunities, and privileges" and the emerging modern idea of rights was not just one of usage. Rights were not understood as inherent in individuals qua individuals; rather they were specific grants of power by the Crown or the state. Jack N. Rakove, *Declaring Rights: A Brief History with Documents* (New York: Palgrave Macmillan, 1997), 19.

[45] See Richard A. Primus, "An Introduction to the Nature of American Rights," in Shain, *Nature of Rights*, 21.

[46] Jack N. Rakove, *Original Meanings: Politics and Ideas in the Making of the Constitution* (New York: Vintage Books, 1997), 294.

[47] As an example, the second charter issued by the Crown to the Virginia Company was reorganized by the king in 1624, with all power placed in the hands of the governor, all of whose actions had to be approved by the Crown-appointed council of state.

extent colonists viewed them as contracts of a most "solemn" nature, these charters provided support for the rights claims being made.

Samuel Smith, a Quaker merchant whose many government positions included serving in the New Jersey Provincial Council (chosen by the Crown), is typical in this respect. He invoked that colony's proprietary charter as a continuing foundation for provincial rights and liberties, notwithstanding the proprietors' surrender of their rights of government to the Crown in 1702.[48] These founding documents had become for Americans a way to bring the English Constitution into view "'to reduce to a certainty the rights and privileges we were entitled to' and 'to point out and circumscribe the prerogatives of the crown,' so that 'these prerogatives [we]re as much limited and confined in the colonies as they [we]re in England.'"[49] Allan Nevins made this point in his pioneering study of the American states between 1775 and 1789: "The settlers did not look upon [the charters] as revocable grants, but as agreements inviolable except by mutual consent."[50] The alteration and suspension of the colonial charters by the Crown were grievances found in both the Declaration and Resolves of the First Continental Congress and the Declaration of Independence. Even after the Declaration of Independence, when most states were adopting new constitutions with new rights provisions, Connecticut and Rhode Island continued to operate under their colonial charters—a reflection of the value accorded these documents.

Moral and Political Philosophy

The idea of a God-created universe ordered by a natural law has deep roots in the Western tradition. Humans, by virtue of possessing reason, are capable of comprehending the requirements of this law—of knowing right from wrong, and determining what is just and unjust. The Catholic tradition of natural law as represented by Thomas Aquinas was introduced

[48] See the treatment of this question in Eugene R. Sheridan, "A Study in Paradox: New Jersey and the Bill of Rights," in *The Bill of Rights and the States: The Colonial and Revolutionary Origins of American Liberties*, ed. Patrick T. Conley and John P. Kaminski (Madison, WI: Madison House, 1992), 263–64; Reid, "Authority of Rights," 97–98.

[49] Gordon S. Wood, *The Creation of the American Republic, 1776–1787* (Chapel Hill: University of North Carolina Press, 1969), 269, quoting John Adams.

[50] *The American States During and After the Revolution, 1775–1789* (New York: Macmillan, 1924), 117.

into English Protestant theology by Richard Hooker, a prominent English theologian.[51]

It was a short step from Hooker's political theology to John Locke's political philosophy. Locke argued that in the state of nature, before humans agreed to enter society and establish a government, they had certain natural rights: the natural rights to life, liberty, and property. Governments are instituted to protect these natural rights and when governments fail in that task, they lose their legitimacy and can be resisted or overthrown.

A further distinction was made between natural rights that were inalienable and those that were alienable. Rights considered inalienable, such as life, liberty, and the pursuit of happiness, could not be transferred without denying one's humanity. Alienable natural rights were capable of being transferred by consent to the community. Though viewed as a natural right, the right to property was not viewed as an inalienable right by any of the major natural law thinkers of the seventeenth and eighteenth centuries, including Locke and Jefferson.[52]

Some thinkers offered a theological basis for unalienable rights: the right to life and the liberty of religious conscience, e.g., were God-given, and no person could alienate or renounce a right derived from a duty imposed by God.[53] Congregationalist minister Elisha Williams preached: "A man may alienate some branches of his property and give up his right in them to others; but he cannot transfer the rights of conscience, unless he could destroy his rational and moral powers...,"[54] that is deny his very nature as a human being. This definition comes closest to addressing, or at least mitigating, the difficulties associated with the concept and best comports with the understanding of rights in eighteenth-century America.[55]

[51] Hooker's most influential work is *Of the Laws of Ecclesiastical Polity*, ed. Arthur Stephen McGrade, critical ed. (Oxford: Oxford University Press, 2013 [1593]).

[52] Morton White, *The Philosophy of the American Revolution* (New York: Oxford University Press, 1981) provides a fuller description of the views of these thinkers.

[53] Ibid., 201.

[54] "The Essential Rights and Liberties of Protestants" (1744), in *Political Sermons of the American Founding Era, 1730–1805*, ed. Ellis Sandoz, 2nd ed. (Indianapolis: Liberty Fund 1998), 1:62.

[55] See the brief but illuminating discussion of the difficulties involved in making sense of the idea in White, *Philosophy of the American Revolution*, 107–123, 195–213, 230–231. Theophilus Parsons offers a thoughtful analysis of the difference between natural and

Natural rights that were alienable may be parted with by consent for an equivalent. The Boston Committee of Correspondence declared in 1772 that "every natural Right not expressly given up or from the nature of a Social Compact necessarily ceded remains."[56] Rights were inalienable when there was no equivalent that could be received in exchange for their transfer; the right to conscience being a prime example.

Locke wrote that "[m]an ... hath by nature a power ... to preserve his property, that is, his life, liberty and estate."[57] God created us with a desire for happiness and a desire to preserve our lives, thus we have a duty to pursue happiness and a duty to preserve that life. It is a logical step to say we have a right to do both. Although Jefferson characterized the pursuit of happiness as necessary and inalienable, the specific form and conditions under which it may be pursued in any given society would be a matter of human choice.

Some state constitutions incorporated the notion of inalienable rights. The Bill of Rights in the 1784 New Hampshire Constitution provided:

> III. When men enter into a state of society, they surrender up some of their natural rights to that society, in order to insure the protection of others; and, without such an equivalent, the surrender is void.
>
> IV. Among the natural rights, some are in their very nature unalienable, because no equivalent can be given or received for them. Of this kind are the RIGHTS OF CONSCIENCE.[58]

unalienable rights. "The Essex Result" (1778), in *American Political Writing During the Founding Era, 1760–1805*, ed. Charles S. Hyneman and Donald S. Lutz (Indianapolis: Liberty Fund, 1983), 1:487.

[56] "The Rights of the Colonists" (1772), in *The Writings of Samuel Adams*, ed. Harry Alonzo Cushing (New York: G.P. Putnam's Sons, 1906), 2:352.

[57] *Two Treatises of Government*, ed. Thomas Hollis (London: A. Millar et al., 1764 [1690]), Bk. II, sec. 87, at 269.

[58] N. H. Decl. 1784, Arts. III, IV. See also Alexander Hamilton, "The Farmer Refuted," in *The Works of Alexander Hamilton*, ed. Henry Cabot Lodge (New York: G.P. Putnam's Sons, 1904), 1:61–64, https://oll.libertyfund.org/titles/hamilton-the-works-of-alexander-hamilton-federal-edition-vol-1.

North Carolina's declaration provides the "natural and unalienable right to worship Almighty God according to the dictates of their own consciences."[59]

For most of the twentieth century, John Locke's ideas of equal creation, natural rights, consent of the governed, and the right to resist tyrannical rule were thought to be the philosophical basis for Jefferson's Declaration of Independence, the American Revolution, and eventually the liberal tradition with its emphasis on individual interests, personal liberty, and government by consent.[60] Over half a century ago, scholars began to challenge this "Locke and nothing else" understanding of the American Revolution. The roots of American Revolutionary thought were to be found in the English version of the classical republican tradition that originated with the Roman Republic, as explicated by Cicero, Polybius, and Livy, and transmitted by way of Machiavelli to republican and radical Whig writers of seventeenth- and eighteenth-century England.[61]

The language was that of civic virtue, public liberty, patriotism, sacrifice, and fear of corruption. The English republicans understood that the English mixed or balanced government was always open to disequilibrium and required a people whose civic virtue would provide the bulwark

[59] N.C. Decl. 1776, Art. XIX. See also Del. Decl. 1776, sec. 2; Pa. Decl. 1776, Art. II; Vt. Decl. 1786, Art. III. Although most writers did not consider property an inalienable right, some constitutions included the rights to acquire and possess property as inalienable. See pp. 50–51, footnote 34 for specific citations.

[60] See, e.g., Carl Lotus Becker, *The Declaration of Independence: A Study on the History of Political Ideas* (New York: Harcourt, Brace and Co., 1922); Louis Hartz, *The Liberal Tradition in America: An Interpretation of American Political Thought Since the Revolution* (New York: Harcourt, Brace and Co., 1955). Becker emphasized the downside of this tradition—economic self-interest and materialist values. C.B. MacPherson, *The Political Theory of Possessive Individualism: Hobbes to Locke* (Oxford: Oxford University Press, 1962) used the term "possessive individualism" to describe Locke's political philosophy.

[61] The *locus classicus* of Whig thinking was a series of articles by John Trenchard and Thomas Gordon, collectively known as *Cato's Letters*. *Cato's Letters, or Essays on Liberty, Civil and Religious, and Other Important Subjects*, ed. Ronald Hamowy, 4 vols. in 2 (Indianapolis: Liberty Fund, 1995 [1720–1723]). See also Trenchard and Gordon's essays written just prior to *Cato's Letters* and collected in *The Independent Whig: Or, a Defence of Primitive Christianity*...., 4 vols. (London: J. Peele, 1741–1747 [1720–1721]), https://oll.libertyfund.org/titles/gordon-the-independent-whig-4-vols-1720-1743.

against dependence, corruption, and tyranny. Eternal vigilance was the price of liberty.[62]

The extended debate between the Lockean and classical republican understandings on the American founding occasioned a massive outpouring of scholarship and polemic.[63] A half-century later, a new consensus emerged. Scholars on both sides acknowledged the presence of both Lockean and republican influences in eighteenth-century America. Gordon S. Wood conceded:

> none of the historical participants ... ever had any sense that he had to choose or was choosing between republicanism and liberalism, between Machiavelli and Locke.... Classical republicanism ... was not a clearly discernible body of thought to which people self-consciously adhered. And what we call Lockean liberalism was even less manifest and palpable.[64]

J. G. A. Pocock admitted that alternative modes of discourse (Liberal/Republican) do not "typically succeed in excluding one another."[65]

Locke Redivivus

The new consensus was spurred in part by scholarship reasserting Locke's significance as a central figure around whom American Revolutionary ideas would coalesce, but it was not the Locke of Becker

[62] A full exploration and analysis of this tradition is available in Caroline Robbins, *The Eighteenth-Century Commonwealthmen: Studies in the Transmission, Development and Circumstance of English Liberal Thought from the Restoration of Charles II Until the War with the Thirteen Colonies* (Cambridge, MA: Harvard University Press, 1959); Bailyn, *Ideological Origins*; Wood, *Creation of the American Republic*; J. G. A. Pocock, *The Machiavellian Moment: Florentine Political Thought and the Atlantic Republican Tradition* (Princeton, NJ: Princeton University Press, 1975); Quentin Skinner, *Liberty Before Liberalism* (Cambridge: Cambridge University Press, 1998).

[63] See excellent summaries of the debate in Jerome Huyler, *Locke in America: The Moral Philosophy of the Founding Era* (Lawrence: University Press of Kansas, 1995), 1–28; Andreas Kalyvas and Ira Katznelson, *Liberal Beginnings: Making a Republic for the Moderns* (Cambridge: Cambridge University Press, 2009), 1–17.

[64] "Afterword," in *The Republican Synthesis Revisited: Essays in Honor of George Athan Billias*, ed. Milton M. Klein, Richard D. Brown, and John B. Hench (Worcester: American Antiquarian Society, 1992), 145.

[65] "The Concept of a Language and the *metier d'historien*: Some Considerations on Practice," in *The Languages of Political Theory in Early-Modern Europe*, ed. Anthony Pagden (Cambridge: Cambridge University Press, 1987), 21.

and Hartz. This reassessment illuminated the communitarian aspect of Locke's political and social philosophy. This Locke is a Christian and a theologian.[66] This is a Locke who is not averse to regulation and takings of property for public purposes.[67] This is a Locke committed to promoting the conditions necessary for a moral community: "No Opinions contrary to human Society, or to those moral Rules which are necessary to the preservation of Civil Society are to be tolerated by the Magistrate."[68] Concerning the absolute right to protect one's life and property in the state of nature, Locke wrote: "[This] power ... *he gives up* to be regulated by laws made by the society... [insofar] as the preservation of himself, and the rest of that society shall require; which laws of the society in many things confine the liberty he had by the law of nature."[69] For Locke, rights and duties were two parts of a single understanding of political life. Locke did not elevate unbridled self-interest; indeed, he condemned its pursuit: "he that knows not how to resist the importunity of present pleasure or pain, for the sake of what reason tells him is fit to be done, wants the true principle of virtue and industry, and is in danger

[66] He writes "A christian I am sure I am, because I believe 'Jesus to be the Messiah,' the King and Saviour promised and sent by God..." "A Second Vindication of the Reasonableness of Christianity," (1695) in John Locke, *The Works of John Locke in Nine Volumes*, 12th ed. (London: Rivington, 1824), 6:359, https://oll.libertyfund.org/titles/locke-the-works-vol-6-the-reasonableness-of-christianity. A partial list of revisionist works includes John Dunn, "What Is Living and What Is Dead in the Political Theory of John Locke?," in Dunn, *Interpreting Political Responsibility: Essays, 1981–1989* (Princeton, NJ: Princeton University Press, 1990), 9–25; Steven M. Dworetz, *The Unvarnished Doctrine: Locke, Liberalism, and the American Revolution* (Durham, NC: Duke University Press, 1990); Victor Nuovo, "Locke's Christology as a Key to Understanding his Philosophy," in *The Philosophy of John Locke: New Perspectives*, ed. Peter R. Anstey (London: Routledge, 2003). Also emphasizing the Christian foundations of Locke's political thinking is Jeremy Waldron, *God, Locke, and Equality: Christian Foundations in Locke's Political Thought* (Cambridge: Cambridge University Press, 2002); Mark Goldie, "Introduction," in John Locke, *A Letter Concerning Toleration and Other Writings*, ed. Mark Goldie (Indianapolis: Liberty Fund, 2010).

[67] Richard Tuck, *Natural Rights Theories: Their Origin and Development* (Cambridge: Cambridge University Press, 1979); James Tully, *A Discourse on Property: John Locke and His Adversaries* (Cambridge: Cambridge University Press, 1980); Richard Ashcraft, *Locke's Two Treatises of Government* (London: Unwin Hyman, 1987).

[68] "A Letter Concerning Toleration," (1689) in Locke, *A Letter Concerning Toleration*, 49–50. Locke refused to grant toleration to atheists or Catholics: both, he argued, posed dangers to the political order.

[69] Locke, *Two Treatises*, Bk. II, sec. 129, at 309 (emphasis in original).

of never being good for any thing."[70] Even more forcefully: "For I think it every man's indispensable duty, to do all the service he can to his country; and I see not what difference he puts between himself and his cattle, who lives without that thought."[71]

Locke's ideas pervade *Cato's Letters*: "[W]hen Cato does move away from Hobbes and Machiavelli, he heads not toward Athens, but in a distinctively Lockean direction."[72] Jerome Huyler writes: "I shall treat *Cato's Letters* as a comprehensive synthesis of Lockean and 'classical' republican principles–a package readily available for colonial consumption during the political crisis to come."[73]

Locke's portrayal as the source of the liberal theory of individual (subjective) rights and its corollary, "possessive individualism," has been vigorously disputed in recent scholarship. John Dunn captured this revised version:

> For Locke all the rights human beings have (and which they certainly do possess prior to and independently of all human political authority) derive from, depend upon, and are rigidly constrained by a framework of objective duty: God's requirements for human agents. Within this setting, but as he supposed only within this setting, the claims of right are indeed decisive and all human beings have a duty to observe them and to enforce them.[74]

No American public figure in the seventeenth or eighteenth century asserted that natural or inalienable rights were underived, primary features of human beings. The moral world of traditional natural law theory was accepted by the dominant Protestant tradition: duties and rights were seen as correlative terms. Rights were not simply powers granted, as is the case with the subjective rights liberal tradition: They were God-given, and they were anchored in some communal purpose. To be recognized, rights claims must not conflict with the moral order as determined by the community. Natural rights existed in a sphere bounded by a natural moral law. This was true of Locke, Scottish Enlightenment philosophers,

[70] "Some Thoughts Concerning Education," (1695), sec. 45.1, in Locke, *Works of John Locke*, 8:36.

[71] Locke, *Works of John Locke*, 8:iii (dedication to Edward Clarke, of Chipley).

[72] Dworetz, *Unvarnished Doctrine*, 109.

[73] *Locke in America*, 39.

[74] Dunn, "What Is Living,"16.

and the natural law thinkers who combined elements of both traditions. The moral philosophy of the Scottish Enlightenment, with its idea that individuals possessed a moral sense-a faculty like the other senses-that embraced virtue, rejected vice, and endowed humans with sociability and benevolence, aligned thinkers like Francis Hutcheson and Adam Smith with the Reformed Protestant and classical republican traditions. All three focused on the corporate or communal pursuit of virtue.[75] That virtue took several forms: in the Protestant tradition, it was moral perfection; in classical republicanism, it was civic virtue (participation in the public realm); and for Scottish Enlightenment thinkers, it was benevolence and sociability. The understanding of rights as subjective and individual-centered would not appear until late in the eighteenth century. It would grow in importance in the nineteenth century and become the dominant understanding in the twentieth.[76]

[75] The Reformed Protestant tradition refers to a broad grouping of Calvinist-inspired denominations that included New England Congregationalists (descendants of the Puritans), Scotch-Irish Presbyterians, French Huguenots, and Dutch and German reformed congregations. In addition to being overwhelmingly Protestant, colonists identified, either by heritage or conviction, with this reformed tradition. Historians estimate that from seventy-five to ninety percent of the colonists came out of the Calvinist, rather than Lutheran, side of the Protestant Reformation. Daniel L. Dreisbach, ***Reading the Bible with the Founding Fathers*** (New York: Oxford University Press, 2017), 11 and studies cited therein, 243, n. 24.

[76] From the time the notion of rights made its appearance, rights had been anchored in and derived from the natural law of God's universe, a law which imposed duties on humans. In eighteenth-century colonial America, rights were "grounded in religion, if not the religion of the New Testament... at least in Judeo-Christian morality." Hutson, "Bill of Rights," 74. That which we have a duty to do we have a right to do. In the former understanding, rights were seen as derived from some higher moral standard. Subjective right, on the other hand, was drawn from attributes (powers) inherent in the subject. Rights were vehicles for expressing "unrestrained personal ambitions and appetites in the name of vindicating individual autonomy." Hutson, "Emergence of the Modern Concept of a Right in America," 54. This latter understanding was inconsistent with the community-wide moral consensus derived from shared Christian convictions that saw a close nexus between rights and duties, a connection deemed indispensable to ordered liberty. The understanding of rights as powers unanchored in the community and "indulged to fulfill autonomous personal goals that transgress traditional moral boundaries," however, was on the horizon. Ibid.

Richard Price, an English "radical" Whig writing in the second half of the eighteenth century, comes closest to a subjective, individualist notion that human beings could have sufficient autonomy to impose obligations upon themselves without any ultimate reference to a higher law or supreme authority. Price spoke of "physical liberty," the self-determination that gave man control over his own actions instead of reducing them to

The Reformed Protestant Tradition

For the overwhelming number of colonial Americans, the source of rights was the Creator—"nature's God." Samuel Adams wrote that "the Religion and public Liberty of a People are intimately connected; their Interests are interwoven, they cannot subsist separately; and therefore they rise and fall together."[77] It is not surprising then that the first freedom for colonists was religious liberty.[78] The Protestant right to individual conscience "was the only Revolutionary-era *individual* right that was seen by most Americans as truly inalienable."[79] Every human being was made in the image of God. God had made them free. Liberty was the highest earthly good; but civil liberty depended on spiritual liberty. The quintessential religious liberty, the freedom of conscience, was given forceful expression by Martin Luther: "my conscience is captive to the Word of God."[80] Locke also appears to have valued freedom of conscience for the Lutheran reason that it was essential to spiritual salvation.[81] John Milton epitomized the argument: "No man who knows ought, can be so stupid to deny that all men naturally were borne free,

being the effect of an outside cause, and "moral liberty," the power to act in accordance with one's own sense of right and wrong in all circumstances. *Observations on the Nature of Civil Liberty, the Principles of Government, and the Justice and Policy of the War with America*, 9th ed. (London: Edward and Charles Dilly and Thomas Cadell, 1776), pt. I, sec. 1. See Colin Bonwick, *English Radicals and the American Revolution* (Chapel Hill: University of North Carolina Press, 1977) for an analysis of the ideas of Price and his peers.

[77] "Article Signed Valerius Poplicola," *Boston Gazette*, October 5, 1772, in Cushing, *Writings of Samuel Adams*, 2:336.

[78] This judgment is reflected in the titles of two scholarly works on religious liberty, William Lee Miller's *The First Liberty: Religion and the American Republic* (New York: Alfred A. Knopf, 1986) and Thomas J. Curry's *The First Freedoms: Church and State in America to the Passage of the First Amendment* (New York: Oxford University Press, 1986).

[79] Barry Alan Shain, *The Myth of American Individualism: The Protestant Origins of American Political Thought* (Princeton, NJ: Princeton University Press, 1994), 242–43.

[80] "Luther at the Diet of Worms, 1521" in Martin Luther, *Luther's Works*, vol. 32, *Career of the Reformer II*, ed. George W. Forell (Philadelphia: Fortress Press, 1958), 112.

[81] See footnote 66, above. See also Calvin's comparable view of Christian obedience to God's word over humans. John Calvin, *Institutes of the Christian Religion*, ed. John T. McNeill, trans. Ford Lewis Battles (Philadelphia: Westminster Press, 1960 [1559]), Bk IV; Ch. XX, sec. 32, at 2:1520–1521.

being the image and resemblance of God...."[82] Locke's influence on American political ideas and the Reformed Protestant clergy was preceded by Calvin's impact on Locke, particularly on the question of the right to resist arbitrary or tyrannical authority. Sixteenth-century Calvinists in France and Geneva generated a body of writings providing justification for limited government and a right to resist.[83] Similar arguments were advanced by John Knox and George Buchanan in Scotland, and Miles Coverdale in England, among others. Locke was familiar with *Defense of Liberty Against Tyrants* and much of the resistance literature.[84] Daniel Dreisbach claims that the *Defense*, via Locke, and the Reformed Protestant clergy who supported that right, stamped its imprint on the American Revolution.[85] The connection is more direct and explicit: Jefferson adopted "Rebellion to Tyrants is Obedience to God" as the motto for his personal seal after that slogan had been unsuccessfully proposed by Benjamin Franklin to be used for the Seal of the United States. Embracing this slogan aligned these founders with Knox, who, a century earlier had written: "'[t]o resist evil' is equal to 'honor[ing] God truly.'"[86]

Thomas Hooker and Roger Williams gave voice to notions of popular sovereignty, majority rule, liberty, and separating religion from government well before Locke penned his *Second Treatise*. Relishing the irony, Lutz writes: "[I]t makes more sense to call Locke an American than it does to call America Lockean."[87]

In colonial America, the Reformed Protestant tradition was pervasive and significant. It was a religion of intense political activism rooted in the

[82] "The Tenure of Kings and Magistrates," in John Milton, *Areopagitica and Other Political Writings of John Milton* (Indianapolis: Liberty Fund, 1999), 58.

[83] The list includes Francois Hotman, *Francogallia* (1573), Theodore Beza, *Du droit des magistrats* [*Right of Magistrates*] (1574) and Philippe du Plessis-Mornay (attrib.), *Vindiciae Contra Tyrranos* [*Defense of Liberty Against Tyrants*] (1579). These works are available in *Constitutionalism and Resistance in the Sixteenth Century: Three Treatises by Hotman, Beza, & Mornay*, ed. and trans. Julian H. Franklin (New York: Pegasus, 1969).

[84] John Witte Jr., "Rights, Resistance, and Revolution in the Western Tradition: Early Protestant Foundations," *Law and History Review* 26, no. 3 (Fall 2008): 570.

[85] Dreisbach, *Reading the Bible*, 26–27.

[86] As quoted in David W. Hall, *The Geneva Reformation and the American Founding* (Lanham, MD: Lexington Books, 2003), 4.

[87] Lutz, *Origins of American Constitutionalism*, 11.

image of the Puritan community as the collective agent of Providence.[88] It was a tradition that made a connection between religion and the political order. Calvinists in Europe and their American counterparts, the Presbyterians, embraced and preached the following ideas: constitutions must be written because self-interest and depravity will subvert law absent fixed, determinate rules; liberty must be defended even if it means resistance to authority; representatives are obligated to act on behalf of the community; and power should not be placed in the hands of one or the few.

Unquestionably the founding principles of the republic can trace their provenance to Enlightenment writers like Locke, but beyond his political writings, Locke was "a major theologian whose interpretation of Christianity was tremendously influential in Britain and America."[89] There was no need to see a "convergence between Locke and Protestantism …because Locke already was a Protestant theologian."[90] Unlike the French Enlightenment and French Revolution, a distinctive feature of the colonial American experience was the synthesis, rather than antithesis, of religious and Enlightenment principles.[91]

The fusion of Lockean and classical republican ideals in the sermons and writings of the Protestant clergy amplified their impact far beyond what otherwise would have been the case. Political philosophers in England and on the continent who wrote on the nature of government, natural laws, and natural rights may have been read by colonial elites, but they were not on the reading lists of most colonists. Until the 1760s, religious publications outnumbered all other categories of publications in

[88] George McKenna, *The Puritan Origins of American Patriotism* (New Haven, CT: Yale University Press, 2007), 4, and the Introduction generally.

[89] Thomas G. West, "The Transformation of Protestant Theology as a Condition of the American Revolution," in *Protestantism and the American Founding*, ed. Thomas S. Engeman and Michael P. Zuckert (Notre Dame, IN: Notre Dame Press, 2004), 188.

[90] Ibid., 190. Steven Dworetz has provided extensive evidence of Locke's impact on the Puritan tradition and the extent to which the clergy, particularly in New England, relied on him to reinforce their political ideas. *Unvarnished Doctrine*, 135–184.

[91] A number of historians have explored this connection. See George M. Marsden, *The Twilight of the American Enlightenment: The 1950s and the Crisis of Liberal Belief* (New York: Basic Books, 2014), xxiii–xxiv; Mark A. Noll, *America's God: From Jonathan Edwards to Abraham Lincoln* (New York: Oxford University Press, 2002); David A. Hollinger "The Accommodation of Protestant Christianity with the Enlightenment: An Old Drama Still Being Enacted," in Hollinger, *After Cloven Tongues of Fire: Protestant Liberalism in Modern American History* (Princeton, NJ: Princeton University Press, 2013).

the colonies and two out of three colonists placed themselves somewhere in the dissenting religious tradition. Religion stood virtually alone as a community and cultural gathering place.[92] Gordon S. Wood described the influence religion had on political understandings:

> [I]t was the clergy who made the Revolution meaningful for most common people… for every gentleman who read a scholarly pamphlet and delved into Whig and ancient history for an explanation of events, there were dozens of ordinary people who read the Bible and looked to their ministers for an interpretation of what the Revolution meant.[93]

What the latter knew about these ideas arrived in the form of sermons, pamphlets, broadsides, newspaper articles, and public gatherings.[94] Patricia U. Bonomi characterized this interplay between the clergy and the Revolution: "By turning colonial resistance into a righteous cause, and by crying the message to all ranks in all parts of the colonies, ministers did the work of secular radicalism and did it better."[95]

[92] Edwin S. Gaustad, "Religion Before the Revolution," in Greene and Pole, *Companion to the American Revolution*, 64.

[93] "Religion and the American Revolution" in *New Directions in American Religious History*, ed. Harry S. Stout and D. G. Hart (New York: Oxford University Press, 1997), 175.

[94] Robert Ferguson noted "[c]olonial Americans, in effect, use[d] their diatribes against episcopacy to recognize each other across denominational affiliations." Robert A. Ferguson, *The American Enlightenment, 1750–1820* (Cambridge, MA: Harvard University Press, 1997), 47. George III's remark that the Revolution was nothing more than a "Presbyterian rebellion" is given scholarly support by J. C. D. Clark in *The Language of Liberty 1660–1832: Political Discourse and Social Dynamics in the Anglo-American World* (Cambridge: Cambridge University Press, 1994). Clark argues that religion (denominational differences) played a central role in mobilizing support for the Revolution. Rival conceptions of liberty were expressed in the conflict created by Protestant dissidents' hostility to Anglican hegemony. In his words: "the conflict among different persuasions of Christians [was] … a chief determinant of the idioms of discourse within which all political conflicts were articulated." Ibid., 146.

[95] *Under the Cope of Heaven: Religion, Society, and Politics in Colonial America*, updated ed. (New York: Oxford University Press, 2003), 216. But see T. H. Breen, *The Marketplace of Revolution: How Consumer Politics Shaped American Independence* (New York: Oxford University Press, 2004), where he suggests the unifying factor was the consumer marketplace: "bourgeois virtues" exercised in that marketplace enabled the communication of political grievances and mobilization of political resistance. The marketplace of goods—the boycotting of goods—was the marketplace of ideas that helped generate and spread a common cause. Ibid., xv–xviii, 264, 329.

Reformed Protestantism could find common cause with American civic republicanism and Lockean liberalism partly because, on key points—consent of the governed, natural rights, commonweal, civic virtue, limited government, right to resist tyrants—they preached the same gospel, or at least parallel gospels. This common nesting ground existed because during the course of the eighteenth century, Lockean ideas had been adopted by both Whig-infused republicans and the Protestant clergy.[96]

It was this confluence of Reformed Protestantism, Lockean liberalism, classical republican themes, and English common law constitutionalism found in the writings of the radical Whigs that shaped the political culture of the American colonists in the first half of the eighteenth century. Although radical or true Whigs provided significant support for the colonists' assertions of their rights under the English Constitution, it was the "identification of English rights with natural rights that made relatively easy the transition from history to political theory."[97] It was this transformation to which John Adams referred when he wrote that the "*radical change in the principles, opinions, sentiments, and affections of the people, was the real American Revolution.*"[98]

[96]Thomas West provides a clear picture of the gradual transformation of the original understanding on which Puritans founded their communities to the Lockean political theology of mid-eighteenth century Congregationalism. West, "Transformation of Protestant Theology," 190. Another earlier and more detailed account of the Protestant clergy's use of Locke or Lockean ideas can be found in Alice M. Baldwin, *The New England Clergy and the American Revolution* (Durham, NC: Duke University Press, 1928).

[97]Trevor Colbourn, *The Lamp of Experience: Whig History and the Intellectual Origins of the American Revolution* (Indianapolis: Liberty Fund, 1998 [1965]), 232. The designations "Radical Whigs" or "True Whigs" were used to differentiate the political thinkers and publicists who supported an amalgam of Lockean and classical republican ideas from the Whig political party that held power during most of the eighteenth century. David N. Mayer has traced "the uniquely American attributes of American constitutionalism directly to the influence on Americans of the Revolutionary era of the ideas of the English radical Whigs of the seventeenth and eighteenth centuries." "The English Radical Whig Origins of American Constitutionalism," *Washington University Law Review* 70, no. 1 (January 1992): 204.

[98]Letter to Hezekiah Niles, February 13, 1818, in John Adams, *The Works of John Adams, Second President of the United States* (Boston: Little, Brown and Co., 1856), 10:283 (emphasis in original).

The Rights Tradition in America's First Constitutions

In this chapter, we provide a summative view of the understanding of rights contained in the constitutions adopted by the former colonies and Vermont between 1776 and 1790.

Rights and Community

Rights in the seventeenth and eighteenth centuries were as likely to be understood as communal and geographic as individual and personal: "Bearers of rights included legislatures, governments, cities, colonies, countries, specific communities, and 'the people' as a collective entity distinct from individuals."[1] We start, therefore, with the view that the rights provisions under examination must be read in the context of the colonists' understanding of conditions necessary for sustaining the community. That assumption leads us to hypothesize that rights functioned differently in state constitutions than in the national Bill of Rights, which explains why these declarations contained items that would not be considered rights in the twentieth and twenty-first centuries. By working through these community conditions, we can reach behind the template established by the

[1] Richard A. Primus, *The American Language of Rights* (Cambridge: Cambridge University Press, 1999), 85. Jefferson, Adams, and Paine, among others, spoke of the rights of the Parliament, legislatures, and municipalities. The 1776 Maryland declaration referred to the rights of the City of Annapolis. Md. Decl. 1776, Art. XXXVII.

P. J. Galie et al., *Bills of Rights Before the Bill of Rights*,
https://doi.org/10.1007/978-3-030-44301-6_3

U.S. Bill of Rights and reveal the rights world of the newly independent Americans.

Donald S. Lutz lays out what he considers the Whig political theory that undergirded colonial communities:

- The population is homogeneous with respect to rights;
- The population has a community of interests in protecting and preserving these rights; and
- Community interests are superior to individual interests.[2]

Colonial governments regulated all sorts of personal behavior, moral and religious, "without any consciousness that they were depriving people of their private liberty or rights."[3] They could do so because liberty had not yet come to mean the right of an individual to a subjective claim against the community. The difficult business of translating the kinds of activities protected by the "life, liberty, and pursuit of happiness" trilogy was undertaken by the community and would not be interpreted in ways inconsistent with the public good. The community claimed the **right** to perform the difficult and protean task of determining what conditions and limits would be placed on liberty, whether based on claims of natural rights or English common law rights.[4]

Once individuals entered civil society, all questions of rights, save those deemed natural *and* inalienable (e.g., the right to life or the right to religious conscience), were matters for the community to decide. American colonists used rights to express community values.[5] Several declarations of rights would follow Pennsylvania's declaration, which speaks of the people's "sole, exclusive and inherent **right** of governing and regulating the

[2] *Popular Consent and Popular Control: Whig Political Theory in the Early State Constitutions* (Baton Rouge: Louisiana State University Press, 1980), 203.

[3] Gordon S. Wood, *The Idea of America: Reflections on the Birth of the United States* (New York: Penguin Press, 2011), 297. Barry Alan Shain summarizes the work of scholars who agree with Wood. *The Myth of American Individualism: The Protestant Origins of American Political Thought* (Princeton, NJ: Princeton University Press, 1994), 30–32.

[4] As Jack N. Rakove noted: "[I]n the eighteenth century...many authorities would still have held that the primary holders of rights were not individuals but rather the collective body of the people." *Declaring Rights: A Brief History with Documents* (New York: Palgrave Macmillan, 1997), 22.

[5] Donald S. Lutz, *A Preface to American Political Theory* (Lawrence: University Press of Kansas, 1992), 72–73.

internal police [power] of the [state]."[6] Viewed today as a power of the community that is often in tension with rights claimed by individuals, the police power was "properly a liberty, because the aggregate of individuals could thereby assert the essential rights of safety, morality, and well-being against the licentious."[7] The community had rights!

Early state constitution writers saw no conflict between a commitment to rights protection as a central purpose of government and the police power of the community. John Jay, one of the architects of the first New York Constitution, spoke for most when he wrote:

> ...civil liberty consists not in a right to every man to do just what he pleases, but it consists in an equal right to all the citizens to have, enjoy, and to do, in peace, security, and without molestation, whatever the equal and constitutional laws of the country admit to be consistent with the public good.[8]

Robert C. Palmer writes of the nexus between community and rights with concision: "[C]ommunal powers, when exercised in a properly structured republican government, maximized freedom."[9]

The early natural rights republics interwove rights and duties into their constitutional tapestries. The word "duty" is used to refer to the duties of both officials and citizens, with the latter including, inter alia, the duty

[6] Pa. Decl. 1776, Art. III (emphasis added). See also Del. Decl. 1776, sec. 4; Md. Decl. 1776, Art. II; N.C. Decl. 1776, Art. II; Vt. Decl. 1777, Art. IV; Vt. Decl. 1786, Art. V.

[7] Robert C. Palmer, "Liberties as Constitutional Provisions: 1776–1791," in *Liberty and Community: Constitution and Rights in the Early American Republic*, ed. William E. Nelson and Robert C. Palmer (New York: Oceana Publications, 1987), 66. The provision asserted the sovereign independence (self-governance) of the state vis-à-vis other states.

[8] Charge to Grand Juries (1790), *The Correspondence and Public Papers of John Jay*, ed. Henry P. Johnston (New York: G. P. Putnam's Sons, 1891), 3:395, http://oll.libertyfund.org/titles/jay-the-correspondence-and-public-papers-of-john-jay-vol-1-1763-1781. As Gordon S. Wood noted, "[I]ndividual liberty and the public good were easily reconcilable because the important liberty in the Whig ideology was public or political liberty." *The Creation of the American Republic, 1776–1787* (Chapel Hill: University of North Carolina Press, 1969), 61.

[9] Palmer, "Liberties as Constitutional Provisions," 55.

to worship God,[10] the duty to defend the state,[11] the duty "to bear witness to the truth,"[12] and the duty "to practise Christian forbearance, love, and charity towards each other."[13] Focusing on the word "duty," however, understates the pervasiveness of the duty/right correlation. Duty is also indicated by phrases such as "bound to contribute"[14] and "being responsible for the abuse of that liberty."[15] When referring to citizen behavior, "ought" also functioned as a synonym for duty.[16] Finally, there are implicit duty provisions. The right of the people to bear arms for the defense of the state and provisions declaring a "well-regulated militia" the proper defense of a free state[17] fuse a duty or obligation with the right to serve in the militia. Pennsylvania's provision is typical: "every member of society hath a right to be protected in the enjoyment of life, liberty and property, and therefore is bound to contribute his proportion towards the expence of that protection, and yield his personal service when necessary, or an equivalent thereto."[18]

[10] See, e.g., Md. Decl. 1776, Art. XXXIII; Mass. Decl. 1780, Art. II. See also Va. Decl. 1776, sec. 16 (describing religion as "the duty which we owe to our Creator").

[11] See N.Y. Const. 1777, Art. XL.

[12] S.C. Const. 1778, Art. XXXVIII.

[13] Va. Decl. 1776, sec. 16.

[14] Del. Decl. 1776, sec. 10; N.H. Decl. 1784, Art. XII; Pa. Decl. 1776, Art. VIII; Vt. Decl. 1777, Art. IX; Vt. Decl. 1786, Art. X.

[15] Pa. Const. 1790, Art. IX, sec. 7.

[16] See, e.g., Mass. Decl. 1780, Art. XVIII; N.H. Decl. 1784, Art. XXXVIII; Pa. Decl. 1776, Art. XIV; Vt. Decl. 1777, Art. XVI; Vt. Decl. 1786, Art. XX (all prescribing that people "ought" to pay particular attention to certain fundamental principles in their selection of representatives).

[17] See Table 3, for specific militia provisions applicable to each state.

[18] Pa. Decl. 1776, Art. VIII. Paying taxes and serving in the militia were expected of citizens, both to fulfill their obligations and to demonstrate their involvement in the community. The maintenance of public order was a community affair, the duty of all citizens. All able-bodied men were part of the militia and were required to possess (and pay for) their arms. England had restricted ownership of arms among commoners as a measure to help enforce game laws and to allay concerns over armed and potentially rebellious subjects. At different times, Catholics and Protestants (depending on the religion of the monarch) were subjected to such restrictions. Colonial conditions produced a less restrictive view on the bearing of arms by the citizenry: militia service was seen as a matter of survival. Robert J. Cottrol and Raymond T. Diamond, "Public Safety and the Right to Bear Arms," in *The Bill of Rights in Modern America: After 200 Years*, ed. David J. Bodenhamer and James W. Ely Jr. (Bloomington: Indiana University Press, 1993), 72–77.

Religion and the Community

The newly independent Americans defined their connection to God, others, and themselves in terms of duties and responsibilities. They shared a belief that a republican government was impossible absent a strong moral foundation in the people, and that moral foundation depended on religion. Where Lutz draws his communitarian assumptions from Whig political theory, Barry Alan Shain sees them rooted in the Reformed Protestant tradition. He notes the vast majority of early Americans lived in "morally demanding agricultural communities shaped by reformed-Protestant social and moral norms."[19] James H. Hutson describes the connection between religion, morality, and republican government as the founding generation's syllogism: "[V]irtue and morality are necessary for free, republican government; religion is necessary for virtue and morality; religion is, therefore, necessary for republican government."[20] Colonial preacher Gad Hitchcock reflected the depths to which human nature would fall absent the liberty acquired through virtue: Men with liberty "can be led to acquire, and support the character of religion and virtue;" conversely, without liberty, they "sink below the primitive standard of humanity… They become stupid, and debased in spirit, indolent and groveling…"[21]

This commitment to civic virtue and morality was as crucial for the republican idea of liberty as self-government as it was for Reformed Protestant theology. A government reflected the degree of civic virtue exhibited among members of the community. In contemporary terms: "people get the government they deserve." The nexus between individual liberty and the health of the state led political and religious leaders to focus on the dangers of the loss of civic virtue, viz., moral decay and corruption of the political order. Nathan O. Hatch noted the ease with which the eighteenth-century commonwealth tradition merged with New England prophetic history as the "rhetoric of the jeremiad and the coming

In the colonies, the right and obligation to bear arms broadened to include commoners, and was not limited by religious considerations.

[19] *Myth of American Individualism*, xvi.

[20] *Religion and the Founding of the American Republic* (Washington, DC: Library of Congress, 1998), 81.

[21] *A Sermon Preached at Plymouth, December 22, 1774* (Boston: Edes and Gill, 1775), 17.

kingdom slipped so imperceptibly into evocations of republican meanings…."[22]

Constitutional Principles

A number of provisions in the early state constitutions were aspirational and hortatory. They proclaimed and sanctified the values by which the community defined itself, and provided the basis for civic education and enlightenment that would make it more difficult for violations of popular sovereignty to occur. The use of hortatory and precatory language to express these principles makes sense if we approach them not as enactments of fundamental law beyond the reach of government, but as the constitutional principles that provide the foundations of the regime.[23] Declaring rights would serve as "a prime agency of that political and moral education of the people on which free republican government depends."[24] In the words of the "Federal Farmer":

> Men, in some countries do not remain free, merely because they are entitled to natural and unalienable rights; men in all countries are entitled to them, not because their ancestors once got together and enumerated them on paper, but because, by repeated negotiations and declarations, all parties are brought to realize them, and of course to believe them to be sacred….[25]
>
> If a nation means its systems, religious or political, shall have duration, it ought to recognize the leading principles of them in the front page of every family book.[26]

[22] *The Sacred Cause of Liberty: Republican Thought and the Millennium in Revolutionary New England* (New Haven, CT: Yale University Press, 1977), 137.

[23] Here we rely on the careful analysis of Jeremy Elkins, "Constitutions and 'Survivor Stories': Declarations of Rights," *University of Chicago Law School Roundtable* 3 (1996): 243–322. That declarations of rights, which did not emanate from and were not granted by governments, were placed before the structures or frames of government is further evidence of their function.

[24] Herbert J. Storing, *What the Anti-Federalists Were For: The Political Thought of the Opponents of the Constitution* (Chicago: University of Chicago Press, 1981), 70.

[25] "Letter from the Federal Farmer to the Republican," Letter 16, January 20, 1788, in *An Additional Number of Letters From the Federal Farmer to the Republican*… (New York: T Greenleaf, 1788), 145.

[26] Ibid., 144.

They were "admirable tablets upon which these new conceptions [of rights would be] publicly and indelibly engraved," a "civic lexicon by which the people teach themselves the grammar and meaning of freedom."[27]

From this perspective, the rights provisions included in these constitutions no longer appear as anomalies or imperfect first attempts. The provisions that took the form of principles or ideals were not seen as judicially enforceable limitations on state action; rather, they were principles on which the polity was founded and to which all citizens should repair. How does one enforce a right to resistance?[28] To whom does one appeal to vindicate the right to alter or abolish a government?[29] The use of the word "ought" rather than "shall" in many of these declarations also suggests that their character and purpose was to enshrine principles and provide aspirational guidance rather than to demand any specific legal action;[30] they were "structural necessities for the basic liberty of republicanism."[31]

The central focus on community that characterized colonial life, reflected in the first constitutions, found support in the civic republican tradition with its emphasis on sovereignty in the people as a collective body and the right to self-government, that is, public liberty. G. Alan Tarr, a leading student of our state constitutional tradition, concluded that the assumptions of modern liberalism as to the fundamental incompatibilities both between majority rule and the protection of rights and between individual rights and the common good were not shared by those who

[27] William Clarence Webster, "A Comparative Study of the State Constitutions of the American Revolution," *The Annals of the American Academy of Political and Social Science* 9 (May 1897): 388; Colleen A. Sheehan, *James Madison and the Spirit of Republican Self-Government* (Cambridge: Cambridge University Press, 2009), 108.

[28] See, e.g., Md. Decl. 1776, Art. IV; N.H. Decl. 1784, Art. X.

[29] See, e.g., Del. Decl. 1776, sec. 5; Md. Decl. 1776, Art. IV; Mass. Decl. 1780, Art. VII; N.H. Decl. 1784, Art. X; Pa. Decl. 1776, Art. V; Pa. Const. 1790, Art. IX, sec. 2; Vt. Decl. 1777, Art. VI; Vt. Decl. 1786, Art. VII; Va. Decl. 1776, sec. 3.

[30] Lutz, *Popular Consent*, 62.

[31] Palmer, "Liberties as Constitutional Provisions," 67, 82. Palmer refers to them as "serious principles by which the government was to abide." Ibid., 69. In the last decade or so of the eighteenth century, a few courts began to treat "ought" in provisions as synonymous with "shall," and thus judicially enforceable.

wrote our first constitutions.[32] It was the vigilant, civic-minded citizen who would ensure that the legislature and executive would remain true to the liberties embodied in these declarations of rights.

All the early state constitutions contained some combination of the following principles: a commitment to natural rights, equality, popular sovereignty (and its related concept, the consent of the governed), and a polity dedicated to serving all—a commonweal.

Natural Rights

The Declaration of Independence opens with the proclamation that all men are created equal, followed by the assertion that all humans possess the unalienable rights to life, liberty, and the pursuit of happiness. The universalistic character of its opening paragraph is in sharp contrast to the seventeenth-century Petition of Right and English Declaration of Rights, which confined their rights claims to the ancient rights and liberties and statutes of the realm. The difference between natural, unalienable rights and natural but alienable rights occasioned much dispute at the philosophic level as well as in the public arena.[33] Polemicists, publicists, and public officials rarely bothered to make distinctions, and the terms were often used synonymously. In any case, nearly all of the newly adopted state declarations committed to some version of natural rights.[34]

[32] *Understanding State Constitutions* (Princeton, NJ: Princeton University Press, 1998), 80.

[33] See pp. 30–37 for analysis of the distinctions offered by European and colonial thinkers.

[34] Natural rights included: (1) liberty of conscience or the right to worship God (see Del. Decl. 1776, sec. 2 ("natural and unalienable"); N.H. Decl. 1784, Arts. IV and V ("natural and unalienable"); N.C. Decl. 1776, Art. XIX ("natural and unalienable"); Pa. Decl. 1776, Art. II ("natural and unalienable"); Pa. Const. 1790, Art. IX, sec. 3 ("natural and indefeasible"); Vt. Decl. 1777, Art. III; Vt. Decl. 1786, Art. III ("natural and unalienable")); (2) rights to enjoy and defend life and liberty, acquire, possess, and protect property, and seek and obtain safety and happiness (see Mass. Decl. 1780, Art. I ("natural, essential, and unalienable"); N.H. Decl. 1784, Art. II ("natural, essential, and inherent"); Pa. Decl. 1776, Art. I ("natural, inherent and inalienable"); Vt. Decl. 1777, Art. I ("natural, inherent, and unalienable"); Vt. Decl. 1786, Art. I (same as 1777 declaration); Va. Decl. 1776, sec. 1 ("inherent rights")); and (3) the right to emigrate from one state to another, or to form a new state in a vacant country or in a country that they purchased (see Pa. Decl. 1776, Art. XV ("natural inherent"); Vt. Decl. 1777, Art. XVII ("natural and inherent"); Vt. Decl. 1786, Art. XXI (same as 1777 declaration)). The preambles of the Massachusetts, Pennsylvania, and Vermont constitutions all affirmed

Equality

Undergirding the justification of republican government and popular sovereignty was the belief that citizens were capable of exercising an independent will. All men were created equal in the sense that they were endowed with natural rights to life and liberty and to pursue happiness. Notwithstanding differences in talent, strength, and intelligence, they all possessed the moral sense to discern right from wrong—the just and unjust. As Jefferson wrote, "[w]hatever be their degree of talent it is no measure of their rights."[35]

The commitment to the view that all men were by nature equal meant that no adult could be subject to the rule of another without his or her consent. They are, in the words of the Virginia Declaration of Rights—"by nature equally free and independent,"[36] possessing an independent value or worth in their own right. The stark juxtaposition of such sentiments with the existence of slavery was to perplex and divide the nation from its inception.

Possessing natural rights to liberty and equality did not, *ipso facto*, entitle one to citizenship: "the political claim to equal citizenship required a different sort of argument than the natural and universal claim to freedom."[37] Civil rights were derived from, but not identical to, natural rights. As one commentator notes, "people are 'free' or 'equal' only as members of society, not as people as such. Eighteenth-century formulations of freedom could carry only the meanings allowed by the contemporary social and cultural market."[38]

that one of the ends of government was to furnish citizens the power of enjoying their natural rights.

[35] Letter to Henri Gregoire, February 25, 1809, *The Works of Thomas Jefferson*, ed. Paul Leicester Ford (New York: G.P. Putnam's Sons, 1905), 11:100. It was not a historical accident that organized anti-slavery politics originated in America. By the beginning of the nineteenth century, nearly all Northern states had abolished or taken steps to abolish slavery.

[36] Va. Decl. 1776, sec. 1. See also Mass. Decl. 1780, Art. I; N.H. Decl. 1784, Art. I; Pa. Decl. 1776, Art. I; Pa. 1790, Art. IX, sec. 1; Vt. Decl. 1777, Art. I; Vt. Decl. 1786, Art. I.

[37] Diana Schaub, Letter in Reply to John Burt's Response to Review of *Lincoln's Tragic Pragmatism: Lincoln, Douglas, and Moral Conflict*, n. d., *Claremont Review of Books* 14, no. 1 (Winter 2013/2014): 7.

[38] Michal Jan Rozbicki, *Culture and Liberty in the Age of the American Revolution* (Charlottesville: University of Virginia Press, 2011), 17. Some, like Jefferson, believed

Critics of the gap between these proclamations of equality and the reality on the ground pass over the significance of the contrast between the new states and English society, where the principle of hierarchy—property, aristocratic lineage, age, and sex—divided the king from his subjects, a principle that extended throughout the social order. The privileges, immunities, and franchises clauses found in many of the colonial charters reflected the fact that some possessed privileges, immunities, and franchises, while others did not. The republic offered all citizens, qua citizens, equal recognition and self-esteem, both of which heretofore had been ascribed to a few. In addition to the "created equally" clauses, seven constitutions contained explicit anti-aristocracy clauses.[39]

Popular Sovereignty

Delegates to the congresses or conventions that drafted the early state constitutions took popular sovereignty seriously; they were determined to ensure that it remained an active principle and did not become what authors would later describe as a "fiction,"[40] "the most formidable abstraction of the Revolutionary era,"[41] or a "riddle inherent in the idea that a people actually could be the sovereign."[42]

The components of this doctrine have been laid out succinctly by Paul K. Conkin:

that granting blacks equal citizenship with whites would precipitate a race war. Letter to John Holmes, April 22, 1820, in Ford, *Works of Thomas Jefferson*, 12:158–160; *Notes on Virginia* (1782), Query 14, in Ford, *Works of Thomas Jefferson*, 4:49–50. See the section below on the right to vote for the suffrage requirements imposed by the states.

[39] See, e.g., Md. Decl. 1776, Art. XL; Mass. Decl. 1780, Art. VI; N.H. Decl. 1784, Art. IX; N.C. Decl. 1776, Art. XXII; Pa. Const. 1790, Art. IX, sec. 24; S.C. Const. 1790, Art. IX, sec. 5; Va. Decl. 1776, sec. 4. Georgia, North Carolina, Pennsylvania, and Vermont adopted provisions designed to eliminate entail, which promoted an aristocracy. See Ga. Const. 1777, Art. LI; Ga. Const. 1789, Art. IV, sec. 6; N.C. Const. 1776, Art. XLIII; Pa. Const. 1776, sec. 37; Vt. Const. 1777, sec. XXXIV; Vt. Const. 1786, sec. XXXIII.

[40] See Edmund S. Morgan, *Inventing the People: The Rise of Popular Sovereignty in England and America* (New York: W. W. Norton, 1988), 306.

[41] Stanley Elkins and Eric McKitrick, *The Age of Federalism: The Early American Republic, 1788-1800* (New York: Oxford University Press, 1993), 482.

[42] Christian G. Fritz, *American Sovereigns: The People and America's Constitutional Tradition Before the Civil War* (New York: Cambridge University Press, 2008), 8.

1. Sovereign power rests originally in the whole people of a commonwealth in a community founded on consent and mutual trust;
2. The people originally exercise their sovereignty by establishing the form and specific powers of their government. This fundamental law (constitution) must not violate natural law or the minimal ends of any society, but is superior to all positive or statutory law;
3. Popular sovereignty does not necessitate any particular form of government, but it does make any government a fiduciary (i.e., a limited trust with effective powers of sovereignty, but never itself sovereign); and
4. The people have continuous access to the fundamental law, either to change it entirely or to amend it.[43]

The Virginia Declaration of Rights, the first declaration adopted by a former colony, specified the first component, proclaiming that "all power is vested in, and consequently derived from, the people; that magistrates are their trustees and servants, and at all times amenable to them."[44] The other states followed suit: every state that adopted a constitution during the period under consideration specified the first component, the heart of the doctrine.

Commonweal

Popular sovereignty was understood to mean that all legitimate power resided in and flowed from the people **united for the common good**. The latter phrase suggests common commitments, agreement on values, and a way of life. It was a right and a duty of the government to promote the commonweal.[45]

[43] *Self-Evident Truths: Being a Discourse on the Origins & Development of the First Principles of American Government—Popular Sovereignty, Natural Rights, and Balance & Separation of Powers* (Bloomington: Indiana University Press, 1974), 25–26.

[44] Va. Decl. 1776, sec. 2. See also Del. Decl. 1776, sec. 1; Ga. Const. 1777, preamble; Md. Decl. 1776, Art. I; Mass. Decl. 1780, Art. V; N.H. Decl. 1784, Arts. I, VIII; N.J. Const. 1776, preamble; N.Y. Const. 1777, Art. I; N.C. Decl. 1776, Art. I; Pa. Decl. 1776, Art. IV; Pa. Const. 1790, Art. IX, sec. 2; S.C. Const. 1790, Art. IX, sec. 1; Vt. Decl. 1777, Art. V; Vt. Decl. 1786, Art. VI.

[45] A "commonwealth" is "a state in which the supreme power is vested in the people." Emily J. Salmon and Edward D. C. Campbell Jr., eds., *The Hornbook of Virginia History*, 4th rev. ed. (Richmond: The Library of Virginia, 1994), 88. Four states (Virginia,

The preamble to the Massachusetts Constitution describes the role the common good plays in the body politic:

> The body politic is formed by a voluntary association of individuals: it is a social compact, by which the whole people covenants with each citizen, and each citizen with the whole people, that all shall be governed by certain laws for the common good. It is the duty of the people, therefore, in framing a constitution of government, to provide for an equitable mode of making laws, as well as for an impartial interpretation and a faithful execution of them; that every man may, at all times, find his security in them.[46]

That same document asserts that "[g]overnment is instituted for the common good; for the protection, safety, prosperity, and happiness of the people; and not for the profit, honor, or private interest of any one man, family, or class of men."[47]

The common good was mentioned most often in connection with provisions concerning the right to assemble, as this provision from the Pennsylvania declaration shows: "That the people have a right to assemble together, to consult for their common good, to instruct their representatives, and to apply to the legislature for redress of grievances, by address, petition, or remonstrance."[48] Other constitutions specified that no person could be bound by any laws except those they had assented to for their common good.[49]

Massachusetts, Pennsylvania, and Kentucky) began to employ that term in the eighteenth century, with Virginia being the first. Ibid.

[46] Mass. Const. 1780, preamble.

[47] Mass. Decl. 1780, Art. VII. Other states having similar provisions are N.H. Decl. 1784, Art. X; Pa. Decl. 1776, Art. V; Vt. Decl. 1777, Art. VI; Vt. Decl. 1786, Art. VII; Va. Decl. 1776, sec. 3.

[48] Pa. Decl. 1776, Art. XVI. Similar provisions are found at Mass. Decl. 1780, Art. XIX; N.H. Decl. 1784, Art. XXXII; N.C. Decl. 1776, Art. XVIII; Pa. Const. 1790, Art. IX, sec. 20; Vt. Decl. 1777, Art. XVIII; Vt. Decl. 1786, Art. XXII.

[49] See Pa. Decl. 1776, Art. VIII; Vt. Decl. 1777, Art. IX; Vt. Decl. 1786, Art. X.

Structural Provisions: The Infrastructure of Liberty

The successful operation of a natural rights republic required structures and procedures that would implement the foundational principles and ensure the protection of rights. The early state constitutions contained mechanisms that would enable citizens to obtain knowledge of and commitment to republican principles and to exercise the vigilance that was indispensable for the success of the republic.

Commitment to legislative supremacy was contingent on a belief that it would be the most effective means for expressing the people's will. The various devices and procedures adopted suggest a fear that power, wherever exercised, required watching and carefully structuring so that there would be little or no gap between citizens and their representatives. To this end, the framers relied on structural safeguards found in their frames of government. These included bicameralism, separation of legislative, judicial, and executive powers, prohibitions against or limitations on plural office-holding, representative assemblies (equally apportioned with broad-based suffrage), requirements that all money bills originate in the lower house (the house closest to the people), short terms for legislators and chief executives, and term limits.[50]

Table 1 indicates structural limitations in the early state constitutions.

In addition to these limitations, a number of early constitutions made the government accessible to the people by providing that the doors of the legislature be kept open,[51] requiring that legislative proceedings

[50] Commitment to the separation of powers ran the gamut, from the weakest in the constitutions of Pennsylvania, Georgia, and Vermont to the strongest in Virginia and Massachusetts, both of which made explicit commitments to the doctrine. The former reflected the radical Whig notion of legislative supremacy, while the latter followed the moderate Whig commitment to balanced regimes. Lee Ward, *The Politics of Liberty in England and Revolutionary America* (Cambridge: Cambridge University Press, 2004), 406ff. Thomas Paine's *Common Sense* and John Adams's rejoinder, "Thoughts on Government," provide arguments for the radical and moderate Whig positions respectively.

[51] See N.Y. Const. 1777, Art. XV; Pa. Const. 1776, sec. 13; Pa. Const. 1790, Art. I, sec. 15; Vt. Const. 1777, sec. XII; Vt. Const. 1786, sec. XIII.

Table 1 Institutional provisions in state constitutions adopted between 1776 and 1790

	No. of houses	*Lower house term (yrs)*	*Upper house term (yrs)*	*Chief exec term (yrs)*	*Explicit sep of powers*	*Money bills orig in lower house*	*Select of chief exec*	*Prohibitions against holding multiple offices*	*Term limits*	*Terms of highest judicial officers*
Delaware (1776)	Two	One	Three	Three	No	Yes	Leg	Yes (*arts. 8, 12, 18*)	P (*art. 7*)	Good behavior
Georgia (1777)	One	One	N/A	One	Yes	No	Leg	Yes (*arts. XVII, XVIII*)	G (*art. XXIII*)	One year
Georgia (1789)	Two	One	Three	Two	No	No	Leg	Yes (*art. I, sec. 10*)	No	Three years
Maryland (1776)	Two	One	Five	One	Yes	Yes	Leg	Yes (**art. XXXII**; *art. XXXVII*)	G (*art. XXXI*); S (*art. XLII*)	Good behavior
Massachusetts (1780)	Two	One	One	One	Yes	Yes	People	Yes (*ch.VI, art. I*)	T, RG (*ch. II, sec. IV, art. I*)	Good behavior
New Hampshire (1776)	Two	One	One	One	No	Yes	Leg	No	No	N/S
New Hampshire (1784)	Two	One	One	One	Yes	Yes	People	Yes (*Const.*)	D (*Const.*)	Good behavior
New Jersey (1776)	Two	One	One	One	No	Yes*	Leg	Yes (*art. XX*)	S (*art. XIII*)	Seven years

	No. of houses	*Lower house term (yrs)*	*Upper house term (yrs)*	*Chief exec term (yrs)*	*Explicit sep of powers*	*Money bills orig in lower house*	*Select of chief exec*	*Prohibitions against holding multiple offices*	*Term limits*	*Terms of highest judicial officers*
New York (1777)	Two	One	Four	Three	No	No	People	Yes (*arts. XXII, XXV, XXVI*)	S, C (*art. XXVI*)	Good behavior or age 60
North Carolina (1776)	Two	One	One	One lePara>	Yes	No	Leg	Yes (*arts. XXV-XXX, XXXV*)	G (*art. XV*); D (*art. XXXVII*)	Good behavior
Pennsylvania (1776)	One	One	N/A	One	No	No	Leg	Yes (*secs. 7, 19, 23*)	R (*sec. 8*); D (*sec. 11*); EC, S(*secs.19, 31*)	Seven years
Pennsylvania (1790)	Two	One	Four	Three	No	Yes	People	*Yes* (*art. I, sec. 18; art. II, secs. 5, 8*)	G (*art. II, sec. 3*); S (*art.VI, sec. 1*)	Good behavior
South Carolina (1776)	Two	Two	Two	N/S	No	Yes	Leg	Yes (*arts. IV, V, X*)	No	Good behavior
South Carolina (1778)	Two	Two	Two	Two	No	Yes*	Leg	Yes (*arts. IV, VII, IX, XX*)	G(*art.VI*); PC (*art. IX*); S, TO (*arts. XXVIII, XXIX*)	Good behavior

(continued)

Table 1 (continued)

	No. of houses	*Lower house term (yrs)*	*Upper house term (yrs)*	*Chief exec term (yrs)*	*Explicit sep of powers*	*Money bills orig in lower house*	*Select of chief exec*	*Prohibitions against holding multiple offices*	*Term limits*	*Terms of highest judicial officers*
South Carolina (1790)	Two	Two	Four	Two	No	Yes	Leg	Yes (*art. I, sec. 21; art. II, sec. 2*)	G (*art. II, sec. 2*); S (*art.VI, sec. 2*)	Good behavior
Vermont (1777)	One	One	N/A	One	No	No	People	No	D (*sec. X*)	N/S
Vermont (1786)	One	One	N/A	One	Yes	No	People	Yes (*sec. XXIII*)	D (*sec. XXVII*)	Annual
Virginia (1776)	Two	One	Four	One	Yes	Yes*	Leg	*Yes*	G (*Const.*)	Good behavior

Legend

N/A = Not applicable; **N/S** = Not specified. For provisions having citations, citations to a state declaration of rights are in bold. Citations to a state constitution are in italics

Money Bills: For states having an * in money bills column, upper house could not even amend money bills

Selection of Chief Executive Provision: Leg—State's chief executive chosen by the state legislative

Term Limits: C = Coroner; D = Delegate to Congress; EC = Executive Council Member; G = Governor; P = President

PC = Privy Council Member; R = Representative; RG = Receiver-General; S = Sheriff; T = Treasurer; TO = Treasury Officer

be published,[52] and ensuring citizens the right to petition or instruct legislators.[53]

A Republican Civic Culture

Constitutionally grounded structures and procedures alone were not sufficient: rights and principles needed to be maintained and fostered. To accomplish this goal, civic culture provisions were included in these charters. An example is found in Article XIV of the Pennsylvania Declaration of Rights: "a frequent recurrence to fundamental principles, and a firm adherence to justice, moderation, temperance, industry, and frugality are absolutely necessary to preserve the blessing of liberty, and keep a government free...."[54] This is not a right, let alone an enforceable one, as rights are now defined. It is, rather, an admonitory provision meant to promote and emphasize the role of moral character and civic virtue in sustaining the republic. Institutions that educated and instilled civic virtue in the citizens included schools, a free press, the jury, and the militia.

Schools

Educating elites and rulers in the West has ancient roots; that tradition, however, did not include civic education for subjects.[55] A singular but significant exception was the Puritan insistence upon all-inclusive, government-enforced, compulsory education. That legacy provided an educated, informed citizenry—an essential component in the making of the new republics.[56] Benjamin Rush, a leading eighteenth-century educational theorist, made it a postulate that a republic required educating the ordinary citizen: "Without learning, men are incapable of

[52] See N.H. Const. 1784; N.Y. Const. 1777, Art. XV; N.C. Const. 1776, Art. XLVI; Pa. Const. 1776, sec. 14; Pa. Const. 1790, Art. I, sec. 14; Vt. Const. 1777, sec. XIII; Vt. Const. 1786, sec. XIV.

[53] See Del. Decl. 1776, sec. 9; Md. Decl. 1776, Art. XI; Mass. Decl. 1780, Art. XIX; N.H. Decl. 1784, Art. XXXII; N.C. Decl. 1776, Art. XVIII; Pa. Decl. 1776, Art. XVI; Pa. Const. 1790, Art. IX, sec. 20; Vt. Decl. 1777, Art. XVIII; Vt. Decl. 1786, Art. XXII.

[54] Pa. Decl. 1776, Art. XIV. See also Mass. Decl. 1780, Art. XVIII; N.H. Decl. 1784, Art. XXXVIII; N.C. Decl. 1776, Art. XXI; Vt. Decl. 1777, Art. XVI; Vt. Decl. 1786, Art. XX; Va. Decl. 1776, sec. 15.

[55] On the role of education in colonial society, see Melvin C. Yazawa, "Creating a Republican Citizenry," in *The American Revolution: Its Character and Limits*, ed. Jack P. Greene (New York: New York University Press, 1987).

[56] Richard D. Brown, *The Strength of a People: The Idea of an Informed Citizenry in America, 1650-1870* (Chapel Hill: University of North Carolina Press, 1996), 3, 51.

knowing their rights, and where learning is confined to a few people, liberty can be neither equal nor universal."[57] Rush epitomized the collective sentiment of public intellectuals and activists when he wrote: "While we inculcate these republican duties upon our pupil, we must not neglect, at the same time, to inspire him with republican principles. He must be taught that there can be no durable liberty but in a republic."[58] The education required to sever the bonds of dependence was concerned not only with reading, writing, and arithmetic, but with transforming subjects into full participating members of the republic. Popular sovereignty gave rise to the idea of every individual as a guardian of public liberty. Education for citizenship had as its goal the creation of a citizen body capable of guarding its liberties jealously against the constant dangers of tyranny.

Giving constitutional status to these ideals and aspirations would provide a beacon light and a readily available measure for determining legitimate government action. Drafters undertook this task by including provisions that recognized and promoted moral integrity, civic virtue, and independence, tying those efforts to the preservation of liberty:

> Wisdom and knowledge, as well as virtue, diffused generally among the body of the people, being necessary for the preservation of their rights and liberties; and as these depend on spreading the opportunities and advantages of education in the various parts of the country, and among the different orders of the people, it shall be the duty of legislatures and magistrates, in all future periods of this commonwealth, to cherish the interests of literature and the sciences, and all seminaries of them; especially the university at Cambridge, public schools and grammar schools in the towns....[59]

[57] Benjamin Rush, "A Plan for Establishing Public Schools in Pennsylvania..." (1786), in Rush, *Essays, Literary, Moral, and Philosophical* (Philadelphia: Thomas and William Bradford, 1806), 1; see also Richard D. Brown, "The Idea of an Informed Citizenry in the Early Republic," in *Devising Liberty: Preserving and Creating Freedom in the New American Republic*, ed. David Thomas Konig (Stanford, CA: Stanford University Press, 1995), 161.

[58] Benjamin Rush, "Of the Mode of Education Proper in a Republic" (1786), in Rush, *Essays, Literary, Moral, and Philosophical*, 12. Eve Kornfeld, *Creating an American Culture, 1775–1800: A Brief History with Documents* (New York: Palgrave Macmillan, 2001), 27ff, examines the extensive network of intellectuals who shared and were active in establishing Rush's vision.

[59] Mass. Const. 1780, Ch. V, sec. II. New Hampshire adopted a similar provision. N.H. Const. 1784.

Six states included the creation of schools in their first state constitutions.[60] The idea that education of the lower ranks of people at public expense was crucial for republican government marked a radical break from past practice.[61]

Free Press

The colonists understood the importance of a free press for self-government and the liberty of the people. Reliance on the watchfulness of the electorate would be ineffective without a press to keep them informed. The indispensable nature of this institution is demonstrated by the fact that nearly all of the early state constitutions protected this freedom.[62] When freedom of the press provisions appeared in these declarations, they served to provide the people the means by which a communal will would form, be communicated, and be effectuated. By the same token, false and seditious statements were not protected and were seen as dangerous disruptors of the community rather than a necessary prerequisite for public liberty and social order.

The Jury

Alexis de Tocqueville captured the communitarian and republican character and functions of the jury. Unlike the jury in England, the jury system in America was a "consequence... of popular sovereignty just as direct... as universal suffrage. Both are equally powerful means of ensuring that

[60] In addition to Massachusetts and New Hampshire, these states included Georgia (Const. 1777, Art. LIV), North Carolina (Const. 1776, Art. XLI), Pennsylvania (Const. 1776, sec. 44; Const. 1790, Art. VII, sec. 1), and Vermont (Const. 1777, sec. XL; Const. 1786, sec. XXXVII).

[61] Initially women, blacks, and Native Americans were excluded from the public realm for which education was intended to be preparation.

[62] See Del. Decl. 1776, sec. 23; Ga. Const. 1777, Art. LXI; Ga. Const. 1789, Art. IV, sec. 3; Md. Decl. 1776, Art. XXXVIII; Mass. Decl. 1780, Art. XVI; N.H. Decl. 1784, Art. XXII; N.C. Decl. 1776, Art. XV; Pa. Decl. 1776, Art. XII; Pa. Const. 1776, sec. 35; Pa. Const. 1790, Art. IX, sec. 7; S.C. Const. 1778, Art. XLIII; S.C. Const. 1790, Art. IX, sec. 6; Vt. Decl. 1777, Art. XIV; Vt. Const. 1777, sec. XXXII; Vt. Decl. 1786, Art. XV; Va. Decl. 1776, sec. 12. In contrast, only the Pennsylvania and Vermont constitutions protected freedom of speech generally. Some states protected speech made during legislative debate. See Ga. Const. 1789, Art. I, sec. 14; Md. Decl. 1776, Art. VIII; Mass. Decl. 1780, Art. XXI; N.H. Decl. 1784, Art. XXX; N.C. Decl. 1776, Art. XLV; Pa. Const. 1790, Art. I, sec. 17; Vt. Decl. 1786, Art. XVI.

the majority reigns."[63] But beyond its role as a mechanism for the active expression of popular sovereignty, the jury provided a major vehicle for civic education and virtue:

> ... when juries are used in civil cases, their work is constantly in the public eye.... Everyone serves on them. Thus they become a part of daily usage. The human mind becomes habituated to the jury's forms, and the jury itself comes to be identified, as it were, with the very idea of justice.[64]

Tocqueville focuses his analysis on what he sees as the central role of the jury—the civic education of the citizen:

> The jury is incredibly useful in shaping the people's judgment.... This, in my view, is its greatest advantage. It should be seen as a free school, and one that is always open, to which each juror comes to learn about his rights, and where he ... receives practical instruction in the law....[65]
>
> * * *
>
> Thus, the jury, which is the most energetic form of popular rule, is also the most effective means of teaching the people how to rule.[66]

The importance of the right to trial by jury is demonstrated by its ubiquity in early state constitutions. All states adopting constitutions during the period under consideration guaranteed that right.[67] Among the states

[63] *Democracy in America,* trans. Arthur Goldhammer (New York: The Library of America, 2004), 314.

[64] Ibid., 315–316.

[65] Ibid., 316.

[66] Ibid., 318. Tocqueville amplifies Madison's view that bills of rights and institutions like the jury can serve as republican schoolmasters, forming the minds and character of the citizens. James Madison, "Spirit of Governments," *National Gazette*, February 18, 1792, in James Madison, *The Papers of James Madison*, ed. William T. Hutchinson, et al. (Charlottesville: University of Virginia Press, 1983), 14:234.

[67] See Del. Decl. 1776, secs. 13, 14; Ga. Const. 1777, Art. LXI; Ga. Const. 1789, Art. IV, sec. 3; Md. Decl. 1776, Arts. III, XIX; Mass. Decl. 1780, Arts. XII, XV; N.H. Decl. 1784, Arts. XVI, XX; N.J. Const. 1776, Art. XXII; N.Y. Const. 1777, Art. XLI; N.C. Decl. 1776, Arts. IX, XIV; Pa. Decl. 1776, Arts. IX, XI, Pa. Const. 1776, sec. 25; Pa. Const. 1790, Art. IX, secs. 6, 9; S.C. Const. 1776, Art. XVIII; S.C. Const. 1790, Art. IX, sec. 6; Vt. Decl. 1777, Arts. X, XIII; Vt. Const. 1777, sec. XXII; Vt. Decl. 1786, Arts. XI, XIV; Vt. Const. 1786, sec. XXVIII; Va. Decl. 1776, secs. 8, 11.

not adopting constitutions, Rhode Island's 1790 Declaration of Rights included a right to a jury trial,[68] and Connecticut had provided for jury trials of criminal and civil cases by 1672.[69] Beyond mere numbers, the power of the jury as an institution is seen in provisions such as Georgia's constitutional grant to the jury of the power to decide the law as well as the facts,[70] and New Jersey's legislative oath providing that the right to a jury trial could not be altered, amended, or repealed.[71]

The Militia

Concern about the danger of standing armies was a prominent issue in seventeenth-century England. The control of such armies by the Crown provided a source of patronage and thus a potential source of corruption. Moreover, a standing army could be turned against the people, weakening the belief that the people retained a right to resist a tyrant.[72] The English Bill of Rights of 1689 banned standing armies during peacetime absent the consent of Parliament. Subjects on both sides of the Atlantic also complained about having to quarter soldiers and maintained that the military power should be subordinate to the civil power.[73]

The fears Americans had of standing armies and a powerful military made the nascent country heavily dependent on the militia, and militia service was understood as a civic obligation. Patriotism was the quintessential republican virtue. A republic depended on citizens who

[68] See R.I. Decl. of Rights (1790), sec. 8, covered in that chapter.

[69] See text accompanying footnotes 71 and 72 of the Connecticut chapter.

[70] See Ga. Const. 1777, Art. XLI.

[71] See N.J. Const. 1776, Art. XXIII.

[72] The resistance to standing armies in England is well told in Stephen Skinner, "Blackstone's Support for the Militia," *American Journal of Legal History* 44, no. 1 (January 2000): 1–18.

[73] London's early charters, dating back to 1130 and 1155, placed restrictions on forced billeting. William S. Fields and David T. Hardy, "The Third Amendment and the Issue of the Maintenance of Standing Armies: A Legal History," *The American Journal of Legal History* 35, no. 4 (October 1991): 399. In turn, Magna Carta provided that the City of London would enjoy its "ancient liberties and free customs," Ch. 13. The English Petition of Right (1628) barred the quartering of soldiers and the imposition of martial law during peacetime. See Table 2, for the states having these provisions.

were willing to fight, and, if necessary, lay down their lives for their country: "A citizen who was not also a soldier had alienated a vital part of his freedom and had lost his independence."[74]

Delegates to the constituent bodies drawing up the constitutions saw militia service as a transformative experience molding members to civic virtue. Militia provisions also demonstrated the government's efforts to preserve the peace and security of the community. They were attempts to ensure that political violence was used for constitutional ends. The natural right to self-defense would be surrendered to the community in return for securing the safety of the republic through a well-regulated militia.[75]

Table 2 depicts the militia provisions adopted by the states. They illustrate the balance constitution-makers struck in providing for the defense and safety of the state, while prohibiting standing armies absent legislative approval, subordinating the military power to the civil, providing that only military personnel could be tried by military courts, and placing restrictions on quartering.

Implicit in the obligation to defend the republic in militia service was the right to bear arms. Cottrol and Diamond write: "By the eighteenth century, the right to possess arms, both for personal protection and as a counterbalance against state power, had come to be viewed as one of the fundamental rights of Englishmen on both sides of the Atlantic."[76] The debate over the individual versus the collective character of the right to bear arms has been carried on in the context of the Second Amendment and not in the context of the militia articles found in the state constitutions adopted prior to that amendment.[77] Any alleged dichotomy would not involve states' rights. The dichotomy, if there be such, would have

[74] H. T. Dickinson, *Liberty and Property: Political Ideology in Eighteenth-Century Britain* (London: Weidenfeld & Nicolson, 1977), 126.

[75] For further elaboration along these lines, see David C. Williams, *The Mythic Meanings of the Second Amendment: Taming Political Violence in a Constitutional Republic* (New Haven, CT: Yale University Press, 2003), Chs. 1–2 and Saul Cornell, *A Well-Regulated Militia: The Founding Fathers and the Origins of Gun Control in America* (New York: Oxford University Press, 2006), Ch. 1.

[76] Cottrol and Diamond, "Public Safety," 91.

[77] See, for example, the discussion of recent attempts at synthesis found in H. Richard Uviller and William G. Merkel, "Scottish Factors and the Origins of the Second Amendment: Some Reflections on David Thomas Konig's Rediscovery of the Caledonian Background to the American Right to Arms," *Law and History Review* 22, no. 1 (Spring 2004): 169–170.

Table 2 Military provisions in state constitutions, 1776 and 1790, and selected sources

	Obligation to contribute towards protection and give personal service[1]	*Right of people to have a well-regulated and disciplined militia*[2]	*Right to bear arms*	*Standing armies not to be kept (or kept only with legislative approval)*	*Military power subordinate to civil power*	*Restrictions on quartering*	*Martial law only for soldiers*
Petition of Right 1628						sec.VI	sec.VII
English Bill of Rights 1689			[art. VI]	[art. V]			
Decl. of Resolves 1774				No. 9, [11]		[No. 11]	
Decl. of Independence 1776				[No. 11]	[No. 12]	[No. 14]	
Delaware 1776	**sec. 10***	**sec. 18**		**sec. 19**	**sec. 20**	**sec. 21**	
Georgia 1777		*art. XXXV*#					
Georgia 1789							
Maryland 1776		**art.XXV**		**art. XXVI**	**art. XXVII**	**art. XXVIII**	**art. XXIX**
Massachusetts 1780	**art. X**		**art. XVII**	**art. XVII**	**art. XVII**	**art. XXVII**	**art. XXVIII**
New Hampshire 1776							
New Hampshire 1784	**art. XII***	**art. XXIV**		**art. XXV**	**art. XXVI**	**art. XXVII**	**art. XXXIV**
New Jersey 1776							
New York 1777	*art. XL**	*art. XL*					
North Carolina 1776			**art. XVII**	**art. XVII**	**art. XVII**		

(continued)

Table 2 (continued)

	Obligation to contribute towards protection and give personal service[1]	*Right of people to have a well-regulated and disciplined militia*[2]	*Right to bear arms*	*Standing armies not to be kept (or kept only with legislative approval)*	*Military power subordinate to civil power*	*Restrictions on quartering*	*Martial law only for soldiers*
Pennsylvania 1776	**art. VIII***	*sec. 5#*	**art. XIII**	**art. XIII**	**art. XIII**		
Pennsylvania 1790	*art. VI, sec. 2**		*art. IX, sec. 21*	*art. IX, sec. 22*	*art. IX, sec. 22*	*art. IX, sec. 23*	
South Carolina 1776							
South Carolina 1778					*art. XLII*		
South Carolina 1790					*art. IX, sec. 3*		
Vermont 1777	**art. IX***	*sec. V#*	**art. XV**	**art. XV**	**art. XV**		
Vermont 1786	**art. X***	*sec. XIX#*	**art. XVIII**	**art. XVIII**	**art. XVIII**		**art. XIX**
Virginia 1776		**sec. 13**		**sec. 13**	**sec. 13**		

Legend

For provisions having citations, citations to a state declaration of rights are in bold. Citations to a state constitution are in italics

Sections having brackets around them (e.g. [No. 11]) did not have a section or article number in the original text

[1]Those states with an * permitted conscientious objectors to pay an equivalent in lieu of giving personal service

[2]Those states with an # did not specifically secure the right of the people to a well-regulated militia, but did contain provisions specifically for the levying, organization, and training of the militia

been between a personal right to self-defense and the communal duty to serve in the militia.[78] But as Nathan R. Kozuskanich argues, "one cannot separate the eighteenth-century conception of rights from its collective implications."[79] He continues:

> The right to bear arms was not exercised solely by the state or by individuals, but rather by citizens in an attempt to ensure public safety. Early attempts to regulate the militia clearly show that individual rights and collective responsibilities were enmeshed. Indeed, the individual right to bear arms was essential if men were to perform their duty of militia service.[80]

David B. Kopel and Clayton E. Cramer also argue persuasively that the Militia Article of the Pennsylvania Constitution was meant to guarantee a personal right to bear arms and to provide for the collective defense of the state.[81]

The militia clauses, along with clauses limiting resort to standing armies and requiring civilian control of the military, were interrelated and tied directly to the character of a republic. The first prevented the government from achieving a monopoly of force and ensured that lawful governments could be forcefully defended and protected by the people as a whole. The second limited the *government's* ability to create a separate power of force. The third ensured that to the limited extent government required its own power of force, such power would be controlled by the people, acting through their civil representatives.[82]

[78] Two states, Pennsylvania and Vermont, explicitly provided individuals with the right to bear arms "for the defence of themselves and the state." Pa. Decl. 1776, Art. XIII; Pa. Const. 1790, Art. IX, sec. 21; Vt. Decl. 1777, Art. XV; Vt. Decl. 1786, Art. XVIII. Article 17 of Rhode Island's 1790 Declaration of Rights, while not explicitly mentioning self-defense, did not limit the right to bear arms to defense of the state.

[79] "Pennsylvania, the Militia, and the Second Amendment," *The Pennsylvania Magazine of History and Biography* 133, no. 2 (April 2009): 123.

[80] Ibid.

[81] "The Keystone of the Second Amendment: The Quakers, the Pennsylvania Constitution, and the Flawed Scholarship of Nathan Kozuskanich," *Widener Law Journal* 19 (2010): 277–320.

[82] Ibid., 291.

Fundamental Rights

In addition to expressing the fundamental values and goals to which the community was committed, declarations contained rights thought to be fundamental.[83] These were generally public liberties or communal rights. This is not to say that individual rights were absent or unimportant. Indeed, the right to due process associated with the protection of life, liberty, and property, appears in all of the declarations and constitutions.[84] Certain rights and privileges afforded to the accused in criminal prosecutions were also individual in nature.

All state constitutions contained a quartet of rights colonists considered fundamental: the right to self-government, implemented by elections and representative institutions; the right to trial by jury; liberty of conscience; and the protections included under the mantle of the due process of law. The first two, participatory and communal in character, were the guarantors of all other rights, and for that reason indispensable to the success of republican government. The liberty of conscience, which contained both individual and communal aspects,[85] reflected the important role religion played in the colonies. The due process clause, which protected the life, liberty, and property of citizens from arbitrary government actions, came closest to guaranteeing protection of individuals qua individuals.

Suffrage

A widespread franchise was a necessary concomitant of popular sovereignty. Combined with an elected legislature, it ensured that the community would not be subject to arbitrary actions by the government.

[83] R. R. Palmer notes "the liberties enumerated within the declarations…do not conform to the individual rights model." "Liberties as Constitutional Provisions," 62.

[84] See Md. Decl. 1776, Art. XXI; Mass. Decl. 1780, Art. XII; N.H. Decl. 1784, Art. XV; N.Y. Const. 1777, Art. XIII; N.C. Decl. 1776, Art. XII; Pa. Decl. 1776, Art. IX; Pa. Const. 1790, Art. IX, sec. 9; S.C. Const. 1778, Art. XLI; S.C. Const. 1790, Art. IX, sec. 2; Vt. Decl. 1777, Art. X; Vt. Decl. 1786, Art. XI; Va. Decl. 1776, sec. 8. In two states, Delaware and New Jersey, the appearance of the due process clause is indirect, applied through incorporation provisions that imported the common law or colonial statutes into the constitution. See Del. Const. 1776, Art. 25; N.J. Const. 1776, Art. XXII. Georgia had a provision incorporating "the principles of the habeas corpus act," Ga. Const. 1777, Art. LX (see also Ga. Const. 1789, Art. IV, sec. 4), and adopted a statute later that year continuing in force the common law of England. See p. 315.

[85] See pp. 72–75, and Table 4 pp. 76–78, for the communal dimensions of that right.

Republican government held out the promise of equal liberty to its citizens, but also determined who would be entitled to full citizenship in the body politic. Criteria for citizenship in eighteenth-century America included age, gender, residency, religion, property ownership, loyalty, and good character (virtue). What united the various conditions requisite for citizenship was personal independence from subjection to others and self-mastery or freedom from internal subjection to one's own passions.[86]

Table 3 shows the suffrage requirements established by the early state constitutions.

Historically, the method of discerning whether an individual possessed the necessary independence for full citizenship was a property test or its alternative, taxpayer status. The freehold requirements for voting, common in colonial times and continued in many of the early state constitutions, demonstrated the importance of property in determining citizenship. It measured the extent of involvement in the community and was a tangible manifestation of the virtues sometimes referred to, appropriately in colonial America, as the "Protestant ethic." A financial base would enable a person to resist bribery or other economic inducements to steal his vote. Abundant land in the colonies made freehold requirements for voting easier to satisfy, allowing for a much larger voting population than in England. Some states, such as Pennsylvania and Georgia, eliminated freehold requirements, implementing taxpayer requirements instead. Vermont went further, eliminating all financial requirements to vote. A residency requirement, in addition to providing stability, enabled a denizen to become acquainted with and integrated into the community before becoming a full participant.[87]

Dramatic evidence of the correlative duty/right character of the right to vote is found in the 1777 Georgia Constitution:

[86] Jack P. Greene, "All Men Are Created Equal: Some Reflections on the Character of the American Revolution," in Greene, *Imperatives, Behaviors, and Identities: Essays in Early American Cultural History* (Charlottesville: University of Virginia Press, 1992), 256, 261.

[87] Donald S. Lutz, *The Origins of American Constitutionalism* (Baton Rouge: Louisiana State University Press, 1988), 75. Participation rates in colonial America are notoriously difficult to calculate. There is evidence that property and religious requirements were not systematically enforced. On the other hand, a majority of residents "did not vote even though many of them were qualified to do so." Gilman Ostrander, *The Rights of Man in America, 1606–1861* (Columbia: University of Missouri Press, 1960), 65 and the studies cited at 62–65.

Table 3 Suffrage in state constitutions adopted between 1776 and 1790

Delaware 1776	As exercised by law (*art. 5*); in 1776, statutory requirements were: (1) natural born subject of Great Britain, or naturalized in England, Delaware, or Pennsylvania; (2) male; (3) 21 years of age; (4) freeholder within Delaware holding 50 acres of land, with 12 acres cleared and improved, or be otherwise worth 40 pounds lawful money; (5) resident of state for two years
Georgia 1777	(1) Male; (2) white; (3) 21 years of age; (4) possessed of 10 pounds value, and liable to pay tax in state, or being of mechanic trade; (5) resident of state for six months (*art. IX*)
Georgia 1789	(1) Citizens and inhabitants of state; (2) 21 years of age; (3) paid tax for year prior to election; (4) resident of county for six months (*art. IV, sec. 1*)
Maryland 1776	(1) Freeman; (2) 21 years of age; (3) freehold of 50 acres, residing in the county (or property above 30 pounds and residing in county for one year) (*arts. II, XIV*)
Massachusetts 1780	(1) Male; (2) 21 years of age; (3) freehold estate of annual income of three pounds, or any estate of the value of 60 pounds (*ch. I, sec. II, art. II; sec. III, art. IV; ch. II, sec. I, art. II*) (property must be owned in same town as residence to vote for lower house).
New Hampshire 1776	Not specified; in 1776, statutory requirements were: (1) male; (2) 21 years of age; (3) taxpayer status
New Hampshire 1784	(1) Male; (2) 21 years of age; (3) paying a poll tax (*Const.*)
New Jersey 1776	(1) Full age; (2) worth 50 pounds proclamation money, clear estate in the same; (3) resident of county for 12 months (*art. IV*)
New York 1777	**Assembly members:** (1) Male; (2) full age (not defined); (3) resided within county for six months; (4) freehold of twenty pounds within county, or have rented tenement of yearly value of forty shillings, and have been rated and actually paid taxes to state; (5) had to take oath of loyalty to state (*arts.VII, VIII*); **Senators and Governor:** (1) Freeholder possessed of freehold of value of 100 pounds over and above all debts charged therein (*arts. X, XVII*)
North Carolina 1776	**House of Commons:** (1) Freeman; (2) 21 years of age; (3) paid public taxes; (4) inhabitant of any one county or town in state for 12 months (*arts. VIII, IX*); **Senators:** (1) Freeman; (2) 21 years of age; (3) inhabitant of any one county in state for 12 months; (4) possessed of freehold within county of 50 acres of land, for six months (*art. VII*).
Pennsylvania 1776	(1) Freeman; (2) 21 years of age; (3) resided in state for one year; (4) paid public taxes during that time (also incl. sons of freeholders aged 21) (*sec. 6*).

Pennsylvania 1790	(1) Citizen; (2) freeman; (3) 21 years of age; (4) resident of state for two years before election; (5) paid a state or county tax assessed at least six months before the election (also incl. sons of qualified electors between ages 21 and 22) (*art. III, sec. 1*)
South Carolina 1776	As required by law (*art. XI*); in 1776, statutory requirements were: (1) free, white (2) male; (3) Protestant; (4) 21 years of age; (5) freeholder holding 100 acres of land, or have paid 10 shillings in taxes; (6) resident/inhabitant of state for one year.
South Carolina 1778	(1) Free, white; (2) male; (3) 21 years of age; (4) acknowledge the being of God and believe in future state of rewards and punishments; (5) resident/inhabitant of state for one year; (6) freehold of 50 acres of land, or town lot, and legally seized and possessed of same for six months before election, or paid tax the preceding year, or was taxable the present year, at least six months before election, in sum equal to tax on 50 acres of land (*art. XIII*)
South Carolina 1790	(1) Free, white; (2) male; (3) 21 years of age; (4) citizen of state; (5) resident in state two years; (6) freehold of 50 acres of land or a town lot which he has been legally seized and possessed at least six months before election, or resident in election district six months before election, and paid tax the preceding year of three shillings sterling (*art. I, sec. 4*)
Vermont 1777	(1) Male; (2) 21 years of age; (3) resident in state for one year; (4) quiet and peacable behavior (*sec. VI*)
Vermont 1786	(1) Male; (2) 21 years of age; (3) resident of state for one year; (4) quiet and peacable behavior (*sec. XVIII*)
Virginia 1776	As exercised as present; in 1776, statutory requirements were: (1) free, white; (2) male; (3) 21 years of age; (4) freehold of 100 acres of unimproved land or 25 acres of improved land, or a house and part of a lot in a city or town, possessed at least a year before voting (*Const.*)

Legend

For provisions having citations, citations to a state declaration of rights are in bold. Citations to a state constitution are in italics

CT: Connecticut did not adopt a constitution during the period under consideration. By 1776, the suffrage requirements for that state were: (1) Freeman; (2) 21 years of age; (3) person of an honest, peaceable, and civil conversation; (4) either real estate assessed at a yearly value of forty shillings or personal property assessed at forty pounds

RI: Rhode Island did not adopt a constitution during the period under consideration. By 1776, the suffrage requirements for that state were: (1) Freeman; (2) Christian, non-Catholic; (3) real estate either worth forty pounds or that rented for forty shillings

> Every person absenting himself from an election, and shall neglect to give in his or their ballot at such election, shall be subject to a penalty not exceeding five pounds; the mode of recovery and also the appropriation thereof, to be pointed out and directed by act of the legislature: *Provided, nevertheless*, That a reasonable excuse shall be admitted.[88]

The Jury

Eighteenth-century Americans considered the jury, along with the representative assembly, "popular powers," which were:

> the heart and lungs, the mainspring and the centre wheel, and without them the body must die, the watch must run down, the government must become arbitrary.... In these two powers consist wholly the liberty and security of the people.... What a satisfaction is it to reflect, that he can lie under the imputation of no guilt, be subjected to no punishment, lose none of his property, or the necessaries...but by the judgment of his peers, his equals, ...men ...who have no end to serve by punishing him...[89]

The jury was understood to be more than a protector of a person's life, liberty, and property from arbitrary actions of the government; in colonial America, juries often decided matters of law as well as of fact, meaning that the "representatives of local communities assembled as jurors generally had effective power to control the content of the province's substantive law."[90]

Liberty of Conscience

Religious thinkers believed that political virtue without a sincere belief in God was untenable. As one pastor noted, "virtue and piety are nearly connected—married by heaven."[91] Hatch summarizes the argument: "[A] belief in God's moral government and the approaching state of reward

[88] Ga. Const. 1777, Art. XII (emphasis in original).

[89] John Adams, "The Earl of Clarendon to William Pym," Letter published in Boston Gazette, January 27, 1766, in John Adams, *The Works of John Adams, Second President of the United States* (Boston: Little, Brown and Co., 1856), 3:482–483.

[90] William Edward Nelson, *Americanization of the Common Law: The Impact of Legal Change on Massachusetts, Society, 1760–1830* (Athens: University of Georgia Press, 1994), 29.

[91] John Murray, *Nehemiah, or the Struggle for Liberty Never in Vain...* (Newburyport, MA: John Mycall, 1779), quoted in Hatch, *Sacred Cause*, 110. Some, but not all,

and punishment would effectively check the unruly passions of men ..... The Christian religion could redirect the very source of human conduct and thus form better citizens in all walks of life."[92] All the colonies held fast to the view that a religious community was essential to the very survival of the state. Colonists, in their charters and laws, articulated theological principles and referred to Christianity, Protestantism, a monotheistic deity, or the inspiration of the Bible in positive terms.[93] Concomitant with this commitment to a polity grounded on religious belief was the commitment to what was known commonly as the "sacred rights of conscience."[94] It is the dialectical relationship between the two commitments that provided the key to understanding the religious provisions of the early state constitutions.

Though liberty of conscience was a goal of Enlightenment thinkers, an important reason Americans embraced religious liberty derived from Christian convictions. Biblical and theological arguments played a key role in protecting the sacred right of conscience: persecution didn't work; the Bible requires religious freedom; and "liberty of conscience causes true religion to flourish...."[95] Reformed Protestants, who constituted the overwhelming number of colonists, were committed to the view that the

republican thinkers did make a connection between civic virtue and religious belief, e.g. Machiavelli, *Discourses on Livy*, Bk III.

[92] Hatch, *Sacred Cause*, 110. Hatch quotes extensively from statements by clergymen throughout New England who echoed this belief.

[93] William G. Miller, *Faith, Reason, and Consent: Legislating Morality in Early American States* (New York: LBF Scholarly Publishing, 2008), 59. Even the most religiously tolerant colony, Rhode Island, was unwilling to consider religion unnecessary for a well-ordered community. Its 1663 charter, retained as its constitution after independence, speaks of the founders as "pursueing... their sober, serious and religious intentions... of edifieing themselves, and one another, in the holie Christian ffaith and worship..." and "preserv[ing] unto them that libertye, in the true Christian ffaith and worshipp of God, which they have sought..." and "true pietye rightly grounded upon gospell principles..." Charter of Rhode Island and Providence Plantations (1663), in Thorpe, *Constitutions*, 6:3211–3212. Moreover this religious liberty did not extend to any differences of opinion that "actually disturb the civill peace" or to "useing this libertie to lycentiousnesse and profanenesse... or outward disturbeance of others...." Ibid., 3213. See above pp. 47–48.

[94] For examples, see Daniel L. Dreisbach and Mark David Hall, *The Sacred Rights of Conscience: Selected Readings on Religious Liberty and Church-State Relations in the American Founding* (Indianapolis: Liberty Fund, 2009), vii–viii.

[95] Mark David Hall, *Did America Have a Christian Founding? Separating Modern Myth from Historical Truth* (Nashville: Nelson Books, 2019), 125.

sacred scripture alone constituted the rule of faith and practice and "that every Christian has *a right of judging for himself* what he is to believe and practice in religion according to that rule..."[96] A defining argument in the Protestant tradition for religious liberty derived from the theological principle that humans have a duty to worship God as their conscience dictates.[97]

Unlike the national Constitution, state constitutions devoted significant attention to religion; they recognized an obligation on the part of the community to promote religion as the foundation of the commonwealth as well as a condition of personal salvation. Even the inalienable right to religious conscience—a condition for personal salvation—was a prerequisite for full membership in the community. States often balanced provisions affording liberty of conscience, such as those barring compelled worship and forced support of sects other than one to which the citizen belonged, with provisions requiring religious oaths and qualifications for office-holding and granting full civil rights only to particular believers.

An understanding of this balance enables us to make sense of the Massachusetts Declaration of Rights, Article II, which speaks of the right *and* the duty to worship the Supreme Being and ensures the right of all citizens to worship as each sees fit unmolested and unrestrained. Immediately following, in Article III, one finds the communitarian dimension of this liberty:

> As the happiness of a people, and the good order and preservation of civil government, essentially depend upon piety, religion, and morality; and as these cannot be generally diffused through a community but by the institution of the public worship of God, and of public instructions in piety, religion, and morality: Therefore, to promote their happiness, and to secure the good order and preservation of their government, the people of this commonwealth have a right to invest their legislature with power to authorize and require, and the legislature shall, from time to time, authorize and require, the several towns, parishes, precincts, and other bodies politic, or religious societies, to make suitable provision, at their own expense, for the

[96] Elisha Williams, "The Essential Rights and Liberties of Protestants" (1744), in *Political Sermons of the American Founding Era, 1730–1805*, ed. Ellis Sandoz, 2nd ed. (Indianapolis: Liberty Fund 1998), 1:55.

[97] Evidence of the widespread commitment to this idea is provided in Hall, *Did America Have a Christian Founding?*, 125–131.

> institution of the public worship of God, and for the support and maintenance of public Protestant teachers of piety, religion, and morality, in all cases where such provision shall not be made voluntarily.[98]

By simultaneously granting liberty of conscience and requiring those who dissented from the Congregational Church to pay taxes to their own pastor or, if they lacked a minister, to contribute to Congregational worship, these provisions fused the protection of an individual's sacred right to conscience with the structural and moral support necessary to sustain the character of the community.[99] Table 4 indicates the extent to which this combination is repeated in other constitutions.

The attempts to reconcile claims to full citizenship for members of diverse religious communities with the belief that religion is an indispensable prerequisite for a stable and decent community are evident in constitutional provisions found in both Massachusetts and New Hampshire. In those states, the commitment to the inalienable right of conscience is followed by a statement of the indispensable role religion plays in the life of the community and an admonition that the community has the right to protect and foster that role by requiring that believers "demean[] themselves peaceably, and as good subjects of the commonwealth …"[100]

The Establishment of Religion

An understanding of the phrase "established religion" in the context of the Revolutionary constitutions cannot be had if we take as our starting point the Establishment Clause of the First Amendment. In large part, that clause reflected the determination of Anti-Federalists to ensure the national government would not interfere with a state's sovereignty over its religious establishments or support for religions. The concern over established religions, attributed to Jefferson and Enlightenment thinkers

[98] Mass. Decl. 1780, Art. III. See also Md. Decl. 1776, Art. XXXIII; N.H. Decl. 1784, Arts. V, VI; S.C. Const. 1778, Art. XXXVIII; Vt. Decl. 1777, Art. III; Vt. Decl. 1786, Art. III.

[99] This balance was made clear when Richard Henry Lee of Virginia, a state with the Church of England as its established church, wrote that "true freedom embraces the Mahomitan [Muslim] and the Gentoo [Hindu] as well as the Xn [Christian] religion…." Letter to James Madison, November 26, 1784, *The Letters of Richard Henry Lee*, ed. James Curtis Ballagh (New York: Macmillan, 1914), 2:305.

[100] Mass Decl. 1780, Art. III. See also N.H. Decl. 1784, Art. VI.

Table 4 Religion in state constitutions adopted between 1776 and 1790

	Persons afforded liberty of conscience/free exercise of religion	*Persons entitled to equal rights and privileges*	*General assessment*	*Religious requirements for public officers*	*Restrictions on ministers holding office*
Delaware (1776)	All (**sec. 2**)	Christians (**sec. 3**)	Forbidden (**sec. 2**)	Any office–Oath (*art. 22*)[4]	Any office (*art. 29*)
Georgia (1777)	All (*art. LVI*)	N/S	Allowed (*art. LVI*)	Leg–Protestant (*art. VI*)	Leg (*art. LXII*)
Georgia (1789)	All (*art. IV, sec. 5*)	N/S	Allowed (*art. IV, sec. 5*)	None	Gen'l Assy (*art. I, sec. 18*)
Maryland (1776)	Christians (**art. XXXIII**)	N/S (but see **art. XXXIII)**	Allowed (**art. XXXIII**)[2]	Any office–Oath (**art. XXXV**; *art. LV*)[5]	Gen'l Assy, Gov Coun (*art. XXXVII*)
Massachusetts (1780)	All (**art. II**)	Christians (**art. III**)	Allowed (**art. III**)[3]	Gen'l Ct, Gov, Lt. Gov, Exec Coun–Oath (*ch.VI, art. I*)[6]	None
New Hampshire (1776)	N/S	N/S	N/S	None	None
New Hampshire (1784)	All (**art. II**)	Christians (**art. VI**)	Allowed (**art. VI**)[3]	Gen'l Ct, Gov–Protestant	None
New Jersey (1776)	All (*art. XVIII*)	Protestants (*art. XIX*)	Forbidden (*art. XVIII*)	Leg, any office–Protestant (*art. XIX*)	None

	Persons afforded liberty of conscience/free exercise of religion	*Persons entitled to equal rights and privileges*	*General assessment*	*Religious requirements for public officers*	*Restrictions on ministers holding office*
New York (1777)	All (*art. XXXVIII*)	N/S	Forbidden (*art. XXXV*)	None	Any office (*art. XXXIX*)
North Carolina (1776)	All (**art. XIX**; *art. XXXIV*)	N/S	Forbidden (**art. XXXIV**)	Any office–Oath (*art. XXXII*)[7]	Gen'l Assy, Coun of State (*art. XXXI*)
Pennsylvania (1776)	All (**art. II**)	Believers in a God (**art. II**)	Forbidden (**art. II**)	House of Reps–Oath (*sec. 10*)[8]	None
Pennsylvania (1790)	All (*art. IX, sec. 3*)	N/S	Forbidden (*art. IX, sec. 3*)	Any office–Oath (*art. IX, sec. 4*)[9]	None
South Carolina (1776)	N/S	N/S	N/S	None	None
South Carolina (1778)	Believers in one God (*art. XXXVIII*)[1]	Protestants (*art. XXXVIII*)	Forbidden (*art. XXXVIII*)	Gen'l Assy, Gov, Lt Gov–Protestant (*art. III*)	Gen'l Assy, Gov, Lt Gov, Privy Coun (*art. XXI*)
South Carolina (1790)	All (*art. VIII, sec. 1*)	N/S	N/S	None	Gen'l Assy, Gov, Lt Gov (*art. I, sec. 23*)
Vermont (1777)	All (**art. III**)	Protestants (**art.III**)	Forbidden (**art.III**)	House of Reps–Oath (*sec. IX*)[10]	None

(continued)

Table 4 (continued)

	Persons afforded liberty of conscience/free exercise of religion	*Persons entitled to equal rights and privileges*	*General assessment*	*Religious requirements for public officers*	*Restrictions on ministers holding office*
Vermont (1786)	All (**art. III**)	All (**art. III**)	Forbidden (**art. III**)	House of Reps–Oath (*sec. XII*)[11]	None
Virginia (1776)	All (**sec. 16**)	N/S	N/S	None	Gen'l Assy, Privy Coun

Legend: Gen'l Assy-General Assembly; Gen'l Ct-General Court; Gov-Governor; Gov Coun-Governor's Council; Leg-Legislature; Privy Coun-Privy Council; N/S-Not Specified

For provisions having citations, citations to a state declaration of rights are in bold. Citations to a state constitution are in italics

Connecticut and Rhode Island did not adopt constitutions during the specified period. For their treatment of religion, see the chapters on those states. The 1776 Maryland and 1778 South Carolina constitutions banned compelled worship but limited free exercise to the groups listed

[1]**SC**: Required to acknowledge: one God; future state of punishments and rewards; and God is to be publicly worshipped

[2]**MD**: Could lay general tax for support of Christian religion, for which individual could designate recipient

[3]**MA** and **NH**: Could tax for support and maintenance of public Protestant teachers of piety, religion, and morality, for which individual could apply to his own denomination, or else it would go towards parish or precinct where it was raised

[4]**DE**: "I, A B, do profess faith in God the Father, and in Jesus Christ His only Son, and in the Holy Ghost, one God, blessed for evermore; and I do acknowledge the holy scriptures of the Old and New Testament to be given by divine inspiration"

[5]**MD**: Had to subscribe declaration of belief in the Christian religion

[6]**MA**: "I, A. B., do declare, that I believe the Christian religion, and have a firm persuasion of its truth..." A candidate for governor was also required to declare himself to be of the Christian religion (Const., Ch. II, sec. I, Art. II)

[7]**NC**: Could not deny being of God, truth of Protestant religion, or divine authority of Old or New Testaments

[8]**PA**: "I do believe in one God, the creator and governor of the universe, the rewarder of the good and the punisher of the wicked. And I do acknowledge the Scriptures of the Old and New Testament to be given by Divine inspiration"

[9]**PA**: Had to acknowledge the being of a God and a future state of rewards and punishments

[10]**VT**: "I do believe in one God, the Creator and Governor of the universe, the rewarder of the good and punisher of the wicked. And I do acknowledge the scriptures of the old and new testament to be given by divine inspiration, and own and profess the protestant religion"

[11]**VT**: Principles of 1786 oath were identical to that of 1777 constitution; only difference was pronoun structure

generally, arose from the danger "lest impious clerks tighten their grip upon the purses and the minds of men."[101] Thinkers committed to the importance of religion, such as Roger Williams, saw the danger coming from a different direction. They worried that the wilderness (the state) might invade or insinuate itself into the garden (religion).

On the eve of the Revolution, churches receiving direct tax aid existed in nine colonies.[102] Even in colonies without tax support, such as Pennsylvania, Delaware, and New Jersey, religious tests for public office and laws promoting Christian morality and practices were present. The Revolutionary-era constitutions saw an expansion of exemptions from the general assessments that were used to support churches, and eventually, to the elimination of direct financial support for religion. Henceforth religions would survive on voluntary contributions.

Of greater importance is the fact that whether or not a state had a single, multiple, or no established church, every state constitution—to one degree or another—established religion: the religion of Christianity. This is made amply clear by the religious requirements for office-holding, the oaths required of officeholders, suffrage requirements,[103] oaths for obtaining citizenship,[104] and related provisions.[105]

Where a religion or religions were officially recognized, this recognition did not constitute a complete union of church and state: Church and state were kept separate in that magistrates managed the political realm, while the spiritual realm was left to the clerics. Of the twelve states adopting constitutions between 1776 and 1790, seven prohibited ministers from serving in the legislature, and several also barred clergymen from holding executive offices.[106] Church and state had their separate spheres of action and "neither was to transgress the domain of the other."[107] In practice, especially in the New England colonies of Massachusetts and

[101] Mark De Wolfe Howe, *The Garden and the Wilderness: Religion and Government in American Constitutional History* (Chicago: University of Chicago Press, 1965), 7.

[102] John K. Wilson, "Religion under the State Constitutions, 1776–1800," *Journal of Church and State* 32, no. 4 (Autumn 1990): 754.

[103] See S.C. Const. 1778, Art. XIII.

[104] See N.Y. Const. 1777, Art. XLII.

[105] See Table 4 for details.

[106] See Table 4 for details.

[107] C. Gregg Singer, *A Theological Interpretation of American History*, 3rd ed. (1964; reprint, Greenville, SC: A Press, 1994), 15.

Connecticut, cooperation between the two created a de facto fusion that effectively limited liberty of conscience to a narrow band of religious beliefs.[108]

Due Process

If there is a central theme that can be traced to Magna Carta, it is the idea that no one should be deprived of life, liberty, or property except by the law of the land or due process of the law.[109] Subsequent iterations of this right included a right to timely access to justice.[110] The due process clause initially provided narrow protections to freemen, but gradually expanded under the influence of common law judges like Edward Coke and parliamentary statutes. Having successfully read a trial by jury protection into the due process clause, Coke addressed the question: Of what value would these protections be to one falsely imprisoned? His answer: the writ of habeas corpus. This writ was sanctioned by the Petition of Right of 1628 and strengthened by the Habeas Corpus Act of 1679. Eventually, the due process clause came to protect all subjects of the realm and to encompass the full panoply of rights we now identify with the term due process of law.

Colonists included these rights in their charters, bodies of liberties, articles, laws and orders, and, after 1776, in their constitutions. Of the twelve states adopting constitutions in the period under consideration, nine included law of the land or due process guarantees, and seven adopted open court or right to remedy clauses. Colonists derived the right to a jury trial from those same chapters, and that right was found in every state constitution. Drawing on Chapter 20 of Magna Carta, ten states prohibited excessive bail or fines. Five state constitutions guaranteed

[108] By the end of the eighteenth century, growing religious pluralism, accompanied by an aggressive and expansive understanding of what liberty of conscience required, prompted the adoption of constitutional provisions expanding religious liberty and full citizens' rights to all Christians, resulting in the breakdown and gradual elimination of general assessment systems for aiding religion typified by the Massachusetts Declaration of Rights. William G. McLoughlin, "The Role of Religion in the Revolution: Liberty of Conscience and Cultural Cohesion in the New Nation," in *Essays on the American Revolution*, ed. Stephen G. Kurtz and James H. Hutson (Chapel Hill: University of North Carolina Press, 1973), 210–229.

[109] Magna Carta, Ch. 39.

[110] Magna Carta, Ch. 40. Both these clauses were merged into Chapter 29 of the 1225 revision.

the writ of habeas corpus.[111] Other provisions derived from that document included those banning the taking of private property without just compensation (Chapter 28) and a right to free emigration into the state (Chapter 42).

The English Constitution, Common Law, and Colonial Grievances

The influence of the common law tradition on American law generally is hard to overstate.[112] Entitlement to the common law was listed among those rights included in the 1774 Declaration and Resolves, and several of the abuses claimed in the Declaration of Independence, e.g., deprivation of the right to a jury trial, were violations of rights secured by the common law. The extensive reliance on the common law that characterized the colonial period continued with the constitution-making during the Revolutionary period. Americans used it to generate the core of their declarations of rights.[113] Seven state constitutions contained clauses directly or indirectly incorporating the common law into the law of the state insofar as that law was consistent with the republican principles adumbrated in the documents, and all the remaining states under consideration besides Connecticut[114] incorporated the common law by statute:

State	*Method*	*Reference*
Connecticut	Neither	Not incorporated by statute or constitution
Delaware	Constitution	Const. 1776, Art. 25
Georgia	Statute	Act of September 16, 1777 (criminal law); Act of November 15, 1778 (all common law); Act of February 25, 1784 (made permanent)
Maryland	Constitution	Decl. 1776, Art. III
Massachusetts	Constitution	Const. 1780, Ch. VI, Art. VI
New Hampshire	Both	Act of April 9, 1777; Const. 1784, Pt. II
New Jersey	Constitution	Const. 1776, Art. XXII
New York	Constitution	Const. 1777, Art. XXXV
North Carolina	Statute	Laws of 1778, Ch. V

(continued)

[111] See p. 86, below for additional discussion of preservation by statute and judicial decision.

[112] See Chapter 2, generally.

[113] Lutz, *Origins of American Constitutionalism*, 60.

[114] See pp. 354, 356–358, for that state's unique treatment of the common law.

(continued)

State	*Method*	*Reference*
Pennsylvania	Statute	Act of January 28, 1777, P.L. 429
Rhode Island	Statute	Act of January, 1798
South Carolina	Combination	Const. 1776, Art. XXIX; Const. 1778, Art. XXXIV; Const. 1790, Art. VII (all continuing Act of December 17, 1712)
Vermont	Statute	Act of February 1779 (common law of New England); Act of June 1782 (common law of England)
Virginia	Statute	Act of May 6, 1776

Any parts of the common law deemed inconsistent with the state's political ideals and constitutional tradition could be revised or nullified by legislative enactment. These umbrella provisions encompassed an extensive body of rights-protecting law. The complaint that these early state constitutions were incoherent and incomplete in their selection process seems to ignore the force of these incorporation clauses.[115]

The inclusion in state constitutions of some rights protected under the common law and statutory law of England and not others suggests that the proximate cause for their inclusion might be their derivation from, among others, the Declarations and Resolves of the First Continental Congress (1774) and the twenty-seven item "train of abuses" listed in the Declaration of Independence. The willingness of British authorities to undermine or ignore their own rights tradition signaled the need to have the endangered rights placed in the fundamental law.[116]

[115] See especially Leonard W. Levy, *Origins of the Bill of Rights* (New Haven, CT: Yale University Press, 1999), 63–64. Levy recognizes the significance of these incorporation clauses by implication, repudiating his earlier claim of haphazard incompleteness, at least with regard to due process and the common law. Moreover, by restricting his examination to rights that appear in the constitutions, he minimizes or ignores the fact that on the eve of the Revolution, a number of states had established solid foundations for the protection of these rights in their charters, statutes, or interpretations of the common law. This was certainly the case with regard to the privilege against self-incrimination, which, by the time of the Revolution, had achieved "nearly universal acceptance." George Dargo, *Roots of the Republic: A New Perspective on Early American Constitutionalism* (New York: Praeger, 1974), 70–71.

[116] Declaration and Resolves of the First Continental Congress, in Barry Alan Shain, ed., *The Declaration of Independence in Historical Context: American State Papers, Petitions, Proclamations, and Letters of the Delegates to the First National Congress* (Indianapolis:

The selection process for specific rights included in the declarations of rights was governed less by principles than by "the need to reject specific adversities of colonial rule."[117] Colonists focused on the rights being threatened by colonial officials, the Crown, and later by Parliament. A majority of the declarations would have included, e.g., freedom from military imposition, security of property, trial by jury in the vicinity, search and seizure protections, representative government, the right to petition, bans on the suspension of laws without legislative consent, and mandates that no taxation could be imposed absent the consent of the people.

Other rights included in most declarations were those that had achieved acceptance among the colonists, even if they were not the subject of a particular grievance against the Crown. Concerning rights for those accused of crimes, all eight declarations adopted between 1776 and 1790 included the right to be informed of the nature of the charges, the right to be confronted with witnesses, and the privilege against self-incrimination; six declarations provided the right to counsel, which had already been expanded well beyond the protections afforded by English common law.[118] Table 5 indicates how the more prevalent rights, whether or not adopted in response to particular grievances, were treated in the early state declarations and constitutions.

The fact that a particular right was not included in the majority of state declarations or constitutions, in and of itself, suggests nothing about the

Liberty Fund, 2014), 211–214. In the "Declaration and Resolves," the sources of rights are listed as "the immutable laws of nature, the principles of the English Constitution and the several charters or compacts…." The rights listed, however, all have their source in the English Constitution and the several charters, not the "immutable laws of nature." In this respect, the Declaration and Resolves anticipates a similar dichotomy found in the 1776 Declaration of Independence between the opening paragraph and the grievances listed in the body of the document. The phrase "immutable laws of nature" is taken from William Blackstone's *Commentaries on the Laws of England in Four Books* (1753; reprint, Philadelphia: J. B. Lippincott Co., 1893), 1:124. Blackstone's use of the phrase offers little support to the natural rights philosophy asserted by the American Revolutionaries. English law "could not be reduced to a rationalist deductive structure, nor was it based on a set of natural law principles." Michael Lobban, "Blackstone and the Science of the Law," *The Historical Journal* 30, no. 2 (June 1987): 334. For the use of nature and natural rights as authority for rights, see above pp. 30–37.

[117] Primus, *American Language of Rights*, 90.

[118] Other departures from the English common law in early state constitutions included protection for debtors, elimination of primogeniture and entail, prohibitions of sanguinary punishments, and elimination of punishment for suicide. See Table 5.

Table 5 Selected provisions in state constitutions adopted between 1776 and 1790, with selected sources

	Due Process/ Law of Land	*Open Courts/ Right to Remedy*	*Jury Trial*	*Trial in Vicinity*	*No Excessive Bail/Fines*
Magna Carta 1215	ch.39	ch.40	ch.39		chs.20,21
Petition of Right 1628	secs. III, IV				
English Bill of Rights 1689			[art.XI]		[art.X]
Stamp Act Grievance 1765			No. VII	No. VIII	
Decl. of Resolves 1774			No. 5	No. 5	
Decl. of Independence 1776			[No. 18]	[No. 19]	
Delaware 1776		**sec.12**	**sec.13**	**sec.13**	**sec.16**
Georgia 1777			*art.LXI*	*art.XXXIX*	*art.LIX*
Georgia 1789			*art.IV,sec.3*	*art.III, sec.4*	
Maryland 1776	**art.XXI**	**art.XVII**	**arts.III,XIX**	**art.XVIII**	**art.XXII**
Massachusetts 1780	**art.XII**	**art.XI**	**arts.XII,XV**	**art.XIII**	**art.XXVI**
New Hampshire 1776					
New Hampshire 1784	**art.XV**	**art.XIV**	**arts.XVI,XX**	**art.XVII**	**art.XXXIII**
New Jersey 1776			*art.XXII*		
New York 1777	*art.XIII*		*art.XLI*		
North Carolina 1776	**art.XII**		**arts.IX,XIV**		**art.X**
Pennsylvania 1776	**art.IX**	*sec.26*	**arts.IX,XI;***sec.25*		*sec.29*
Pennsylvania 1790	*art.IX,sec.9*	*art.IX,sec.11*	*art.IX,secs.6,9*	*art.IX, sec.9*	*art.IX, sec.13*
South Carolina 1776			*preamble*	*preamble*	
South Carolina 1778	*art.XLI*				
South Carolina 1790	*art.IX, sec.2*		*art.IX, sec.6*		*art.IX, sec.4*
Vermont 1777	**art.X**	*sec.XXIII*	**arts.IX,XIII;***sec.XXII*	**art.XIX**	*sec.XXVI*
Vermont 1786	**art.XI**	**art.IV**	**arts.XI,XIV;***sec.XXVIII*	**art.XXIII**	*sec.XXX*
Virginia 1776	**sec.8**		**secs.8,11**	**sec.8**	**sec.9**

	Right to Counsel	*Restrictions on Search/ Seizure*	*Confront Witnesses*	*No Self-Incrimination*	*Informed of Charges*
Magna Carta 1215					
Petition of Right 1628					
English Bill of Rights 1689					
Stamp Act Grievance 1765					
Decl. of Resolves 1774					
Decl. of Independence 1776					
Delaware 1776	**sec.14**	**sec.17**	**sec.14**	**sec.15**	**sec.14**
Georgia 1777					
Georgia 1789					
Maryland 1776	**art.XIX**	**art.XXIII**	**art.XIX**	**art.XX**	**art.XIX**
Massachusetts 1780	**art.XII**	**art.XIV**	**art.XII**	**art.XII**	**art.XII**
New Hampshire 1776					
New Hampshire 1784	**art.XV**	**art.XIX**	**art.XV**	**art.XV**	**art.XV**
New Jersey 1776	*art.XVI*		*art.XVI*		
New York 1777	*art.XXXIV*				
North Carolina 1776		**art.XI**	**art.VII**	**art.VII**	**art.VII**
Pennsylvania 1776	**art.IX**	**art.X**	**art.IX**	**art.IX**	**art.IX**
Pennsylvania 1790	*art.IX, sec.9*	*art.IX, sec.8*	*art.IX, sec.9*	*art.IX, sec.9*	*art. IX, sec.9*
South Carolina 1776					
South Carolina 1778					
South Carolina 1790					
Vermont 1777	**art.X**	**art.XI**	**art.X**	**art.X**	**art.X**
Vermont 1786	**art.XI**	**art.XII**	**art.XI**	**art.XI**	**art.XI**
Virginia 1776		**sec.10**	**sec.8**	**sec.8**	**sec.8**

(continued)

Table 5 (continued)

	No Cruel/Unusual Punishment	*Habeas Corpus*	*Right to Petition*	*Only Legislature can Suspend Laws*	*Taxation only with Consent*
Magna Carta 1215					ch.12
Petition of Right 1628		sec.V			secs. I,II
English Bill of Rights 1689	[art.X] (and)		[art.V]	[art.I]	[art. IV]
Stamp Act Grievance 1765			No. XIII		Nos. III-V, VIII
Decl. of Resolves 1774			No. 8	[No.11]	Nos.4,[11]
Decl. of Independence 1776				[Nos. 6,21,22]	[No. 17]
Delaware 1776	**sec.16 (or)**		**sec.9**	**sec.7**	
Georgia 1777		*art.LX*			
Georgia 1789		*art.IV, sec.4*			
Maryland 1776	**art.XXII (or)**		**art.XI**	**art.VII**	**art.XII**
Massachusetts 1780	**art.XXVI (or)**	*ch.VI, art.VII*	**art.XIX**	**art.XX**	**art.XXIII**
New Hampshire 1776					
New Hampshire 1784	**art.XXXIII (or)**	*Const.*	**art.XXXII**	**art.XXIX**	**art.XXVIII**
New Jersey 1776					
New York 1777					
North Carolina 1776	**art.X (or)**	**art.XIII**	**art.XVIII**	**art.V**	**art.XVI**
Pennsylvania 1776			**art.XVI**		*sec.41*
Pennsylvania 1790	*art.IX, sec.13(cruel)*	*art.IX, sec.14*	*art.IX, sec.20*	*art.IX, sec.12*	
South Carolina 1776					*preamble*
South Carolina 1778					
South Carolina 1790	*art.IX, sec.4(cruel)*				
Vermont 1777			**art.XVIII**		*sec.XXXVII*
Vermont 1786			**art.XXII**	**art.XVII**	**art.X**
Virginia 1776	**sec.9 (and)**			**sec.7**	**sec.6**
	Restrictions on Gov't Takings	*No Ex Post Facto Laws*	*No Punishment for Suicide*	*Sanguinary Laws Discouraged*	*No Prison for Debt*
Magna Carta 1215	chs.28-31				
Petition of Right 1628					
English Bill of Rights 1689					
Stamp Act Grievance 1765					
Decl. of Resolves 1774					
Decl. of Independence 1776					
Delaware 1776	**sec.10**	**sec.11**			
Georgia 1777					
Georgia 1789					
Maryland 1776		**art.XV**		**art.XIV**	
Massachusetts 1780	**art.X**	**art.XXIV**			
New Hampshire 1776					
New Hampshire 1784	**art.XII**	**art.XXIII**	*Const.*	**art.XVIII**	
New Jersey 1776			*art.XVII*		
New York 1777					
North Carolina 1776		**art.XXIV**			*art.XXXIX*
Pennsylvania 1776	**art.VIII**			*sec.38*	*sec.28*
Pennsylvania 1790	*art.IX, sec.10*	*art.IX, sec.17*	*art.IX, sec.19*		*art.IX, sec.16*
South Carolina 1776					
South Carolina 1778				*art.XL*	
South Carolina 1790		*art.IX, sec.2*			
Vermont 1777	**arts. II,IX**			*sec.XXXV*	*sec.XXV*
Vermont 1786	**arts.II,X**		*sec.XXXV*	*sec.XXXIV*	*sec.XXX*
Virginia 1776	**sec.6**				

Legend: For provisions having citations, citations to a state declaration of rights are **in bold**. Citations to a state constitution are *in italics*. Sections having brackets around them (e.g., [No. 11]) did not have a section or article number in the original text

extent of colonial commitment to that right. Rights guarantees were also found in the statutes and common law of the states. The writ of habeas corpus is a case in point. Complaints about the suspension of this writ by the British appeared in a "Letter to the Inhabitants of the Province of Quebec" (1774).[119] British authorities had repeatedly rebuffed colonial attempts to provide a statutory basis for the writ. As one commentator noted, "[b]y practice, precedent, proclamation, or enactment the common law privilege of the writ of habeas corpus was also enjoyed by the colonists at the time of the Revolution."[120] Following the Declaration of Independence, five state constitutions specifically guaranteed the writ, while other states protected it through statutes and the incorporation of the common law.[121] The prohibition against double jeopardy in America dated back to the Massachusetts Body of Liberties (1641), yet it was only included in two of the state constitutions under consideration. The protection, however, was included in the common law that the states incorporated and in decisional law prohibiting the practice.[122]

The multiple sources of rights protection reflected the relationship of the colonies to the English constitutional common law tradition, their special solicitude for religious conscience, and the strikingly different environment in which the colonists operated. States were still working through the relationships between statute law and common law on one hand and constitutional provisions on the other. The distinction between the two would become a bedrock principle of American constitutionalism.[123]

We return to the question posed in Chapter 1: Were the rights merely an "agglomerated…unrationalized patchwork" or did they reflect a coherent pattern? Given the fifteen-year span in which they were adopted, the wartime conditions under which the conventions operated, the diverse

[119] Reprinted in Shain, *Declaration of Independence*, 229; Dargo, *Roots of the Republic*, 71–72.

[120] Neil Douglas McFeeley, "The Historical Development of Habeas Corpus," *Southwestern Law Journal* 30, no. 3 (1976): 593.

[121] A.H. Carpenter, "Habeas Corpus in the Colonies," *The American Historical Review* 8, no. 1 (October 1902): 26.

[122] David S. Rudstein, "A Brief History of the Fifth Amendment Guarantee Against Double Jeopardy," *William & Mary Bill of Rights Journal* 14, no. 1 (2005): 221–226.

[123] See the Epilogue pp. 389–394 for examples of this unsettled relationship.

nature of the separate states, and, standing above all these, the unprecedented task of founding constitutional republics, full coherency might be too much to expect. What we did find was a coherent political philosophy, a consensus on fundamental rights, and the inclusion of English common law and statutory law that reflected the English heritage of the newly independent states—and their grievances—with the British Empire.

Popular Sovereignty and the Enforcement of Rights

The men who wrote the constitutions provided a variety of mechanisms for revising their fundamental law, ostensibly obviating or mitigating the need for citizens to resort to revolution, which they viewed as a natural right. Nonetheless, delegates in seven of the twelve states adopting new constitutions inserted clauses recognizing the right of the citizens to alter or abolish governments that abused their power. Why? We believe the answer is found in the inability of the states to agree upon or even include provisions offering citizens a direct role in revising or amending their constitutions, that is the desire to keep popular sovereignty a vital, active principle.

The first wave of constitutions did not reach a consensus on the question of how and by whom these constitutions could be changed. Pennsylvania and Vermont each created a council of censors, a version of a continuing constitutional convention with the power to monitor the constitution and determine what was and was not working, report any violations, and recommend changes.[124] Three states, Georgia, Massachusetts, and New Hampshire, provided for an automatic constitutional convention call.[125] Delaware, South Carolina, and Maryland authorized constitutional amendments by the legislature. Concerning what majority was required in the legislature to effectuate an amendment, South Carolina's 1778 constitution required a simple majority,[126] Delaware required five-sevenths of the assembly (plus seven members of the nine-member

[124] See Pa. Const. 1776, sec. 47; Vt. Const. 1777, sec. XLIV.

[125] See Ga. Const. 1789, Art. IV, sec. 7; Mass. Const. 1780, Ch. VI, Art. X; N.H. Const. 1784.

[126] See S.C. Const. 1778, Art. XLIV.

legislative council),[127] and Maryland's constitution and South Carolina's 1790 document mandated a vote of two successive legislatures.[128,129] In Virginia, New Jersey, New York, and North Carolina, revision was not addressed, presumably leaving the task to the legislature. Constitution-makers had not yet found a solution consistent with their commitment to popular sovereignty.

One means by which the framers attempted to keep the sovereign will of the citizens intact was through entrenchment or inviolate clauses. These clauses placed certain parts of a constitution—usually rights related—off limits to either legislative amendment or abolition. Five states included such clauses in their constitutions.[130]

"Alter or abolish" clauses constituted another means framers adopted to keep the Revolutionary embers burning and to maintain an active, vigilant citizenry. These clauses sanctioned the sovereign right of the people to express their will directly.[131] Versions of the natural right to reform, alter, or abolish a rogue government were not legally enforceable rights; they functioned as admonitions to all power holders that their governing power was a power in trust, revocable by legal and extra-legal means when that trust had been breached. They were part of a fundamental law to which ordinary legislation was subordinated; judicial standards, however, could not be and were not expected to be fashioned for these clauses:

[127] See Del. Const. 1776, Art. 30.

[128] Md. Const. 1776, Art. LIX; S.C. Const. 1790, Art. XI. In South Carolina, all amendments required a two-thirds vote for both passages; amendments to the Maryland Constitution related to the "eastern shore" required a similar margin.

[129] Eventually, all the states did provide means of revising their constitutions by procedures more demanding than the ordinary legislative process. Today, every state but Delaware requires ratification of constitutional amendments by the public.

[130] See Del. Const. 1776, Art. 30 (declaration of rights and certain other provisions); Ga. Const. 1777, Art. LXI (freedom of press and trial by jury); Ga. Const. 1789, Art. IV, sec. 3 (same as 1777); N.J. Const. 1776, Art. XXIII (annual terms, religious liberty, and jury trial); N.Y. Const. 1777, Art. XLI (trial by jury); Pa. Const. 1790, Art. IX, secs. 9 (trial by jury), 26 (entire rights article).

[131] See footnote 29, above. Two states, Vermont and Delaware, subsequently revised their constitutions to mute the invitations to direct action by the people. Compare Vt. Decl. 1777, Art. VI, with Vt. Decl. 1786, Art. VII; and Del. Decl. 1776, sec. 5, with Del. Const. 1792, preamble.

enforcement was expected to come through the people's "interpretive authority."[132]

"Frequent recurrence to fundamental principles" clauses were meant to establish consent as the *sine qua non* of free government as well as to provide a measure of the government's legitimacy. The frequent recurrence language suggests that citizens would be expected to act through frequent elections and other participatory mechanisms found in the constitutions or to invoke the alter or abolish clauses when such elections proved futile. What united these procedures and structural devices was the determination to constitutionalize an active role for the citizens.

Preserving the Constitution and Protecting Rights

Commitment to the doctrine of popular sovereignty was one thing; preventing it from becoming dormant or dissolving like Lewis Carroll's Cheshire cat was another. The newly independent citizens played an active role in the Revolution and the establishment of the new constitutions: What assurances would there be that the constitutions, once adopted, would be properly monitored and guarded and that the rights and principles ensconced in their declarations would be observed? The newly independent republics expected that enforcement would be the duty of the citizenry. How would this monitoring take place?

The key to understanding how these principles were to be honored and rights enforced is found in the concept of popular sovereignty. All the state constitutions, explicitly or implicitly, made it the foundation of their polities. By their actions, legal and extra-legal, the colonists secured American independence and were expected to maintain that independence by their vigilance and political action.

The new republican orders expected people to exercise their sovereignty in a series of ascending steps from preventative to public resistance:

[132] See Larry D. Kramer, *The People Themselves: Popular Constitutionalism and Judicial Review* (New York: Oxford University Press, 2004), 24–29.

1. **Admonitions and hortatory clauses** urging citizens to become informed and politically active,[133] and to choose elected officials and jurors wisely.
2. **Chambered political institutions and devices**, such as annual terms, rotation in office, frequent and open legislative proceedings printed in newspapers, mandatory voting, instructions, petitions, requirements that money bills originate in the legislative house most accountable to the people, local juries, and constitutionally mandated procedures for revising or amending the constitution.
3. **Citizens out of doors,** including sermons, formal statements of grievances and protest, e.g., the remonstrance,[134] assembling, pamphleteering, and use of broadsides in public squares, schools, and taverns.
4. **Citizens out of doors (active resistance)**, including protests, demonstrations, mobbing, and resistance. Unlike the activities in the first two steps, which encompass citizens speaking through or speaking to their representatives, steps three and four involve citizens taking direct action to alter government policies or the government itself. The militia, citizens armed and disciplined, was seen as an institutional mechanism by which alter or abolish clauses—the right to resist tyranny—could be implemented without the anarchy of mob violence.[135]

Larry D. Kramer claims that mobbing was an acceptable form of political action in the colonies and England.[136] Pauline Maier writes sympathetically about resistance in the form of mobs and attempts to bring focus

[133] See provisions accompanying footnote 54, above, for the principles voters were to employ when selecting officials.

[134] A remonstrance was an aggressive expression of protest or reproof and formal statement of grievances. Prominent and successful examples include the Flushing Remonstrance in New York (1657), http://www.nycourts.gov/history/legal-history-new-york/legal-history-eras-03/history-era-03-flushing-remonstrance.html, and Madison's Memorial and Remonstrance Against Religious Assessment. "To the Honorable the General Assembly of the Commonwealth of Virginia: A Memorial and Remonstrance," June 20, 1785, *The Papers of James Madison*, ed. William T. Hutchinson, et al. (Chicago: University of Chicago Press, 1973), 8:298–304.

[135] The role of the military in providing "well-regulated liberty" is explored in Cornell, *A Well-Regulated Militia*, 2–7.

[136] *The People Themselves*, 26–27.

and "order" to their activities, which she describes as "disciplined collective coercion."[137] Not all eighteenth-century American supporters of an active citizenry viewed this unrest with equanimity. Sporadic riots and unrest plagued the states between 1776 and the 1790s: ugly mobbing was direct action that did not need encouraging.[138] The increasing diversity of communities made it more likely that dissent, protest, and urban unrest would take the form of factions rather than expressions of the general community's discontent. These changes in the social order would have profound consequences for natural rights republics.

[137] *From Resistance to Revolution: Colonial Radicals and the Development of American Opposition to Britain, 1765–1776* (New York: W. W. Norton, 1992), 280 and generally, 272–287.

[138] The urban and agrarian protests that continued in the last quarter of the eighteenth century are explored in Alfred F. Young, "American Historians Confront 'the Transforming Hand of Revolution,'" in Alfred F. Young and Gregory H. Nobles, *Whose American Revolution was It? Historians Interpret the Founding* (New York: New York University Press, 2011), 111–113. Elizabeth Beaumont, though committed to popular constitutionalism or constitutionalism outside the courts, would exclude such activities under her civic constitutionalism model. *The Civic Constitution: Civic Visions and Struggles in the Path toward Constitutional Democracy* (New York: Oxford University Press, 2014).

States Adopting Declarations of Rights

Virginia

Virginia's heritage of constitutionalism and the protection of rights can be traced back to its very first charter, granted by King James I to the Virginia Company on April 10, 1606. This founding document contained, in the words of Virginia statesman Edmund Randolph, a "ray of freedom"[1]:

> Also we do, for Us, our Heirs, and Successors, DECLARE, by these Presents, that all and every the Persons being our Subjects, which shall dwell and inhabit within every or any of the said several Colonies and Plantations, and every of their children, which shall happen to be born within any of the Limits and Precincts of the said several Colonies and Plantations, shall HAVE and enjoy all Liberties, Franchises, and Immunities, within any of our other Dominions, to all Intents and Purposes, as if they had been abiding and born, within this our Realm of England, or any other of our said Dominions.[2]

This promise that settlers would be guaranteed the rights enjoyed by Englishmen was echoed in the second charter of Virginia in 1609, which further instructed the Virginia Company to operate a legal system "as near as conveniently may be…to the Laws, Statutes, Government, and Policy

[1] Edmund Randolph, *History of Virginia* (Charlottesville: University Press of Virginia, 1970), 19.

[2] The First Charter of Virginia (1606), in Thorpe, *Constitutions*, 7:3788.

P. J. Galie et al., *Bills of Rights Before the Bill of Rights*,
https://doi.org/10.1007/978-3-030-44301-6_4

of this our Realm of England."[3] Together, these two clauses would seem to guarantee to the settlers all the benefits of the common law, although the common law would not begin to take root in Virginia until it became a royal colony in 1624.[4]

In 1618, Sir Edwin Sandys, Virginia Company investor and member of the royally appointed Council of Virginia (located in England), helped prepare a commission to the governor that provided for a new system of representative governance, with a popularly elected, unicameral legislature.[5] This general assembly was to be made up of the governor, the members of the council of state (chosen by the Company) and two representatives (burgesses) elected from each town and plantation.[6] The first

[3] The Second Charter of Virginia (1609), in Thorpe, *Constitutions*, 7:3800, 3801.

[4] Some historians, such as W. H. Bryson, have concluded that the common law and its attendant privileges were in force in Virginia from its founding, W. H. Bryson, "The Prerogative of the Sovereign in Virginia: Royal Law in a Republic," *Tijdschrift voor Rechtsgeschiedenis* 73 (2005): 372, 374, accessed June 18, 2018, https://scholarship.richmond.edu/cgi/viewcontent.cgi?referer=https://www.google.com/&httpsredir=1&article=1442&context=law-faculty-publications; see also John Ruston Pagan, "English Statutes in Virginia," in *"Esteemed Bookes of Lawe" and the Legal Culture of Early Virginia*, ed. Warren M. Billings and Brent Tarter (Charlottesville: University of Virginia Press, 2017), 60. William Nelson's comprehensive four-volume work on the common law in colonial America describes a gradual implementation of the common law in Virginia, one that did not begin until after the Virginia Company's control of the colony was relinquished to the Crown in 1624. William E. Nelson, *The Common Law in Colonial America*, vol. 1, *The Chesapeake and New England, 1607–1660* (New York: Oxford University Press, 2008). The Virginia Company ruled with an iron fist, withholding from Virginia's early settlers the common law staples of private property rights and the right to trial by jury. Ibid., 125.

[5] Theodore K. Rabb, "Sir Edwin Sandys (1561–1629)," *Encyclopedia Virginia*. Virginia Humanities, February 18, 2014, https://www.encyclopediavirginia.org/sandys_sir_edwin_1561-1629, accessed January 17, 2020. Sandys earned the sobriquet "the father of colonial self-government." Matthew Page Andrews, *Virginia, the Old Dominion* (Garden City, NY: Doubleday, Doran & Company, Inc., 1937), 43, as quoted by Alf J. Mapp Jr., *The Virginia Experiment: The Old Dominion's Role in the Making of America 1607–1781* (Lanham, MD: Hamilton Press, 1987), 13. He was an early voice for social contract theory in England, having delivered a speech before the House of Commons in 1614 essentially declaring that a king's authority originated in, and was therefore limited by, the consent of the people. Mapp, *Virginia Experiment*, 15–16.

[6] A. E. Dick Howard, *Commentaries on the Constitution of Virginia* (Charlottesville: University Press of Virginia, 1974), 1:317, 321. The actions of the general assembly were subject to the governor's veto power. In 1643 the general assembly was made bicameral, with the house of burgesses sitting as one house and the governor's council sitting as the other house.

meeting of the Virginia General Assembly, on July 30, 1619, marked the beginning of political self-government for those who came to the New World.[7]

In 1624, the Virginia Company's charter was revoked, and Virginia became a royal colony governed by the rule of law. This change in political affairs did not alter the fact that colonists considered the liberty guarantees afforded by the colonial charters as their birthright.[8] The popularly elected house of burgesses began to meet separately as the lower house of the general assembly after 1643; it operated largely unchecked by royal authority for much of the seventeenth century, encouraging the growth of self-government in the colony. Crown policies that infringed on the assembly's legislative authority provoked dissatisfaction and protest. The Virginia Assembly asserted the "rights of Englishmen" guaranteed by the charters when it passed resolutions protesting the Revenue Act of 1764 and the Stamp Act of 1765.[9] The assembly's resolutions of 1774 in response to the Intolerable Acts added natural rights theory to the arguments based on colonial charters and the English Constitution.[10]

Royal authority in Virginia began to collapse in the latter part of the eighteenth century. The governor dissolved the house of burgesses in May 1774; nevertheless, the house continued to meet on its own until May 1776. During this period, a series of extra-legal conventions exercised de facto governance of the colony.[11] On May 15, 1776, the Fifth Virginia Convention passed a resolution instructing its delegates to the Continental Congress to move for a declaration of independence from England.[12] Having decided to sever ties with the mother country, the convention next resolved to form a committee "to prepare a DECLARATION OF RIGHTS and such a plan of government as will be most likely to maintain peace and order in this colony, and secure substantial and equal liberty to

[7] Mapp, *Virginia Experiment*, 44.

[8] A. E. Dick Howard, "From Mason to Modern Times: 200 Years of American Rights," in *The Legacy of George Mason*, ed. Josephine E. Pacheco (Cranbury, NJ: Associated University Presses, 1983), 97.

[9] Howard, *Commentaries*, 1:3–4.

[10] Ibid., 5–6.

[11] Ibid., 34.

[12] Ibid.

the people."[13] Legal historian A. E. Dick Howard explains the significance of the placement of the declaration of rights ahead of a plan of government:

> The members of the 1776 Convention, steeped in Lockean notions of the social contract, might well have considered themselves in a state of nature upon the dissolution of the bond with Great Britain. Heirs to a tradition of written liberties, they found it a natural step to declare man's inherent rights.[14]

Consistent with the idea that rights are declared, not granted, by governments and to emphasize the importance of rights, delegates wrote and adopted a declaration of rights prior to adoption of the body, or frame, of the constitution.

The task of drafting the first American state bill of rights fell to George Mason. Regarded as "one of the most thorough students of constitutional law in the American colonies,"[15] Mason had previously penned annotated extracts from the colonial charters (1773), the Fairfax Resolves (1774), and Remarks on Annual Elections for the Fairfax Independent Company (1775). Significant portions of these documents found their way into the Virginia Declaration of Rights.[16] After a few alterations and additions in committee, the declaration was passed unanimously by the convention on June 12, 1776.[17] Mason's influence is evident in all but two sections of the final product.[18] The constitution was adopted shortly thereafter on June 29.

[13] "Resolutions of the Virginia Convention Calling for Independence," in *The Papers of Thomas Jefferson*, ed. Julian P. Boyd (Princeton, NJ: Princeton University Press, 1950), 1:290–291.

[14] Howard, *Commentaries*, 1:34–35.

[15] Mapp, *Virginia Experiment*, 410.

[16] See "Extracts from the Colonial Charters, With Some Remarks on Them Made in the Year 1773," in *The Life of George Mason 1725–1792*, ed. Kate Mason Rowland (New York: G.P. Putnam's Sons, 1892), 1:393–414; Josephine F. Pacheco, "Introduction" to Pacheco, *Legacy of George Mason*, 17; *The Papers of George Mason 1725–1792*, ed. Robert A. Rutland (Chapel Hill: University of North Carolina Press, 1970), 1:232.

[17] *Revolutionary Virginia, the Road to Independence*, ed. Brent Tarter and Robert L. Scribner, vol. 7, *Independence and the Fifth Convention, 1776* (Charlottesville: University Press of Virginia, 1983), pt. 1, 10.

[18] Jeff Broadwater, *George Mason: Forgotten Founder* (Chapel Hill: University of North Carolina Press, 2006), 87.

Constitutional Developments: 1776 Declaration and Constitution

The Virginia Declaration of Rights illustrates the predominantly communal context for understanding rights shared by most early state constitution writers. It was written, as its preamble states, to the people of Virginia to set forth the rights that were the foundation of the new government, and to inform citizens of their duties and obligations to preserve liberty. Edmund Randolph, a member of the convention's drafting committee, would later assert that the declaration of rights was "the cornerstone" of the constitution and had been written with a two-fold purpose: "that the legislature should not in their acts violate any of those canons;" and "that in all the revolutions of time, of human opinion, and of government, a perpetual standard should be erected, around which the people might rally and by notorious record be forever admonished to be watchful, firm, and virtuous."[19]

After asserting in section 1 that men had inherent rights they were not divested of when leaving a state of nature to form a social compact, the declaration then defined popular sovereignty in sections 2 and 3. These provisions proclaimed that a government's legitimate authority was derived from the people; government was established for the common benefit of the people; and public officials were the servants of the people. When adopted, these sections announced to Virginians, to the newly-independent states, and to the world the political philosophy of the state's first constitution.

Many of the essential rights of the people proclaimed in the declaration had implicit corresponding duties, such as the right and duty to vote, the right to trial by jury and the duty of jury service, the right to serve in a militia and the duty of militia service, and the right and duty to worship. The religious liberty provision (Decl. 1776, sec. 16) especially demonstrates the interwoven character of rights and duties, postulating that the *right* to free religious exercise arises out of a *duty* to worship our Creator as conscience dictates. The last clause of section 16, "that it is the mutual duty of all to practise Christian forbearance, love, and charity toward each other," was an aspirational provision—not legally enforceable, but rather meant to exhort the people to practice civic and religious virtue, which was believed to be crucial for effective self-government and

[19] Randolph, *History of Virginia*, 255.

ordered liberty. The preceding section was also an admonition to the people. Section 15 stated: "That no free government, or the blessings of liberty, can be preserved to any people, but by a firm adherence to justice, moderation, temperance, frugality, and virtue, and by frequent recurrence to fundamental principles." The emphasis on the corresponding duties associated with fundamental rights demonstrates that Mason and his colleagues were relying on the independence, integrity, and vigilance of the electorate as the primary safeguards of liberty. If this failed, section 3 asserted that the majority of the people had an inalienable right to alter or abolish a wayward government.

The declaration also contained provisions denouncing offensive governmental actions fresh in the delegates' minds as grievances the colonists had against the Crown and Parliament: taxing the people or taking their property without their consent (Decl. 1776, sec. 6); issuing general warrants, which lacked a sufficiently particularized description of the person or thing to be seized or the place to be searched (ibid., sec. 10); having standing armies (ibid., sec. 13); restraining the freedom of the press (ibid., sec. 12); and suspending or executing laws without the consent of the people's representatives (ibid., sec. 7). Section 7 was derived from the English common law, as were trial by a jury of one's peers and due process (ibid., sec. 8) and the prohibition on excessive bail, fines, and cruel and unusual punishments (ibid., sec. 9).

Suffrage

Section 6 of the declaration claimed that "all men, having sufficient evidence of permanent common interest with, and attachment to, the community, have the right of suffrage." The constitution specified: "the right of suffrage in the election of members for both Houses shall remain as exercised at present." Under the standing colonial election laws, suffrage was generally limited to free white males, twenty-one years or older, with a freehold[20] of 100 acres of unimproved land or twenty-five acres of

[20] In addition to the outright ownership of land, a freehold under Virginia law included a life tenancy. There were special rules for joint tenants and tenants in common, and some exceptions pertaining to certain towns. For a thorough history of Virginia's pre-Revolutionary suffrage laws, see Robert E. and B. Katherine Brown, *Virginia, 1705–1786: Democracy or Aristocracy?* (East Lansing: Michigan State University Press, 1964), 125–135.

improved land, or a house and part of a lot in a city or town, possessed at least a year before voting.[21]

Structural Provisions

Virginia included structural provisions in its frame of government that would implement the principles enshrined in the declaration. Section 5 of the declaration provided that the three branches of government should be separate and distinct: the constitution executed this principle by prohibiting plural office-holding.[22] The constitution also established that judges were to hold office during good behavior and to have "fixed and adequate salaries,"[23] key components of judicial independence.

Sections 5 and 6 of the declaration called for free and frequent elections to allow the people to remove from office politicians who were not attentive to their constituents' desires, which the constitution implemented by establishing annual elections for representatives and by requiring senators, governors, and privy councilors to take periodic breaks from office-holding. Members of the house of delegates were elected for annual terms, and the legislature was required to meet at least once per year.[24] These short terms provided a more responsive legislature, making it unlikely a gap would develop between community sentiment and legislative action. The annual turnover expected in the house of delegates was balanced by the staggered rotation of four-year senate terms, which ensured some continuity and experience. The staggered senate terms also served as a limit on the length of time one could serve, as a senator displaced at the end of his four-year term had to wait four years (until his seat was once again up for election) to run again.

[21] An act for prevention of undue election of Burges[s]es (1699) in *The Statutes at Large; Being a Collection of All the Laws of Virginia from the First Session of the Legislature in the Year 1619*, ed. William Waller Hening (Philadelphia: Thomas Desilver, 1823), 3:172 (setting gender and age requirements for suffrage); An act...for the better government of Negros, Mulattos, and Indians, bond or free (1723) in Hening, *Statutes at Large* (Richmond, VA: Franklin Press, 1820), 4:133–134 (setting race restrictions for suffrage); An act to declare who shall have a right to vote... (1736), in Hening, *Statutes at Large*, 4:475–476 (setting property requirements for suffrage).

[22] The frame of government of the 1776 constitution did not contain specific section numbers.

[23] Const. 1776, in Thorpe, *Constitutions* 7:3817.

[24] Ibid., 3815–3816.

The constitution included other restrictions on reelection. The governor, whose term was one year, could be reelected twice (holding office a total of three years in a row) but then had to wait four years before running again, and privy councilors once removed (two were required to be removed by joint ballot of both houses every three years) were ineligible for the next three years.[25] Virginia's was the first state constitution to include such limitations on its officials.[26]

Although the declaration announced that all men were equally free and independent (Decl. 1776, sec. 1), both the declaration and the constitution had qualifications for participating in the political life of the state. The qualifications for office-holding were established in the frame of government as follows:

Office	*Minimum Age*	*Estate*	*Residency*	*Religion*
Governor	No age specified	None specified	None specified	None specified
Senator	25 years	Freehold within his district	Must reside within his district	None specified
Representative	No age specified	Freehold within his county	Must reside within his county	None specified

Alternatively, senators and representatives could serve if they were "duly qualified according to law," leaving the interpretation of qualification requirements in the hands of the legislature.

Rights Not Included in Virginia's Declaration

The influence of the Virginia Declaration of Rights was pervasive. Most states adopting bills of rights before the adoption of the U.S. Bill of Rights in 1791 relied either directly or indirectly on the work of the Virginia convention when crafting their rights provisions.[27] However, Virginia's declaration has come under criticism from some historians for

[25] Ibid., 3816 (restrictions on governor), 3817 (restrictions on council members).

[26] Willi Paul Adams, *The First American Constitutions*, rev. ed. (Lanham, MD: Rowman & Littlefield Publishers, Inc., 2001), 251.

[27] Rowland, *Life of George Mason*, 250, claims all succeeding bills of rights were modeled on Virginia's. As an example, Pennsylvania's declaration, which borrowed from the

leaving out such protections as freedom of speech, assembly, and petition, restrictions against the quartering of troops, freedom from double jeopardy, the right to habeas corpus and grand jury indictment, and freedom from attainders and ex post facto laws.[28] Historian Leonard Levy has chalked up the omission of these rights to "thoughtlessness,"[29] but there are other explanations.

One possibility is Mason's belief that only fundamental rights should be included in the declaration, which implies his draft was a list of what he considered primary rights, not a catalog of all the people's rights.[30] Rights colonists considered the basis for all other rights—jury trial, self-government (representation), due process (common law), and liberty of conscience—were present in Virginia's declaration.

Historian Brent Tarter believes Mason and the other contributing committee members chose to include the rights they thought to have been of "essential importance" and most threatened by the actions of

Virginia declaration, was, in turn, the model for Vermont's declaration. It should be noted that most of the state conventions and assemblies relied upon the May 27 draft of the declaration rather than the final version. John E. Selby, *The Revolution in Virginia, 1775–1783* (Williamsburg, VA: The Colonial Williamsburg Foundation, 1988), 102; Rutland, *Papers of George Mason*, 1:276. This can be attributed to the fact that the draft was circulating up and down the eastern seaboard almost three weeks before the final version was adopted. Rutland, *Papers of George Mason*, 1:276. The *Virginia Gazette* (Dixon & Hunter) first placed the draft in general circulation on June 1. Ibid. It was then published in the *Pennsylvania Evening Post* on June 6, the *Pennsylvania Ledger* on June 8, the *Pennsylvania Gazette* on June 12, the *Maryland Gazette* on June 13, and was eventually printed in almost every other American newspaper. Ibid; Tarter and Scribner, *Revolutionary Virginia*, vol. 7, pt. 1:278.

[28] Leonard W. Levy, *Origins of the Fifth Amendment: The Right Against Self-Incrimination* (New York: Oxford University Press, 1968), 408. Robert P. Sutton, *Revolution to Secession: Constitution Making in the Old Dominion* (Charlottesville: University Press of Virginia, 1989), 33, agrees with Levy that the declaration of rights had "serious weaknesses".

[29] Levy, *Origins of the Fifth Amendment*, 408.

[30] Mason rejected an association with sections 12 and 16 because they were "not of fundamental nature." Rutland, *Papers of George Mason*, 1:286. Mason "may not have intended his list to be exclusive, and perhaps he thought the addition of other provisions was unnecessary." Broadwater, *George Mason*, 89. The members of the Fifth Convention "purposefully refrained from cataloguing the liberties of free people down to the last jot and tittle." Warren M. Billings, "'That All Men Are Born Equally Free and Independent': Virginians and the Origins of the Bill of Rights," in *The Bill of Rights and the States: The Colonial and Revolutionary Origins of American Liberties*, ed. Patrick T. Conley and John P. Kaminski (Madison, WI: Madison House, 1992), 343.

Great Britain in the preceding years.[31] A number of the rights in the declaration were included as a direct result of actions occurring either in the colony or in England. The absence of other rights is most likely explained by the fact that those rights had not been put in jeopardy by the Crown.[32]

Furthermore, the absence of a right from the declaration did not mean it had no protection. Rights not included in the declaration were often assumed to be already protected by the common law, which remained in force in Virginia by statute enacted in May 1776.[33] The right to counsel and the writ of habeas corpus were well established in the state by the time the declaration was drafted.[34] A guarantee against double jeopardy may have been overlooked because of the concept's universal acceptance.[35] A prohibition against bills of attainder was likely left out because of the perceived need for the device to deal with Josiah Phillips, a renegade who led a band of rebels and thieves that terrorized southeastern Virginia from 1775 to 1778.[36] Also purposely excluded from the declaration was a prohibition against ex post facto laws, having been stricken from the final draft after Patrick Henry successfully argued for its removal with the hypothetical example of a public enemy endangering the populace.[37] These last two intentional omissions illustrate the communitarian context for rights: the rights of the community (the commonweal) took

[31] Brent Tarter, "The Virginia Bill of Rights," in *To Secure the Blessings of Liberty: Rights in American History*, ed. Josephine F. Pacheco (Fairfax, VA: George Mason University Press, 1993), 44–45.

[32] Ibid., 47.

[33] Sutton, *Revolution to Secession*, 32; An ordinance to enable the present magistrates and officers to continue the administration of justice, and for settling the general mode of proceedings in criminal and other cases till the same can be more amply provided for, May 1776, in Hening, *Statutes at Large* (Richmond, VA: J. & G. Cochran, 1821), 9:127.

[34] Broadwater, *George Mason*, 89. An act passed by the colonial assembly in 1734 declared: "in all trials for capital offences, the prisoner, upon his petition to the court, shall be allowed counsel." An Act for better regulating the trial of Criminals, for Capital Offenses, August, 1734, in Hening, *Statutes at Large*, 4:404. "Virginia was specifically made beneficiary of the 1679 [Habeas Corpus] Act through a proclamation issued by Governor Spotswood." Howard, *Commentaries*, 1:161 n. 71; Daniel John Meador, *Habeas Corpus and Magna Carta: Dualism of Power and Liberty* (Charlottesville: University Press of Virginia, 1966), 30–31.

[35] Howard, *Commentaries*, 1:136.

[36] Sutton, *Revolution to Secession*, 32; see also Howard, *Commentaries*, 1:168.

[37] Howard, *Commentaries*, 1:171.

precedence over rights claims made by the individual; and the community determined the extent to which rights, natural or social, would be recognized.

Whatever the merit of modern criticisms, the people of revolutionary Virginia appear to have been satisfied with the selection of rights in Virginia's declaration. In their instructions to their representatives in the general assembly, the inhabitants and freeholders of Albemarle County described the Virginia Declaration of Rights as "truly a master piece."[38]

Postscript: Following a constitutional convention authorized by popular referendum, the voters ratified Virginia's second constitution in 1830. Article I incorporated the 1776 declaration of rights into the new constitution, stating that it "requir[ed] in the opinion of this convention no amendment." Article II, section 11, however, contained a list of additional rights protections. This section prohibited suspension of the writ of habeas corpus, bills of attainder, ex post facto laws, laws impairing the obligation of contracts, takings of private property without just compensation, and laws abridging the freedom of speech, press, or religion. The constitution also reduced—but did not eliminate—the property requirements for suffrage and made representation more proportional to population.

Constitution of Virginia [1776]

[DECLARATION OF RIGHTS]

A declaration of rights made by the representatives of the good people of Virginia, assembled in full and free convention; which rights do pertain to them and their posterity, as the basis and foundation of government.[39]

Section 1. That all men are by nature equally free and independent, and have certain inherent rights, of which, when they enter into a state of society, they cannot, by any compact, deprive or divest their posterity;

[38] "Albemarle County Instructions concerning the Virginia Constitution," in Boyd, *Papers of Thomas Jefferson*, 6:285.

[39] Despite the mounting pressures of war, the framers felt it imperative to put in writing the rights on which their new order would be built. By addressing "the good people of Virginia...and their posterity," delegates signaled their desire to legislate not only for themselves and their contemporaries, but for all future Virginians. Howard, *Commentaries*, 1:57.

namely, the enjoyment of life and liberty, with the means of acquiring and possessing property, and pursuing and obtaining happiness and safety.[40]

SEC. 2. That all power is vested in, and consequently derived from, the people; that magistrates[41] are their trustees and servants, and at all times amenable to them.[42]

SEC. 3. That government is, or ought to be, instituted for the common benefit, protection, and security of the people, nation, or community; of all the various modes and forms of government, that is best which is capable of producing the greatest degree of happiness and safety, and

[40] This section declared man's natural rights in the tradition of John Locke. Dan Friedman, *Tracing the Lineage: Textual and Conceptual Similarities in the Revolutionary-Era State Declarations of Rights of Virginia, Maryland, and Delaware* (2002): 87, accessed January 10, 2019, https://msa.maryland.gov/megafile/msa/stagsere/se1/se14/000027/html/writing_it_all_down/msa/speccol/sc2200/sc2221/000004/000000/pdf/friedman04.pdf. George Mason expressed similar sentiments in his address to the Fairfax Independent Company a year earlier: "All men are by nature born equally free and independent…men entered into compacts to give up some of their natural rights, that by union and mutual assistance they might secure the rest; but they gave up no more than the nature of the thing required." "Remarks on Annual Elections for the Fairfax Independent Company, *ca.* 17–26 April 1775," in Rutland, *Papers of George Mason*, 1:229. Mason had originally drafted the first clause of this section to read: "all men are born equally free," but in the final draft the convention substituted "by nature" for "born" and added "when they enter into a state of society" to allay fears that the original language would lead to a slave revolt. Ibid., 279, 289, restating Locke "That all men by nature are equal," and Cato: "All Men are born free." This alteration excluded slaves as they were not considered to be full members of the community. Randolph, *History of Virginia*, 253. Despite these changes, anti-slavery proponents relied upon this section when petitioning the assembly for abolition of that institution. Ibid., 329.

[41] Although a contemporary understanding of "magistrates" may be limited to judicial officers, the term during the eighteenth century likely referred to public civil officers. Howard, *Commentaries*, 1:69 n. 1.

[42] This was the first statement of the "American version of the republican theory of sovereignty….in constitutionally binding form." Adams, *First American Constitutions*, 133. Mason had identified popular sovereignty in his previous writings as a necessary condition for freedom. In his address to the Fairfax Independent Company, he cautioned: "let us never lose sight of this fundamental maxim—that all power was originally lodged in, and consequently is derived from, the people." "Remarks on Annual Elections," 231. Commitment to popular sovereignty was reflected in several provisions of the frame of government concerning legislation. All bills were required to originate in the branch closest and most accountable to the people, the house of delegates; the senate could not make any amendments to money bills. Const. 1776, in Thorpe, *Constitutions*, 7:3816.

is most effectually secured against the danger of maladministration; and that, when any government shall be found inadequate or contrary to these purposes, a majority of the community hath an indubitable, inalienable, and indefeasible right to reform, alter, or abolish it, in such manner as shall be judged most conducive to the public weal.[43]

SEC. 4. That no man, or set of men, are entitled to exclusive or separate emoluments or privileges from the community, but in consideration of public services; which, not being descendible, neither ought the offices of magistrate, legislator, or judge to be hereditary.[44]

SEC. 5. That the legislative and executive powers of the State should be separate and distinct from the judiciary; and that the members of the two first may be restrained from oppression, by feeling and participating the burdens of the people, they should, at fixed periods, be reduced to a private station, return into that body from which they were originally taken, and the vacancies be supplied by frequent, certain, and regular elections, in which all, or any part of the former members, to be again eligible, or ineligible, as the laws shall direct.[45]

[43] The third section sets forth the purposes of government and the natural right of the majority to reform, alter, or abolish the government should it fail to meet its obligations. Mason had previously expressed his belief in this principle in his address to the Fairfax Independent Company: "Every society, all government…is or ought to be, calculated for the general good and safety of the community." "Remarks on Annual Elections," 229.

[44] The first clause of this section denouncing emoluments and privileges may have been influenced by the abuses and corruption perpetrated by county sheriffs. A sheriff's duties included serving as escheat officer, clerk of the court, and surveyor of public lands, and these officers often took advantage of advance information about bankruptcies, property about to escheat, or removal of Indians for their own financial gain. William E. Dodd, *The Old South Struggles for Democracy* (New York: The Macmillan Company, 1937), 100–101. Although appointed annually by the governor, in practice a sheriff retained his position for as long as he desired, thus perpetuating this cycle of corruption. Ibid., 100. The second provision prohibiting hereditary succession to offices reflected the belief that political office-holding should be based on merit. See Gordon S. Wood, *The Creation of The American Republic, 1776–1787* (Chapel Hill: University of North Carolina Press, 1969), 70–75. Connected to this belief was Mason's "guiding political principle" of frequent elections, addressed more specifically in the next section. Rutland, *Papers of George Mason*, 1:280.

[45] The independent judiciary provision seems only to separate the judiciary from the other branches of government and does not appear to separate the legislative and executive branches. This was likely not Mason's intent, however, since he also drafted the separation of powers provision found in the state constitution's frame of government: "[t]he legislative, executive, and judiciary department, shall be separate and distinct, so

SEC. 6. That elections of members to serve as representatives of the people, in assembly, ought to be free; and that all men, having sufficient evidence of permanent common interest with, and attachment to, the community, have the right of suffrage, and cannot be taxed or deprived of their property for public uses, without their own consent, or that of their representatives so elected, nor bound by any law to which they have not, in like manner, assembled for the public good.[46]

that neither exercise the powers properly belonging to the other: nor shall any person exercise the powers of more than one of them, at the same time..." Howard, *Commentaries*, 1:82. This interpretation is also consistent with the view of convention member Edmund Randolph, who later wrote that the declaration's fifth section "separates the legislative, executive, and judicial functions." Randolph, *History of Virginia*, 253. Virginia's efforts to implement the principle of separation of powers in its constitution included eliminating powers that were seen as improper appropriations of legislative functions, such as the prerogatives of the governor and his veto power. The former has been defined as:

> [t]he special power or peculiar right possessed by an official by virtue of his or her office. In English law a discretionary power that exceeds and is unaffected by any other power; the special preeminence that the monarch has over and above all others, as a consequence of his or her sovereignty.

West's Encyclopedia of American Law, 2nd ed., s.v. "prerogative," (2008), accessed November 1, 2018, https://legal-dictionary.thefreedictionary.com/prerogative.

The remaining provisions of the section dealt with rotation in office for legislators and executives. In Mason's address to the Fairfax Independent Company in 1775, he attributed the fall of the Roman Republic to its abandonment of the practice of rotation in office. "Remarks on Annual Elections," 230–231. To prevent government from becoming oppressive "the most effectual means that human wisdom hath ever been able to devise, is frequently appealing to the body of the people, to those constituent members from whom authority originated, for their approbation or dissent." Ibid., 230. This was a familiar concept for most Virginians, who had a long history of electing public officials and frequently exercised their right to vote officials out of office. Howard, *Commentaries*, 1:83.

[46]The belief that electors should have a stake in society through ownership of property (i.e., a freehold requirement) had been a permanent part of Virginia's suffrage law since 1677. Howard, *Commentaries*, 1:87, 318. The constitution's frame of government continued freehold suffrage as it had existed under colonial law. Const. 1776, in Thorpe, *Constitutions*, 7:3816. See footnotes 25 and 26 above.

The latter half of the section addressed taxes and takings, aimed at the Crown's practice of imposing taxes and fees without legislative consent. The general assembly had questioned Lieutenant Governor Robert Dinwiddie's authority to impose a fee on land patents in the early 1750s, declaring "the Rights of the Subject are so secured by Law, that they cannot be deprived of the least part of their Property, but by their own Consent: Upon this excellent Principle is our Constitution founded...," as quoted

SEC. 7. That all power of suspending laws, or the execution of laws, by any authority, without consent of the representatives of the people, is injurious to their rights, and ought not to be exercised.[47]

SEC. 8. That in all capital or criminal prosecutions a man has a right to demand the cause and nature of his accusation, to be confronted with the accusers and witnesses, to call for evidence in his favor, and to a speedy trial by an impartial jury of twelve men of his vicinage, without whose unanimous consent he cannot be found guilty; nor can he be compelled to give evidence against himself; that no man be deprived of his liberty, except by the law of the land or the judgment of his peers.[48]

by Clinton Rossiter, *Seedtime of the Republic: The Origin of the American Tradition of Political Liberty* (New York: Harcourt, Brace and Co., 1953), 254. Although this section did not require just compensation to be paid for government takings, such language may have been unnecessary since this was already the practice in Virginia when people or their property were impressed to help on public works. Helen Hill, *George Mason, Constitutionalist* (Cambridge, MA: Harvard University Press, 1938), 51.

[47] This provision was derived from the English Bill of Rights (1689), which provided "[t]hat the pretended power of suspending of laws, or the execution of laws, by regal authority, as it hath been assumed and exercised of late, is illegal." English Bill Of Rights (1689), in Bernard Schwartz, *The Bill of Rights: A Documentary History* (New York: Chelsea House, 1971), 1:42.

[48] This section, a product of Mason's experience as a justice of the peace, "provided the first post-colonial American catalog of rights for those accused of crimes." Friedman, *Tracing the Lineage*, 32; Rutland, *Papers of George Mason*, 1:280. It would serve as a precedent for later state conventions. Howard, *Commentaries*, 1:95; Eben Moglen, "Taking the Fifth: Reconsidering the Origins of the Constitutional Privilege Against Self-Incrimination," *Michigan Law Review* 92, no. 5 (1994): 1118. The rights listed, covering accusation, confrontation, evidence, venue, jury trial, and unanimous verdict, were part of what has been termed the "trial-rights cluster," which developed throughout English history from Magna Carta to the Treason Trials Act of 1696. Ibid., 1113, 1118–1119.

The protection against self-incrimination has been called unnecessary in light of the common law's prohibition against defendants testifying under oath. Levy, *Origins of the Fifth Amendment*, 406–407; Howard, *Commentaries*, 1:95. However, if the purposes of the declaration included binding future generations regardless of changes in governments and opinions and proclaiming fundamental rights as a form of civic education, protection of this right beyond the common law was required. Randolph, *History of Virginia*, 255; see also the declaration's preamble. Another criticism of the provision is that it is more limiting than Virginia's 1677 law extending the right against self-incrimination to parties and witnesses in both civil and criminal proceedings. Levy, *Origins of the Fifth Amendment*, 407, 409–410; Howard, *Commentaries*, 1:95; Hening, *Statutes at Large*, 2:422. Perhaps Mason, who suggested the declaration should contain only fundamental rights and handwrote in a personal copy of the declaration that certain articles the convention added were "not of fundamental nature," Rowland, *Life of George Mason*, 436, was tacitly

SEC. 9. That excessive bail ought not to be required, nor excessive fines imposed, nor cruel and unusual punishments inflicted.[49]

SEC. 10. That general warrants, whereby an officer or messenger may be commanded to search suspected places without evidence of a fact committed, or to seize any person or persons not named, or whose offense is not particularly described and supported by evidence, are grievous and oppressive, and ought not to be granted.[50]

SEC. 11. That in controversies respecting property, and in suits between man and man, the ancient trial by jury is preferable to any other, and ought to be held sacred.[51]

SEC. 12. That the freedom of the press is one of the great bulwarks of liberty, and can never be restrained but by despotic governments.[52]

acknowledging that the consequences of criminal prosecution (where life and liberty were at stake) were of a different order than a civil trial and justified a different standard.

[49] This section, taken verbatim from the English Bill of Rights, is often seen as the inspiration for similar provisions in eight other states' early constitutions (see Table 5, pp. 84–85) and for the U.S. Constitution's Eighth Amendment. Even though the provision employed the word "ought" rather than the legally binding "shall," the Virginia Court of Appeals ruled in a 1799 case that this section *prohibited* excessive fines--effectively making the language mandatory. *Jones v. Commonwealth* (1799), cited in Suzanna Sherry, "The Early Virginia Tradition of Extratextual Interpretation," in *Toward a Useable Past: Liberty Under State Constitutions*, ed. Paul Finkelman and Stephen E. Gottlieb (Athens: University of Georgia Press, 2009), 165.

[50] This section represented Virginia's efforts to outlaw general warrants, a device whose use had become a point of contention in the colonies when the British were attempting to enforce the Navigation Acts. Howard, *Commentaries*, 1:176. Mason believed that right was "not of fundamental nature," but the persistent use of these warrants in the preceding decades made his position a losing one. Rutland, *Papers of George Mason*, 1:286.

[51] The eighth section of the declaration mandated the right to trial by jury in criminal prosecutions; this section provided the same for civil cases. Notwithstanding the section's description of this right as "sacred," Randolph believed this provision was not absolute and exceptions could be made. Randolph, *History of Virginia*, 254. Intended beneficiaries of this section were Virginians with British creditors, Mason believing jury trials might better protect the property of individuals sued for these debts. Brent Tarter, "George Mason and the Conservation of Liberty," *The Virginia Magazine of History and Biography* 99, no. 3 (1991): 303.

[52] This section contained the first ever constitutional protection for freedom of the press. Roger P. Mellen, *The Origins of a Free Press in Prerevolutionary Virginia: Creating a Culture of Political Dissent* (Lewiston: NY: The Edwin Mellen Press, 2009), 225. Unlike other rights protected in this declaration that can be traced to English precedents or Enlightenment thinkers, the origins of Virginia's constitutional right to a free press arose "out of a cultural transformation within the colony." Ibid., 263. The conflict between

SEC. 13. That a well-regulated militia, composed of the body of the people, trained to arms, is the proper, natural, and safe defence of a free State; that standing armies, in time of peace, should be avoided, as dangerous to liberty; and that in all cases the military should be under strict subordination to, and governed by, the civil power.[53]

SEC. 14. That the people have a right to uniform government; and, therefore, that no government separate from, or independent of the government of Virginia, ought to be erected or established within the limits thereof.[54]

SEC. 15. That no free government, or the blessings of liberty, can be preserved to any people, but by a firm adherence to justice, moderation,

printers and the royal governor over the publishing of dissenting material caused Virginians to view government control, through prior restraints or prosecutions for seditious libel, as stifling civic discourse. Ibid., 284. In 1736 the first Virginia newspaper asserted that liberty of the press did not allow for criticism of government authorities; thirty years later such criticism was considered an essential safeguard of liberty, and seditious libel prosecutions were disfavored by the courts. Ibid., 274, 282. Although section 12 may have captured the sentiment of the times, it did not annul seditious libel laws or protect British sympathizers.

[53]This section pronounced the communal right and duty of citizens to serve in the militia, prohibited standing armies in peacetime, and declared the supremacy of civil over military authority. Although added in committee, it was likely written by Mason, who promulgated a plan (ultimately adopted) to create the first independent company of volunteer militia on the continent. Rutland, *Papers of George Mason*, 1:286; Hill, *George Mason, Constitutionalist*, 117. In this plan he explained how the communitarian duty of militia service would serve to protect liberty: "a well regulated Militia…is the natural Strength and only safe & stable security of a free Government," making it "unnecessary to keep any standing Army (ever dangerous to liberty) in this Colony." "Fairfax County Militia Plan 'for Embodying the People', Enclosure of 6 February 1775," in Rutland, *Papers of George Mason*, 1:215.

[54]Mason thought this section should not have been included in the declaration, writing on a copy in his personal collection that it was not a fundamental right. Rowland, *Life of George Mason*, 436; Rutland, *Papers of George Mason*, 1:286. A device to keep western territory within Virginia's jurisdiction, the section was occasioned by contentious boundary disputes with Maryland and Pennsylvania, and by mounting pressure for independent government in the territory that is now Kentucky. Ibid.; Howard, *Commentaries*, 1:278–279. Randolph explained that it was a response to "royal fiats in favor of Lord Baltimore and Lord Fairfax" that altered the chartered boundaries of Virginia "much to the discontent of the people." Randolph, *History of Virginia*, 254. Whatever its primary impetus, the fourteenth section is unique—the right to uniform government was not found in any other early state bill of rights.

temperance, frugality, and virtue, and by frequent recurrence to fundamental principles.[55]

SEC. 16. That religion, or the duty which we owe to our Creator, and the manner of discharging it, can be directed only by reason and conviction, not by force or violence; and therefore all men are equally entitled to the free exercise of religion, according to the dictates of conscience; and that it is the mutual duty of all to practise Christian forbearance, love, and charity toward each other.[56]

THE CONSTITUTION OR FORM OF GOVERNMENT, AGREED TO AND RESOLVED UPON BY THE DELEGATES AND REPRESENTATIVES OF THE SEVERAL COUNTIES AND CORPORATIONS OF VIRGINIA

* * *

The legislative, executive, and judiciary department, shall be separate and distinct, so that neither exercise the powers properly belonging to the other: nor shall any person exercise the powers of more than one of them, at the same time; except that the Justices of the County Courts shall be eligible to either House of Assembly.

[55] This section, a declaratory and aspirational provision, enshrined in the constitution an admonition to the citizenry regarding the qualities and moral character believed to be essential for the preservation of a constitutional republic. It passed the Virginia convention unopposed. Rutland, *Papers of George Mason*, 1:281.

[56] Mason's original section on religious freedom called for "fullest toleration" rather than free exercise. Mason, who served as a vestryman of his parish in Fairfax, believed morality and civic virtue were vital principles of republican government. Daniel L. Dreisbach, "George Mason's Pursuit of Religious Liberty in Revolutionary Virginia," *Virginia Magazine of History and Biography* 108, no. 1 (2000): 6–7. Mason's draft drew on ideas found in Locke's *Letter Concerning Toleration* and "went further [toward the goal of religious liberty] than any previous declaration in force in Virginia." Ibid., 12–13. It did not go far enough for James Madison, who viewed Mason's original language affording "toleration" as conferring upon the exercise of religion the status of a mere privilege granted by the state rather than an inalienable right. Ibid., 13. Madison drafted the amendment to the declaration providing for the "free exercise" of religion. Madison's amendment also contained a clause that would have disestablished the Anglican Church, but that portion was rejected by the convention. Selby, *Revolution in Virginia*, 109. Disestablishment would come a decade later with the passage of Thomas Jefferson's Statute for Establishing Religious Freedom in 1786. Dreisbach, "George Mason's Pursuit of Religious Liberty," 28.

* * *

The right of suffrage in the election of members for both Houses shall remain as exercised at present...[57]

[57] See the discussion of suffrage supra pp. 100–101 and footnote 21.

Pennsylvania

Five colonies—Massachusetts, Connecticut, Rhode Island, Maryland, and Pennsylvania—had religion as the primary motivating factor for their existence: That foundation would stamp each with an identity long after the religious impulse had dissipated. Unique among the four with their combination of religious commitment and utopian ideals were the Quakers of Pennsylvania. The 1776 Pennsylvania Constitution offered an unparalleled combination of communitarian assumptions, humanitarian aspirations, and commitment to the common law.

In 1680/1681, King Charles II, as repayment for a debt owed William Penn's late father, granted Penn a tract of land named Pennsylvania ("Penn's Woods" in Latin), in honor of the elder Penn. It was to be a refuge for persecuted Quakers, a place where tolerance and freedom of conscience would give rise to a peaceable kingdom, a society that was godly and virtuous. Penn acknowledged that "though I desire to extend religious freedom, yet I want some recompense for my trouble."[1] The charter granting the land, although replete with phrases giving Penn "full and absolute power" and affording him status as the "true and absolute Proprietarie,"[2] also made it clear that any laws had to "bee consonant to reason, and bee not repugnant or contrarie ... to the Lawes and Statutes,

[1] As quoted in William Robert Shepherd, *History of Proprietary Government in Pennsylvania* (New York: Columbia University Press, 1896), 175.

[2] Charter for the Province of Pennsylvania (1681), in Thorpe, *Constitutions*, 5:3037, 3040, 3042.

P. J. Galie et al., *Bills of Rights Before the Bill of Rights*,
https://doi.org/10.1007/978-3-030-44301-6_5

and rights of this Our Kingdome of England...."[3] The king reserved the right to hear any plea "touching any Judgement to bee there made or given."[4]

In August 1682, James, Duke of York, issued Penn a series of documents conveying to him what is now Delaware. The counties of Newcastle, Kent, and Sussex, known as the Three Lower Counties on Delaware, became part of Pennsylvania. Before setting sail for his new, combined colony, Penn drafted a "Frame of Government" and an accompanying set of "Laws Agreed upon in England." The preamble to the frame is like no other found in the colonies:

> ...government seems to me a part of religion itself, a thing sacred in its institution and end. For, if it does not directly remove the cause, it crushes the effects of evil, and is as such, (though a lower, yet) an emanation of the same Divine Power, that is both author and object of pure religion; the difference lying here, that the one is more free and mental, the other more corporal and compulsive in its operations: but that is only to evil doers; government itself being otherwise as capable of kindness, goodness and charity, as a more private society. They weakly err, that think there is no other use of government, than correction, which is the coarsest part of it: daily experience tells us, that the care and regulation of many other affairs, more soft, and daily necessary, make up much of the greatest part of government....
>
> * * *
>
> Governments, like clocks, go from the motion men give them; and as governments are made and moved by men, so by them they are ruined too. Wherefore governments rather depend upon men, than men upon governments. Let men be good, and the government cannot be bad; if it be ill, they will cure it. But, if men be bad, let the government be never so good, they will endeavor to warp and spoil it to their turn.[5]

Penn drew the following conclusion from these propositions:

[3] Ibid., 3038.

[4] Ibid.

[5] Frame of Government of Pennsylvania (1682), preface, in Thorpe, *Constitutions*, 5:3053–3054.

> That, therefore, which makes a good constitution, must keep it, viz.: men of wisdom and virtue, qualities, that because they descend not with worldly inheritances, must be carefully propagated by a virtuous education of youth; for which after ages will owe more to the care and prudence of founders, and the successive magistracy, than to their parents, for their private patrimonies.[6]

Notably absent from Penn's political writings were references to Old Testament exegesis; nor did he theorize about how individuals might behave in a natural state in the fashion of Locke or Grotius. His political ideas were rooted in the English Constitution which, he asserted, "is antecedent to either protestancy or popery."[7]

This preamble reflected and epitomized the communitarian character and assumptions of colonial governments.[8] It provided the *raison d'etre* for the admonitions and exhortations found in the frame and the Laws Agreed upon in England. It enables us to understand how provisions declaring acts contrary to the "liberties, franchises, and properties" of the people to be of no force could be juxtaposed with provisions addressing education and moral character and restricting a wide range of behaviors from sex to swearing.

The 1682 frame and accompanying laws provided that all who believed the "one Almighty and eternal God, to be the Creator, Upholder and Ruler of the world" and lived "peaceably and justly in civil society" were free to worship as their conscience dictated.[9] Nobody could be compelled to support any ministry or religious endeavor.[10] The frame established a bicameral legislature consisting of a provincial council and a representative assembly, chosen in free and voluntary elections by the freemen of the

[6] Ibid., 3054.

[7] "Petition to Parliament," circa November 1680, in *The Papers of William Penn*, ed. Richard S. Dunn and Mary Maples Dunn (Philadelphia: University of Pennsylvania Press 1982), 2:52. As part of Penn's, "The Excellent Priviledge of Liberty and Property: Being the Birth-Right of the Free-Born Subjects of England" (1687), he appended the 1225 version of Magna Carta—its first printing on American soil. A reprint can be found at *The Excellent Priviledge of Liberty and Property: Being a Reprint and Fac-simile of the First American Edition of Magna Charta* (1897; reprint, Clark, NJ: The Lawbook Exchange, Ltd., 2005).

[8] See our discussion, pp. 3–17.

[9] Frame of Government of Pennsylvania (1682), Laws Agreed upon in England, &C. (1682) [hereinafter cited as "Laws Agreed upon in England"], sec. XXXV, in Thorpe, *Constitutions*, 5:3063.

[10] Ibid.

colony. It required a secret ballot and rotation in office.[11] Penn prohibited non-Christians from holding public office and denied Catholics the right to vote or hold office, believing their loyalty would lie with the pope in Rome, a foreign power.[12] For non-Protestants, freedom of religion meant freedom to worship and practice their faith, not full citizenship. Penn's frame did not extend its protections to slaves, though Pennsylvania Quakers would later be in the vanguard of the crusade to abolish slavery.

The laws contained procedural and substantive rights for those accused of crimes, including grand jury and petit jury for criminal cases,[13] open courts,[14] speedy justice,[15] plain language requirements,[16] a right to bail,[17] and punishments that were not oppressive and for rehabilitation only. The founding documents of the colony also provided care for the needy,[18] the building and maintenance of public schools,[19] humane prison conditions,[20] and some protection for indentured servants.[21]

Wishing to submit the frame and laws to a representative body in the colony, Penn issued writs calling for the election of representatives to a general assembly in October 1682. Once elected, the assembly displayed independence that surprised and disconcerted Penn: it failed to approve

[11] Frame of Government of Pennsylvania (1682), sec. IV, 3056.

[12] William C. Kashatus, "William Penn's Legacy: Religious and Spiritual Diversity," *Pennsylvania Heritage* 37, no. 2 (Spring 2011), http://www.phmc.state.pa.us/portal/communities/pa-heritage/william-penn-legacy-religious-spiritual-diversity.html.

[13] Laws Agreed upon in England, sec. VIII, 3060. A right to a jury trial in civil cases was also provided.

[14] Ibid., sec. V, 3060.

[15] Ibid., sec. VII, 3060.

[16] Ibid.

[17] Ibid., sec. XI, 3061.

[18] *Charter to William Penn, and Laws of the Province of Pennsylvania, Passed Between the Years 1682 and 1700* (Harrisburg: L.S. Hart, State Printer, 1879), Ch. XXXII. Online at https://catalog.hathitrust.org/Record/010315596.

[19] Frame of Government of Pennsylvania (1682), sec. XII, 3056.

[20] Laws Agreed upon in England, sec. XIII, 3061.

[21] Ibid., sec. XXIX, 3062.

the frame, presaging Penn's relationship with that body. Similarly, the Laws Agreed upon in England were never approved by the settlers; rather, they were superseded by a series of statutes adopted in December 1682 known as the "Great Law."[22] The preamble to the Great Law set forth the purpose of government: "to Make and Establish Such Laws as shall best preserve true Christian and Civill Liberty…."[23]

The Great Law afforded, among others, liberty of conscience for all who acknowledged one Almighty God,[24] a right to jury trial in both civil and criminal proceedings (and a grand jury presentment in the case of the latter),[25] and an open courts provision traceable back to Magna Carta.[26] The law also limited the death penalty to only cases of murder.

Following the rejection of the 1682 frame, a compromise was reached among the governor, council, and assembly, and the 1683 Frame of Government was agreed to by all parties. Subsequent frames were adopted in 1696 (known as Markham's Frame) and in 1701, with the latter referred to as the Charter of Privileges.[27] The Charter of Privileges contained a reaffirmation of the liberty of conscience, which was required to "be kept and remain, without any alteration, inviolably for ever."[28] The document also provided defendants in criminal cases with the same privileges of witness and counsel as their prosecutors,[29] and mandated that no person answer any complaint other than in the ordinary course of justice.[30]

The successive frames, coupled with the Great Law, governed the colony until 1776. The frames and laws approved by the freemen of the province established a tradition of written bills of rights, and by the end

[22] The Great Law (1682) is reprinted in *The Statutes at Large of Pennsylvania from 1682 to 1700*, comp. Robert L. Cable (Harrisburg: Legislative Reference Bureau, 2001), 1:5–26, http://www.palrb.us/statutesatlarge/16001699/1682/0/misclaw/grlawlv.pdf.

[23] Ibid., preamble, 5.

[24] Ibid., Ch. 1, 5.

[25] Ibid., Ch. 46, 18–19.

[26] Ibid., Ch. 42, 17.

[27] Each revision of the frame reduced the power of the governor and increased the power of the assembly. The last major change in governmental structure took place in 1701 with the creation of a unicameral legislature.

[28] Charter of Privileges Granted by William Penn, Esq. to the Inhabitants of Pennsylvania and Territories (1701), sec. VIII, in Thorpe, *Constitutions*, 5:3080.

[29] Ibid., sec. V, 3079.

[30] Ibid., sec. VI, 3079.

of the seventeenth century, Pennsylvania had in place three fundamental rights, namely, freedom of religious conscience, trial by jury, and self-government. All would find their way into the 1776 constitution.

Constitutional Developments 1776–1790

The Pennsylvania Constitution of 1776 was framed by an elected convention called by the Pennsylvania Provincial Conference following the express directive of the Continental Congress to the states to inaugurate new forms of government. Chaired by Benjamin Franklin, the convention sat in Philadelphia from July 15 until September 28. The convention authorized a draft of the constitution to be printed as a pamphlet and published in the *Pennsylvania Evening Post*.[31] The convention responded to criticisms provoked by the posting and made some changes; the final document, however, was not submitted to the people for ratification. At the signing, twenty-three of the ninety-six members of the convention—nearly twenty-five percent—signified their dissatisfaction with the constitution by refusing to affix their names to it. The lack of consensus from the beginning, atypical of constitutional conventions of the day, undermined support for the constitution and ultimately would prove fatal.

The preamble of the 1776 constitution encapsulated the communitarian, egalitarian, and visionary ideals of the Quakers. It contained a natural rights clause, but the first listed purpose of government was "the security and protection of the community as such," followed by a commitment to "the individuals who compose it to enjoy their natural rights." The preamble's communitarian character was also reflected in its focus on the commonweal: "the people of this State, by common consent, and without violence... promote the general happiness of the people...and provide for future improvements, without partiality for, or prejudice against any particular class, sect, or denomination..." (Const. 1776, preamble).[32]

[31] John N. Shaeffer, "Public Consideration of the 1776 Pennsylvania Constitution," *The Pennsylvania Magazine of History and Biography* 98, no. 4 (October 1974): 419. For the influence of Thomas Paine on the 1776 constitution, see Robert F. Williams, "The Influences of Pennsylvania's 1776 Constitution on American Constitutionalism During the Founding Decade," *The Pennsylvania Magazine of History and Biography* 112, no. 1 (January 1988): 28–32.

[32] Penn was committed to civil unity. The notion of civil interest as the cement of society is a constant theme throughout his work as it was in the colonies generally. The extensive and intrusive character of his laws regulating civil conduct was at least

The declaration of rights built on these ideals, beginning with the principle that "all men are born equally free and independent, and have certain natural, inherent and inalienable rights, amongst which are, the enjoying and defending life and liberty, acquiring, possessing and protecting property, and pursuing and obtaining happiness and safety" (Decl. 1776, Art. I). The declaration provided a full-throated affirmation of the liberty of conscience: all men "have a natural and unalienable right to worship Almighty God according to the dictates of their own consciences and understanding" (ibid., Art. II), and no man "ought or of right [could] be" forced to attend any religious worship, support any place of worship, or maintain any ministry against his will. Taken together, these liberty provisions provide a summative statement of William Penn's vision expressed in the governing documents adopted between 1682 and 1701.

Section 46 of the frame of government erased any doubt as to whether the declaration was part of the constitution: "The declaration of rights is hereby declared to be a part of the constitution of this commonwealth, and ought never to be violated on any pretence whatever." For twenty-first century students of the law, such provisions are likely to be seen as stating little more than a truism but in 1776, the view that statutory law must conform to the limits and conditions laid down in the constitution was not firmly established.

The doctrine of popular sovereignty is present in three articles of the declaration. Article III confirmed the people as having the sole and exclusive right of governing and regulating the police power of the state. Article IV affirmed that all power was originally inherent in, and derived from the people and that all government officers were accountable to the people. Article V contained an alter or abolish clause, affording the community "an indubitable, unalienable and indefeasible right to reform, alter, or abolish government in such manner as shall be by that community judged most conducive to the public weal."

Structural provisions for implementing the constitution's commitment to popular sovereignty included a requirement for reapportionment based on taxpayer population (Const. 1776, sec. 17) and elimination of property qualifications for suffrage (ibid., sec. 6).[33] To ensure that the actions

comparable to the Puritan codes of laws. See his draft of the "Fundamental Constitution of Pennsylvania." Dunn and Dunn, *Papers of William Penn*, 2:190.

[33] The convention rejected a proposal that would have reduced unequal distributions of wealth.

of the legislature accurately mirrored the will of the people, the frame of government mandated the following: the doors of the house of representatives remain open during sessions unless otherwise demanded by the welfare of the state (ibid., sec. 13); the votes and proceedings of the general assembly be printed weekly (ibid., sec. 14); and bills of public nature state their motives in the preambles, be printed for consideration by the people before final reading, and, in all but cases of "sudden necessity," not be passed until the following session (ibid., sec. 15). Collectively, these provisions constituted the most systematic attempt to ensure the openness of the legislative process in eighteenth-century America. One commentator asserts that it was unlikely that "the concept of the people as the ultimate constitution-makers and lawgivers (popular sovereignty) was as clearly asserted anywhere else in the United States as it was in Pennsylvania."[34] In place of the checks and balances identified with the mixed or balanced government model, the Pennsylvania Constitution placed almost complete reliance on the independence, integrity, and watchfulness of the people for the preservation of liberty—what has been called republican or popular constitutionalism.[35]

Suffrage

Property ownership, long identified with political competence as well as a commitment to and a stake in the community, was eliminated as a condition for voting. Suffrage was granted to all freemen, aged twenty-one and over, who resided in the state for one year and who paid public taxes during that time (Const. 1776, sec. 6). Sons of freeholders who were at least twenty-one were also eligible to vote, regardless of whether they had paid taxes. These changes brought close to ninety percent of free adult males into the political community, creating the most liberal franchise known in the Western world to that date.[36] This sharp break with nearly a century of elections in England and its colonies reflected a new understanding of representation, bolstered by the arguments advanced to justify that revolution. "Associators," men who had volunteered to associate in

[34] Douglas McNeil Arnold, "Political Ideology and the Internal Revolution in Pennsylvania, 1776–1790" (PhD diss., Princeton University, 1976), 2, 46.

[35] See, e.g., the analysis above, pp. 89–91.

[36] Gary B. Nash, *The Unknown American Revolution: The Unruly Birth of Democracy and the Struggle to Create America* (New York: Viking Press, 2005), 269.

militia-like units as bands of brothers, who were twenty-one, residents of the state for one year, and paid any taxes (regardless of amount) were eligible to vote.[37] The commitments to popular sovereignty and militia duty—patriotic service in defense of the country—worked in tandem to undercut the arguments for property qualifications.[38]

Structural Provisions

Under the influence of Thomas Paine's unalloyed republicanism, the convention downplayed the separation of powers, identifying the notion with the English Constitution's mixture of aristocratic, monarchic, and popular elements. Some features of separation were included. The frame afforded the unicameral house of representatives legislative power unchecked by an executive veto, while lodging executive power in a president and council. Plural office-holding was prohibited: representatives could hold no other office except in the militia (Const. 1776, sec. 7); council members could not serve as members of the general assembly or as congressional delegates (ibid., sec. 19); and supreme court judges could not hold any civil or military office (ibid., sec. 23). Judicial independence was wanting, as judges of the supreme court only received seven-year terms of office.

The declaration called for rotation in office and regular elections (Decl. 1776, Art. VI), and the frame gave members of the house of representatives one-year terms (Const. 1776, sec. 9) and a limit of no more than four years in seven (ibid., sec. 8). Representatives were required to reside in their city or county of selection for two years before the election (ibid., sec. 7), and to swear an oath declaring belief in one God and acknowledging the Old and New Testaments to have been given by divine inspiration (ibid., sec. 10). Members of the supreme executive council were given three-year terms following a transition period, and any person who served three consecutive years was ineligible for four years afterward (ibid., sec. 19). The drafters adopted section 36 of the frame, which recognized that public service should be compensated, but sought to avoid offices of

[37] Ibid.

[38] See Marc W. Kruman, *Between Authority and Liberty: State Constitution Making in Revolutionary America* (Chapel Hill: University of North Carolina Press, 1997), 92–93. See Decl. 1776, Art. VII.

profit that might encourage "dependence and servility."[39] The rotation in office provisions and short terms, along with this warning, support the conclusion that legislative office-holding was meant to be an act of citizenship, not a means to earn a livelihood.

The Pennsylvania Constitution was the first to contain a method for its revision. The frame specified that the legislature "shall have no power to add to, alter, abolish, or infringe any part of this constitution" (Const. 1776, sec. 9). Instead, a council of censors, consisting of two people elected once every seven years from each city and county in the state, possessed the power to amend or revise the constitution (ibid., sec. 47). Charged with reviewing legislation and executive actions for conformity with the constitution and suggesting corrective action, the council was empowered to call a constitutional convention if it believed amendment an "absolute necessity." In those situations, the council was required to publish any proposed amendments six months before the date of the convention.

The communitarian assumptions about civic virtue and homogeneity expressed in the 1776 constitution were tested and undermined by an increasingly heterogeneous population, a competitive, entrepreneurial spirit, rapid economic development, and internal unrest.[40] These tensions intensified demands for a new constitution, and a convention was held in 1789–90, which adopted the state's second constitution.

The 1790 constitution reflected these changes by adopting structures and institutions more like those found in the national Constitution. Convention delegates removed the declaration of rights as a free-standing component of the constitution and placed most of its contents in a newly added Article IX. It was the first state to do so,[41] eliminating the division that had characterized state constitutions during the period under study. If there was any meaning intended by the original placement before the body or frame of government, it was lost in the move.

[39] Vermont was the only other state to include a similar provision in its constitution. See Vt. Const. 1777, sec. XXXIII; Vt. Const. 1786, sec. XXII.

[40] The extent of civil unrest and violence in Pennsylvania is chronicled in Jack D. Marietta and G. S. Rowe, *Troubled Experiment: Crime and Justice in Pennsylvania, 1682–1800* (Philadelphia: University of Pennsylvania Press, 2006), 263–265.

[41] South Carolina's 1790 constitution, adopted three months before the Pennsylvania Constitution, included an article (Article IX) enumerating rights, but its previous constitution had no declaration of rights.

Signaling the end of a political order reliant upon a legislature that reflected the general will of a homogeneous community, the new constitution moved in the direction of the Federalist understanding as epitomized by James Madison. The delegates replaced the frame of government enacted in the early months of the Revolution with a document reflecting the influence of the federal model including: a bill of rights containing judicially enforceable rights over and against the community; a stronger commitment to the separation of powers (including an independent judiciary), and a significantly altered relationship among the branches of government. Gone was the weak, plural executive and the all-powerful unicameral assembly; in their place, the delegates provided for a governor, elected directly by the people and equipped with veto power, and a bicameral legislature elected from districts based on an equitable distribution of the population.

Evidence of the influence of the federal model is also manifest in the rights article. The lengthy preamble was reduced to one sentence and a number of nearly verbatim copies of rights provisions found in the national Constitution were added. Of greatest significance was the elimination or shortening of provisions in the 1776 constitution that contained aspirational or hortatory language.[42] The transformation from the most democratic constitution in the country to a republican Federalist model was complete.

Postscript: Pennsylvania adopted new constitutions in 1838, 1874, and 1968. The rights article in the 1790 constitution remains substantially intact.

Constitution of Pennsylvania [1776]

A Declaration of the Rights of the Inhabitants of the Commonwealth, or State of Pennsylvania

I. That all men are born equally free and independent, and have certain natural, inherent and inalienable rights, among which are, the enjoying

[42] Articles IV, VI, VII, VIII and XIV of the 1776 declaration and sections 42, 43, 44, and 45 of the 1776 frame were eliminated.

and defending life and liberty, acquiring, possessing and protecting property, and pursuing and obtaining happiness and safety.[43]

II. That all men have a natural and unalienable right to worship Almighty God according to the dictates of their own consciences and understanding: And that no man ought or of right can be compelled to attend any religious worship, or erect or support any place of worship, or maintain any ministry, contrary to, or against, his own free will and consent: Nor can any man, who acknowledges the being of a God, be justly deprived or abridged of any civil right as a citizen, on account of his religious sentiments or peculiar mode of religious worship: And that no authority can or ought to be vested in, or assumed by any power whatever, that shall in any case interfere with, or in any manner control, the right of conscience in the free exercise of religious worship.[44]

III. That the people of this State have the sole, exclusive and inherent right of governing and regulating the internal police of the same.[45]

IV. That all power being originally inherent in, and consequently derived from, the people; therefore all officers of government, whether legislative or executive, are their trustees and servants, and at all times accountable to them.[46]

V. That government is, or ought to be, instituted for the common benefit, protection and security of the people, nation or community; and not for the particular emolument or advantage of any single man, family, or sett of men, who are a part only of that community; And that the community hath an indubitable, unalienable and indefeasible right to

[43] The phraseology setting forth the natural rights of man is closer to George Mason's version in section 1 of the Virginia Declaration of Rights than Jefferson's version in the Declaration of Independence.

[44] This article reflected Penn's commitment and support for religious liberty expressed in the colony's governing documents adopted between 1682 and 1701. This liberty was not absolute. Chapter 10 of the frame of government mandated assembly members swear to an oath of office requiring belief in the Old and New Testaments.

[45] This provision, one of many designed to ensure that the state did not surrender its sovereign police powers to a confederation, does not appear in the 1790 constitution. The Federalist sympathies of a good number of delegates to the convention drafting that document and the existence of a federal Union mitigated earlier fears of what a possible union might mean to the sovereignty of the states.

[46] Similar to Va. Decl. 1776, sec. 2.

reform, alter, or abolish government in such manner as shall be by that community judged most conducive to the public weal.[47]

VI. That those who are employed in the legislative and executive business of the State, may be restrained from oppression, the people have a right, at such periods as they may think proper, to reduce their public officers to a private station, and supply the vacancies by certain and regular elections.[48]

VII. That all elections ought to be free; and that all free men having a sufficient evident common interest with, and attachment to the community, have a right to elect officers, or to be elected into office.[49]

VIII. That every member of society hath a right to be protected in the enjoyment of life, liberty and property, and therefore is bound to contribute his proportion towards the expence of that protection, and yield his personal service when necessary, or an equivalent thereto: But no part of a man's property can be justly taken from him, or applied to public uses, without his own consent, or that of his legal representatives: Nor can any man who is conscientiously scrupulous of bearing arms, be justly compelled thereto, if he will pay such equivalent, nor are the people bound by any laws, but such as they have in like manner assented to, for their common good.[50]

[47] Similar to Va. Decl. 1776, sec. 3. This article offered a muted right to revolution or, at the very least, a right to take extra-constitutional means to change the government if deemed necessary. Pennsylvanians may have had in mind the incendiary claims made in the Declaration of Independence; more likely they intended to legitimize the extra-constitutional provincial conference that sprung up and, without firing a shot, assumed control of the government and called for the election of delegates to establish the new constitution.

[48] This was a rotation in office provision, but it left the specifics of the rotation scheme to the frame of government. See text accompanying "Structural Provisions," above. It was a prompt to the citizens acting directly and through their representatives to monitor the operation of the government to prevent the rise of an "inconvenient aristocracy."

[49] The initial clause of this article first appeared in the English Bill of Rights of 1689 and was repeated, with slightly different wording, in Markham's Frame. See Frame of Government of Pennsylvania (1696), in Thorpe, *Constitutions*, 5:3073. The second part laid down the general principle that suffrage should be granted to those who have a "sufficient evident common interest with and attachment to the community." See section 6 of the frame of government for the specific requirements in the document.

[50] This article, found in several state constitutions, reflected the commonly held view that rights and privileges were accompanied by duties and obligations. See pp. 43–46, above. In addition, it repeated the fundamental principle of Magna Carta that no person's property could be taken without due process of law, in this case, consent of the duly

IX. That in all prosecutions for criminal offences, a man hath a right to be heard by himself and his council, to demand the cause and nature of his accusation, to be confronted with the witnesses, to call for evidence in his favour, and a speedy public trial, by an impartial jury of the country, without the unanimous consent of which jury he cannot be found guilty; nor can he be compelled to give evidence against himself; nor can any man be justly deprived of his liberty except by the laws of the land, or the judgment of his peers.[51]

X. That the people have a right to hold themselves, their houses, papers, and possessions free from search and seizure, and therefore warrants without oaths or affirmations first made, affording a sufficient foundation for them, and whereby any officer or messenger may be commanded or required to search suspected places, or to seize any person or persons, his or their property, not particularly described, are contrary to that right, and ought not to be granted.[52]

elected representatives. The conscientious objection exemption was eliminated in the 1790 constitution. The pacifism and loyalty of Quakers to the British during the Revolutionary War did not endear them to convention delegates.

[51] Most of the criminal procedure rights found in this article can be traced to common law and English statutes. Chapters 39 and 40 of Magna Carta set forth the due process clause that concluded this article and the principle that justice would be neither delayed nor denied that underlies the speedy trial requirement. Penn embraced these ideas. Section V of the Laws Agreed upon in England provided that "all courts shall be open, and justice shall neither be sold, denied nor delayed," and section VIII secured the right to a jury trial. Laws Agreed upon in England, secs. V, VIII, 3060 (both cites). The 1701 Charter of Privileges protected the rights to counsel and evidence on an equality principle. Charter of Privileges, sec. V, 3079.

[52] The language of this article banning general warrants more closely resembled the prohibition found in article 12 of the widely-circulated committee report of the Virginia Declaration of Rights than the final version of that declaration. The first part of the article, setting forth the "right" of "the people" to be free from search and seizure, was a Pennsylvania addition. Thomas Y. Davies concludes that this language was probably not meant to prohibit warrantless arrests or searches. "Correcting Search-and-Seizure History: Now-Forgotten Common-Law Warrantless Arrest Standards and the Original Understanding of 'Due Process of Law'," *Mississippi Law Journal*, 77, no. 1 (Fall 2007): 106.

XI. That in controversies respecting property, and in suits between man and man, the parties have a right to trial by jury, which ought to be held sacred.[53]

XII. That the people have a right to freedom of speech, and of writing, and publishing their sentiments; therefore the freedom of the press ought not to be restrained.[54]

XIII. That the people have a right to bear arms for the defence of themselves and the state; and as standing armies in the time of peace are dangerous to liberty, they ought not to be kept up; And that the military should be kept under strict subordination to, and governed by, the civil power.[55]

XIV. That a frequent recurrence to fundamental principles, and a firm adherence to justice, moderation, temperance, industry, and frugality are absolutely necessary to preserve the blessings of liberty, and keep a government free: The people ought therefore to pay particular attention to these points in the choice of officers and representatives, and have a right to exact a due and constant regard to them, from their legislatures and magistrates, in the making and executing such laws as are necessary for the good government of the state.[56]

[53] This article provided the right to a jury trial in civil cases, which dated back to Chapter 46 of the Great Law. Cable, *Statutes at Large*, 1:18–19. See the 1776 frame of government, section 25 below, for another provision on jury trials.

[54] The Pennsylvania Constitution was one of the few early state constitutions that protected both press and speech. It also added a section in the frame of government (section 35) requiring that the printing press be free to all who would examine the government. It was intended to guarantee to citizens the freedom of speech and of the press sanctioned by the common law. *Respublica v. Oswald, 1 Dallas*, 319 (1788). Both of these provisions were intended to preserve, not extend, the freedom of the press.

[55] The Constitution of Pennsylvania guaranteed the right to bear arms, including for defense of self, with no mention of the militia (at the time, Pennsylvania had no organized militia). See pp. 63–67 for a thorough description of these clauses. The right to bear arms and the prohibition against standing armies can be found in the English Bill of Rights of 1689.

The first clause of the article stated the "people have a **right** to bear arms," the second clause concerning standing armies used "ought," and the framers used "should" in the third clause. If there is a difference in the use of the terms "have" and "ought to," as some scholars have claimed, then only the right to bear arms was a legally enforceable command. One explanation for the difference is that the first right has as its focus individuals; the other two clauses focus respectively on an institution, standing armies, and the conditions under which those armies should operate.

[56] Similar to Va. Decl. 1776, sec. 17. See also commentary at p. 112.

XV. That all men have a natural inherent right to emigrate from one state to another that will receive them, or to form a new state in vacant countries, or in such countries as they can purchase, whenever they think that thereby they may promote their happiness.[57]

XVI. That the people have a right to assemble together, to consult for their common good, to instruct their representatives, and to apply to the legislature for redress of grievances, by address, petition, or remonstrance.[58]

Plan or Frame of Government for the Commonwealth or State of Pennsylvania

* * *

SECT. 6. Every freemen of the full age of twenty-one years, having resided in this state for the space of one whole year next before the day of election for representatives, and paid public taxes during that time, shall enjoy the right of an elector: Provided always, that sons of freeholders of the age of twenty-one years shall be intitled to vote although they have not paid taxes.

* * *

[57] The "natural inherent right" of "all men" to emigrate from one country to another whenever they believed by so doing they "might promote their own happiness and welfare" had always been asserted by Americans. English common law did not permit subjects to voluntarily relinquish their allegiance—once a subject always a subject. "An Englishman who removes to France, or to China, owes the same allegiance to the king of England there as at home, and twenty years hence as well as now. For it is a principle of universal law, that the natural-born subject of one prince cannot by any act of his own, no, not by swearing allegiance to another, put off or discharge his natural allegiance to the former." William Blackstone, *Commentaries on the Laws of England in Four Books* (1753; reprint, Philadelphia: J.B. Lippincott Co., 1893), 1:369. This article explicitly repudiated that doctrine, adopting an approach more in line with the status of a citizen in a natural rights republic.

[58] Pennsylvania became the first state to provide its citizens with a constitutional guarantee of the right to assemble and petition their representatives, although this right was asserted in the Declaration and Resolves adopted by the First Continental Congress in 1774. These rights were a piece with other articles in the declaration aimed at ensuring the people would have constitutionally protected means to act as a check on the government.

SECT. 25. Trials shall be by jury as heretofore: And it is recommended to the legislature of this state, to provide by law against every corruption or partiality in the choice, return, or appointment of juries.[59]

SECT. 26. Courts of sessions, common pleas, and orphans courts shall be held quarterly in each city and county; and the legislature shall have power to establish all such other courts as they may judge for the good of the inhabitants of the state. All courts shall be open, and justice shall be impartially administered without corruption or unnecessary delay: All their officers shall be paid an adequate but moderate compensation for their services: And if any officer shall take greater or other fees than the law allows him, either directly or indirectly, it shall ever after disqualify him from holding any office in this state.[60]

* * *

SECT. 28. The person of a debtor, where there is not a strong presumption of fraud, shall not be continued in prison, after delivering up, ***bona fide***, all his estate real and personal, for the use of his creditors, in such manner as shall be hereafter regulated by law. All prisoners shall be bailable by sufficient sureties, unless for capital offences, when the proof is evident, or presumption great.[61]

SECT. 29. Excessive bail shall not be exacted for bailable offences: And all fines shall be moderate.[62]

[59] Trial by jury is a right proclaimed in the declaration (Arts. IX and XI) and repeated here in the frame. Why make it explicit twice? Perhaps it was another example of the role of a constitution as a civic schoolmaster, admonishing the legislature to ensure that this most fundamental of rights was not corrupted. Penn's experience as a defendant in a criminal case in England gave him an appreciation of the importance of the jury. Contempt charges against recalcitrant jurors who refused to convict him led to Bushell's Case (1670), 124 E.R. 1006, which established jury independence.

[60] Open courts clauses traced their origins to Chapter 40 of Magna Carta. More directly, the protection was included in Penn's Laws Agreed upon in England, sec. V, 3060, and the subsequently adopted Great Law. Great Law, Ch. 42, 17. Without open and transparent legislative and judicial proceedings, public vigilance would be ineffective.

[61] Colonial laws permitted imprisoning individuals for failure to pay their debts, and the laws were enforced. The effect of this provision was to require passage of insolvency laws, which would provide a method by which debtors could obtain discharge from custody upon surrendering their property. The last sentence is nearly verbatim from section XI of the Laws Agreed upon in England. Laws Agreed upon in England, sec. XI, 3061.

[62] Similar to Va. Decl. 1776, sec. 9. The first appearance in Pennsylvania of a requirement that fines be moderate was section XVIII of the Laws Agreed upon in England:

* * *

SECT. 32. All elections, whether by the people or in general assembly, shall be by ballot, free and voluntary: And any elector, who shall receive any gift or reward for his vote, in meat, drink, monies, or otherwise, shall forfeit his right to elect for that time, and suffer such other penalties as future laws shall direct. And any person who shall directly or indirectly give, promise, or bestow any such rewards to be elected, shall be thereby rendered incapable to serve for the ensuing year.[63]

* * *

SECT. 35. The printing presses shall be free to every person who undertakes to examine the proceedings of the legislature, or any part of government.[64]

* * *

SECT. 37. The future legislature of this state, shall regulate intails in such a manner as to prevent perpetuities.

"That all fines shall be moderate, and saving men's contenements [a holding of property], merchandize or wainage [means of transporting goods]." Laws Agreed upon in England, sec. XVIII, 3061.

[63] Antecedents begin with the English Bill of Rights (1689) ("That election of members of Parliament ought to be free") and the Laws Agreed upon in England:

> That all elections of members, or representatives of the people and freemen of the province of Pensilvania, to serve in provincial Council, or General Assembly, to be held within the said province, shall be free and voluntary: and that the elector, that shall receive any reward or gift, in meat, drink, monies, or otherwise, shall forfeit his right to elect; and such person as shall directly or indirectly give, promise, or bestow any such reward as aforesaid, to be elected, shall forfeit his election, and be thereby incapable to serve as aforesaid....

Laws Agreed upon in England, sec. III, 3060; see also Great Law, Ch. 68, 24–25 and Frame of Government of Pennsylvania (1696), 3073.

[64] During colonial times, a printer in Pennsylvania had been compelled to flee for publishing a paper written by a Quaker, criticizing his brethren who were in positions of authority, and on several occasions measures were taken to suppress books in print deemed to offend against public authority. While controls on the press had dissipated or disappeared by the 1770s, the memory of these attacks and the possibility of their revival prompted this section.

SECT. 38. The penal laws as heretofore used shall be reformed by the legislature of this state, as soon as may be, and punishments made in some cases less sanguinary, and in general more proportionate to the crimes.[65]

SECT. 39. To deter more effectually from the commission of crimes, by continued visible punishments of long duration, and to make sanguinary punishments less necessary; houses ought to be provided for punishing by hard labour, those who shall be convicted of crimes not capital; wherein the criminals shall be imployed for the benefit of the public, or for reparation of injuries done to private persons: And all persons at proper times shall be admitted to see the prisoners at their labour.

* * *

SECT. 41. No public tax, custom or contribution shall be imposed upon, or paid by the people of this state, except by a law for that purpose: And before any law be made for raising it, the purpose for which any tax is to be raised ought to appear clearly to the legislature to be of more service to the community than the money would be, if not collected; which being well observed, taxes can never be burthens.[66]

[65] Sections 38 and 39 were directives to the legislature to undertake penal reforms. The assembly implemented those directives in 1786 and revised the penal code to make it less harsh. Capital punishment was replaced by fines and incarceration for many crimes; physical mutilation was forbidden. John K. Alexander, "Pennsylvania: Pioneer in Safeguarding Personal Rights," in *The Bill of Rights and the States: The Colonial and Revolutionary Origins of American Liberties*, ed. Patrick T. Conley and John P. Kaminski (Madison, WI: Madison House, 1992), 314. This provision received high praise from French observers, who saw it as a manifestation of Enlightenment thought and a step towards the perfectibility of man: "I regard the Constitution of Pennsylvania as the model of an excellent government, under which, when peace has restored public tranquillity, there will be very little crime." J. Paul Selsam, "Brissot de Warville on the Pennsylvania Constitution of 1776," *Pennsylvania Magazine of History and Biography* 72, no. 1 (January 1948): 28.

[66] Section 41 addressed the common practice by Crown authorities of assessing taxes or requiring gifts or loans without the consent of Parliament or the colonial legislature. The Stamp Act Congress, in its "Declaration of Rights and Grievances, October 19, 1765," listed this complaint as one of its grievances. Barry Alan Shain, ed., *The Declaration of Independence in Historical Context: American State Papers, Petitions, Proclamations, and Letters of the Delegates to the First National Congresses* (New Haven, CT: Yale University Press, 2014), 88–89. This provision required that when taxes were going to be raised, the public had a right to know explicitly what purposes those taxes were to serve. Additionally, the council of censors was charged to "enquire whether the public taxes had been justly laid and collected in all parts of the commonwealth…" (Const. 1776, sec. 46).

SECT. 42. Every foreigner of good character who comes to settle in this state, having first taken an oath or affirmation of allegiance to the same, may purchase, or by other just means acquire, hold, and transfer land or other real estate; and after one year's residence, shall be deemed a free denizen thereof, and entitled to all the rights of a natural born subject of this state, except that he shall not be capable of being elected a representative until after two years residence.[67]

SECT. 43. The inhabitants of this state shall have liberty to fowl and hunt in seasonable times on the lands they hold, and on all other lands therein not inclosed; and in like manner to fish in all boatable waters, and others not private property.[68]

SECT. 44. A school or schools shall be established in each county by the legislature, for the convenient instruction of youth, with such salaries to the masters paid by the public, as may enable them to instruct youth at low prices: And all useful learning shall be duly encouraged and promoted in one or more universities.[69]

[67] English common law and statute law imposed alien property disabilities that restricted a foreigner's access to land. This section removed these impediments, giving foreigners all the rights of native-born freemen after they fulfilled a residency requirement of one year (to allow familiarity and identification with the community) and took an oath of allegiance. This provision was designed to encourage foreigners to acquire property in the state, settle the vacant lands, and become citizens. Marilyn C. Baseler, *Asylum for Mankind: America, 1607–1800* (Ithaca, NY: Cornell University Press, 1998), 218.

[68] William Penn himself recognized Pennsylvanians' 'liberty to fowl and hunt upon the lands they hold....', with that right being secured in the second Frame of Government of Pennsylvania (1683), sec. XXII, in Thorpe, *Constitutions*, 5:3068, and in Markham's Frame. Frame of Government of Pennsylvania (1696), 3075. This reaffirmation of Penn's position was a reaction against the English practices, under which "the freeholders of moderate estates [were] deprived of a natural right ... [T]he body of the people kept from the use of guns are utterly ignorant of the arms of modern war, and the kingdom effectually disarmed, except of the standing forces...." As quoted in Stephen P. Halbrook, "The Constitutional Right to Hunt: New Recognition of an Old Liberty in Virginia," *William & Mary Bill of Rights Journal* 19, no. 1 (October 2010): 200.

The section is unique among the early state constitutions. Most likely, it was meant to assure residents and prospective settlers that these opportunities would remain protected.

[69] Education guaranteed by the constitution and provided at a cost enabling the less well-off to attend school further evidenced the central importance of education, as well as religion, in maintaining a well-ordered, self-governing community. See pp. 59–61 for a more thorough discussion of this connection.

SECT. 45. Laws for the encouragement of virtue, and prevention of vice and immorality, shall be made and constantly kept in force, and provision shall be made for their due execution: And all religious societies or bodies of men heretofore united or incorporated for the advancement of religion or learning, or for other pious and charitable purposes, shall be encouraged and protected in the enjoyment of the privileges, immunities and estates which they were accustomed to enjoy, or could of right have enjoyed, under the laws and former constitution of this state.[70]

SECT. 46. The declaration of rights is hereby declared to be a part of the constitution of this commonwealth, and ought never to be violated on any pretence whatever.[71]

[70]The first clause reflected Penn's belief, embodied in the frame of 1682, that "men of wisdom and virtue, qualities, that because they descend not with worldly inheritances, must be carefully propagated by a virtuous education of youth; for which after ages will owe more to the care and prudence of founders, and the successive magistracy, than to their parents, for their private patrimonies." Frame of Government of Pennsylvania (1682), preamble, 3052. Penn recognized that liberty required nurture and that nurturing was a communal responsibility.

Explicit guarantees of religious rights were placed in the constitution but some church leaders were uneasy about the lack of any guarantee for the existing privileges of churches and schools that had been incorporated by the colonial government. A group of ministers led by the Rev. Henry Melchior Muhlenberg petitioned the convention for specific consideration. In response to this concern, the convention added the second clause of this section. Drafted by Muhlenberg, it was a constitutional guarantee that existing religious and charitable organizations would be protected in their privileges and estates. Shaeffer, "Public Consideration," 426.

[71]This clause, a retrospective response to multiple threats by British authorities to nullify colonial legislation, drove the delegates to declare that no government had the legitimate authority to trench on these rights. It removed any lingering doubt about the legal status of the declaration.

Constitution of Pennsylvania [1790]

Article III

Section 1. In elections by the citizens, every freeman of the age of twenty-one years, having resided in the State two years next before the election, and within that time paid a State or county tax, which shall have been assessed at least six months before the election, shall enjoy the rights of an elector: *Provided.* That the sons of persons qualified as aforesaid, between the ages of twenty-one and twenty-two years, shall be entitled to vote, although they shall not have paid taxes.[72]

Article VII

Section 1. The legislature shall, as soon as conveniently may be, provide, by law, for the establishment of schools throughout the State, in such manner that the poor may be taught gratis.

Sec. 2. The arts and sciences shall be promoted in one or more seminaries of learning.

Sec. 3. The rights, privileges, immunities, and estates of religious societies and corporate bodies shall remain as if the constitution of this State had not been altered or amended.

Article IX

That the general, great, and essential principles of liberty and free government may be recognized and unalterably established, we declare—

Section 1. That all men are born equally free and independent, and have certain inherent and indefeasible rights, among which are those of enjoying and defending life and liberty, of acquiring, possessing, and protecting property and reputation, and of pursuing their own happiness.[73]

Sec. 2. That all power is inherent in the people, and all free governments are founded on their authority and instituted for their peace, safety, and happiness. For the advancement of those ends, they have at all times an unalienable and indefeasible right to alter, reform, or abolish their government, in such manner as they may think proper.[74]

[72] This section increased the residency requirement from one to two years, and capped at twenty-two the age at which sons of freeholders could vote without paying taxes. The added phrase "by the citizens" meant that non-naturalized foreign-born residents would be ineligible to vote. Cf. Const. 1776, sect. 6.

[73] Similar to Decl. 1776, Art. I. The word "indefeasible" was substituted for "inalienable."

[74] Similar to Decl. 1776, Arts. IV, V.

SEC. 3. That all men have a natural and indefeasible right to worship Almighty God according to the dictates of their own consciences; that no man can of right be compelled to attend, erect, or support any place of worship, or to maintain any ministry, against his consent; that no human authority can, in any case whatever, control or interfere with the rights of conscience; and that no preference shall ever be given, by law, to any religious establishments or modes of worship.[75]

SEC. 4. That no person, who acknowledges the being of a God and a future state of rewards and punishments, shall, on account of his religious sentiments, be disqualified to hold any office or place of trust or profit under this commonwealth.[76]

SEC. 5. That elections shall be free and equal.

SEC. 6. That trial by jury shall be as heretofore, and the right thereof remain inviolate.

SEC. 7. That the printing-presses shall be free to every person who undertakes to examine the proceedings of the legislature, or any branch of government, and no law shall ever be made to restrain the right thereof. The free communication of thoughts and opinions is one of the invaluable rights of man; and every citizen may freely speak, write, and print on any subject, being responsible for the abuse of that liberty. In prosecutions for the publication of papers investigating the official conduct of officers or men in a public capacity, or where the matter published is proper for public information, the truth thereof may be given in evidence; and in all indictments for libels the jury shall have a right to determine the law and the facts, under the direction of the court, as in other cases.[77]

[75] Similar to Decl. 1776, Art. II. In addition to truncating the earlier provision, the 1790 version substituted "ought or of right can be compelled" with "can be compelled" and added a clause forbidding preference to any religious establishment or mode of worship.

[76] The increasing diversity within the state meant an increasing number of deists and Jews, among others, would be barred from holding office under the restrictions of the 1776 constitution. Section 4 eliminated that inequity by extending the right to hold office to all who "acknowledge[d] the being of a God and a future state of rewards and punishments."

[77] Section 7 explicitly modified the common law of seditious libel in two ways. It recognized truth as a defense, placing it at odds with the law in England and most of the colonies. Just as important, given the colonists' view that the jury was indispensable for securing the protection of liberty, the section made juries the deciders of law as well as fact, in effect giving them the final decision as to how the law should be read and applied.

Sec. 8. That the people shall be secure in their persons, houses, papers, and possessions from unreasonable searches and seizures; and that no warrant to search any place, or to seize any person or things, shall issue, without describing them as nearly as may be, nor without probable cause, supported by oath or affirmation.[78]

Sec. 9. That in all criminal prosecutions the accused hath a right to be heard by himself and his counsel, to demand the nature and cause of the accusation against him, to meet the witnesses face to face, to have compulsory process for obtaining witnesses in his favor, and, in prosecutions by indictment or information, a speedy public trial, by an impartial jury of the vicinage; that he cannot be compelled to give evidence against himself, nor can he be deprived of his life, liberty, or property, unless by the judgment of his peers or the law of the land.[79]

Sec. 10. That no person shall, for any indictable offence, be proceeded against criminally by information, except in cases arising in the land or naval forces, or in the militia, when in actual service in time of war or public danger, or, by leave of the court, for oppression and misdemeanor in office. No person shall, for the same offence, be twice put in jeopardy of life or limb; nor shall any man's property be taken or applied to public use without the consent of his representatives, and without just compensation being made.[80]

Sec. 11. That all courts shall be open, and every man, for an injury done him in his lands, goods, person, or reputation, shall have remedy by the due course of law, and right and justice administered without sale, denial, or delay. Suits may be brought against the commonwealth in such manner, in such courts, and in such cases as the legislature may by law direct.[81]

[78] Similar to U.S. Const., amend IV.

[79] Section 9 added the phrase "of vicinage" to the jury requirements (previously a jury "of the country" was the standard). Requiring a jury to be from the area reinforced the role of the jury in reflecting community understandings of rights and justice in rendering their verdicts. This section removed the unanimity requirement of the 1776 declaration.

[80] This provision afforded the right to a grand jury in all but certain specified cases, and prohibited double jeopardy. Noteworthy is the removal of the duty/right connection to the due process clause found in Article VIII of the 1776 declaration.

[81] This section extended the open courts clause of the 1776 constitution (sec. 26) to include a right to remedy clause and made explicit the guarantee of justice free from corruption or delay.

SEC. 12. That no power of suspending laws shall be exercised, unless by the legislature or its authority.[82]

SEC. 13. That excessive bail shall not be required, nor excessive fines imposed, nor cruel punishments inflicted.[83]

SEC. 14. That all prisoners shall be bailable by sufficient sureties, unless for capital offences, when the proof is evident or presumption great; and the privilege of the writ of *habeas corpus* shall not be suspended, unless when, in cases of rebellion or invasion, the public safety may require it.[84]

SEC. 15. That no commission of oyer and terminer or jail-delivery shall be issued.[85]

SEC. 16. That the person of a debtor, where there is not strong presumption of fraud, shall not be continued in prison, after delivering up his estate for the benefit of his creditors, in such manner as shall be prescribed by law.[86]

SEC. 17. That no *ex post facto* law, nor any law impairing contracts, shall be made.[87]

SEC. 18. That no person shall be attainted of treason or felony by the legislature.

SEC. 19. That no attainder shall work corruption of blood, nor, except during the life of the offender, forfeiture of estate to the commonwealth; that the estates of such persons as shall destroy their own lives shall

[82] It was not uncommon for the Crown to suspend the operation or execution of the laws of Parliament. The practice was outlawed by the English Bill of Rights of 1689. This provision placed the suspension power exclusively in the hands of the legislature or its authority.

[83] Similar to Const. 1776, sec. 29; U.S. Const., amend VIII.

[84] Similar to Const. 1776, sec. 28; U.S. Const., Art. I, sec. 9, cl. 2 (habeas corpus).

[85] The use of special commissions to try prisoners for certain offenses was a practice of the Crown. Colonists saw the use of these commissions of oyer and terminer (to hear and decide) as a way of predetermining the result because the courts would be selected from judges sympathetic to the Crown's view of the defendant. This provision prohibited their issue. See *Commonwealth v. Flanagan*, 7W. & S. 68 (1842) for an application of this article.

[86] Similar to Const. 1776, sec. 28.

[87] The U.S. Constitution, ratified shortly before adoption of the 1790 Pennsylvania Constitution, prohibited states from adopting ex post facto laws, bills of attainder (i.e., bills announcing the conviction and punishment of a person without benefit of trial), or laws impairing contracts (U.S. Const., Art. I, sec. 10, cl. 1). This section and the following one reflected those prohibitions.

descend or vest as in case of natural death; and if any person shall be killed by casualty, there shall be no forfeiture by reason thereof.[88]

SEC. 20. That the citizens have a right, in a peaceable manner, to assemble together for their common good, and to apply to those invested with the powers of government for redress of grievances, or other proper purposes, by petition, address, or remonstrance.[89]

SEC. 21. That the right of citizens to bear arms, in defence of themselves and the State, shall not be questioned.[90]

SEC. 22. That no standing army shall, in time of peace, be kept up without the consent of the legislature; and the military shall in all cases and at all times be in strict subordination to the civil power.[91]

SEC. 23. That no soldier shall, in time of peace, be quartered in any house without the consent of the owner, nor in time of war but in a manner to be prescribed by law.[92]

SEC. 24. That the legislature shall not grant any title of nobility or hereditary distinction, nor create any office the appointment of which shall be for a longer term than during good behavior.[93]

SEC. 25. That emigration from the State shall not be prohibited.[94]

[88] The first clause of this section negated all common law rules regarding the forfeiture of an estate as a penalty for conviction of a crime. The section also constitutionalized the provision of the 1701 Charter of Privileges eliminating the practice by which suicide destroyed a family's right to inherit because it was attainted by blood. Charter of Privileges, sec. VIII, 3079.

[89] Similar to Decl. 1776, Art. XVI. The 1790 version substituted the word "citizens" for people.

[90] The 1790 constitution limited the right to bear arms to "citizens." During the American Revolution, Pennsylvania, like other states, severely limited the civil rights of denizens who refused to swear an oath of allegiance to the Revolutionary government.

[91] Similar to Decl. 1776, Art. XIII.

[92] Similar to U.S. Const., amend. III.

[93] Similar to U.S. Const., Art. I, sec. 9. The founders believed titles of nobility were inconsistent with a republican form of government and contrary to the fundamental principle that all men are created equal.

[94] Similar to Decl. 1776, Art. XV. The prior declaration spoke of a "natural inherent right … to form a new state in vacant countries or countries they can purchase, whenever they think…they may promote their own happiness." One suspects the removal of the last clause was intended to eliminate a potential mischief-maker. Vermont eliminated a similar clause in its 1786 constitution.

SEC. 26. To guard against transgressions of the high powers which we have delegated, we declare, that everything in this article is excepted out of the general powers of government, and shall forever remain inviolate.[95]

[95] Similar to Const. 1776, sec. 46. This section made explicit that the rights in the declaration were inviolate, that is, not susceptible to change.

Maryland

Maryland was established in 1632 as a Catholic refuge under the proprietorship of Cecil Calvert, Second Baron Baltimore. The charter issued by King Charles I to Lord Baltimore, granted him and his proprietors the absolute powers of a feudal lord—"the true and absolute Lords and Proprietaries"[1]—while simultaneously promising colonists a role in government and protection of fundamental rights. This arrangement set the stage for a conflict between the proprietors and colonists that would play out for the colony's entire existence. Although the charter did not require that Lord Baltimore recognize the Anglican Church, in a largely Protestant world, he understood that to maintain control of the colony and attract financial backers and settlers, Maryland needed to welcome Protestants as well as be a haven for oppressed Catholics.

The charter directed that "with the Advice, Assent, and Approbation of the Free-Men of the same Province, or the greater Part of them, or of their Delegates or Deputies…[an Assembly] shall be called together for the framing of Laws, when, and as often as Need shall require…."[2]

The charter granted to those who settled the colony

> …all Privileges, Franchises and Liberties of this our Kingdom of England, freely, quietly, and peaceably to have and possess, and the same may use and enjoy in the same manner as our Liege-Men born, or to be born

[1] The Charter of Maryland (1632), sec. V, in Thorpe, *Constitutions*, 3:1679.

[2] Ibid., sec. VII, 1679–1680.

P. J. Galie et al., *Bills of Rights Before the Bill of Rights*,
https://doi.org/10.1007/978-3-030-44301-6_6

> within our said Kingdom of England, without Impediment, Molestation, Vexation, Impeachment, or Grievance of Us, or any of our Heirs or Successors; any Statute, Act, Ordinance, or Provision to the contrary thereof, notwithstanding.[3]

Tensions between the proprietor and the assembly were not long in coming. The assembly of 1638/1639 proposed "An Act for the Liberties of the People."[4] It has been called the "first American Bill of Rights."[5] In addition to securing to the inhabitants of the province all rights and liberties enjoyed by any natural born subject of England "by force or vertue of the common law or Statute Law of England...," the act also paraphrased Chapter 39 of Magna Carta, the clause that came to be known as the law of the land or due process clause.[6] Whether the statute deserves its title is debatable, but pride of place remains with Maryland. The same year, the assembly extended all the rights and liberties accorded by Magna Carta and English law to the inhabitants of the colony and guaranteed rights to a grand jury indictment and trial by a twelve-man jury for all serious crimes.[7]

In 1649, at the instruction of Lord Baltimore, the assembly approved the Maryland Toleration Act, described as offering the "broadest definition of religious freedom during the seventeenth century and ... an

[3] Ibid., sec. X, 1681.

[4] Donald S. Lutz, ed., *Colonial Origins of the American Constitution: A Documentary History* (Indianapolis: Liberty Fund, 1998), 308, https://oll.libertyfund.org/pages/1638-act-for-the-liberties-of-the-people-maryland.

[5] The claim, made by Bernard Schwartz in *The Bill of Rights: A Documentary History* (New York: Chelsea House, 1971), 1:67, is based on the fact that the act predated the Massachusetts Body of Liberties by two years. Charles A. Rees has challenged that designation on several grounds. See "The First American Bill of Rights: Was It Maryland's 1639 Act for the Liberties of the People?," *University of Baltimore Law Review* 31, no. 1 (Fall 2001): 53–61. For one, Rees claims the act was never duly enacted. Ibid.

[6] Lutz, *Colonial Origins*, 308.

[7] An act ordeining certain Laws for the Goverment of this Province, March 19, 1638/1639, in William Hand Browne, ed., *Archives of Maryland*, vol. 1, *Proceedings and Acts of the General Assembly of Maryland, January 1637/8–September, 1664* (Baltimore: Maryland Historical Society, 1883), 82–83.

important step toward true freedom of religion."[8] It provided: "noe person ... professing to beleive in Jesus Christ, shall ... bee any waies troubled, Molested, or discountenanced for or in respect to his or her religion not in the free exercise thereof within this Province... nor in any way be compelled to the beliefe or exercise of any other Religion against his or her consent...."[9] Upon gaining control of the colony in 1654, the Puritans rescinded the act. Three years later, Lord Baltimore regained power and the statute was restored. In 1658, Quakers were permitted to offer a pledge of loyalty to the government instead of an oath of allegiance, enabling them to hold public office.[10] At the time, only Rhode Island offered a similar opportunity.

Maryland's record on protecting the rights of other groups was less satisfactory. Gregory A. Stiverson writes that "[w]hite servants had few rights, and Indians had even fewer."[11] In 1664, Maryland declared all slaves residing in the colony, and any imported in the future, slaves for life.[12] Subsequently adopted manumission laws, however, made it easier for slaveholders to emancipate their slaves.[13]

The Glorious Revolution in England in 1688 led to the overthrow of the proprietary government the following year. In 1691, Maryland became a royal colony, marking the end of religious equality for the colony's Catholics. A test oath requirement adopted in 1699 excluded all Catholics from public office.[14] In 1702, the Church of England was

[8] Lutz, *Colonial Origins*, 309. For a careful and less laudatory evaluation of the act in the context of previous and subsequent actions on the question of toleration in Maryland, see Carl N. Everstine, "Maryland's Toleration Act: An Appraisal," *Maryland Historical Magazine* 79, no. 2 (Summer 1984): 99–116.

[9] An Act Concerning Religion, April 21, 1649, in Lutz, *Colonial Origins*, 312.

[10] Gregory A. Stiverson, "'To Maintain Inviolate Our Liberties': Maryland and the Bill of Rights," in *The Bill of Rights and the States: The Colonial and Revolutionary Origins of American Liberties*, ed. Patrick T. Conley and John P. Kaminski (Madison, WI: Madison House, 1992), 377.

[11] Ibid.

[12] Ibid.

[13] By the first decade of the nineteenth century, twenty-five percent of Maryland blacks were free—a tenfold increase. Richard S. Dunn, "Black Society in the Chesapeake, 1776–1810," in *Slavery and Freedom in the Age of the American Revolution*, ed. Ira Berlin and Ronald Hoffman (Urbana: University of Illinois Press, 1983), 50.

[14] The test oath is replicated at Browne, *Archives*, vol. 25, *Proceedings of the Council of Maryland, 1698–1731* (Baltimore: Maryland Historical Society, 1905), 68.

established in the colony.[15] Barred from publicly practicing their religion in 1704,[16] Catholics were disenfranchised in 1718.[17] Royal control of the colony ended in 1715 with the return of Anglican convert, the Fifth Baron Baltimore, though the change did little to alleviate the political paralysis that characterized the colony's government. Marylanders joined the other colonists in opposing British legislation, their opposition an extension of their ongoing resistance to proprietary prerogatives, which continued to be a source of discontent in the colony.

By the mid-1770s opposition had congealed: an extra-legal provincial convention met in June 1774, to be followed by eight more. In July 1775, the fifth convention set up a council of safety to perform executive functions, effectively assuming control of the government.[18] Marylanders entered the Revolutionary period with over a century of struggles to define, assert, and secure rights. This history led them to believe that written documents—constitutions in which their rights were spelled out—were the only effective means to prevent arbitrary government. Their more immediate experience with government by convention, however, raised concerns about that body's absorption of all government power.[19] Maryland had declared independence but needed a government that did not concentrate all power in one body.

The corollary to independence came on July 3, 1776, when the Eighth Provincial Convention called for the election of delegates to a new convention:

[15] An Act for the Establishment of Religious Worship in this Province According to the Church of England: and for the Maintenance of Ministers, March 16, 1701/1702, in Browne, *Archives*, vol. 24, *Proceedings and Acts of the General Assembly of Maryland, April 26, 1700–May 3, 1704* (Baltimore: Maryland Historical Society, 1904), 265–273. This act followed several similar bills in previous years that had passed the general assembly but failed to secure royal assent.

[16] An Act to prevent the Growth of Popery within this Province, September 30, 1704, in Browne, *Archives*, vol. 26, *Proceedings and Acts of the General Assembly of Maryland, September, 1704–April, 1706* (Baltimore: Maryland Historical Society, 1906), 340–341.

[17] A Supplementary Act to the Act directing the Manner of Electing and Summoning Delegates and Representatives to serve in succeeding Assemblies, in Clayton Colman Hall, ed., *Archives of Maryland*, vol. 33, *Proceedings and Acts of the General Assembly of Maryland, May, 1717–April, 1720* (Baltimore: Maryland Historical Society, 1913), 288.

[18] Stiverson provides a concise description of these developments. "To Maintain Inviolate," 379–386.

[19] Marc W. Kruman, *Between Authority and Liberty: State Constitution Making in Revolutionary America* (Chapel Hill: University of North Carolina Press, 1997), 112.

> Resolved, That a new convention be elected for the express purpose of forming a new government, by the authority of the people only, and enacting and ordaining all things for the preservation, safety, and general weal of this colony.[20]

The resulting convention chose a drafting committee to prepare "a declaration and charter of rights, and a plan of government agreeable to such rights as will best maintain peace and good order, and most effectually secure happiness and liberty to the people of this state."[21] The committee spent ten days drafting a declaration of rights containing forty-four articles. Debate on the declaration took place almost every day between October 10 and November 3, 1776, whereupon the committee circulated a draft of the document throughout the state for public comment. The convention adopted the forty-two article "Declaration of Rights" on November 3; five days later, it approved and put in effect the declaration and the form of government. Neither document was submitted to the voters for ratification.

Constitutional Developments: 1776 Declaration and Constitution

The Maryland Declaration of Rights is the longest and most comprehensive enumeration of rights adopted by an American state between 1776 and 1790—over twice the length of the Virginia declaration. Only New Hampshire's declaration, adopted in 1784 as part of its second constitution, comes close in size to the Maryland declaration. A comparison with the Virginia declaration indicates the Maryland drafting committee relied substantially on the May 27th draft of that document.[22]

Although the Maryland declaration contained commitments to popular sovereignty and the commonweal, it lacked much of the natural rights

[20] *Archives of Maryland*, vol. 78, *Proceedings of the Conventions of the Province of Maryland, Held at the City of Annapolis, in 1774, 1775, and 1776* (Baltimore: James Lucas and E.K. Deaver, 1836), 184.

[21] Ibid., 220.

[22] Dan Friedman, *The Maryland State Constitution: A Reference Guide* (Westport, CT: Praeger, 2006), 2, and Dan Friedman, "Tracing the Lineage: Textual and Conceptual Similarities in the Revolutionary-Era State Declarations of Rights of Virginia, Maryland, and Delaware," *Rutgers Law Journal* 33, no. 4 (Summer 2002): 929–1028. Maryland largely ignored the Pennsylvania declaration, which would have been available. Ibid., 942–943.

and equality language found in other declarations. Natural rights are mentioned only once, in the context of a command that no person shall injure the natural rights of others in their exercise of religious liberty (Decl. 1776, Art. XXXIII). The declaration lacked any statement that all men were either born or were otherwise inherently equal (although equality in Christian worship was guaranteed). The common law and statutory law of England were specifically incorporated (ibid., Art. III).

Maryland's constitution established a Christian commonwealth. It offered religious freedom only to persons professing the Christian religion (Decl. 1776, Art. XXXIII), and required all officeholders to declare belief in Christianity (ibid., Art. XXXV; Const. 1776, Art. LV). Contrariwise, the declaration ended the financial privileges of the Anglican Church and stipulated that a person could no longer be compelled to attend any particular place of worship or support a particular ministry; it did, however, provide a system of multiple establishments in which the legislature could assess an equal tax for all Christian religions, with the taxpayer selecting the denomination that he would support. These achievements were the work of both Reformed Protestants and Roman Catholics like Charles and John Carroll. Maryland attempted to balance its commitment to religious liberty with its belief that a religious foundation, in this case, Christianity, was necessary for the maintenance of civic virtue and ordered liberty, if not the survival of the government.[23]

Suffrage

Suffrage was granted to all freemen over twenty-one who resided in the county one year preceding the election and possessed either a freehold of fifty acres of land in the county in which they resided or property in the state worth over thirty pounds (Const. 1776, Arts. II, XIV). These requirements made Maryland's one of the least democratic state constitutions.[24]

[23] See pp. 72–80 for further discussion of the importance religion played in the early state constitutions.

[24] See Article V and accompanying commentary, p. 152.

Structural Provisions

The declaration made an explicit commitment to the separation of powers (Decl. 1776, Art. VI). Provisions implementing that doctrine included tenure for judges "during good behaviour" (Const. 1776, Art. XL) and bans on plural office-holding (Decl. 1776, Art. XXXII; Const. 1776, Art. XXXVII).

Legislative power in the state was exercised by a two-house general assembly: a senate elected for five-year terms (Const. 1776, Arts. XIV, XV) and a house of delegates chosen annually (ibid., Arts. II, IV, V). The general assembly was directed to meet no less often than annually (ibid., Art. XXIII). The senate was not permitted to originate or amend money bills (ibid., Art. XXII). The constitution created a governor, chosen for an annual term by joint ballot of both houses (ibid., Art. XXV), and an executive council. The governor did not have a veto power.

Requirements for holding office were as follows:

Office	*Minimum Age*	*Estate*	*Residency*	*Religion*
Governor	25 years	5000 pounds real and personal; 1000 pounds being freehold	At least 5 years within state	Christian
Senator	25 years	1000 pounds real and personal	At least 3 years within state	Christian
House of Delegates	21 years	500 pounds real and personal	At least 1 year within state	Christian
Council	25 years	Freehold estate of 1000 pounds	At least 3 years within state	Christian
Congress Delegate	21 years	1000 pounds real and personal	At least 5 years within state	Christian
Sheriff	21 years	1000 pounds real and personal	Inhabitant of the county	Christian

Ministers or preachers of the gospel could not serve as legislators (Const. 1776, Art. XXXVII). The prohibition followed the English practice of barring clergy from serving in the House of Commons where the Crown's authority over the Church of England would provide the church with undue influence on its decisions. The governor and sheriffs had term limits—after serving for three years they were rendered ineligible for four years (ibid., Arts. XXXI, XLII).

The constitution provided that no part of the frame of government or the declaration of rights could be altered unless the bill making the alteration passed two consecutively elected sessions of the general assembly and was published three months before the election (Const., Art. LIX). Any alterations relating to the eastern shore required two-thirds majority on both passages (ibid.). This provision recognized that constitutional change was not on a par with legislative action, with the former requiring additional consultation with the citizens and the extraordinary procedure of re-passage by a post-election legislature.

Postscript: The 1776 constitution remained in effect until 1851, when a new constitution was adopted. Amendments affecting rights during the operation of the 1776 charter included a 1795 amendment allowing Quakers to make an affirmation instead of an oath, enabling them to serve in public office if the other qualifications were met, and an 1810 amendment eliminating all property qualifications for voting. Although the declaration has been subject to significant amendments during the lifetime of Maryland's four constitutions, over two-thirds of the provisions in the 1776 declaration remain in some form.

Constitution of Maryland [1776]

A Declaration of Rights, and the Constitution and Form of Government agreed to by the Delegates of Maryland, in free and full Convention assembled.

A Declaration of Rights, &C

THE parliament of Great Britain, by a declaratory act, having assumed a right to make laws to bind the Colonies in all cases whatsoever, and, in pursuance of such claim, endeavoured, by force of arms, to subjugate the United Colonies to an unconditional submission to their will and power, and having at length constrained them to declare themselves independent States, and to assume government under the authority of the people;—Therefore we, the Delegates of Maryland, in free and full Convention assembled, taking into our most serious consideration the best means of establishing a good Constitution in this State, for the sure foundation and more permanent security thereof, declare,

I. That all government of right originates from the people, is founded in compact only, and instituted solely for the good of the whole.[25]

II. That the people of this State ought to have the sole and exclusive right of regulating the internal government and police thereof.[26]

III. That the inhabitants of Maryland are entitled to the common law of England, and the trial by jury, according to the course of that law, and to the benefit of such of the English statutes, as existed at the time of their first emigration, and which, by experience, have been found applicable to their local and other circumstances, and of such others as have been since made in England, or Great Britain, and have been introduced, used and practised by the courts of law or equity; and also to acts of Assembly, in force on the first of June seventeen hundred and seventy-four, except such as may have since expired, or have been or may be altered by acts of Convention, or this Declaration of Rights—subject, nevertheless, to the revision of, and amendment or repeal by, the Legislature of this State: and the inhabitants of Maryland are also entitled to all property, derived to them, from or under the Charter, granted by his Majesty Charles I. to Caecilius Calvert, Baron of Baltimore.[27]

IV. That all persons invested with the legislative or executive powers of government are the trustees of the public, and, as such, accountable for their conduct; wherefore, whenever the ends of government are perverted, and public liberty manifestly endangered, and all other means of redress are ineffectual, the people may, and of right ought, to reform the old or establish a new government. The doctrine of non-resistance,

[25] Article I proclaimed the doctrine of popular sovereignty. A more immediate influence was the Virginia Declaration of Rights (sec. 2), where the first expression in a state constitution appears.

[26] Proposals for confederations at the Continental Congress prompted convention delegates to assert their right to internal government—a state's right as a sovereign entity. In particular, the Congress had ordered Robert Eden, Maryland's last governor, arrested—an act the convention believed was interference in Maryland's internal affairs. Friedman, "Tracing the Lineage," 998. This concern foreshadowed the states' anxiety over the formation of a national government.

[27] Derived from Maryland's colonial charters, this article, found in nearly all early state constitutions, served to ease the transition to statehood and give constitutional status to the extensive rights and liberties encompassed by the common law and statutes that made up the English Constitution. The common law had been adopted in Maryland by statutes between 1635 and 1639. William E. Nelson, *The Common Law in Colonial America*, vol. 1, *The Chesapeake and New England, 1607–1660* (New York: Oxford University Press, 2008), 106.

against arbitrary power and oppression, is absurd, slavish, and destructive of the good and happiness of mankind.[28]

V. That the right in the people to participate in the Legislature is the best security of liberty, and the foundation of all free government; for this purpose, elections ought to be free and frequent, and every man, having property in, a common interest with, and an attachment to the community, ought to have a right of suffrage.[29]

VI. That the legislative, executive and judicial powers of government, ought to be forever separate and distinct from each other.[30]

VII. That no power of suspending laws, or the execution of laws, unless by or derived from the Legislature, ought to be exercised or allowed.[31]

VIII. That freedom of speech and debates, or proceedings in the Legislature, ought not to be impeached in any other court or judicature.[32]

[28] Article IV provided a statement of the political ideas that underpinned the American Revolution. It fused popular sovereignty, announced in the first article, with ideas proclaimed in the Declaration of Independence. It was not a provision that could be judicially enforced; rather it served as an aspirational reminder of the ideals on which the polity was founded and, if necessary, sustained. It contained a right/ought combination: the people may and by right ought to reform or alter their governments.

[29] This article provided reaffirmation and formal recognition of the right to self-government, implemented by suffrage requirements for the right to vote. Suffrage provisions first appeared in the colony's founding charter. In response to interference by King James II with parliamentary elections, the English Bill of Rights declared that "election of members of Parliament ought to be free." English Bill of Rights (1689), in Schwartz, *Bill of Rights*, 1:42. The frame of government outlined the frequency of elections to the various offices and the level of "attachment to the community" required.

[30] Article VI provided a succinct statement of the doctrine of the separation of powers. That it was included in a declaration of rights is evidence of the broad understanding of rights in eighteenth-century America. Here, the separation of powers was understood as a structural right meant to prevent abuse of power and provide security for other rights.

[31] Article VII was a corollary to the separation of powers, specifying the legislature's role as sole law-maker and representative of the people. In response to the suspension of laws by the Crown, often done to afford religious toleration to Catholics and dissenters, the English Bill of Rights included a precursor to this article. English Bill of Rights, 42. More than just a reaction to interference with the operation of the colony's affairs by the Crown and colonial governors, the article also anticipated the possibility of a colonies-wide government, having the potential of limiting the state's sovereignty.

[32] Maryland was the first American state to include the parliamentary privilege of speech and debate in its declaration of rights, likely a response to prosecutions of several members of the English House of Commons for offering bills displeasing to the monarch. See Leon R. Yankwich, "The Immunity of Congressional Speech-Its Origin, Meaning and Scope,"

IX. That a place for the meeting of the Legislature ought to be fixed, the most convenient to the members thereof, and to the depository of public records; and the Legislature ought not to be convened or held at any other place, but from evident necessity.[33]

X. That, for redress of grievances, and for amending, strengthening and preserving the laws, the Legislature ought to be frequently convened.[34]

XI. That every man hath a right to petition the Legislature, for the redress of grievances, in a peaceable and orderly manner.[35]

University of Pennsylvania Law Review 99, no. 7 (1951): 962–963. The English Bill of Rights included a speech and debate clause. English Bill of Rights, 42. Such provisions were seen as necessary to ensure that the legislature would be able to deliberate without interference from intrusions by the executive or judicial branches of the government.

[33] At first glance, Article IX seems out of place in a declaration of rights, but it was a means to protect the right of the legislature to be free from external manipulation or interference. It appears to be derived from the fourth grievance listed in the Declaration of Independence, which accused the Crown of calling legislative bodies at unusual and distant places to force them, through fatigue, into compliance. This article and the one immediately preceding were part of a package of provisions meant to protect and implement the separation of powers and popular sovereignty.

[34] Articles X and XI, along with Articles IV, V, and IX of the declaration and Article II of the "Form of Government" made it clear that legislators were to reflect the wishes of their constituents. Article X is taken almost verbatim (substituting "the Legislature" for "parliaments") from the English Bill of Rights. English Bill of Rights, 42. Royal abuses of the power to summon and dissolve Parliament had contributed to the English Civil War. Suspension of colonial legislatures was mentioned in three separate grievances listed in the Declaration of Independence.

[35] The idea that legislative bodies were to represent or mirror their constituents' policy preferences was an underlying assumption of these early constitutions. They instantiated and operationalized Maryland's commitment to popular sovereignty. Several colonial charters, beginning with the Massachusetts Body of Liberties (1641), included similar provisions concerning petition rights. The right preceded Magna Carta and appeared in the 1215 version of that charter (Chapter 61), as well as the English Bill of Rights. A detailed analysis of the right in England and in the colonies is provided by Gregory A. Marks, "The Vestigial Constitution: The History and Significance of the Right to Petition," *Fordham Law Review* 66, no. 6 (May 1998): 2153. The right to petition, historically a formal process, was taken more seriously by colonists than it is today. Professor Marks asserts that petitioning was "originally a central feature of the relationship between the governed and the government…." Ibid., 2155. Note Article XXXI of the frame calling for rotation in office, another measure directed at keeping the government close to the people as well as limiting opportunities for corruption.

XII. That no aid, charge, tax, fee, or fees, ought to be set, rated, or levied, under any pretence, without consent of the Legislature.[36]

XIII. That the levying taxes by the poll is grievous and oppressive, and ought to be abolished; that paupers ought not to be assessed for the support of government; but every other person in the State ought to contribute his proportion of public taxes, for the support of government, according to his actual worth, in real or personal property, within the State; yet fines, duties, or taxes, may properly and justly be imposed or laid, with a political view, for the good government and benefit of the community.[37]

[36]The principle that free people ought not to be taxed without their consent or that of their elected representatives is seen in Magna Carta, the English Petition of Right (1628), the English Bill of Rights, the Resolutions of the Stamp Act Congress of 1765, the Declaration and Resolves of the First Continental Congress, and the grievances listed in the Declaration of Independence. See Table 5, pp. 84–85. But the proprietary fee controversy in the colony was the immediate motivating factor for this provision, rather than the more general colonial complaints against parliamentary taxation.

Proprietary officials were paid by fees on the transactions of their offices, such as real estate activities, tobacco inspections, control of shipping, execution of documents, and the collection of proprietary dues and rentals. H. H. Walker Lewis, *The Maryland Constitution of 1776* (Baltimore: Bicentennial Committee, Maryland State Bar Association, 1976), https://msa.maryland.gov/megafile/msa/speccol/sc2200/sc2221/000004/000000/html/00000005.html. As the colony grew, so did the volume of transactions, enlarging significantly the revenue collected. The exorbitant fees created temptations too strong to resist, and the offices collecting these fees become patronage plums to be granted to favored individuals.

[37]The prohibition against poll taxes arose out of Maryland's colonial experience. It was a reaction to the highly unpopular use of poll taxes to support the Church of England and its clergy. As Professor Lewis notes: "This explanation of the prohibition of poll taxes in the 1776 Declaration of Rights is supported by the fact that no comparable restriction was adopted by the neighboring colonies of Delaware, Pennsylvania and Virginia, where poll taxes do not appear to have been used for the support of the church." H. H. Walker Lewis, "The Tax Articles of the Maryland Declaration of Rights," *Maryland Law Review* 13, no. 2 (Spring 1953): 89. The second clause in this article exempts paupers from taxes to support the government. Lewis claims that the third clause proposing taxes in proportion to a person's actual worth can be traced to Adam Smith's *An Inquiry into the Nature and Causes of the Wealth of Nations*, ed. R. H. Campbell and A. S. Skinner (1976; reprint, Indianapolis: Liberty Fund, 1981 [1776]), 2:825, which states the following as the first maxim concerning taxes:

> I. The subjects of every State ought to contribute towards the support of the government, as nearly as possible, in proportion to their respective abilities; that is,

XIV. That sanguinary laws ought to be avoided, as far as is consistent with the safety of the State: and no law, to inflict cruel and unusual pains and penalties, ought to be made in any case, or at any time hereafter.[38]

XV. That retrospective laws, punishing facts committed before the existence of such laws, and by them only declared criminal, are oppressive, unjust, and incompatible with liberty; wherefore no *ex post facto* law ought to be made.[39]

XVI. That no law, to attaint particular persons of treason or felony, ought to be made in any case, or at any time hereafter.[40]

XVII. That every freeman, for any injury done him in his person or property, ought to have remedy, by the course of the law of the land, and ought to have justice and right freely without sale, fully without any denial, and speedily without delay, according to the law of the land.[41]

> in proportion to the revenue which they respectively enjoy under the protection of the state.

The two clauses are not identical, but both have equality as their underlying principle. The fourth clause, that fines, duties, or taxes, may properly and justly be imposed or laid, for the good government and benefit of the community, was a response to an earlier proposal that would have outlawed all taxes other than property taxes. Lewis suggests that this clause, by expressly authorizing other types of taxes, settled the matter: "property was not to be the exclusive source of taxes." Lewis, *Maryland Constitution of 1776.*

[38] Although the English Bill of Rights had forbidden the imposition by courts of cruel and unusual punishments, see commentary to Article XXII, below, this clause discouraging the use of sanguinary laws (i.e., laws imposing punishments deemed unnecessary or disproportionate to the crimes committed) had as its goal limiting the power of the legislature to adopt such laws. Friedman, "Tracing the Lineage," 1018–1020. The addition of the sanguinary language may have been influenced by the Pennsylvania Constitution. Pa. Const. 1776, secs. 38, 39.

[39] This was the first appearance of the ex post facto protection in an American constitution. It derived from English common law. See William Blackstone, *Commentaries on the Laws of England in Four Books* (1753; reprint, Philadelphia: J.B. Lippincott Co., 1893), 1:46. Bernard Schwartz calls this "the most significant innovation made by the Maryland Declaration of Rights." Schwartz, *Bill of Rights*, 1:279.

[40] A legislative act attainting a person without a judicial trial was known as a bill of attainder. The power of Parliament to declare guilt and impose punishment by such measures was well established by the fifteenth century. This provision banned such acts.

[41] This article authorized the judiciary to provide a remedy where the legislature had unreasonably failed to do so. See Article XXI, which provided additional protection. The impetus behind the measure can be traced to Magna Carta, Chs. 39–40. Colonists often read Magna Carta through the filter provided by Edward Coke, whose interpretation of Chapter 40 read: "...every Subject of this Realme, for injury done to him in [goods,

XVIII. That the trial of facts where they arise, is one of the greatest securities of the lives, liberties and estates of the people.[42]

XIX. That, in all criminal prosecutions, every man hath a right to be informed of the accusation against him; to have a copy of the indictment or charge in due time (if required) to prepare for his defence; to be allowed counsel; to be confronted with the witnesses against him; to have process for his witnesses; to examine the witnesses, for and against him, on oath; and to a speedy trial by an impartial jury, without whose unanimous consent he ought not to be found guilty.[43]

XX. That no man ought to be compelled to give evidence against himself, in a common court of law, or in any other court, but in such cases as have been usually practised in this State, or may hereafter be directed by the Legislature.

XXI. That no freeman ought to be taken, or imprisoned, or disseized of his freehold, liberties, or privileges, or outlawed, or exiled, or in any manner destroyed, or deprived of his life, liberty, or property, but by the judgment of his peers, or by the law of the land.[44]

lands, or person], ... may take his remedy by the course of the Law, and have justice, and right for the injury done to him, freely without sale, fully without any deniall, and speedily without delay." Edward Coke, *The Second Part of the Institutes of the Lawes of England*, in *Selected Writings and Speeches of Sir Edward Coke*, ed. Steve Sheppard (Indianapolis: Liberty Fund Inc., 2003), 2:870. Such clauses are now referred to as open courts or right to remedy provisions.

[42] This provision limited the power of the state to arbitrarily select the vicinage (venue) for trials. During the Revolutionary period, English authorities would sometimes require a person who committed a crime in the colonies to stand trial in Canada or England. Complaints about this practice were seen in both the Declaration and Resolves of the First Continental Congress (Declaration No. 5) and the grievances listed in the Declaration of Independence.

[43] Articles XIX and XX contained several criminal procedure rights derived from the accusatory system of justice developed in England as part of the common law and expanded by such statutes as the Petition of Right and the Bill of Rights of 1689. Maryland deviated from the common law of juries, permitting juries to decide matters of law as well as facts, making the jury central to Maryland's legal order. William E. Nelson, *The Common Law in Colonial America*, vol. 3, *The Chesapeake and New England, 1660–1750* (New York: Oxford University Press, 2016), 16ff.

[44] The origin of this article, found in Maryland's first governing charter and repeated in subsequent statutes, can be traced to Chapter 39 of Magna Carta. Frequently quoted, the colonists viewed Chapter 39 as epitomizing the idea of the rule of law.

XXII. That excessive bail ought not to be required, nor excessive fines imposed, nor cruel or unusual punishments inflicted, by the courts of law.[45]

XXIII. That all warrants, without oath or affirmation, to search suspected places, or to seize any person or property, are grievous and oppressive; and all general warrants—to search suspected places, or to apprehend suspected persons, without naming or describing the place, or the person in special—are illegal, and ought not to be granted.[46]

XXIV. That there ought to be no forfeiture of any part of the estate of any person, for any crime except murder, or treason against the State, and then only on conviction and attainder.[47]

XXV. That a well-regulated militia is the proper and natural defence of a free government.[48]

XXVI. That standing armies are dangerous to liberty, and ought not to be raised or kept up, without consent of the Legislature.

XXVII. That in all cases, and at all times, the military ought to be under strict subordination to and control of the civil power.

[45] The wording of this article is all but verbatim from the 1689 English Bill of Rights. That bill had as its primary objective prohibiting the imposition of punishments not authorized by statute or within the jurisdiction of the court to impose. Anthony F. Granucci, "Nor Cruel and Unusual Punishments Inflicted: The Original Meaning," *California Law Review* 57, no. 4 (October 1969): 859. The language at the end of this article made clear the article was a command to the judiciary.

[46] Similar to Va. Decl. 1776, sec. 10. This article represents Maryland's attempt to deal with general warrants, which had been commonly used by the British during the Revolutionary period and were a major grievance of the colonists. The language used, emphasizing that any such warrants were "illegal," was stronger than its Virginia counterpart.

[47] Under English law, forfeiture of an estate (to the Crown) was a consequence of conviction for a felony. During the Revolution, British authorities would confiscate estates with similar justifications. This article limited that procedure to certain well-defined exceptions.

[48] Articles XXV and XXVI were intended to protect the citizens' right to form militias that would enable them to fight in the defense of their country and "not be dependent an alien soldiery commanded by men who are not responsible to law ..." E. A. Dick Howard, *Commentaries on the Constitution of Virginia* (Charlottesville: University of Virginia Press, 1974), 1: 277. Article XXVII made clear that the military power would always be subordinate to the civil power. Most likely these articles have their origin in similarly worded provisions in the draft of Virginia's declaration of rights, available to the Maryland convention delegates. Friedman, "Tracing the Lineage," 971–972.

XXVIII. That no soldier ought to be quartered in any house, in time of peace, without the consent of the owner; and in time of war, in such manner only, as the Legislature shall direct.[49]

XXIX. That no person, except regular soldiers, mariners, and marines in the service of this State, or militia when in actual service, ought in any case to be subject to or punishable by martial law.[50]

XXX. That the independency and uprightness of Judges are essential to the impartial administration of justice, and a great security to the rights and liberties of the people; wherefore the Chancellor and Judges ought to hold commissions during good behaviour; and the said Chancellor and Judges shall be removed for misbehaviour, on conviction in a court of law, and may be removed by the Governor, upon the address of the General Assembly; *Provided*, That two-thirds of all the members of each House concur in such address. That salaries, liberal, but not profuse, ought to be secured to the Chancellor and the Judges, during the continuance of their commissions, in such manner, and at such times, as the Legislature shall hereafter direct, upon consideration of the circumstances of this State. No Chancellor or Judge ought to hold any other office, civil or military, or receive fees or perquisites of any kind.[51]

XXXI. That a long continuance, in the first executive departments of power or trust, is dangerous to liberty; a rotation, therefore, in those departments, is one of the best securities of permanent freedom.[52]

[49] The quartering of troops by the British was a major grievance of the colonists. This provision, the first American constitutional limitation on this practice, would ensure that quartering, if deemed necessary ("in time of war"), obtained the approval of the legislature.

[50] This provision, along with Article XXVII, reinforced the supremacy of the civil power over the military, in this instance by subjecting only military personnel to martial law.

[51] Article XXX began with a compelling expression of the importance of an independent judiciary to the rights and liberties of the people, followed by a series of structural measures designed to ensure that independence. This guarantee of independence was repeated in Article XL of the frame, which also afforded the attorney general, the clerks of court, and certain registers tenure during good behavior. Removal for misbehavior required a "conviction in a court of law," a two-thirds vote of each house, and agreement by the governor.

[52] This article called rotation in office "one of the best" safeguards of permanent freedom. The mechanics of rotation were addressed in the frame of government. The governor could not serve longer than three years successively, nor be eligible to serve again until the expiration of four years after leaving office (Const. 1776, Art. XXXI). Regarding other executive officials who wielded power, the measure was essentially admonitory.

XXXII. That no person ought to hold, at the same time, more than one office of profit, nor ought any person, in public trust, to receive any present from any foreign prince or state, or from the United States, or any of them, without the approbation of this State.[53]

XXXIII. That, as it is the duty of every man to worship God in such manner as he thinks most acceptable to him; all persons, professing the Christian religion, are equally entitled to protection in their religious liberty; wherefore no person ought by any law to be molested in his person or estate on account of his religious persuasion or profession, or for his religious practice; unless, under colour of religion, any man shall disturb the good order, peace or safety of the State, or shall infringe the laws of morality, or injure others, in their natural, civil, or religious rights; nor ought any person to be compelled to frequent or maintain, or contribute, unless on contract, to maintain any particular place of worship, or any particular ministry; yet the Legislature may, in their discretion, lay a general and equal tax, for the support of the Christian religion; leaving to each individual the power of appointing the payment over of the money, collected from him, to the support of any particular place of worship or minister, or for the benefit of the poor of his own denomination, or the poor in general of any particular county: but the churches, chapels, glebes, and all other property now belonging to the church of England, ought to remain to the church of England forever. And all acts of Assembly, lately passed, for collecting monies for building or repairing particular churches or chapels of ease, shall continue in force, and be executed, unless the Legislature shall, by act, supersede or repeal the same: but no county court shall assess any quantity of tobacco, or sum of money, hereafter, on the application of any vestrymen or church-wardens; and every encumbent of the church of England, who hath remained in his parish, and performed his duty, shall be entitled to receive the provision and support established by the act, entitled "An act for the support of the clergy of the church of England, in this Province," till the November court of this present year, to be held for the county in which his parish shall lie, or

[53] By prohibiting multiple office-holding and gifts from the U.S. government or any other nation, this provision insured the independence of public officials from any other sources.

partly lie, or for such time as he hath remained in his parish, and performed his duty.[54]

XXXIV. That every gift, sale, or devise of lands, to any minister, public teacher, or preacher of the gospel, as such, or to any religious sect, order or denomination, or to or for the support, use or benefit of, or in trust for, any minister, public teacher, or preacher of the gospel, as such, or any religious sect, order or denomination—and every gift or sale of goods, or chattels, to go in succession, or to take place after the death of the seller or donor, or to or for such support, use or benefit—and also every devise of goods or chattels to or for the support, use or benefit of any minister, public teacher, or preacher of the gospel, as such, or any religious sect, order, or denomination, without the leave of the Legislature, shall be void; except always any sale, gift, lease or devise of any quantity of land, not exceeding two acres, for a church, meeting, or other house of worship, and for a burying-ground, which shall be improved, enjoyed or used only for such purpose—or such sale, gift, lease, or devise, shall be void.[55]

XXXV. That no other test or qualification ought to be required, on admission to any office of trust or profit, than such oath of support and fidelity to this State, and such oath of office, as shall be directed by this Convention, or the Legislature of this State, and a declaration of a belief in the Christian religion.[56]

[54] See p. 148 above for the treatment of religion by the 1776 constitution and see pp. 72–80 for the role of religion generally in the colonies. Article XXXIII disestablished the Anglican Church but allowed the state to provide general support for all Christian religions. None was ever authorized.

[55] Article XXXIV limited gifts to any religious activity or organization. It was designed to prevent deathbed wills that left money to religious institutions. As one scholar wrote, "[u]nderlying the laws was the image –or fantasy—of the wicked priest preying on the dying man or woman, manipulating their fears of eternal damnation to squeeze out gifts for the church…." Lawrence M. Freidman, *Dead Hands: A Social History of Wills, Trusts, and Inheritance Law* (Palo Alto, CA: Stanford University Press, 2009), 29. Further justification for this provision was the prevention of considerable amounts of property being granted to the church, leading to an "overgrown establishment holding fast a large portion of the property in this State." *The Debates of the Constitutional Convention of the State of Maryland, Assembled at the City of Annapolis, Wednesday, April 27, 1864* (Annapolis: Richard P. Bayly, Printer, 1864), 1:382.

[56] Maryland was among several states requiring all officeholders to swear a belief in the Christian religion. See the discussion of religion in the 1776 constitution, p.150.

XXXVI. That the manner of administering an oath to any person, ought to be such, as those of the religious persuasion, profession, or denomination, of which such person is one, generally esteem the most effectual confirmation, by the attestation of the Divine Being. And that the people called Quakers; those called Dunkers, and those called Menonists, holding it unlawful to take an oath on any occasion, ought to be allowed to make their solemn affirmation, in the manner that Quakers have been heretofore allowed to affirm; and to be of the same avail as an oath, in all such cases, as the affirmation of Quakers hath been allowed and accepted within this State, instead of an oath. And further, on such affirmation, warrants to search for stolen goods, or for the apprehension or commitment of offenders, ought to be granted, or security for the peace awarded, and Quakers, Dunkers or Menonists ought also, on their solemn affirmation as aforesaid, to be admitted as witnesses, in all criminal cases not capital.[57]

XXXVII. That the city of Annapolis ought to have all its rights, privileges and benefits, agreeable to its Charter, and the acts of Assembly confirming and regulating the same, subject nevertheless to such alteration as may be made by this Convention, or any future Legislature.[58]

XXXVIII. That the liberty of the press ought to be inviolably preserved.[59]

[57] Article XXXVI demonstrated the state's commitment to religious liberty, by exempting Quakers, Mennonites, and Dunkers (German Church of the Brethren) from the requirement of swearing an oath of allegiance and permitting them to serve as witnesses in "all criminal cases not capital."

[58] Among the "rights and privileges" afforded to the City of Annapolis, which had been chartered in 1704, was the protection of the city's right to elect its own representatives. Dan Friedman suggests that delegates may have pointed to a precedent in Magna Carta wherein corporate entities like London were given certain privileges and immunities. Magna Carta, Ch. 13. Besides the powers and privileges relative to the organization of a municipality, Annapolis obtained the privilege of electing two delegates to the general assembly. Elihu S. Riley, *The Ancient City: A History of Annapolis, in Maryland, 1649–1887* (Annapolis: Record Printing Office, 1887), 85. The closing of the Port of Boston by the British in 1774 aroused intense concern in Baltimore that the port city of Annapolis would be next. This provision reaffirmed the city's long standing liberties and privileges to trade and to use its port. Richard A. Primus, *The American Language of Rights* (Cambridge: Cambridge University Press, 1999), 121–123.

[59] The word "ought" was employed to describe a right that, by the force of the word "inviolably," cannot be removed or violated. "Ought to" suggests that the right was not judicially enforceable, placing it in the category of an admonition—a reminder to the

XXXIX. That monopolies are odious, contrary to the spirit of a free government, and the principles of commerce; and ought not to be suffered.[60]

XL. That no title of nobility, or hereditary honours, ought to be granted in this State.[61]

XLI. That the subsisting resolves of this and the several Conventions held for this Colony, ought to be in force as laws, unless altered by this Convention, or the Legislature of this State.[62]

XLII. That this Declaration of Rights, or the Form of Government, to be established by this Convention, or any part or either of them, ought not to be altered, changed or abolished, by the Legislature of this State, but in such manner as this Convention shall prescribe and direct.[63]

community of its duty to maintain a free press. Like most early state constitutions, there was no protection afforded for speech.

[60] Maryland was the first American state to incorporate an anti-monopoly provision into its constitution, though it was not the first appearance in an American document declaring liberties. Over a hundred years earlier, the Massachusetts Body of Liberties provided: "No monopolies shall be granted or allowed amongst us, but of such new Inventions that are profitable to the Countrie, and that for a short time." [Massachusetts Body of Liberties] (1641), sec. 9, in Lutz, *Colonial Origins*, 72. The purpose was to provide equal opportunity for invention and enterprise. It was a companion to the removal of ascribed or inherited privileges found in Article XL.

[61] Similar to Va. Decl. 1776, sec. 4. Titles of nobility were considered inconsistent with the equality of citizens in a republican form of government, and this article banned them. The article was superseded by Article I, section 10 of the national Constitution, prohibiting states from granting such titles.

[62] Article XLI was a transitional clause meant to keep in effect those resolves passed during the period between the Declaration of Independence and the adoption of the new constitution.

[63] The final article revealed both the ambiguities created by the use of the word "ought" and the inchoate understanding on the part of the delegates that what they were creating would be, in some way, permanent or at least more fundamental than ordinary legislation. The use of the word "ought" may reflect the fact that notions of judicially enforceable rights and courts voiding acts of the legislature or the governor had not yet been established or asserted. If the judiciary was not understood to be the enforcement agent of these provisions, then that enforcement rested with and was the duty of the citizenry and members of the government. This article served as an admonitory reminder of that duty. The method of amending the document was provided in Article LIX of the frame of government.

The Constitution, or Form of Government, &C

* * *

II. That the House of Delegates shall be chosen in the following manner: All freemen, above twenty-one years of age, having a freehold of fifty acres of land, in the county in which they offer to vote, and residing therein—and all freemen, having property in this State above the value of thirty pounds current money, and having resided in the county, in which they offer to vote, one whole year next preceding the election, shall have a right of suffrage, in the election of Delegates for such county: ....[64]

* * *

XIV. That the Senate be chosen in the following manner: All persons, qualified as aforesaid to vote for county Delegates, shall, on the first day of September, 1781, and on the same day in every fifth year forever thereafter, elect, *viva voce*, by a majority of votes, two persons for their respective counties (qualified as aforesaid to be elected county Delegates) to be electors of the Senate...

[64] The initial draft of the constitution proposed the same qualifications that had been in effect under the proprietary and that had been used in electing delegates to the convention. The convention reduced that requirement from forty pounds sterling to thirty pounds current money. As H. H. Walker Lewis noted, this was a substantial change as "[l]ocal currency was considerably debased and became more so." *Maryland Constitution, 1776.* In addition to the suffrage granted by this article, the constitution afforded all persons qualified by the charter of the city of Annapolis to vote for burgesses and all inhabitants of Baltimore having the qualifications of electors in the county the right to elect two delegates annually.

Delaware

William Penn was "the father of representative government in Delaware."[1] Penn was not, however, the founder of the colony. That honor went to Peter Minuit who, acting on behalf of the New Sweden Company, landed on the banks of the Delaware River in the year 1638. After purchasing land from the Native Americans extending westward from the Delaware River between Bombay Hook and the mouth of the Schuylkill River, which became known as New Sweden, Minuit set up an outpost, Fort Christina (now Wilmington). Between that founding and the time Penn was granted the territory from James, the Duke of York, in 1682, the three counties constituting what is now Delaware had passed through the hands of the Swedes, the Dutch, the English under the Duke of York, the Dutch again, and then the English—with each group having a separate charter.

The first charter was the 1642 "Instruction" from Sweden's regency council to Governor Johan Printz. This document did not mention specific rights but included due process requirements—an early example of these protections in a colonial document originating outside the English legal tradition. The instruction required Printz to administer any controversial matters "according to Swedish law and justice, custom and

[1] Carol E. Hoffecker, *Democracy in Delaware: The Story of the First State's General Assembly* (Wilmington, DE: Cedar Tree Books, 2004), 9.

P. J. Galie et al., *Bills of Rights Before the Bill of Rights*,
https://doi.org/10.1007/978-3-030-44301-6_7

usage."[2] The governor was also given the power to punish, including the administration of capital punishment, yet could only do so "in no other than in a regular manner, and after a careful hearing and consideration of the case, with the foremost people and the most prudent associate judges, who can be found in the country for assistance and counsel."[3] Concerning religious liberty, the instruction commanded:

> Above all things the Governor shall endeavor and see to it that to God the most High be paid in all [things] a true and befitting worship and proper honor, laud and praise, and therefore take all good care that divine service be zealously performed according to the true Augsburg Confession, the Council of Uppsala, and the ceremonies of the Swedish Church; and [he shall see to it that] all persons, especially the young, be well instructed in the articles of their Christian faith, and besides [that] all good church discipline be [duly] held and exercised. But so far as relates to the Holland colonists that live and settle under the government of [Her] Roy[al] Maj[esty] and the Swedish Crown, the Governor shall not disturb them in that which was granted them in the Royal Charter, as to the exercise of the Reformed religion.[4]

Rights to individual land ownership were afforded in a 1654 ordinance drafted by Governor Johan Risingh, allowing anyone who bought land to keep possession for himself and his heirs forever and freeing any indentured servants after six years of labor.[5]

In 1655, the Dutch, led by Peter Stuyvesant, took over the colony of New Sweden and held it as part of New Netherland. The Dutch afforded the conquered liberty of conscience, but only the Dutch Reformed faith was encouraged.[6] Although jury trials and the right to counsel were

[2] *The Instruction for Johan Printz, Governor of New Sweden*, trans. Amandus Johnson (Philadelphia: The Swedish Colonial Society, 1930), 92, 94.

[3] Ibid., 94.

[4] Ibid., 94, 96.

[5] Gaspare J. Saladino, "Delaware: Armed in the Cause of Freedom," in *The Bill of Rights and the States: The Colonial and Revolutionary Origins of American Liberties*, ed. Patrick T. Conley and John P. Kaminski (Madison, WI: Madison House, 1992), 277.

[6] Ibid., 278.

not provided in the territory, the courts were open with appeals to the director-general and council in Amsterdam permitted in cases involving serious crimes.[7]

In September 1664, Stuyvesant surrendered New Amsterdam to English Colonel Richard Nicolls. The following month, Sir Robert Carr, representing Nicolls, seized the Dutch settlements on the Delaware for the Duke of York. Save for a brief reclamation by the Dutch in 1673–1674, the next eighteen years saw the territory administered as part of the Province of New York.

In 1665, the Duke of York's Laws for the Government of the Colony of New York were compiled under the direction of Governor Nicolls. This first body of statute law for the colony would, except for the Dutch reclamation period, remain in place until 1682.[8] During this time, Governor Francis Lovelace introduced the common law trial to the colony (1669), and by 1676, "a nascent English common law system was in place," providing "some personal, religious and political freedom."[9]

In 1680/1681, Charles II granted an idealistic English Quaker, William Penn, proprietorship of Pennsylvania. In 1682, the Duke of York granted Penn land that included what would become known as the Three Lower Counties on Delaware. In December 1682, an Act of Union joined Penn's two holdings, promising the Lower Counties would "be governed by the same laws and enjoy the same privileges in all respects as the inhabitants of Pennsylvania do..."[10]

The charter and laws of Pennsylvania adopted between 1682 and 1701 afforded the Lower Counties substantial rights.[11] Religious freedom was

[7] Ibid.

[8] Ordinance Introducing the Duke's Laws, Establishing Courts of Justice and Making Various Other Rules for the Government of the Delaware River, in *Foundations of Colonial America: A Documentary History*, ed. W. Keith Kavenagh (New York: Chelsea House, 1973), 2:828. It is available online at: https://www.nycourts.gov/history/legal-history-new-york/documents/charters-duke-transcript.pdf.

[9] Saladino, "Delaware: Armed in the Cause of Freedom," 274.

[10] Act of Union, December 7, 1682, in Kavenagh, *Foundations*, 2:862.

[11] For a thorough description of the frames and other charter documents governing Pennsylvania, see the treatment of them in that chapter.

afforded to all who acknowledged an almighty God,[12] and the state was prohibited from requiring anyone to maintain religious worship or ministry.[13] The charter document of the colony also promised inhabitants a role, albeit a minor one, in lawmaking, required consent to any taxes levied, and provided open courts,[14] a right to bail,[15] a right to a grand jury indictment and a jury trial in criminal proceedings,[16] and care for the needy.[17]

Differences in population growth, disputes over representation in the assembly, and tensions stemming from events in England and Europe, among others, brought the unified assembly to an end in 1701.[18] The assembly of the Lower Counties met for the first time as a separate legislative body in 1704. For the remainder of the colonial period, Pennsylvania and the Lower Counties shared a governor, but their representative assemblies met separately.

By the mid-eighteenth century, consent of the governed, representative institutions, a guarantee of due process of law, trial by jury, and religious liberty were established rights in the Lower Counties. Suffrage was guaranteed to adult, white, male subjects of Great Britain (or otherwise naturalized in England, Delaware, or Pennsylvania), who resided in the colony for a term of two years and possessed fifty acres of land with twelve cleared, or were otherwise worth forty pounds.[19] These requirements excluded women, free and enslaved blacks, and Indians. Harsh measures

[12] The Great Law (1682), Ch. 1, is reprinted in *The Statutes at Large of Pennsylvania from 1682 to 1700*, comp. Robert L. Cable (Harrisburg: Legislative Reference Bureau, 2001), 1:5.

[13] Ibid.

[14] Ibid., Ch. 42, 17.

[15] Ibid., Ch. 62, 22–23.

[16] Ibid., Ch. 46, 18–19.

[17] Ibid., Ch. 37, 15.

[18] Carol E. Hoffecker provides an informative description of these developments in *Democracy in Delaware*, 34ff.

[19] An Act for Regulating Elections, and Ascertaining the Number of the Members of Assembly, 7 Geo. II (1734), Ch. LXI, sec. 2, in *Laws of the State of Delaware from the Fourteenth Day of October, One Thousand Seven Hundred, to the Eighteenth Day of August, One Thousand Seven Hundred and Ninety-Seven* (Newcastle: Samuel and John Adams, 1797), 1:148.

were adopted respecting black slaves and indentured servants, including whipping and cropping of ears.[20]

Those receiving poor relief were required to wear a badge on their outer clothing.[21] The colony reflected the anti-Catholic sentiment that papists could not be allowed full membership in the community because they owed allegiance to a foreign power (the Pope). An election law passed in 1734 required assembly members to swear an oath of allegiance to the king and deny the authority and doctrines of the Roman Catholic Church.[22] A 1744 law permitted only Protestant religious societies to acquire real property.[23]

Between 1763 and 1776 differences between the Lower Counties and the proprietary governors and English authorities were exacerbated by a number of gubernatorial vetoes and intrusive Crown legislation imposed on the colonists. The breaking point occurred in July 1774, when a meeting of Sussex County men held in response to the Boston port closing declared unconstitutional all parliamentary acts "respecting the internal police"[24] of the colony, that is, the right of the colony to regulate its internal affairs without outside interference.

The assembly of the Lower Counties adopted a resolution on June 15, 1776, formally declaring an end to its status as a colony of Great Britain.[25] The assembly not only declared itself free from the British Empire but also asserted its independence as a state entirely separate from Pennsylvania, becoming the de facto State of Delaware.

Believing that it was not the appropriate body to reconstitute the government, the assembly voted on July 27, 1776, to call elections for a

[20] See Saladino, "Delaware: Armed in the Cause of Freedom," 290.

[21] Ibid., 291.

[22] Act for Regulating Elections, Ch. LXI, sec. 10, 1:154–156.

[23] An Act for the Enabling Religious Societies of Protestants within This Government, to Purchase Lands for Burying-Grounds, Churches, Houses for Worship, Schools, etc., 17 Geo. II (1744), Ch. CVIII, in *Laws of the State of Delaware*, 1:271. A more detailed discussion of these measures is found in Saladino, "Delaware: Armed in the Cause of Freedom," 291–292.

[24] J. Thomas Scharf, *History of Delaware: 1609–1888* (Philadelphia: L. J. Richards & Co., 1888), 1:219.

[25] Claudia L. Bushman, Harold B. Hancock, and Elizabeth Moyne Homsey, eds., *Proceedings of the Assembly of the Lower Counties on Delaware, 1770–1776, of the Constitutional Convention of 1776, and of the House of Assembly of the Delaware State, 1776–1781* (Newark: University of Delaware Press, 1986), 199–200.

special convention, in effect, voting itself out of existence.[26] It urged "the good people of the several Counties in this Government to chuse a suitable Number of Deputies to meet in *Convention* there to ordain and declare the future Form of Government for this State."[27] Delaware claims to be the first state to employ the "now generally accepted method of calling a popularly elected convention to adopt a new constitution."[28]

The selection of delegates to the convention took place while British ships patrolled Delaware Bay. The convention met from August 27 through September 21, 1776. A committee was appointed by the convention to prepare a declaration of rights and fundamental rules for the governance of the state. The convention approved the declaration on September 11th. It was published in the *Pennsylvania Gazette* on October 2, 1776, and in the *Maryland Gazette* the following day. The constitution was approved by the convention on September 20, 1776, but not submitted to the public or to the assembly for their approval.[29]

Constitutional Developments: 1776 Declaration and Constitution

George Read, the convention president and chair of the committees to draft a declaration of rights and a constitution, reported: "there being nothing particular in it I did not think it an object of much curiosity, it is made out of ye Pensilvania & Maryland Draughts…."[30] The provisions in the Delaware declaration concerning popular sovereignty (Decl. 1776, sec. 1), consent of the governed (ibid., secs. 1, 6–9), natural rights (ibid., sec. 10), English common law constitutional rights (ibid., secs. 10–17), state sovereignty (ibid., sec. 4), liberty of conscience (ibid., secs. 2–3), a right to alter or abolish tyrannical government (ibid., sec. 5), and citizen

[26] Ibid., 201.

[27] Ibid. (emphasis added).

[28] Randy J. Holland, *The Delaware State Constitution* (2002; reprint, New York: Oxford University Press, 2011), 5. See also John A. Munroe, *Federalist Delaware, 1775–1815* (New Brunswick, NJ: Rutgers University Press, 1954), 84 and the studies cited in the footnote at page 298. Cf. the claims made on behalf of New Hampshire, see below p. 251.

[29] A reliable and more detailed account of the events leading to the calling of the convention, the selection of delegates, the debates, and decision making can be found in Richard Lynch Mumford, "Constitutional Development in the State of Delaware, 1776–1897" (PhD. diss., University of Delaware, 1968).

[30] Letter of George Read to Caesar Rodney, September 17, 1776, reprinted in H. Clay Reed, "The Delaware Constitution of 1776," *Delaware Notes* 6 (1930): 41.

soldiers and civic virtue (ibid., secs. 18–20) closely resembled those other two states. As one historian wrote, "[t]wenty-one of the twenty-three Delaware articles match those of an earlier Maryland draft in ideas and even in words, while the others show obvious features similar to the Pennsylvania Declaration of Rights."[31] This borrowing, referred to as horizontal federalism, reflected the consensus among the states on the principles, rights, and structures that collectively have been labeled natural rights republics.[32] The common law and statute law of England remained in full force (Const. 1776, Art. 25).

From its inception, the status of Delaware's Declaration of Rights was in doubt. Article 30 of the constitution spoke of the declaration and the constitution as if they were separate entities.[33] Saladino goes further: "The declaration was not part of the constitution but was appended to it as a legislative bill by Article 30 of that document."[34] In one of the earliest commentaries on the 1776 declaration, Max Farrand writes, "for some inexplicable reason this bill of rights is not included by Poore in his *Charters and Constitutions*."[35] Thorpe did not include the declaration in his 1909 compilation of constitutions.

The state's commitment to popular sovereignty received pride of place in the declaration, opening that document (Decl. 1776, sec. 1). The declaration also included a series of provisions designed to allow voters to participate in their government at different levels: It affirmed the right of

[31] Mumford, "Constitutional Development," 61.

[32] Michael P. Zuckert, *The Natural Rights Republic: Studies in the Foundation of the American Political Tradition* (Notre Dame, IN: University of Notre Dame Press, 1996). Fuller analysis of these rights and aspirations is provided in Chapter 1.

[33] That article read:

> No article of the declaration of rights and fundamental rules of this State, agreed to by this convention, nor the first, second, fifth, (except that part thereof that relates to the right of suffrage,) twenty-sixth, and twenty-ninth articles of this constitution, ought ever to be violated on any pretence whatever. No other part of this constitution shall be altered, changed, or diminished without the consent of five parts in seven of the assembly, and seven members of the legislative council (Const. 1776, Art. 30).

[34] "Delaware: Armed in the Cause of Freedom," 290.

[35] Max Farrand, "The Delaware Bill of Rights of 1776," *The American Historical Review* 3, no. 4 (July 1898), 641.

the citizens to petition legislators (ibid., sec. 9), required the legislature to convene frequently to carry out that popular will (ibid., sec. 8), mandated frequent elections so that legislators not conforming to the public will could be removed (ibid., sec. 6), and provided a right to "establish a new, or reform the old government" when the ends of government became perverted (ibid., sec. 5).

Suffrage

The right to suffrage itself was not debated; however, the requirements for exercising that right were. Ultimately, the convention decided that the right of suffrage "shall remain as exercised by law at present" (Const. 1776, Art. 5).[36]

Structural Provisions

The constitution created a bicameral general assembly and mandated that it meet at least annually (Const. 1776, Art. 2). Members of the larger "House of Assembly" were chosen for one-year terms (ibid., Art. 3), while members of "The council" were elected for three years (ibid., Art. 4). Money bills were required to originate in the house of assembly (ibid., Art. 6). Members of both houses were required to be freeholders, and the upper house had a minimum age of twenty-five (ibid., 1776, Art. 4). Representatives were required to swear an oath professing faith in "God the Father, and in Jesus Christ His only Son, and in the Holy Ghost, one God, blessed for evermore," and acknowledging the Old and New Testaments to be the product of divine inspiration (ibid., Art. 22). This article banned practicing atheists, deists, and Jews from holding office.[37] Clergy members were ineligible to serve in the legislature or in any civil office (ibid., Art. 29). The chief executive, titled the president, was elected by joint ballot of the general assembly. Although afforded a comparatively lengthy term of three years (ibid., Art. 7), a president was required to sit out of office for three years after finishing one three-year term (ibid.). The president did not have veto power. Beyond privy councilors not being eligible to serve in the general assembly (ibid., Art. 8), no other

[36] See p. 168 for details of that requirement.

[37] This requirement was abolished in the 1792 constitution.

restrictions on plural office-holding existed at the legislative or executive levels.[38] Supreme court judges were allowed to hold office "during good behavior" (ibid., Art. 12).

The Delaware Constitution contained an entrenchment clause (Const. 1776, Art. 30), permanently designating its declaration of rights and certain parts of the frame inviolable. In doing so, delegates created two levels of constitutional provisions: the inviolable and those that could be changed by a super-majority of five-sevenths of the assembly and seven members of the nine-member legislative council (ibid.). No procedure for calling a future constitutional convention was included.

Postscript: In 1787, Delaware became the first state to ratify the national Constitution. Four years later, the concern that the Delaware Constitution did not provide sufficient separation of powers prompted calls for revision. Despite the absence of a provision for a convention in the 1776 constitution, the legislature passed a resolution calling for the election of delegates to a second constitutional convention. That convention met in 1792 and adopted Delaware's second constitution without submission to the people.

Any doubt as to whether the declaration of rights was part of the document were removed by the 1792 constitution, as that constitution relocated the rights provisions to Article I and dropped the separate name.[39] The 1792 constitution also spelled out procedures for calling future conventions (Const. 1792, Article X).

Constitution of Delaware [1776]

[Declaration of Rights]

SECTION 1. That all government of right originates from the people, is founded in compact only, and instituted solely for the good of the whole.[40]

SECT. 2. That all men have a natural and unalienable right to worship Almighty God according to the dictates of their own consciences and understandings; and that no man ought or of right can be compelled

[38] Supreme court judges were prohibited from holding any other office than a military one (Const. 1776., Arts. 12, 18).

[39] Constitution of Delaware (1792), in Thorpe, *Constitutions*, 1:568–570.

[40] Similar to Md. Decl. 1776, Art. I. This section was removed from the 1792 constitution.

to attend any religious worship or maintain any ministry contrary to or against his own free will and consent, and that no authority can or ought to be vested in, or assumed by any power whatever that shall in any case interfere with, or in any manner control the right of conscience in the free exercise of religious worship.[41]

SECT. 3. That all persons professing the Christian religion ought forever to enjoy equal rights and privileges in this state, unless, under colour of religion, any man disturb the peace, the happiness or safety of society.[42]

SECT. 4. That people of this state have the sole exclusive and inherent right of governing and regulating the internal police of the same.[43]

SECT. 5. That persons entrusted with the Legislative and Executive Powers are the Trustees and Servants of the public, and as such accountable for their conduct; wherefore whenever the ends of government are perverted, and public liberty manifestly endangered by the Legislative singly, or a treacherous combination of both, the people may, and of right ought to establish a new, or reform the old government.[44]

SECT. 6. That the right in the people to participate in the Legislature, is the foundation of liberty and of all free government, and for this end all elections ought to be free and frequent, and every freeman, having

[41] Similar to Pa. Decl. 1776, Art. II.

[42] The qualifier "Christian religion" to this section affording equal rights and privileges suggests that there were some "equal rights and privileges" that non-Christians could not enjoy. Article 22 of the frame of government supported that inference, requiring officeholders to be Christians who acknowledged Holy Scriptures to be divinely inspired. When Delaware revised its constitution in 1792, it removed this section. The restriction reflected the delegates' belief that religion, and specifically the Christian religion, was a necessary prerequisite for a well-ordered moral community. For elaboration on colonial assumptions about the nature of community see pp. 43–48. Article 29 of the frame prohibited the establishment of any particular religion.

[43] Similar to Pa. Decl. 1776, Art. III. The declaration by Sussex County in 1774 that all parliamentary acts respecting the "internal police" were unconstitutional indicates that Delaware, even as a colony, zealously guarded the right to control its internal police. See discussion above, p. 169. This section constitutionalized that exercise of sovereignty. This section was removed from the 1792 constitution. By then, Delaware's independent status had been recognized, it had joined the Union, and a Bill of Rights had been added to the national Constitution. Combined, they rendered this section redundant.

[44] Similar to Md. Decl. 1776, Art. IV. The 1792 convention confined this sentiment to a preamble, where the people "may…as circumstances require, from time to time, alter their constitution of government."

sufficient evidence of a permanent common interest with, and attachment to the community, hath a right of suffrage.[45]

SECT. 7. That no power of suspending laws, or the execution of laws, ought to be exercised unless by the Legislature.[46]

SECT. 8. That for redress of grievances, and for amending and strengthening of the laws, the Legislature ought to be frequently convened.[47]

SECT. 9. That every man hath a right to petition the Legislature for the redress of grievances in a peaceable and orderly manner.[48]

SECT. 10. That every member of society hath a right to be protected in the enjoyment of life, liberty and property, and therefore is bound to contribute his proportion towards the expense of that protection, and yield his personal service when necessary, or an equivalent thereto; but no part of a man's property can be justly taken from him or applied to public uses without his own consent or that of his legal Representatives: Nor can any man that is conscientiously scrupulous of bearing arms in any case be justly compelled thereto if he will pay such equivalent.[49]

[45] Similar to Md. Decl. 1776, Art. V. The Delaware version replaced "ought to have a right to suffrage" with "hath a right to suffrage."

The requirements for demonstrating a "permanent common interest with, and attachment to the community," were placed in Article 2 of the frame of government, which in turn referred to the law then in effect concerning suffrage requirements. The existing law levied fines on those who did not vote, making explicit the connection between rights and obligations.

[46] Similar to Md. Decl. 1776, Art. VII; Va. Decl. 1776, sec. 8.

[47] Similar to Md. Decl. 1776, Art. X.

[48] Similar to Md. Decl. 1776, Art. XI. The constitution of 1792 included freedom of assembly in its rights article (Const. 1792, Art. I, sec. 16).

[49] Similar to Pa. Decl. 1776, Art. VIII. Like its Pennsylvania counterpart, this section protected the religious conscience of Quakers.

The 1792 constitution eliminated this section. The notion of communal obligation—taking property for public use and serving in the militia—balanced by fair compensation for the taking and exemption from military service for the conscientious objector, was prefaced by what, under a contemporary rights regime, would be placed in a preamble. The removal of the exemption for those who in conscience could not bear arms, occasioned objections at the 1792 convention. Quaker delegate Warner Mifflin addressed the convention, pleading for an exemption from military service for those whose religious consciences prohibited such service. A deputation of Quakers representing Pennsylvania, New Jersey, and Delaware urged the convention to respect the "rights of conscience." Claudia L. Bushman, Harold B. Hancock, and Elizabeth Moyne Homsey, eds., *Proceedings of the House of Assembly of the Delaware State, 1781–1792 and of the Constitutional*

SECT. 11. That retrospective laws, punishing offences committed before the existence of such laws, are oppressive and unjust, and ought not to be made.[50]

SECT. 12. That every freeman for every injury done him in his goods, lands or person, by any other person, ought to have remedy by the course of the law of the land, and ought to have justice and right for the injury done to him freely without sale, fully without any denial, and speedily without delay, according to the law of the land.[51]

SECT. 13. That trial by jury of facts where they arise is one of the greatest securities of the lives, liberties and estates of the people.[52]

SECT. 14. That in all prosecutions for criminal offences, every man hath a right to be informed of the accusation against him, to be allowed counsel, to be confronted with the accusers or witnesses, to examine evidence on oath in his favor, and to a speedy trial by an impartial jury, without whose unanimous consent he ought not to be found guilty.[53]

SECT. 15. That no man in the courts of Common Law ought to be compelled to give evidence against himself.[54]

Convention of 1792 (Newark: University of Delaware Press, 1988), 844–846, 855–857. Their pleas were unsuccessful. Quaker attitudes towards warfare during the Revolutionary War did not endear them to fellow Delawareans. Munroe, *Federalist Delaware*, 169. The existence and terms of any religious exemptions would be left to the legislature.

[50] Similar to Md. Decl. 1776, Art. XV. The 1792 declaration removed the protection against ex post facto laws, perhaps to avoid redundancy in the wake of the national Constitution's ban on states adopting such laws (U.S. Const., Art. I, sec. 10, cl. 1).

[51] Similar to Md. Decl. 1776, Art. XVII.

[52] Similar to Md. Decl. 1776, Art. XVIII. The Maryland provision on which this section was based did not specify that the local trial would be a jury trial, notwithstanding that a jury trial was provided in other articles of that state's declaration. This section removed any doubt.

[53] Similar to Md. Decl. 1776, Art. XIX. Absent from the Delaware declaration are the rights to have a "copy of the indictment or charge in due time—if required—to prepare for his defense" and "process for his witnesses." The 1792 constitution added additional provisions strengthening the protections for those accused of crimes, such as allowing all prisoners to be bailable by sufficient sureties (bond) except for capital cases (1792 Const., Art. I, sec. 12), and protection of the writ of habeas corpus mirroring that found in the U.S. Constitution (ibid., Art. I, sec. 13).

[54] Similar to Md. Decl. 1776, Art. XX. The Maryland document permitted evidence against one's self to be compelled in cases "as have been usually practised in this State, or may hereafter be directed by the Legislature." The Delaware version contained no such exception to the right.

SECT. 16. That excessive bail ought not to be required, nor excessive fines imposed, nor cruel or unusual punishments inflicted.[55]

SECT. 17. That all warrants without oath to search suspected places, or to seize any person or his property, are grievous and oppressive; and all general warrants to search suspected, or to apprehend all persons suspected, without naming or describing the place or any person in special, are illegal and ought not to be granted.[56]

SECT. 18. That a well-regulated militia is the proper, natural and safe defense of a free government.[57]

SECT. 19. That standing armies are dangerous to liberty, and ought not to be raised or kept up without the consent of the Legislature.[58]

SECT. 20. That in all cases and at all times the military ought to be under strict subordination to and governed by the civil power.[59]

SECT. 21. That no soldier ought to be quartered in any house in time of peace without the consent of the owner; and in time of war in such manner only as the Legislature shall direct.[60]

SECT. 22. That the independency and uprightness of judges are essential to the impartial administration of justice, and a great security to the rights and liberties of the people.[61]

SECT. 23. That the liberty of the press ought to be inviolably preserved.[62]

[Frame of Government]

* * *

[55] Similar to Md. Decl. 1776, Art. XXII.

[56] Similar to Md. Decl. 1776, Art. XXIII.

[57] Similar to Md. Decl. 1776, Art. XXV.

[58] Similar to Md. Decl. 1776, Art. XXVI.

[59] Similar to Md. Decl. 1776, Art. XXVII.

[60] Similar to Md. Decl. 1776, Art. XXVIII.

[61] Similar to Md. Decl. 1776, Art. XXX. The section said nothing about how such independency and uprightness was to be achieved. The frame of the constitution specified that judges of the supreme court and the court of appeals (the actual court of last resort) would serve "during good behavior" (Const. 1776, Arts. 12, 17), a key prerequisite for achieving judicial independence. The 1792 constitution eliminated this section.

[62] Similar to Md. Decl. 1776, Art. XXXVIII.

ART. 5. The right of suffrage in the election of members for both houses shall remain as exercised by law at present…[63]

* * *

ART. 25. The common law of England, as-well as so much of the statute law as has been heretofore adopted in practice in this State, shall remain in force, unless they shall be altered by a future law of the legislature; such parts only excepted as are repugnant to the rights and privileges contained in this constitution, and the declaration of rights, &c., agreed to by this convention.[64]

ART. 26. No person hereafter imported into this State from Africa ought to be held in slavery under any presence whatever; and no negro, Indian, or mulatto slave ought to be brought into this State, for sale, from any part of the world.[65]

* * *

[63] See Suffrage section, above.

[64] Given the heavy reliance by the colonists throughout the eighteenth century on the rights embodied in the English common law, it is not surprising that, one way or another, all states incorporated the protections of that body of law. See the table at above pp. 81–82. This article gave constitutional status to the extensive rights and liberties encompassed by the common law and the statutes that made up the English Constitution. Because the colonies had come to rely on the common law for the administration of justice, the provision also served to ease the transition to statehood. It also made clear that any parts of that law repugnant to the constitution of the state were void and the legislature was authorized to alter or supersede those parts as it saw fit.

[65] A majority of the newly independent states took some formal action by legislation or constitutional provision to curb the slave trade and move gradually towards its elimination. The importance of this ban was underscored by its inclusion among the provisions listed in Article 29 that were not to be violated "on any pretence whatsoever." Moreover, individual manumissions increased after independence. The percentage of free blacks among the black population in Delaware grew from thirty percent in 1790 to seventy-six percent in 1810. Winthrop D. Jordan, *White over Black: American Attitudes Towards the Negro, 1550–1812* (Chapel Hill: University of North Carolina Press, 1968), 407.

The 1792 constitution removed this article. One of the main supporters of this change, delegate John Dickinson, though opposed to the extension of slavery, insisted that the power to prohibit the importation of slaves must be left to the national government under the U.S. Constitution. Thomas G. West, *Vindicating the Founders: Race, Sex, Class, and Justice in the Origins of America* (Lanham, MD: Rowman & Littlefield, 1997), 11.

ART. 29. There shall be no establishment of any one religious sect in this State in preference to another; and no clergyman or preacher of the gospel, of any denomination, shall be capable of holding any civil office in this State, or of being a member of either of the branches of the legislature, while they continue in the exercise of the pastoral function.[66]

[66]There was no established church in pre- or post-constitution Delaware. This provision ensured that none would be established. Christianity was, however, given a privileged position. See Decl. 1776, sec. 3 (granting equal rights only to Christians); Const. 1776, Art. 22 (requiring legislators to swear Christian oath). The first clause prohibited the establishment of a particular religion but the wording appears to allow multiple establishments on an equal footing. Section 2 of the declaration, however, seems to foreclose that possibility by making clear that no individual could be taxed to support any faith against his will. The companion clause prohibited clergy of any faith from holding public office. Reed suggests that this ban was directed against Presbyterian clergymen who were radical, numerous, and active in the Revolutionary struggle. "Delaware Constitution of 1776," 31.

North Carolina

On March 24, 1663, King Charles II granted the first Charter of Carolina to eight friends he credited with helping restore the monarchy. Although the charter gave full authority to the proprietors to govern the territory that now encompasses North and South Carolina, it did include several important checks on their powers.[1] All laws were to be enacted with the "advice, assent and approbation of the freemen of the said province, or of the greater part of them, or of their delegates or deputies," with the proviso that the proprietors could enact orders and ordinances when it was not "convenient" to call an assembly of freeholders.[2] Additionally, all laws had to be "near as may be conveniently, agreeable to the laws and customs of this our kingdom of England," and prospective colonists were to be guaranteed "all liberties, franchises and priviledges of this our kingdom of England … and may freely and quietly have, possess and enjoy, as our liege people born within the same, without the least molestation, vexation, trouble or grievance."[3] The charter also granted religious toleration for those "who really in their Judgments, and for conscience sake"

[1] Scott D. Gerber, "The Origins of an Independent Judiciary in North Carolina, 1663–1787," *North Carolina Law Review* 87 (2009): 1777–1778.

[2] Charter of Carolina (1663), in Thorpe, *Constitutions*, 5:2745, 2746.

[3] Ibid., 2746, 2747. Phrases such as "all liberties, franchises and privileges" appeared frequently in colonial charters. See pp. 22–30. Presumably, it afforded the colonists the protections of the English common law, which North Carolina incorporated by statute in 1715.

P. J. Galie et al., *Bills of Rights Before the Bill of Rights*,
https://doi.org/10.1007/978-3-030-44301-6_8

could not conform to the religious practices of the established Church of England.[4]

To encourage settlement, the proprietors issued the Concessions and Agreements of the Lords Proprietors of the Province of Carolina in 1665. This document each county (Albemarle and Clarendon in the north, and Craven in the south) separate governors, councils, and popularly elected general assemblies, and guaranteed liberty of conscience to those who did not "disturbe the civill peace."[5] The toleration guarantees in the charters and the concessions encouraged the growth of dissenting sects, especially Quakers, in the Albemarle region of the colony.[6] By the end of the seventeenth century, Quakers had secured a number of prominent roles in the government, including the governorship.[7]

[4] Charter of Carolina (1663), 2752–2753. Carolina received a second charter in 1665 that was identical to the first save for an extension of the province's northern border. See Charter of Carolina (1665), in Thorpe, *Constitutions*, 5:2761–2771.

[5] Concessions and Agreements of the Lords Proprietors of the Province of Carolina (1665), in Thorpe, *Constitutions*, 5:2757.

[6] Robert L. Ganyard, "North Carolina During the American Revolution: The First Phase, 1774–1777" (PhD diss., Duke University, 1962), 442. Ganyard subsequently published his doctoral dissertation as, *The Emergence of North Carolina's Revolutionary State Government* (Raleigh: North Carolina Department of Cultural Resources, 1978), which is cited in this chapter instead of the dissertation except where the materials do not overlap.

[7] Ganyard, "North Carolina During the American Revolution," 442–443; Hugh Talmage Lefler and Albert Ray Newsome, *The History of a Southern State: North Carolina*, 3rd ed. (Chapel Hill: University of North Carolina Press, 1973), 59. "Dissenters secured such a substantial foothold in polity and society at such an early date that their rights could not be easily dismissed." William S. Price, Jr., "'There Ought to Be a Bill of Rights': North Carolina Enters a New Nation," in *The Bill of Rights and the States: The Colonial and Revolutionary Origins of American Liberties*, ed. Patrick T. Conley and John P. Kaminski (Madison, WI: Madison House, 1992), 427. In 1705 Quakers and Presbyterians united to secure an Anglican governor's removal because he supported an act that required all assembly members to take an oath affirming their membership in the Church of England. Lefler and Newsome, *History of a Southern State*, 60. The Quakers continued to actively oppose and seek the removal of every subsequent governor that enforced the oath requirement, even to the point of supporting an armed rebellion in 1711–1712. Ibid., 60–61; Price, "There Ought to Be a Bill of Rights," 426. The Quakers were finally appeased in 1715 when the legislature passed an "Act for Liberty of Conscience" giving them the right of affirmation and providing legal protection for all dissenters. Lefler and Newsome, *History of a Southern State*, 67. The influence and growth of dissenting sects continued throughout the eighteenth century. Their toleration was never again jeopardized, and ultimately led to the disestablishment of the Anglican Church in North Carolina's 1776 constitution. Price, "There Ought to Be a Bill of Rights," 427; Charles Lee Raper, *North Carolina, a Study in English Colonial Government* (New York: Macmillan, 1904), 14.

Fearing that these charter provisions were fostering a "democratic spirit" among the settlers,[8] Carolina's proprietors issued the Fundamental Constitutions of Carolina of 1669 to "avoid erecting a numerous democracy."[9] Unlike the 1665 Concessions and Agreements, the new plan concentrated power in a hereditary nobility, limiting the role of the freemen.[10] These feudal elements, ill-suited to the democratic spirit of provincial Carolina, were never fully implemented.[11] The Fundamental Constitutions did, however, guarantee some individual liberties such as religious toleration, trial by jury, and protection against double jeopardy.[12]

The part of the colony that would become South Carolina took shape in the spring of 1670, when 150 settlers sailed from Bermuda into modern-day Charleston. This settlement became the hub of the southern province, and grew more quickly than the northern settlements. In

[8] Raper, *North Carolina*, 20, 22; Gerber, "Origins of an Independent Judiciary," 1781.

[9] The Fundamental Constitutions of Carolina (1669), in Thorpe, *Constitutions*, 5:2772. John Locke played a role in the creation of the 1669 document, although the nature of his role is disputed. That constitution explicitly supported hereditary nobility and slavery, while Locke's *Two Treatises of Government* (1690) argued against the very root of slavery: inherited status, which derived from the same set of ordering ideas and commitments as the monarchy—the divine and hereditary rights of kings. Some scholars have accused Locke of hypocrisy; others find justification for slavery in his own writings. Professor Holly Brewer concludes:

> Locke was a secretary – he drafted a legal document as a lawyer drafts a will. He composed it for the eight men who owned the Carolinas (given to them as a reward by Charles II). These men desired 'that the government of this province may be made most agreeable to the monarchy under which we live'. They sought to 'avoid erecting a numerous democracy'. The principles it espoused – including hereditary nobility and slavery – both predated Locke's involvement, and reflected the ideals of the owners. It is a deep error, therefore, to contend that Locke's role in the Carolina constitutions should guide interpretation of his later work, much less liberalism.

Holly Brewer, "John Locke Took Part in Administering the Slave-Owning Colonies: Does That Make Him, and Liberalism Itself, Hypocritical?" accessed February 9, 2019, https://aeon.co/essays/does-lockes-entanglement-with-slavery-undermine-his-philosophy. For the argument that Locke was more deeply implicated in the defense of slavery, see James Farr, "Locke, Natural Law, and New World Slavery," *Political Theory* 36, no. 4 (August 2008): 495–522.

[10] Gerber, "Origins of an Independent Judiciary," 1781–1782 n. 51.

[11] Price, "There Ought to Be a Bill of Rights," 427; Raper, *North Carolina*, 22.

[12] Gerber, "Origins of an Independent Judiciary," 1783.

1676, the proprietors directed the governor of the Albemarle province, which by then included the former Clarendon County, to take "spetiall care that Justice be duly administered and the wayes to attaine it may neither be tedious, troublesome nor chargeable for men of prudence and of estates have noe reason to venture themselves in any place where liberty and property are not well secured."[13] The instructions also required the governor "to promote and propose in the Assembly the makinge of such Lawes as may best secure the antient and native rights of Englishmen, and in particular the tryall of all Criminall Causes and matters of fact by a jury of 12 sufficient freeholders…"[14]

The two provinces had separate governors until 1691 when Philip Ludwell was appointed governor of the entire colony. This move did not unify government in the provinces, as the proprietors empowered Ludwell "to apoint [sic] a Deputy in North Carolina," and the north retained its own assembly and council.[15] Following several power struggles, the proprietors decided to appoint a separate governor for northern Carolina. Edward Hyde was commissioned on January 24, 1711/1712, and received royal approval on May 9 of that year, effectively severing the colonies. As one of its first actions, the new colony incorporated the common law, providing statutory protection for procedural rights and due process of law.[16]

In 1728, the Lords Proprietors sold their interests in North Carolina to King George II. Following parliamentary approval, a year later North Carolina became a Crown colony. The newly appointed royal governor

[13] William L. Saunders, ed., *The Colonial Records of North Carolina* (Raleigh: P. M. Hale, 1886), 1:230–231.

[14] Ibid., 231.

[15] "Carolina Under the Lords Proprietors' Rule: Lords Proprietors Commission to Governor Philip Ludwell," accessed February 2, 2019, http://www.carolana.com/Carolina/Governors/pludwell_instructions.html. See Saunders, *Colonial Records*, xxv–xxvi.

[16] An Act for the More Effectual Observing of the Queen's Peace, and Establishing a Good and Lasting Foundation of Government in North Carolina (1715), Ch. 31, in *The State Records of North Carolina*, ed. Walter Clark (Goldsboro, NC: Nash Brothers, 1904), 23:38. The common law remained in force after separation from England via state statute in 1778. An Act to Enforce Such Parts of the Statute and Common Laws as Have Been Heretofore in Force and Use Here; and the Acts of Assembly Made and Passed when this Territory was under the Government of the Late Proprietors and the Crown of Great Britain, and for Reviving the Several Acts therein Mentioned (1778), Ch. 5, in Clark, *State Records*, 24:162.

was instructed to permit liberty of conscience to all except Catholics, so long as it was exercised peacefully.[17] Governors were also instructed to provide due process, ensure that all incarcerated persons (except those charged with treason and felony) had the immediate privilege of habeas corpus, and see that a person who had been freed not be "recommitted for the same offence except by the court in which he was bound to appear."[18]

The relationship with England gradually soured over what North Carolinians saw as violations of their charter rights. Beginning in the summer of 1774, a series of unicameral provincial congresses began meeting in locations throughout the colony. The governor issued proclamations the following year condemning the "illegal" provincial congress and demanding the assembly exercise its role as "the only true and lawful Representation of the People."[19] In response, both the assembly and the provincial congress passed resolutions asserting the people's "undoubted right" to petition for a redress of grievances.[20] By August 1775, the governor had departed the province, bringing royal rule of the colony to an end.[21] When the Fourth Provincial Congress met in Halifax on April 12, 1776, North Carolina became the first colony to pass a resolution in support of independence.[22] The following day, the congress appointed a committee to draw up a temporary constitution. The committee relied on South Carolina's recently adopted constitution and Connecticut's 1662 charter

[17] Lefler and Newsome, *History of a Southern State*, 133; Raper, *North Carolina*, 31.

[18] Saunders, *Colonial Records*, 3:90–118.

[19] "Proclamation of Governor Martin, March 6, 1775," in Saunders, *Colonial Records*, 9:1145–1146; "Proclamation of Governor Martin, April 3, 1775," in Saunders, *Colonial Records*, 9:1177–1178.

[20] "Legislative Journals, April 6, 1775," in Saunders, *Colonial Records*, 9:1198–1200; "Journals of the Second Provincial Congress, April 7, 1775," in Saunders, *Colonial Records*, 9:1185.

[21] E. W. Sikes, *The Transition of North Carolina from Colony to Commonwealth* (Baltimore: John Hopkins Press, 1898), 41.

[22] Ganyard, *Emergence of North Carolina's Revolutionary State Government*, 60; Jeffrey J. Crow, *A Chronicle of North Carolina During the American Revolution, 1763–1789* (Raleigh: North Carolina Division of Archives and History, 1975), 28.

for its inspiration.[23] However, the congress failed to approve even a rudimentary constitution, putting in place a temporary government headed by a council of safety until elections for a special convention could be called.[24]

The council of safety ordered elections for a Fifth Provincial Congress that would function as a constitutional convention, while simultaneously impressing on voters the importance of choosing delegates to frame a constitution.[25] This provincial congress convened on November 12, and appointed an eighteen-member committee to draft a constitution and a bill of rights.[26] Regarding the bill of rights, delegates were instructed by the people of Mecklenburg County: "….you shall endeavor that the form of Government shall set forth a bill of rights containing the rights of the people and of individuals which shall never be infringed in any future time by the law-making power or other derived powers in the State."[27] The placement of communal "rights of the people" before individual rights is noteworthy, and reflects the precedence of the former over the latter.

The convention adopted a declaration of rights on December 17, 1776, one day before the adoption of the constitution or frame of government, even though the proposed constitution was reported to the convention six days earlier than the declaration.[28] This sequence suggests "that the convention looked upon the Bill of Rights as more fundamental than the constitution."[29] Rights were declared and recognized, not

[23] Frank Nash, "The North Carolina Constitution of 1776 and its Makers," *The James Sprunt Historical Publications* 11, no. 2 (1912): 11–12; Fletcher M. Green, *Constitutional Development in the South Atlantic States, 1776–1860: A Study in the Evolution of Democracy* (Chapel Hill: University of North Carolina Press, 1930), 49.

[24] Ganyard, *Emergence of North Carolina's Revolutionary State Government*, 63–67.

[25] Ibid., 68. "Voters were asked 'to pay the greatest attention' to the election of delegates who were 'not only to make Laws for the good Government of, but also to form a Constitution for this State, that this last as it is the Corner Stone of all Law, so it ought to be fixed and Permanent, and that according as it is well or ill Ordered it must tend in the first degree to promote the happiness or Misery of the State.'" Lefler and Newsome, *History of a Southern State*, 220.

[26] Ibid., 221.

[27] "Instructions from Inhabitants of Mecklenburg County to Their Delegates for the Provincial Congress of North Carolina," in Saunders, *Colonial Records*, 10:870a.

[28] Ibid., 954, 967, 973–974.

[29] Green, *Constitutional Development in the South Atlantic States*, 71.

granted by governments, making a declaration of rights an independent pre-condition for the creation of a frame of government.

Constitutional Developments: 1776 Declaration and Constitution

The twenty-five articles that made up the declaration reflected the influence of the constitutions of several other states, most notably those of Virginia, Maryland, and Pennsylvania.[30] However, the particular selection and fine-tuning of provisions demonstrated that the aim was to form a new government suited to the unique circumstances and democratic spirit of the people of North Carolina. The delegates crafted a document that both reflected what the people had requested in their instructions (e.g., popular sovereignty [Decl. 1776, Art. I], trial by jury [ibid., Art. XIV], and frequent elections [ibid., Art. XX]), and addressed contentious issues like state sovereignty (ibid., Art. II), taxation (ibid., Art. XVI), and judicial independence (ibid., Art. IV). The new constitution was not submitted to the voters for ratification, unsurprising given the ongoing war, the infancy of constitution-making generally, and the absence of a clear demarcation "between ordinary and fundamental law."[31]

The new constitution rested on popular sovereignty, the foundation of republican government. The declaration began with the unalloyed assertion "[t]hat all political power is vested in and derived from the people only." Unlike neighboring Virginia and South Carolina, in North Carolina, no great wealth differential existed in the colony,[32] and the anti-aristocracy provisions in the declaration and constitution indicated resistance to any measures that might create one. Unearned and inherited emoluments and privileges were prohibited (Decl. 1776, Arts. III, XXII), and perpetuities (restrictions making an estate inalienable perpetually) and monopolies disallowed (ibid., Art. XXIII; Const. 1776, Art.

[30] John V. Orth, "Fundamental Principles in North Carolina Constitutional History," *North Carolina Law Review* 69, no. 5 (1991): 1358. William Hooper, North Carolina's delegate to the Continental Congress, sent a letter to the convention with copies of other states' newly adopted constitutions. John V. Orth and Paul Martin Newby, *The North Carolina State Constitution*, 2nd ed. (New York: Oxford University Press, 2013), 5.

[31] Orth, "Fundamental Principles," 1358; Lefler and Newsome, *History of a Southern State*, 221.

[32] Roger Ekirch, *'Poor Carolina': Politics and Society in Colonial North Carolina, 1729–1776* (Chapel Hill: University of North Carolina Press, 1981), 32.

XLIII). Schools for the instruction of youth were to be established by the legislature with teachers supported by the public, "at low prices" (Const. 1776, Art. XLI).

Several provisions in the document solidified the notion that the community had an architectonic right to determine the nature and scope of liberties and to balance them against the interests and well-being of society as a whole. Even the "natural and inalienable" right to worship God according to the dictates of one's conscience (Decl. 1776, Art. XIX) did not include allowing non-Protestants to hold state office.[33] Communal rights and duties were correlative and were linked to the preservation of republican government. They included, among others, the right/duty to serve on juries (ibid., Arts. IX, XIV); the right/duty to bear arms to defend the state (ibid., Art. XVII); and the right/duty of the people to assemble to consult for their common good and instruct their representatives (ibid., Art. XVIII).

Suffrage

While the declaration announced that political power was derived from the people, the form of government defined the "people" who would grant such power. Freemen twenty-one years of age or older—white or black[34]—who had been inhabitants of the state for at least twelve months and paid public taxes were eligible to vote for members of the house of commons. Owners of fifty acres of land could vote for members of the senate.[35]

[33] Const. 1776, Art. XXXII provided: "That no person, who shall deny the being of God or the truth of the Protestant religion, or the divine authority either of the Old or New Testaments, or who shall hold religious principles incompatible with the freedom and safety of the State, shall be capable of holding any office or place of trust or profit in the civil department within this State".

[34] Orth and Newby, *North Carolina State Constitution*, 14. Free blacks did vote in some counties and "their numbers in a few places were substantial." Ibid. In a close vote, they were disenfranchised by constitutional amendment in 1835. Ibid.

[35] Const. 1776, Arts. VII–VIII.

Structural Provisions

Officeholders were required to meet the following qualifications:

Office	*Minimum age*	*Estate*	*Residency*	*Religion*
Governor	30 years	Freehold above 1000 pounds	At least 5 years within state	Protestant
Senator	No age specified	Freehold estate of 300 acres possessed for 1 year within county he represents	At least 1 year within county he represents	Protestant
Representative	No age specified	Freehold or life estate of 100 acres possessed for 6 months within county he represents	At least 1 year within county he represents	Protestant

Placing time requirements on property ownership ensured that the people's representatives had developed a vested interest in the county they would serve.

North Carolina's declaration and form of government worked in tandem—the former announced the principles, the latter provided substantive and procedural implementation. The declaration called for frequent elections; the form of government established annual elections for both branches of the legislature (Decl. 1776, Art. XX; Const. 1776, Arts. II, III). The declaration announced a commitment to the separation of powers (Decl. 1776, Art. IV); the form of government created a new upper house of the legislature—the senate—to replace the former executive council, thereby transferring the legislative powers formerly practiced by an executive agency to the legislative branch,[36] and prohibited high-ranking government officials, including judges, from plural officeholding (Const. 1776, Arts. XXVIII–XXX, XXXV). The independence of the judiciary was protected through constitutional provisions providing that judges of the supreme courts of law and equity and admiralty courts were to serve during good behavior (ibid., Arts. XIII, XXXIII), and receive adequate salaries (ibid., Art. XXI). The governor was also

[36] Const. 1776, Art. I.

guaranteed an adequate salary (ibid., Art. XXI), and could serve no more than three out of every six years (ibid., Art. XV).

North Carolina's first state governor, Thomas Burke, recognized the importance of an independent judiciary as a barrier to government violations of the people's rights. In 1781, he objected to a court bill that would have created a treason tribunal whose judges were to be chosen by the governor and would serve at his pleasure, arguing that it violated the separation of powers provision in the declaration of rights.[37] An independent judiciary was a structural precondition that made judicial review possible. In 1787, the North Carolina Court of Conference (which later became the Supreme Court of North Carolina) was one of the first state courts to declare an act of the legislature unconstitutional.[38] In that case, *Bayard v. Singleton*, the high court ruled that an anti-Loyalist statute barring suits brought by individuals to recover confiscated property violated the right to jury trial in controversies respecting property found in Article XIV of the declaration.[39]

Postscript: North Carolina's first constitution, as amended and revised, served as the state's governing document for nearly a century. Three years after the Civil War ended, a new constitution was adopted by popular vote. The 1868 constitution contained a lengthy declaration of rights that began with an equality clause notably absent from its predecessor: "That we hold it to be self-evident that all men are created equal." With the institution of slavery abolished, this was no longer an inconvenient truth. Property and race requirements for voters and officeholders were eliminated in the frame of government, two years before the latter was banned by the Fifteenth Amendment. The declaration articulated the new understanding that "political rights and privileges are not dependent upon or modified by property, therefore no property qualifications ought to affect the right to vote or hold office."

[37] Gerber, "Origins of an Independent Judiciary," 1816.

[38] Ibid., 1817.

[39] Orth and Newby, *North Carolina State Constitution*, 11. *Bayard* was decided sixteen years before *Marbury v. Madison* (1803), and was cited by Chief Justice John Marshall in *Marbury*. Price, "There Ought to Be a Bill of Rights," 435.

Constitution of North Carolina [1776]

A Declaration of Rights, &C.

I. That all political power is vested in and derived from the people only.[40]

II. That the people of this State ought to have the sole and exclusive right of regulating the internal government and police thereof.[41]

III. That no man or set of men are entitled to exclusive or separate emoluments or privileges from the community, but in consideration of public services.[42]

IV. That the legislative, executive, and supreme judicial powers of government, ought to be forever separate and distinct from each other.[43]

[40] Similar to Va. Decl. 1776, sec. 2. The instructions sent by the people of Mecklenburg and Orange counties emphasized this notion, stating that "[p]olitical power is of two kinds, one principal and superior, the other derived and inferior," and "[t]he principal supreme power is possessed by the people at large, the derived and inferior power by the servants which they employ." Saunders, *Colonial Records*, 10:870b, 870f. Both counties referred to government throughout their instructions as the "derived inferior power." Ibid., 870b, 870f–h.

[41] This declaration of state sovereignty, taken verbatim from Maryland's declaration of rights, was the culmination of efforts to assert the state's rights as an independent entity. In 1775, the Third Provincial Congress required its members and all public officials to sign a "Test" denying the authority of Parliament to tax or "regulate the internal police" of the colonies. "Minutes of the Provincial Congress of North Carolina," Saunders, *Colonial Records*, 10:171–172. After authorizing Continental Congress delegates to support independence, the Fourth Provincial Congress reserved "to this Colony the Sole, and Exclusive right of forming a Constitution and Laws for this Colony, and of appointing delegates from time to time...to meet the delegates of the other Colonies." "Proceedings of the Fourth Provincial Congress, April 12, 1776," in Saunders, *Colonial Records*, 10:512.

[42] Similar to Va. Decl. 1776, sec. 4. This article likely served as an anti-corruption measure, directed at the use of public office for patronage purposes. It also implemented the directive in the Mecklenburg instructions: "you shall oppose everything that leans to aristocracy or power in the hands of the rich and chief men exercised to the oppression of the poor." Saunders, *Colonial Records*, 10:870a. This antipathy towards an aristocratic power structure was consistent with North Carolina's pre-Revolutionary experience. The province's colonial legislature repeatedly refused to formally approve the Fundamental Constitutions (five versions were promulgated between 1669 and 1698), which attempted to establish a hereditary nobility. Lefler and Newsome, *History of a Southern State*, 39–40.

[43] Nearly identical to Md. Decl. 1776, Art. VI, and accords with instructions from the people of Mecklenburg and Orange. See Saunders, *Colonial Records*, 10:870b, 870g, 870h. The lifetime tenure afforded judges by the constitution (Arts. XIII and XXXIII) ended a longstanding dispute between the colony's general assembly, which wanted to

V. That all powers of suspending laws, or the execution of laws, by any authority, without consent of the Representatives of the people, is injurious to their rights, and ought not to be exercised.[44]

VI. That elections of members, to serve as Representatives in General Assembly, ought to be free.[45]

VII. That, in all criminal prosecutions, every man has a right to be informed of the accusation against him, and to confront the accusers and witnesses with other testimony, and shall not be compelled to give evidence against himself.[46]

VIII. That no freeman shall be put to answer any criminal charge, but by indictment, presentment, or impeachment.

IX. That no freeman shall be convicted of any crime, but by the unanimous verdict of a jury of good and lawful men, in open court, as heretofore used.

make judges independent of royal authority by giving them tenure during good behavior, and the Crown, which allowed judges to serve only at its pleasure and vetoed any laws to the contrary. Earle H. Ketcham, "Sources of the North Carolina Constitution of 1776," The North Carolina Historical Review 6, no. 3 (July 1929):235; Gerber, "Origins of an Independent Judiciary," 1798–1807.

[44] The fifth article, identical to Va. Decl. 1776, sec. 7 and paraphrasing the 1689 English Bill of Rights, highlighted the legislature's role as exercising the sole authority to suspend laws. This principle was alluded to in both the Mecklenburg and Orange instructions. See Saunders, *Colonial Records*, 10:870b, 870f–g.

[45] Similar to Va. Decl. 1776, sec. 6. Delegates did not specifically include a right of suffrage in the declaration, but included liberal voter qualifications in the frame of government (Decl. 1776, Arts. VII–IX).

[46] The seventh, eighth, and ninth articles offered protections for those accused of crimes. The language of the seventh and ninth articles closely resembled that of the Virginia declaration's eighth section. Jury trials in criminal cases had been a long-standing practice in North Carolina, guaranteed both in the instructions to the Lords Proprietors and by acts of the assembly. Other procedural protections had been enshrined in early law, such as "An Act to Direct the Method to be observed in the Examination & Commitment of Criminals" (1715), which specified that no person within the province could be imprisoned "until Examination thereof be first had before some Magistrate." *The Earliest Printed Laws Of North Carolina, 1669–1751*, ed. John D. Cushing (Wilmington, DE: M. Glazier, 1977), 2:19. North Carolina's requirement of indictment, presentment, or impeachment in Article VIII added substance and another layer of protection to an accused's right to be informed of the accusation against him.

X. That excessive bail should not be required, nor excessive fines imposed, nor cruel or unusual punishments inflicted.[47]

XI. That general warrants—whereby an officer or messenger may be commanded to search suspected places, without evidence of the fact committed, or to seize any person or persons, not named, whose offenses are not particularly described, and supported by evidence—are dangerous to liberty, and ought not to be granted.[48]

XII. That no freeman ought to be taken, imprisoned, or disseized of his freehold, liberties or privileges, or outlawed, or exiled, or in any manner destroyed, or deprived of his life, liberty, or property, but by the law of the land.[49]

XIII. That every freeman, restrained of his liberty, is entitled to a remedy, to inquire into the lawfulness thereof, and to remove the same, if unlawful; and that such remedy ought not to be denied or delayed.[50]

XIV. That in all controversies at law, respecting property, the ancient mode of trial, by jury, is one of the best securities of the rights of the people, and ought to remain sacred and inviolable.[51]

[47] In the clause concerning punishments North Carolina followed Maryland's lead by replacing the conjunctive "and" found in the English Bill of Rights (1689) with the disjunctive "or," potentially broadening the protection offered by the clause. See Md. Decl. 1776, Art. XXII. The North Carolina Assembly had included "imposing excessive fines," among the complaints listed in the articles of impeachment against Crown appointed Chief Justice William Smith in 1740. Gerber, "Origins of an Independent Judiciary," 1797.

[48] Similar to Va. Decl. 1776, sec. 10.

[49] Article XII echoed nearly word for word the due process clause (Chapter 39) of Magna Carta. North Carolinians held this provision in high esteem: they had incorporated it into their statute books in 1749. Act of 1749, Ch. 1, in Clark, *State Records*, 23:317. The wording closely resembled a provision in the Maryland Declaration of Rights, except North Carolina's framers, inexplicably, chose to leave out the phrase "the judgment of his peers" customarily found near the end of the clause. They may have assumed that jury trials, protected in the ninth and fourteenth articles, were part of "the law of the land." See Md. Decl. 1776, Art. XXI.

[50] This article was likely inspired by the thirteenth article of Maryland's declaration of rights, and a portion of Chapter 29 of the 1225 confirmation of Magna Carta which stated: "to no one will [we] refuse or delay right or justice." By including this provision, the Fifth Provincial Congress implied a right to habeas corpus and enhanced the role of the judiciary in protecting the liberties of the people.

[51] Similar to Va. Decl. 1776, sec. 11. The ninth article of the declaration guaranteed jury trials in all criminal prosecutions; this article provided no less for civil trials. Although the use of "ought" suggests this article may have been precatory, North Carolina's highest court held it to be a legally enforceable right when it struck down an anti-Loyalist statute

XV. That the freedom of the press is one of the great bulwarks of liberty, and therefore ought never to be restrained.[52]

XVI. That the people of this State ought not to be taxed, or made subject to the payment of any impost or duty, without the consent of themselves, or their Representatives in General Assembly, freely given.[53]

XVII. That the people have a right to bear arms, for the defence of the State; and, as standing armies, in time of peace, are dangerous to liberty, they ought not to be kept up; and that the military should be kept under strict subordination to, and governed by, the civil power.[54]

XVIII. That the people have a right to assemble together, to consult for their common good, to instruct their Representatives, and to apply to the Legislature, for redress of grievances.[55]

XIX. That all men have a natural and unalienable right to worship Almighty God according to the dictates of their own consciences.[56]

barring suits brought by individuals to recover confiscated property in the landmark case of *Bayard v. Singleton* (1787).

[52] Similar to Va. Decl. 1776, sec. 12.

[53] Although this article prohibiting taxation without consent bore some resemblance to Article XII in Maryland's declaration, it is one of the few sections that North Carolina's delegates put entirely in their own words. Perhaps they were reflecting the animus North Carolinians traditionally felt toward taxation. Ganyard, "North Carolina During the American Revolution," 52. The taxes imposed by the British were the main grievance in the colony apart from the non-functioning court system. Crow, *Chronicle of North Carolina*, 14. This article also implemented the earlier assertion of state sovereignty in Article II, asserting another specific self-governing right of "the people of this State".

[54] This article is identical to Pa. Decl. 1776, Art. XIII, except for the omission of Pennsylvania's right of the people to bear arms for the defense of themselves... North Carolina's delegates limited the right to "the defence of the state," thereby placing it solely in a communal context. The language suggests that the purpose of this phrase was to establish the militia—a citizen-army as opposed to a standing army—as the proper custodian of public liberty; nevertheless, in 1843 the North Carolina Supreme Court interpreted it to allow citizens to carry guns "[f]or any lawful purpose—either of business or amusement." *State v. Hunley*, 25 N.C. 418, 422 (1843).

[55] Similar to Pa. Decl. 1776, Art. XVI. This article set forth the communitarian rights of assembly and petition—rights the freeholders of North Carolina had asserted when they met and formed county committees to address their grievances against royal governance during the summer of 1774. See p. 185, above; Sikes, *Transition of North Carolina*, 36–37.

[56] Similar to Pa. Decl. 1776, Art. II. Article XIX proclaimed the "unalienable" right of conscience. The framers disestablished the Church of England in the frame of government (Const. 1776, Art. XXXIV) and expanded their understanding of freedom of worship as

XX. That, for redress of grievances, and for amending and strengthening the laws, elections ought to be often held.[57]

XXI. That a frequent recurrence to fundamental principles is absolutely necessary, to preserve the blessings of liberty.[58]

XXII. That no hereditary emoluments, privileges or honors ought to be granted or conferred in this State.[59]

XXIII. That perpetuities and monopolies are contrary to the genius of a free State, and ought not to be allowed.[60]

freedom from compelled attendance or financial support of religion contrary to one's beliefs.

[57] Article XX contained wording similar to Md. Decl. 1776, Art. X, with a subtle but meaningful alteration. North Carolina's delegates changed the phrase "the legislature ought to be frequently convened," to "elections ought to be often held"—suggesting that their goal was popular sovereignty, not legislative supremacy. The choice of words implied that it was the people's responsibility to hold public officials accountable with their vote. This admonition was enforced in the constitution by the requirement of annual elections, just as the Mecklenburg instructions had requested. Const. 1776, Arts. II, III; Saunders, *Colonial Records*, 10:870c.

[58] Similar to Pa. Decl. 1776, Art. XIV. This was a call to recollect the "fundamental principles" of the natural rights republic. It was an aspirational provision not susceptible to legal enforcement, meant as a reminder and encouragement to citizens of their indispensable role in preserving liberty.

[59] Nearly identical to Md. Decl. 1776, Art. XL. Hereditary privileges were not uncommon in colonial North Carolina, as the Fundamental Constitutions of Carolina conferred upon the proprietors the power to issue patents for titles. The commitment to equality that formed the underpinnings of the Declaration of Independence was inconsistent with privileges, and both North Carolina and Maryland took steps to make sure no further titles would be granted.

[60] Consistent with the commitment to equality and popular sovereignty reflected in the Mecklenburg and Orange instructions, this article prohibited perpetuities and monopolies. Maryland's declaration also contained a provision barring monopolies, reflecting the popular contemporary view that artificial barriers to equality should be eliminated. Md. Decl. 1776, Art. XXXIX; see Joshua C. Tate, "Perpetuities and the Genius of a Free State," *Vanderbilt Law Review* 67, no. 6 (November 2014): 1823, 1831. Perpetuities were railed against by Blackstone, who argued that such devices made estates "incapable of answering those ends of social commerce, and providing for the sudden contingencies of private life, for which property was first established." Ibid., 1832, quoting William Blackstone, *Commentaries on the Laws of England* (Oxford: Printed at the Clarendon Press, 1765–1769), 2:174. The framers may have had in mind the persistent instability of land ownership arising out of the mismanagement of a portion of state land owned by absentee English Lord Carteret, the Second Earl Granville (who had inherited the latter title through heredity), a mismanagement that led to the 1759 Enfield Riot and several subsequent episodes of civil unrest. Ibid., 1826–1829.

XXIV. That retrospective laws, punishing facts committed before the existence of such laws, and by them only declared criminal, are oppressive, unjust, and incompatible with liberty; wherefore no *ex post facto* law ought to be made.[61]

XXV. The property of the soil, in a free government, being one of the essential rights of the collective body of the people, it is necessary, in order to avoid future disputes, that the limits of the State should be ascertained with precision; and as the former temporary line between North and South Carolina, was confirmed, and extended by Commissioners, appointed by the Legislatures of the two States, agreeable to the order of the late King George the Second, in Council, that line, and that only, should be esteemed the southern boundary of this State as follows: that is to say, beginning on the sea side, at a cedar stake, at or near the mouth of Little River (being the southern extremity of Brunswick county,) and running from thence a north-west course, through the boundary house, which stands in thirty-three degrees fifty-six minutes, to thirty-five degrees north latitude; and from thence a west course so far as is mentioned in the Charter of King Charles the Second, to the late Proprietors of Carolina. Therefore all the territories, seas, waters, and harbours, with their appurtenances, lying between the line above described, and the southern line of the State of Virginia, which begins on the sea shore, in thirty-six degrees thirty minutes, north latitude, and from thence runs west, agreeable to the said Charter of King Charles, are the right and property of the people of this State, to be held by them in sovereignty; any partial line, without the consent of the Legislature of this State, at any time thereafter directed, or laid out, in anywise notwithstanding: —*Provided always*, That this Declaration of Rights shall not prejudice any nation or nations of Indians, from enjoying such hunting-grounds as may have been, or hereafter shall be, secured to them by any former or future Legislature of this State: —*And provided also*, That it shall not be construed so as to prevent the establishment of one or more governments westward of this State, by consent of the Legislature: —*And provided further*, That nothing herein contained shall affect the titles or possessions of individuals holding or claiming under the laws heretofore in force, or

[61] Identical to Md. Decl. 1776, Art. XV. Orange County had included a similar prohibition in its instructions to the delegates. Saunders, *Colonial Records*, 10:870h.

grants heretofore made by the late King George the Second, or his predecessors, or the late lords proprietors, or any of them.[62]

The Constitution, or Form of Government, &C.

* * *

VII. That all freemen, of the age of twenty-one years, who have been inhabitants of any one county within the State twelve months immediately preceding the day of any election, and possessed of a freehold within the same county of fifty acres of land, for six months next before, and at the day of election, shall be entitled to vote for a member of the Senate.

VIII. That all freemen of the age of twenty-one years, who have been inhabitants of any one county within this State twelve months immediately preceding the day of any election, and shall have paid public taxes, shall be entitled to vote for members of the House of Commons for the county in which he resides.

* * *

XXXIV. That there shall be no establishment of any one religious church or denomination in this State, in preference to any other; neither shall any person, on any pretence whatsoever, be compelled to attend any place of worship contrary to his own faith or judgement, nor be obliged to pay, for the purchase of any glebe, or the building of any house of worship, or for the maintenance of any minister or ministry, contrary to what he believes right, or has voluntarily and personally engaged to perform; but all persons shall be at liberty to exercise their own mode of worship:—*Provided*, That nothing herein contained shall be construed to exempt preachers of treasonable or seditious discourses, from legal trial and punishment.[63]

[62] Much of the language contained in this article seems better suited to a property deed than a bill of rights; however, the delegates to the Fifth Provincial Congress believed that establishing the boundary line of their state's territory was necessary to protect the collective property right of the people. Additionally, it expressed solicitude for the rights of Indian nations, and included a grandfather clause protecting property granted by English monarchs prior to independence.

[63] See footnote 56 above. Leonard Levy reads the second clause as banning even preferential aid. But the practice of banning general assessments but requiring support of

* * *

XXXIX. That the person of a debtor, where there is not a strong presumption of fraud, shall not be continued in prison, after delivering up, *bona fide*, all his estate real and personal, for the use of his creditors, in such manner as shall hereafter be regulated by law. All prisoners shall be bailable by sufficient sureties, unless for capital offenses, when the proof is evident, or the presumption great.[64]

XL. That every foreigner, who comes to settle in this State, having first taken an oath of allegiance to the same, may purchase, or, by other means, acquire, hold, and transfer land, or other real estate; and after one year's residence, shall be deemed a free citizen.[65]

XLI. That a school or schools shall be established by the Legislature, for the convenient instruction of youth, with such salaries to the masters, paid by the public, as may enable them to instruct at low prices; and, all useful learning shall be duly encouraged, and promoted, in one or more universities.[66]

the church of one's choice employed in other states belies that reading. See Leonard W. Levy, *The Establishment Clause: Religion and the First Amendment*, 2nd ed. (Chapel Hill: University of North Carolina Press, 1994), 53.

[64] Nearly identical to Pa. Const. 1776, sec. 28. Despite gaining an early reputation as a haven for debtors based upon a 1669 Albemarle County statute protecting new settlers from foreign creditors for a period of five years, North Carolina generally followed traditional English debtor-creditor law, including imprisonment for debt. This article provided relief from confinement for debtors who had not engaged in fraud and who had previously tendered all of their assets to satisfy their creditors. The article also provided a right of bail for all non-capital offenses.

[65] Article XL encouraged settlement by easing the property restrictions on foreigners that had existed in English law, and by giving foreigners the same rights as native-born freemen after they took an oath of allegiance and had integrated into the community through a one-year residency requirement. It was likely inspired by section 42 of the 1776 Pennsylvania Constitution, which contained the same guarantees but with slightly more stringent requirements: Foreign settlers had to be "of good character," and were required to reside in the state for two years before becoming eligible to run for legislative office.

[66] Similar to Pa. Const. 1776, sec. 44. The drafters viewed public education as an indispensable prerequisite for successful self-government and for sustaining a moral, well-ordered community. This article provided for the establishment of public schools, and mandated that the public cover the cost of these schools—thus making education a communal responsibility. The government of North Carolina did not establish a public school fund until 1825. "Chapter One: The Beginning of North Carolina's Public Schools &

* * *

XLIII. That the future Legislature of this State shall regulate entails, in such a manner as to prevent perpetuities.[67]

XLIV. That the Declaration of Rights is hereby declared to be part of the Constitution of this State, and ought never to be violated, on any pretence whatsoever.[68]

The Literary Fund," North Carolina State Board of Education, accessed October 12, 2018, https://stateboard.ncpublicschools.gov/about-sbe/history/chapter-one.

67 Identical to Pa. Const. 1776, sec. 37. Entailment was the practice by which land could only be inherited or transferred to a lineal descendant, in perpetuity, so that wealth remained in a single family. John V. Orth, "North Carolina Constitutional History," *North Carolina Law Review* 70, no. 6 (1992): 1767. The general assembly ended the practice in 1784, explaining that "entails of estates tend only to raise the wealth and importance of particular families and individuals, giving them an unequal and undue influence in a republic, and prove in manifold instances the source of great contention and injustice." Act to Regulate the Descent of Real Estates, to do away Entails, to Make Provision for Widows, and Prevent Frauds in the Execution of Last Wills and Testaments, 1784, Ch. 22, sec. 5, in Clark, *State Records*, 24:574.

68 North Carolina followed Pennsylvania's example by incorporating its declaration of rights into the frame of government.

Vermont

Vermont's path to becoming the fourteenth state was unique in several respects. An independent republic for fourteen years until its admission into the Union in 1791, Vermont was never a colony with a founding charter. It had no fundamental orders, agreements, compact, or "laws and liberties." There was no previous government to accommodate, no commercial enterprise, and no errand into the wilderness. Peter S. Onuf writes, "[i]n this sense, Vermont was the only true American republic, for it alone had truly created itself."[1]

The area now known as Vermont consisted of land claimed by New York, based on that colony's 1664 English royal charter from King Charles II to his brother James, the Duke of York. The province of Massachusetts Bay also claimed a portion of the territory based on the 1628/1629 charter of the Massachusetts Bay Colony issued by King Charles I. Following a 1740 decree of King George II fixing the Massachusetts-New Hampshire boundary, New Hampshire argued that its western boundary was made coterminous with those of Massachusetts and Connecticut and thus incorporating Vermont.

In 1749, New Hampshire governor Benning Wentworth began to sell parcels of the disputed land, known as the "New Hampshire Grants," to settlers. New York objected to these grants, setting the stage for further royal intervention. The parties submitted their dispute to the Crown in

[1] *The Origins of the Federal Republic: Jurisdictional Controversies in the United States, 1775–1787* (Philadelphia: University of Pennsylvania Press, 1983), 145.

P. J. Galie et al., *Bills of Rights Before the Bill of Rights*,
https://doi.org/10.1007/978-3-030-44301-6_9

1754, but it was not until 1764 that King George III issued a decree—upholding New York's claim to the disputed territory but not explicitly voiding Wentworth's transfers. New York officials treated the New Hampshire Grants as invalid and began issuing conflicting patents. In 1770, following successful eviction actions in New York courts by the new landowners to displace the New Hampshire grantees, Ethan Allen organized an independent militia, "The Green Mountain Boys," to defend the claims of those holding New Hampshire Grants. The precariousness of their land titles meant that "security of property came first; the other freedoms guaranteed by the Bill of Rights would follow."[2]

Between 1764 and 1777 Vermont existed in a state of nature. Absent a legitimate government, law and order were in short supply. Anti-court mobs and sporadic armed conflict with New York punctuated the territory. Vermonters were in revolt against New York and against the British—a revolution within the Revolution. Thomas Chittenden, the first governor of Vermont, described the first settlers as having "lived in a state of independence from their first settlement, governing themselves, until their State government was formed in January, 1777, by committees and conventions in the manner afterward followed in the other States on their first separation from the British government."[3]

Allen's supporters began a drumbeat for independence from New York. By early 1774, resistance to that state had become an organized rebellion. Notwithstanding some initial differences of opinion between eastern and western Vermonters, at a convention held in April 1775 in Westminster both parts of the territory united to renounce New York rule. A series of conventions between January 1776 and January 1777 petitioned the Continental Congress for recognition of the New Hampshire Grants area as a separate entity from New York—pleas that fell on deaf ears.

Bereft of a colonial charter and unable to obtain congressional recognition, Vermonters embraced what was an article of faith among Americans,

[2] H. Nicholas Muller III, "Freedom and Unity: Vermont's Search for Security of Property, Liberty, and Popular Government," in *The Bill of Rights and the States: The Colonial and Revolutionary Origins of American Liberties*, ed. Patrick T. Conley and John P. Kaminski (Madison, WI: Madison House, 1992), 183. Muller provides a more detailed explanation of these land claim disputes. Ibid., 184–195.

[3] As quoted in *Genealogical and Family History of the State of Vermont: A Record of the Achievements of Her People in the Making of a Commonwealth and the Founding of a Nation*, comp. Hiram Carleton (New York: Lewis Publishing Company, 1903), viii.

that "self-determination exercised through representative forms of government and republican government are synonymous expressions of the same ideal."[4] Founding documents were playing a critical role in defining these principles and rights as well as providing legitimacy for states in the process of writing and adopting their constitutions. The enormous prestige and importance accorded charters in defining rights during the Revolutionary period were demonstrated by Vermont's dubious claim that it possessed a "charter of liberty from Heaven."[5]

Following the Declaration of Independence and the directive from the Continental Congress that states prepare governing charters, convention delegates met at Westminster in January 1777 and formally declared independence from the Crown and New York as the state of "New Connecticut." It was the state's first formal act of self-government. Delegates obtained counsel from Dr. Thomas Young, a well-known radical and close friend of Ethan Allen living in Pennsylvania. Recognizing that the colony had no historical existence prior to declaring independence and no charter on which to rely, Young sent a copy of the constitution adopted by Pennsylvania in 1776 as a model. He also suggested that the state rename itself Vermont.[6]

On June 4, 1777, delegates met in Windsor, appointed a committee to draft a constitution, and scheduled a second session for July second. Joseph Bowker, the convention president, sent a letter to the towns advising of the convention's activities and recommending they elect delegates "to meet the grand convention at Windsor ... to form a constitution for the state of Vermont."[7]

The convention met as planned. Threatened by British military victories, delegates were forced to move quickly. They endorsed unanimously a constitution on July eighth; called for elections for a general assembly to be held in December; set up a council of safety to govern Vermont until the elections were held; and then rushed off to defend their homes. The convention reconvened in December, made some modifications to

[4] Gary J. Aichele, "Making the Vermont Constitution: 1777–1824," *Vermont History* 56, no. 3 (Summer 1988): 182.

[5] Peter S. Onuf, "State-Making in Revolutionary America: Independent Vermont as a Case Study," *Journal of American History* 67, no. 4 (March 1981): 805.

[6] Aichele, "Making the Vermont Constitution," 179.

[7] Ibid., citing Nathaniel Hendricks, "The Experiment in Vermont Constitutional Government," *Vermont History* 34, no. 1 (January 1966): 63.

the document, and rescheduled elections for the newly created legislature in March of the following year.

Scholarly disagreement exists as to whether the constitution was ratified by the people. Ira Allen's *The Natural and Political History of the State of Vermont* (1798) notes that the town of Bennington objected to the constitution, due to the lack of popular ratification.[8] H. Nicholas Muller notes that some towns did consider the draft constitution.[9] Nathaniel Hendricks goes further: "To conclude, we may say with a great deal of certainty that the constitution of the new state was indeed submitted to the people for their approval at the regular town meetings held in the spring of 1778."[10]

To remove any doubt about the constitution's validity, in 1779 and 1782, the Vermont legislature took the unusual step of enacting statutes declaring the constitution adopted by the 1777 convention "be forever considered, held, and maintained, as part of the laws of this State."[11] It took this action "[t]o prevent disputes respecting the legal force of the constitution of this State…."[12]

Constitutional Developments: 1777 Declaration and Constitution

The preamble to the 1777 constitution provides a striking example of the independent path Vermont followed. It opened and closed with views consonant with other state constitutions: that governments rest on the consent of the governed; are instituted "for the security and protection of the community;" enable members of the community to enjoy their natural rights; and, upon failing in their duties, are subject to alteration or abolition by the people. The preamble specified two additional rights:

[8] Cited in Nathaniel Hendricks, "A New Look at the Ratification of the Vermont Constitution of 1777," *Vermont History* 34, no. 2 (April 1966): 136.

[9] Muller, "Freedom and Unity," 200.

[10] Hendricks, "A New Look," 139.

[11] An Act for securing the general privileges of the people, and establishing common law and the constitution, as part of the laws of this State, February 1779, *Vermont State Papers; Being a Collection of Records and Documents, Connected with the Assumption and Establishment of Government by the People of Vermont*, comp. William Slade (Middlebury, VT: J. W. Copeland, 1823), 287–288; An Act establishing the Constitution of Vermont, and securing the Privileges of the People, June 1782, Slade, *Vermont State Papers*, 449.

[12] Act establishing the Constitution of Vermont, 449.

the right to withdraw allegiance when protection has been withheld and the right to separate when the property of part of the community has been disowned. The former was aimed at Great Britain; the latter at New York.

The opening and closing paragraphs containing these sentiments were taken nearly word for word from the preamble to Pennsylvania's 1776 constitution. But the Vermont preamble was much longer and consisted of fourteen paragraphs of complaints about New York. The audience for this declaration was the Continental Congress, which had yet to take decisive action on the demands of Vermont's dissidents. It was the first attempt on the American continent to apply the principles enunciated in the Declaration of Independence to a member (New York) of the Continental Congress that had approved that declaration.[13]

A unique feature of the Vermont Constitution was the absence of provisions found in other state constitutions meant to eliminate, prohibit, or continue practices that were part of their colonial heritage. Because Vermont was a new jurisdiction, words such as "heretofore" were unnecessary.[14]

The Vermont Constitution contained several rights provisions similar in wording and substance to the Pennsylvania Constitution.[15] Unique to the Vermont Constitution was a prohibition against adult slavery (Decl. 1777, Art. I)—a first among the American states.[16] Although Vermont's first constitution did not specifically incorporate English common law, the common law was incorporated by statute in 1779.[17]

Vermont's constitution expressed a strong commitment to popular sovereignty (Decl. 1777, Art. V), and provided various procedures to ensure that the will of the legislature accurately reflected the will of the

[13] The 1786 Vermont Constitution kept the preamble, but it was removed from the constitution adopted in 1793. By that time, the dispute with New York had been resolved.

[14] Paul Gillies provides examples of these differences by contrasting Vermont's provisions with those of Pennsylvania. "Not Quite a State of Nature: Derivations of Early Vermont Law," *Vermont Law Review* 23, no. 1 (Fall 1998): 99–131.

[15] The Vermont constitutions of 1777 and 1786 each had two parts: a declaration of rights (Chapter I) and a plan or frame of government (Chapter II). For ease of the reader, references to Chapter I will be noted as "Decl." and references to Chapter II will be noted as "Const.".

[16] See footnote 25 for a more through description of that provision.

[17] Act for securing the general privileges of the people, 287.

people. It mirrored Pennsylvania's in terms of giving citizens the tools to monitor the assembly by keeping the doors of the general assembly (house of representatives) open except when the general welfare required otherwise (Const. 1777, sec. XII) and requiring the votes and proceedings of that body to be printed weekly with the yeas and nays recorded when requested by one-third of the members (ibid., sec. XIII).[18] Vermont also adopted the Pennsylvania requirements that all bills be printed for the public before passage whenever possible, that bills not be passed until the session after their introduction, and that the purposes of the bills be stated in their preambles (ibid., sec. XIV). The rights to assemble and to instruct the legislature, by way of address, petition, or remonstrance, were also protected (Decl. 1777, Art. XVIII).

Suffrage

Vermont was the first state to grant universal manhood suffrage in its constitution. Paying taxes was not a prerequisite to voting for any state legislative office (Const. 1777, sec. VI). By eliminating the taxpayer requirement, Vermont went one step further than Pennsylvania in creating an unencumbered majoritarian order. Consistent with the belief that citizens should have some connection with the community, the constitution required one year of residency, the taking of a freeman's oath or affirmation, and "quiet and peaceable behavior" (ibid.).

Absent a charter defining its status as a colony and lacking recognition by the Continental Congress and surrounding colonies, Vermont relied heavily on popular consent for its legitimacy. As Peter Onuf noted, "nowhere in America did local communities become so thoroughly accustomed to such a high degree of political self-determination."[19] Not surprisingly, home rule powers featured prominently in the constitution. Members of the unicameral house of representatives, the governor, and members of the executive council were chosen by the freemen of every town in the state (Const. 1777, secs. VII, XVII), with voters exhorted to choose representatives known for their wisdom and virtue (ibid., sec. VII).

[18] The Pennsylvania Constitution required that yeas and nays be taken when two members required it. Pa. Const. 1776, sec. 14.

[19] Onuf, "State-Making," 813.

Structural Provisions

Although the Vermont Constitution lacked a formal declaration of separation of powers, it did contain sections specifying the different institutions that would exercise legislative and executive power (Const. 1777, secs. II, III) as well as mandating the establishment of courts of justice in each county (ibid., sec. IV). Members of the unicameral house of representatives served annual terms (ibid., sec. VIII). In addition to being freemen, members were required to have been residents of the town for one year before the election and to swear an oath acknowledging the Old and New Testaments and professing the Protestant religion (ibid., secs. VIII, IX). The constitution did not prohibit ministers from holding office.

The 1777 constitution required rotation in office for members of Congress: No Congressman could serve longer than two years sequentially, and would then be ineligible for reelection for three years (Const. 1777, sec. X). In two significant departures from the Pennsylvania model (and many other early state constitutions), Vermont did not require rotation for state offices and permitted plural office-holding. A document lauded as "the most democratic constitution of its time"[20] in practice operated "about as conservative as that in any of the states" with an "executive branch… noted for conservative stability because of its control by an entrenched oligarchy."[21] Constitutional amendment was off-limits to the legislature (Const. 1777, sec. VIII); revisions could only be initiated by a convention called by the council of censors (ibid., sec. XLIV), a thirteen-member body chosen every seven years to ensure the constitution was not being violated and that the branches of government were properly performing their duties.

[20] Michael A. Bellesiles, *Revolutionary Outlaws: Ethan Allen and the Struggle for Independence on the Early American Frontier* (Charlottesville: University Press of Virginia, 1993), 5.

[21] John N. Shaeffer, "A Comparison of the First Constitutions of Vermont and Pennsylvania," *Vermont History* 43, no. 1 (Winter, 1975): 36. A similar judgment is offered by Aichele, "Making the Vermont Constitution," 185.

Constitutional Developments: 1786 Declaration and Constitution

The 1777 constitution remained in effect less than a decade. The lack of separation of powers proved problematic. Judicial independence was lacking. Judges were elected annually by joint ballot of the governor, executive council, and assembly, and then later by the legislature. Nearly all supreme court judges were council members.[22] At its inaugural meeting in 1785, the council of censors issued a call for a constitutional convention. The state was beset with internal and external threats. Tensions with New York remained and internal divisions had precipitated a series of laws dealing with treason, rioting, and "inimical conduct."[23] The council proposed a constitution that would provide stability and legitimacy to the government. A constitutional convention met in June 1786 in Manchester and adopted a constitution containing most of the changes proposed by the council.

The most significant change involved adopting an explicit commitment to the separation of powers: "The legislative, executive and judiciary departments shall be separate and distinct, so that neither exercise the powers properly belonging to the other" (Const. 1786, sec. VI). The 1786 constitution also implemented restrictions on plural office-holding (ibid., sec. XXIII), and increased judicial independence by eliminating the legislature's role as a court of appeals. Vermont added four new rights sections closely resembling those found in Massachusetts's 1780 constitution: a "speech and debate clause" for legislators (Decl. 1786, Art. XVI); an article providing that only the legislature could suspend laws (ibid., Art. XVII); a prohibition against the use of law-martial against non-military personnel (ibid., Art. XIX); and a section barring judgments of felony guilt by the legislature (Const. 1786, sec. XVII).

Postscript: Vermont was admitted as the fourteenth state to the Union in 1791. In 1792, the council of censors recommended a constitutional convention. That convention, held in 1793, adopted a third constitution that, as amended, now governs the state. The current declaration of rights contains a number of the original rights provisions found in the 1786 declaration.

[22] Aichele, "Making the Vermont Constitution," 186–187, provides a fuller analysis of the methods of judicial selection and their consequences.

[23] Paul S. Gillies and D. Gregory Sanford, eds., *Records of the Council of Censors of the State of Vermont* (Montpelier, VT: Secretary of State, 1991), 19.

CONSTITUTION OF VERMONT [1777] AND CONSTITUTION OF VERMONT [1786][24]

Chapter I: A Declaration of the Rights of the Inhabitants of the State of Vermont

I. THAT all men are born equally free and independent, and have certain natural, inherent and unalienable rights, amongst which are, the enjoying and defending life and liberty;[-] acquiring, possessing and protecting property,[-] and pursuing and obtaining happiness and safety. Therefore, no male person, born in this country, or brought from over sea, ought to be holden by law, to serve any person, as a servant, slave[,] or apprentice, after he arrives to the age of twenty-one years,[;] nor female, in like manner, after she arrives to the age of eighteen years,[;] unless they are bound by their own consent, after they arrive to such age,[;] or bound by law, for the payment of debts, damages, fines, costs, or the like.[25]

II. That private property ought to be subservient to public uses, when necessity requires it; nevertheless, whenever any particular man's property is taken for the use of the public, the owner ought to receive an equivalent in money.[26]

III. That all men have a natural and unalienable right to worship ALMIGHTY GOD, [Almighty God] according to the dictates of their own

[24] Text that is not underlined or bracketed appeared in both constitutions. Text that is underlined appeared in the 1777 constitution but not the 1786 document. Text that is bracketed appeared in the latter but not the former.

[25] Vermont relied on Pennsylvania's declaration of inalienable rights, a reworded version of section 1 of the Virginia Declaration of Rights. Vermont took the principles to their logical conclusion, becoming the first state to abolish slavery. Notwithstanding the language of this article, recent research by Harvey Amani Whitfield indicates "that [t]he 1777 constitutional abolition of adult slavery did not end slavery... the end of Vermont slavery was contested, contingent, complicated and messy. Vermont made steps toward abolition, but slaveholding, kidnapping of free blacks, and child slavery continued until the early nineteenth century. Those who continued to own slaves were among the most respectable inhabitants of the state." *The Problem of Slavery in Early Vermont, 1777–1810* (Barre: Vermont Historical Society, 2014), 3.

[26] Article II announced the principle that the community had the final determination on how property would be used and for what purposes—in contemporary terms, the power of eminent domain. The article required that owners receive an equivalent of money, now referred to as "just compensation." Article IX of the declaration duplicated this provision with one important difference: it required the consent of the individual or his legal representatives without mentioning compensation. Article II marked the first appearance in an American state constitution of a just compensation requirement, but not the first appearance in the American colonies. The protection was found in section 8 of

consciences and understanding[s], [as in their opinion shall be] regulated by the word of GOD[God]; and that no man ought, or of right can be compelled to attend any religious worship, or erect, or support any place of worship, or maintain any minister, contrary to the dictates of his conscience; nor can any man who professes the protestant religion, be justly deprived or abridged of any civil right, as a citizen, on account of his religious sentiment[s], or peculiar mode of religious worship,[;] and that no authority can, or ought to be vested in, or assumed by, any power whatsoever, that shall, in any case, interfere with, or in any manner controul,[control] the rights of conscience, in the free exercise of religious worship: nevertheless[Nevertheless], every sect or denomination of people[Christians] ought to observe the Sabbath, or the Lord's day, and keep up, and support, some sort of religious worship, which to them shall seem most agreeable to the revealed will of GOD[God].[27]

the Massachusetts Body of Liberties (1641). Donald S. Lutz, ed., *Colonial Origins of the American Constitution: A Documentary History* (Indianapolis: Liberty Fund, 1998), 72.

[27] Vermont's religious liberty article guaranteed liberty of conscience, referring to such a right as "natural and unalienable." But the 1777 declaration's guarantee against being unjustly deprived or abridged of any civil right applied only to those who "professe[d] the protestant religion." This was in sharp contrast to the Pennsylvania Constitution, which allowed full protections to "any man, who acknowledge[d] the being of a God." (Pa. Decl. 1776, Art. II). What accounts for this divergence? Muller suggests this was an appeal to the east side of the state where the Congregational Church had taken root: "[I]ndeed, the background of the Grants' settlers was almost totally Protestant." Muller, "Freedom and Unity," 203. Egbert Benson, in a letter to Continental Congress President John Jay, suggested this was an attempt to preserve and protect the Protestant character of the community:

> ...Governor Chittenden *himself* is determined at all events not to reunite with us, for we may undoubtedly suppose such his determination, when with apparent Sincerity he says that his *religious* rights and privilidges would be in danger from a Union with a Government, by the fundamental [law] of which all Religions are tolerated and all Establishments expressly excluded.

Letter to John Jay, July 6, 1779, John Jay, *The Correspondence and Public Papers of John Jay*, ed. Henry P. Johnston (New York: G.P. Putnam's Sons, 1891), 1:212, http://oll.libertyfund.org/titles/jay-the-correspondence-and-public-papers-of-john-jay-vol-1-1763-1781. Consistent with this Protestant orientation, the frame of government required all members of the house of representatives to profess the "protestant religion" (Const. 1777, sec. IX). The 1786 declaration made several changes to this article. It eliminated the requirement that every denomination "support" some sort of religious worship, removing any perceived constitutional obligation to provide financial support. It also broadened the non-discrimination provision to include all men, not

[IV. Every person within this Commonwealth ought to find a certain remedy, by having recourse to the laws, for all injuries or wrongs which he may receive in his person, property, or character: he ought to obtain right and justice freely, and without being obliged to purchase it—completely, and without any denial—promptly, and without delay; conformably to the laws.][28]

IV. [V.] That the people of this State[, by their legal representatives,] have the sole, exclusive and inherent right of governing and regulating the internal police of the same.[29]

V. [VI.] That all power being originally inherent in, and consequently, derived from, the people; therefore, all officers of government, whether legislative or executive, are their trustees and servants, and at all times[, in a legal way,] accountable to them.[30]

VI. [VII.] That government is, or ought to be, instituted for the common benefit, protection, and security of the people, nation or community;[:] and not for the particular emolument or advantage of any single man, family or set of men, who are a part only of that community; and that the community hath an indubitable, unalienable[,] and indefeasible right[,] to reform, [or] alter, or abolish, government, in such manner as

just those professing the Protestant religion, and substituted "Christians" for "people" as those obligated to observe the Sabbath, likely a recognition of religious sects that do not observe a Sabbath. The retention of the duty to observe the Sabbath and "keep up some sort of religious worship" indicates Vermont was reluctant to sever completely the connection between a citizenry that worshipped regularly and a stable, well-ordered polity.

[28] This article, inserted into the 1786 declaration, provided citizens a right to a remedy for injuries or wrongs, "promptly" and "freely." Such clauses are referred to as right to remedy or open court provisions.

[29] Similar to Pa. Decl. 1776, Art. III. Adding the qualifier "by their legal representatives" in 1786 made clear the power of the people to govern and regulate the internal policies of the state was to be exercised through legitimate governmental means. With the Revolution behind them and the state plagued by rioting and other radical impulses, the actions of the extra-constitutional bodies that led the Revolutionary movement and engineered the creation of most of the other state constitutions seemed less appealing.

[30] Similar to Pa. Decl. 1776, Art. IV. The 1786 declaration modified this provision to specify that officers of the government were accountable to the people "in a legal way." Without such a qualification, the means chosen to ensure accountability could include extra-legal, as well as legal, actions.

shall be, by that community, judged [to be] most conducive to the public weal.[31]

VII. [VIII.] That those who are employed in the legislative and executive business of the State, may be restrained from oppression, the people have a right, at such periods as they may think proper, to reduce their public officers to a private station, and supply the vacancies by certain and regular elections[by their legal representatives, to enact laws for reducing their public officers to a private station, and for supplying their vacancies in a constitutional manner, by regular elections, at such periods as they may think proper].[32]

VIII. [IX.] That all elections ought to be free [and without corruption]; and that all freemen, having a sufficient, evident, common interest with, and attachment to, the community, have a right to elect officers, or[and] be elected into office.[33]

IX. [X.] That every member of society hath a right to be protected in the enjoyment of life, liberty and property,[;] and therefore, is bound to contribute his proportion towards the expense of that protection, and yield his personal service, when necessary, or an equivalent thereto;[:] but no part of a man's property can be justly taken from him, or applied to public uses, without his own consent, or that of his legal representatives[the representative body of the freemen]; nor can any man[,] who is conscientiously scrupulous of bearing arms, be justly compelled thereto, if he will pay such equivalent; nor are the people bound by any law, but such as they have, in like manner, assented to, for their common good. [And previous to any law being made to raise a tax, the

[31] Similar to Pa. Decl. 1776, Art. V. The 1786 revision eliminated the right of citizens to "abolish" their government, leaving them with the less incendiary rights to "reform" and "alter."

[32] Similar to Pa. Decl. 1776, Art. VI. In 1786, this right to reduce public officers to a private station was qualified with the language "by their legal representatives." Also, supplying vacancies was modified by the phrase "in a constitutional manner" and "certain" was added to "regular" as a modifier of elections. Delegates realized that without such specification, the implementation of the right would be uncertain, if not troubling. Vermont's 1793 constitution eliminated this article.

[33] Similar to Pa. Decl. 1776, Art. VII.

purpose, for which it is to be raised ought to appear evident to the Legislature to be of more service to the community, than the money would be if not collected.][34]

X. [XI.] That, in all prosecutions for criminal offences, a man hath a right to be heard, by himself and his counsel—to demand the cause and nature of his accusation—to be confronted with the witnesses—to call for evidence in his favor[favour], and a speedy public trial, by an impartial jury of the country;[,] without the unanimous consent of which jury, he cannot be found guilty;[–] nor can he be compelled to give evidence against himself;[–]nor can any man be justly deprived of his liberty, except by the laws of the land[,] or the judgment of his peers.[35]

XI. [XII.] That the people have a right to hold themselves, their houses, papers and possessions[,] free from search or seizure;[:] and therefore warrants, without oaths or affirmations first made, affording a sufficient foundation for them, and whereby any officer or messenger may be commanded or required to search suspected places, or to seize any person or persons, his, her or their property, not particularly described, are contrary to that right, and ought not to be granted.[36]

XII. [XIII.] That no warrant or writ to attach the person or estate, of any freeholder within this State, shall be issued in civil action, without the person or persons, who may request such warrant or attachment, first make oath, or affirm, before the authority who may be requested to issue the same, that he, or they, are in danger of losing his, her or their debts.[37]

[34] Similar to Pa. Decl. 1776, Art. VIII. The 1786 declaration retained the exemption for conscientious objectors that Pennsylvania would later remove from its 1790 constitution (see p. 128, footnote 50). Alterations made by the 1786 convention included changing the consenting party for the taking of private property for public use from an individual's "legal representatives" to the "representative body of the freemen" and specifying that any law raising taxes ought to appear evident to the legislature that the community would be better off with than without the tax—an attempt to ensure transparency and accountability.

[35] Similar to Pa. Decl. 1776, Art. IX.

[36] Similar to Pa. Decl. 1776, Art. X. This provision made two minor changes from its Pennsylvania counterpart: The Vermont provision used "search or seizure" instead of "search and seizure," and made the provision gender-neutral.

[37] Given the tangle of land claims, the extensive debt incurred by Vermont settlers, and the decisions of New York courts denying land titles and upholding creditors' claims, it is not surprising Vermonters were wary of courts. See Charles A. Jellison, *Ethan Allen: Frontier Rebel* (Taftsville, VT: Countryman Press, 1969), 22–26 and Matt Bushnell Jones, *Vermont in the Making, 1750–1777* (1939; reprint, Hamden, CT: Archon Books, 1968),

XIII. [XIV.] That, in controversies respecting property, and in suits between man and man[when an issue in fact, proper for the cognizance of a jury, is joined in a court of law], the parties have a right to a trial by jury; which ought to be held sacred.[38]

XIV. [XV.] That the people have a right to[of] freedom of speech, and of writing and publishing their sentiments;[, concerning the transactions of government—and] therefore, the freedom of the press ought not be restrained.[39]

[XVI. The freedom of deliberation, speech, and debate, in the legislature, is so essential to the rights of the people, that it can not be the foundation of any accusation or prosecution, action or complaint, in any other court or place whatsoever.][40]

[XVII. The power of suspending laws, or the execution of laws, ought never to be exercised, but by the Legislature, or by authority derived from it, to be exercised in such particular cases only as the Legislature shall expressly provide for.][41]

XV. [XVIII.] That the people have a right to bear arms[,] for the defence of themselves and the State; and, as standing armies, in the time of peace, are dangerous to liberty, they ought not to be kept up; and that the military should be kept under strict subordination to, and governed by, the civil power.[42]

chapter 12. Protection for debtors was manifest in several provisions of the 1777 constitution. This article allowed no writs against property or persons except in extreme circumstances.

[38] Similar to Pa. Decl. 1776, Art. XI. The 1786 constitution expanded jury purview by substituting the phrase "an issue in fact, proper for the cognizance of a jury...." for "controversies respecting property."

[39] Similar to Pa. Decl. 1776, Art. XII. Of the early American constitutions, only Pennsylvania and Vermont protected speech as well as press. Vermont also followed Pennsylvania's lead in adding a section in the frame of government (Const. 1777, sec. XXXII) requiring the printing presses to be free to all who would examine the government. The 1786 revision limited the freedoms of speech and press to "the transactions of government," presumably allowing private suits involving defamation.

[40] Similar to Mass. Decl. 1780, Art. XXI. This article, new to the 1786 declaration, intended to protect legislators from legal reprisals for anything said in the course of their legislative duties.

[41] Similar to Mass. Decl. 1780, Art. XX. An addition to the 1786 declaration, the article specified that the power to suspend the law could only be exercised on authority of the legislature and only in cases "expressly provided for."

[42] Similar to Pa. Decl. 1776, Art. XIII (also including the right to bear arms for defense of the individual). Section V of the 1777 Vermont frame of government provided for the

[XIX. That no person in this Commonwealth can, in any case, be subject to law-martial or to any penalties or pains, by virtue of that law, except those employed in the army, and the militia in actual service.][43]

XVI. [XX.] That frequent recurrence to fundamental principles, and a firm adherence to justice, moderation, temperance, industry[,] and frugality, are absolutely necessary to preserve the blessings of liberty, and keep government free. The [; the] people ought, therefore, to pay particular attention to these points, in the choice of officers and representatives,[;] and have a right[, in a legal way] to exact a due and constant regard to them, from their legislators and magistrates, in the making and executing such laws as are necessary for the good government of the State.[44]

XVII. [XXI.] That all people have a natural and inherent right to emigrate from one State to another, that will receive them; or to form a new State in vacant countries, or in such countries as they can purchase, whenever they think that thereby they can promote their own happiness.[45]

XVIII. [XXII.] That the people have a right to assemble together, to consult for their common good—to instruct their representatives, and to apply to the legislature[Legislature] for redress of grievances, by address, petition or remonstrance.[46]

XIX. [XXIII.] That no person shall be liable to be transported out of this State[,] for trial, for any offence committed within this State [the same].[47]

organizing and training of the militia and guaranteed its democratic character by giving the people the right to choose colonels and commissioned officers.

[43] Similar to Mass. Decl. 1780, Art. XXVIII. This article, added to the 1786 declaration, complemented the previous article making the military subordinate to the civil power by ensuring the only persons that could be subjected to law martial were those employed in the army or in actual service in the militia.

[44] Similar to Pa. Decl. 1776, Art. XIV. With the addition of "in a legal way," the 1786 convention made clear that the provision did not sanction extra-legal means of compulsion.

[45] Similar to Pa. Decl. 1776, Art. XV.

[46] Similar to Pa. Decl. 1776, Art. XVI. The rights provided in this article complemented other articles in the declaration designed to ensure the people would have constitutionally protected means to monitor legislative actions and communicate effectively with their representatives.

[47] Opposition to New York land titles and jurisdiction provoked resistance—sometimes armed—on the part of Vermont landholders to ejectment proceedings. This resistance prompted New York to enact the infamous "Outlawry Act" in 1774, which provided

Chapter II: Plan or Frame of Government

* * *

SECTION VI. [XVIII.] Every man[,] of the full age of twenty-one years, having resided in this State for the space of one whole year, next before the election of representatives, and who is of a quiet and peaceable behaviour, and will take the following oath (or affirmation) shall be entitled to all the privileges of a freeman of this State.

I ——— ——— [You] solemnly swear, by the ever living God, (or affirm, in the presence of Almighty God,) [(or affirm)] that whenever I am called to[you] give my[your] vote or suffrage, touching any matter that concerns the State of Vermont, I [you] will do it so, as in my[your] conscience, I[you] shall judge will most conduce to the best good of the same, as established by the constitution[Constitution], without fear or favor[favour] of any man.[48]

* * *

[XVII. No person ought, in any case, or in any time, to be declared guilty of treason or felony by the Legislature.][49]

* * *

SECTION XXII. [XXVIII.] Trials [of issues, proper for the cognizance of a jury, in the Supreme and County Courts,] shall be by jury[, except where parties otherwise agree:]; and it is recommended to the legislature of this State to provide by law, against every[and great care ought to be

severe punishment, including death, to resistors. Article XIX was based on the state's "sole, exclusive and inherent right of governing and regulating the internal police" (Decl. 1777, Art. IV), in this case protecting its citizens from being transported out of state for trial for any offense committed within the state. Extensive treatment of these complex issues can be found in Jones, *Vermont in the Making*, and Jellison, *Ethan Allen*, especially chapter 2.

[48] This section set forth the suffrage requirements described above. The 1786 revisions removed all references to God from the oath.

[49] Similar to Mass. Decl. 1780, Art. XXV.

taken to prevent] corruption or partiality in the choice, and return, or appointment, of juries.[50]

SECTION XXIII. [IV.] All [Courts of justice shall be maintained in every county in this State, and also in new counties when formed; which] courts shall be open [for the trial of all causes proper for their cognizance], and justice shall be [therein] impartially administered, without corruption[,] or unnecessary delay; all their officers shall be paid an adequate, but moderate, compensation for their services; and if any officer shall take greater or other fees than the laws allow him, either directly or indirectly, it shall ever after disqualify him from holding any office in this State[. The Judges of the Supreme Court shall be Justices of the Peace throughout the State; and the several Judges of the County Courts, in their respective counties, by virtue of their offices, except in the trial of such cases as may be appealed to the County Court].[51]

* * *

SECTION XXV. [XXX.] The person of a debtor, where there is not a strong presumption of fraud, shall not be continued in prison, after delivering up [and assigning over], *bona fide*, all his estate, real and personal, [in possession, reversion, or remainder,] for the use of his creditors, in such manner as shall be hereafter regulated by law. All [And all] prisoners[, unless in execution, or committed for capital offences, when the proof is evident or presumption great,] shall be bailable by sufficient securities, unless for capital offences, when the proof is evident or presumption great[sureties: no shall excessive bail be exacted for bailable offenses].[52]

[50] Similar to Pa. Const. 1776, sec. 25. The Vermont clause deleted "as heretofore" at the end of the first clause. Never having been a colony, there was no "heretofore" in Vermont.

[51] Similar to Pa. Const. 1776, sec. 26. This section was a companion to the transparency requirements imposed upon the legislative body. What constituted "open" courts, "unnecessary delay," and "impartially administered" were not spelled out, leaving one to assume they awaited legislative implementation or were, despite the command word "shall," admonitory. The Vermont provision added a clause requiring adequate pay for all officers and mandating permanent disqualification from any state office should there be a violation of fee allowances.

[52] Similar to Pa. Const. 1776, sec. 28. The protection of debtors took on additional significance given the tangle of land claims and jurisdictional disputes between Vermont on the one hand and New York and New Hampshire on the other.

SECTION XXVI. Excessive bail shall not be exacted for bailable offences: and all fines shall be moderate.[53]

* * *

SECTION XXIX. [XXXI.] All elections, whether by the people[,] or in General Assembly, shall be by ballot, free and voluntary: and any elector[,] who shall receive any gift or reward for his vote, in meat, drink, monies or otherwise, shall forfeit his right to elect at that time, and suffer such other penalty as future laws shall direct. And[: and] any person who shall, directly or indirectly, give, promise, or bestow, any such rewards to be elected, shall, thereby, be rendered incapable to serve for the ensuing year[, and be subject to such further punishment as a future Legislature shall direct].[54]

SECTION XXXII. The printing presses shall be free to every person who undertakes to examine the proceedings of the legislature, or any part of government.[55]

* * *

SECTION XXXIV. [XXXIII.] The future legislature[Legislature] of this State, shall regulate entails[,] in such manner as to prevent perpetuities.

SECTION XXXV. [XXXIV.] To deter more effectually from the commission of crimes, by continued visible punishment[,] of long duration, and to make sanguinary punishments [punishment] less necessary; houses[, means] ought to be provided for punishing, by hard labor[labour], those who shall be convicted of crimes not capital; wherein[, whereby] the criminal shall be employed for the benefit of the public, or for reparation of injuries done to private persons;[:] and all persons, at proper times, shall[ought to] be admitted[permitted] to see the prisoners[them] at their labor[labour].[56]

[53] Similar to Pa. Const. 1776, sec. 29.

[54] Similar to Pa. Const. 1776, sec. 32. The 1786 constitution added a clause allowing the legislature to adopt further punishments for violators.

[55] Similar to Pa. Const. 1776, sec. 35.

[56] Similar to Pa. Const. 1776, sec. 39. The Pennsylvania Constitution directed its legislature to reform the penal law "as heretofore used" to make it less sanguinary (Pa. Const. 1776, sec. 38). Vermont did not need to copy this provision as no such laws were in existence in the newly-established republic. A 1786 revision provided that persons "ought

[XXXV. The estates of such persons as may destroy their own lives, shall not for that offence be forfeited, but descend or ascend in the same manner as if such persons had died in a natural way. Nor shall any article, which shall accidentally occasion the death of any person, be henceforth deemed a deodand, or in anywise forfeited on account of such misfortune.][57]

* * *

SECTION XXXVII. No public tax, custom or contribution shall be imposed upon, or paid by, the people of this State, except by a law for that purpose; and before any law be made for raising it, the purpose for which any tax is to be raised ought to appear clear to the legislature to be of more service to the community than the money would be, if not collected; which being well observed, taxes can never be burthens.[58]

SECTION XXXVIII. [XXXVI.] Every foreigner[person] of good character, who comes to settle in this State, having first taken an oath or affirmation of allegiance to the same, may purchase, or by other just means[,] acquire, hold, and transfer, land or other real estate; and[,] after one years[year's] residence, shall be deemed a free denizen thereof, and intitled[entitled] to all the rights of a natural born subject of this State;[,] except that he shall not be capable of being elected a representative[Governor, Lieutenant-Governor, Treasurer, Counsellor, or Representative in Assembly], until after two years['] residence.[59]

SECTION XXXIX. [XXXVII.] That the[The] inhabitants of this State, shall have liberty[, in seasonable times,] to hunt and fowl, in seasonable times, on the lands they hold, and on other lands (not enclosed;)[not inclosed;] and, in like manner, to fish in all boatable and other waters,

to be permitted" to see the prisoners in place of the earlier "shall be admitted." Moving from the mandatory "shall" to the precatory "ought" ran counter to the trend in state constitution writing of the time.

57 Similar to N.J. Const. 1776, Art. XVII; N.H. Const. 1784. This provision, ending the practice of a suicide's estate reverting to the state, was a new addition to the 1786 document.

58 Similar to Pa. Const. 1776, sec. 41. Additionally, the council of censors was charged to "enquire whether the public taxes ha[d] been justly laid and collected, in all parts of this Commonwealth...." (Const. 1777, sec. XLIV).

59 Similar to Pa. Const. 1776, sec. 42. The 1786 constitution expanded the list of offices subject to the two-year residency requirement to include governor, lieutenant-governor, treasurer, and counsellor.

not private property, under proper regulations, to be hereafter made and provided by the General Assembly.[60]

SECTION XL. A school or schools shall be established in each town, by the legislature, for the convenient instruction of youth, with such salaries to the masters, paid by each town; making proper use of school lands in each town, thereby to enable them to instruct youth at low prices. One grammar school in each county, and one university in this State, ought to be established by direction of the General Assembly.[61]

SECTION XLI. [XXXVIII.] Laws for the encouragement of virtue[,] and prevention of vice and immorality, shall be made and[ought to be] constantly kept in force; and provision shall be made for their due execution;[, and duly executed; and a competent number of schools ought to be maintained in each town for the convenient instruction of youth; and one or more grammar schools be incorporated, and properly supported in each county in this State.] and[And] all religious societies[,] or bodies of men, that have or may be hereafter united and[or] incorporated, for the advancement of religion and learning, or for other pious and charitable purposes, shall be encouraged and protected in the enjoyment of the privileges, immunities[,] and estates[,] which they, in justice, ought to enjoy, under such regulations, as the General Assembly of this State shall direct.[62]

* * *

[60] Similar to Pa. Const. 1776, sec. 43. The Supreme Court of Vermont, in a case decided 200 years later, concluded that this constitutional provision modified the early American preference for agriculture over hunting and changed the English law by "extend[ing] rights to citizens which the common law had not recognized" and recognized "rights to hunt and fish … in what had previously been the landowner's private domain." Cabot v. Thomas, 514 A.2d 1034, 1037–1038 (VT 1986). Only Pennsylvania and Vermont included this right in their constitutions, though other states provided such protection by statute.

[61] Similar to Pa. Const. 1776, sec. 44. Reflecting the importance towns played in Vermont, this section required a school in each town; its Pennsylvania counterpart mandated one in each county. The Vermont provision went further by mandating the creation of a university. The requirements that a school be established in each town and that a university be established were removed from the 1786 constitution.

[62] Similar to Pa. Const. 1776, sec. 45. The 1786 revision offered another example of the substitution of the word "ought" for the word "shall."

SECTION XLIII. [XXXIX.] The declaration of rights[the political rights and privileges of the inhabitants of this State,] is hereby declared to be a part of the Constitution of this State,[Commonwealth;] and ought never[not] to be violated, on any pretence whatsoever.[63]

[63] Similar to Pa. Const. 1776, sec. 46. This section settled the question of whether the declaration was part of the constitution. Frequently quoted by the courts, it is considered to be a solemn injunction, a directive to ensure none of the powers expressly reserved to the people and denied to the general government shall ever be exercised by the latter in violation of the fundamental law. The 1786 constitution replaced one instance of the word "State" with "Commonwealth." Both constitutions used the latter word in various places.

Massachusetts

The Commonwealth of Massachusetts, as it became known upon adoption of its 1780 constitution, was the successor to the Province of Massachusetts Bay, which encompassed, inter alia, the Plymouth Colony founded by Puritan separatists later known as Pilgrims, the Massachusetts Bay Colony founded by the Puritans, and the Province of Maine.

Plymouth Colony

The Plymouth Colony began life without a charter, initially possessing only a patent issued on February 2, 1619/1620 by the Virginia Company of London for the northern part of the land owned by that company (which extended to northern New Jersey).[1] During their voyage, bad weather caused the Pilgrims to anchor on November 11, 1620, in what is now Provincetown, Massachusetts, which fell under the jurisdiction of the Council for New England and outside the reach of the patent.

[1] William Bradford, *Of Plymouth Plantation, 1620–1647*, ed. Samuel Eliot Morison (1952; reprint, New York: Knopf, 2002[1651]), 39. The Plymouth Colony was a "particular plantation," a device created by the Virginia Company in which investors would receive an allotment of land in exchange for shares purchased in the company and for settlers they brought to the territory. Lorena S. Walsh, *Motives of Honor, Pleasure, and Profit: Plantation Management in the Colonial Chesapeake, 1607–1763* (Chapel Hill: University of North Carolina Press, 2010), 39–41. Adventurers had a "free hand in administering their enterprises," so long as their regulations "were not contrary to the laws of England or to the general orders of the Company." Ibid., 39, 40.

P. J. Galie et al., *Bills of Rights Before the Bill of Rights*,
https://doi.org/10.1007/978-3-030-44301-6_10

To avoid settlers "us[ing] their own liberty; for none had power to command them [in light of the void patent],"[2] the majority of the male passengers signed the Mayflower Compact, which read:

> Having undertaken for the glory of God, and advancement of the Christian Faith, and the Honour of our K[i]ng and Countrey, a Voyage to plant the first Colony in the Northern parts of *Virginia*; Do by these Presents, solemnly and mutually, in the presence of God and one another, Covenant and Combine our selves together into a Civil Body Politick, for our better ordering and preservation, and furtherance of the ends aforesaid: and by virtue hereof do enact, constitute, and frame, such just and equal Laws, Ordinances, Acts, Constitutions and Officers, from time to time, as shall be thought most meet and convenient for the general good of the Colony; unto which we promise all due submission and obedience.[3]

The colony operated as a well-functioning democracy. Elections were held for members of the general court (legislature), and most colonists occupied at least one public office. Attendance at town meetings was enforceable by fines. As one commentator noted, "[g]overnment and politics in seventeenth-century Plymouth was a participatory system in the best sense of the term."[4]

On November 15, 1636, the Plymouth colony established the Pilgrim Code of Law, which has been described as "the first American constitution."[5] The preamble to this document laid out that the colonists had brought the laws of England with them: "as freeborn subjects of the state

[2] Bradford, *Of Plymouth Plantation*, 75.

[3] [Agreement Between the Settlers at New Plymouth] (1620) in *Colonial Origins of the American Constitution: A Documentary History*, ed. Donald S. Lutz (Indianapolis: Liberty Fund, 1998), 31–32. In June 1621, the settlers received a temporary patent from the correct entity, and in January 1629/1630, the colony finally obtained a permanent patent [Plymouth Patent] (1629/1630), *Select Charters and Other Documents Illustrative of American History, 1606–1775*, ed. William MacDonald (1899; reprint, New York: Macmillan, 1910), 51–53. While some scholars call this document a "charter," see, e.g., Thorpe, *Constitutions*, 3:1841, MacDonald notes none of the patents were ever confirmed by the Crown, and the colony never obtained a royal charter. MacDonald, *Select Charters*, 51.

[4] H. Roger King, *Cape Cod and Plymouth Colony in the Seventeenth Century* (Lanham, MD: University Press of America, 1993), 171.

[5] George L. Haskins, "The Legal Heritage of Plymouth Colony," *University of Pennsylvania Law Review* 110 (1962): 848. Harry M. Ward shares that view. *Statism in Plymouth Colony* (Port Washington, NY: Kennikat Press, 1973), 71. Donald S. Lutz refers to the

of England, we hither came endowed with all and singular the privileges belonging to such…"[6] This code provided that laws would be made only with the consent of the governed, "according to the free liberties of the state and kingdom of England and no otherwise."[7] Jury trials were provided in both criminal and civil cases.[8] The governor and members of the executive council were to be elected annually by the people.[9] This code lasted until 1671, when it was replaced.

Massachusetts Bay Colony

The Massachusetts Bay Colony operated under a royal charter granted by King Charles I in March 1628/1629 to the Puritan leaders of the New England Company. The charter did not require meetings to be held in England.[10] In April 1630, one year after Charles permanently dissolved Parliament, a large group of grantees migrated to America—transforming a trading company into a political entity. The directors of the company were empowered to elect a governor and a deputy governor, act as a general court (legislature), and enact any laws they saw fit so long as they did not contradict the laws of England. The charter made clear that the colonists "shall have and enjoy all liberties and Immunities of free and naturall Subiects … as yf they and everie of them were borne within the Realme of England."[11]

In 1641, the general court of the colony adopted a code of laws, drafted by Nathaniel Ward, known as the Massachusetts Body of Liberties. Part codification of the existing laws of the colony and part constitution, the document has been called "the first postmedieval, or modern,

document as "a candidate for the honor of being the first true written constitution in the modern world." *Colonial Origins*, 61.

[6] [Pilgrim Code of Law] (1636), in Lutz, *Colonial Origins*, 62.

[7] Ibid.

[8] Ibid., 67.

[9] Ibid., 62.

[10] Much has been made over the centuries about the omission of such a requirement. Ronald Dale Kerr concludes the charter's exclusion of a particular meeting place was "neither unprecedented nor particularly noteworthy." "The Missing Clause: Myth and the Massachusetts Bay Charter of 1629," *The New England Quarterly* 77, no. 1 (March 2004): 106.

[11] The Charter of Massachusetts Bay (1629), in Thorpe, *Constitutions*, 3:1857.

bill of rights."[12] The opening article of this document contained the due process clause from Magna Carta:

> No mans life shall be taken away, no mans honour or good name shall be stayned, no mans person shall be arested, restrayned, banished, dismembred, nor any wayes punished, no man shall be deprived of his wife or children, no mans goods or estaite shall be taken away from him, nor any way indammaged under Coulor of law, or Countenance of Authoritie, unlesse it be by vertue or equitie of some expresse law of the Country warranting the same, established by a generall Court and sufficiently published, or in case of the defect of a law in any partecular case by the word of god....[13]

The Body of Liberties also provided freedom of speech at town meetings and councils,[14] afforded freedom from double jeopardy,[15] and prohibited "inhumane Barbarous or cruell" bodily punishments.[16] It granted religious freedom for those who worshiped "in a Christian way, with due observation of the rules of Christ revealed in his word."[17] The criminal code in the body of liberties contained a strong Old Testament cast: It mandated death for violations of most of the Ten Commandments.[18]

Province of Massachusetts Bay

Displeased with Massachusetts Bay's assertions of independence, the king revoked the colony's charter in 1684. The colony became part of the short-lived Dominion of New England from 1686 to 1689; in 1691, William and Mary issued a charter for the Province of Massachusetts

[12] Lutz, *Colonial Origins*, 70.

[13] [Massachusetts Body of Liberties] (1641), sec. 1 in Lutz, *Colonial Origins*, 71. One of the earliest appearances in the colonies of the law of the land clause, it is derived from Chapter 39 of Magna Carta.

[14] Ibid., sec. 12, 72–73. The document also provided that anybody who behaved "offensively" at any town meeting could be sentenced by the rest of the freemen in attendance. Ibid., sec. 56, 78.

[15] Ibid., sec. 42, 76.

[16] Ibid., sec. 46, 77.

[17] Ibid., sec. 95(1), 85.

[18] Ibid., sec. 94, 83–84.

Bay.[19] The charter limited the autonomy enjoyed by the earlier colony, providing for a royally appointed governor with veto power.[20] The general court was made bicameral, with the lower house elected by the townspeople, and a governor's council chosen by the deputies of the lower house. The charter made property, not religion, the key qualification for the suffrage,[21] and provided that "there shall be a liberty of Conscience allowed in the Worshipp of God to all Christians (Except Papists)...."[22] The privileges and immunities clause of the 1628/1629 charter was retained.[23]

Deteriorating relations between colonists and the Crown in the 1760s led to the formation of the Boston Committee of Correspondence. In 1772, the committee issued the 'Boston Pamphlet,' which derived claims of rights from a blend of natural law, the New Testament, and the English Constitution, while specifying British violations of these rights. After the Boston Tea Party, Parliament annulled the 1691 charter, curtailed self-government in the colony, gave the governor the power to appoint certain previously elective offices, and authorized the king to appoint and remove members of the governor's council. After the governor dissolved the provincial assembly in 1774, a series of extra-legal conventions were held throughout Massachusetts Bay; ultimately an autonomous provincial congress was organized.

Constitutional Developments: Proposed Constitution of 1778

In 1775, the provincial congress ordered the election of a general court under the provincial charter, and "amended" that charter to give the executive power to a council elected by the house of representatives. This amended charter governed Massachusetts until it adopted its first (and

[19] In addition to the territory of the Massachusetts Bay Colony, the province included what had previously been the Plymouth Colony, as well as Martha's Vineyard, Nantucket, Maine, Nova Scotia, and New Brunswick.

[20] Charter of Massachusetts Bay, 1883.

[21] The charter granted suffrage to men who owned freehold having a "value of Forty Shillings per Annũ [Annum] at the least or other estate to the value of Forty pounds Sterl." Ibid., 1879.

[22] Ibid., 1881.

[23] Ibid.

only) constitution in 1780.[24] In the interim, the state "grappled with the problem of converting the consent of the governed from a political theory into a political process."[25] In 1776, the house canvassed the towns for permission to convene along with the council as a constitutional convention. Most of the towns that did respond (less than half) requested that any constitution be submitted to the people for ratification, and at least four argued that a constitution should be written by a convention specially elected for that purpose.[26] The general court ignored the latter request, and in June, 1777, resolved itself into a constitutional convention.

In February 1778, the convention adopted a constitution to be ratified at town meetings open to all males over age twenty-one.[27] The constitution lacked a declaration of rights.[28] Separation of powers did not feature prominently in the document; the senate acted both as the upper house of the general court and the governor's council. The constitution expanded suffrage, with no property qualification to vote for members of the house of representatives.[29] The absence of a bill of rights and the general court's failure to

[24] Samuel Eliot Morison, *A History of the Constitution of Massachusetts* (Boston: Wright & Potter, 1917), 13.

[25] Oscar Handlin and Mary Handlin, eds., *The Popular Sources of Political Authority: Documents on the Massachusetts Constitution of 1780* (Cambridge, MA: Belknap Press, 1966), 18.

[26] Ibid., 106–107 (Town of Stoughton), 124–125 (Town of Norton), 152–153 (Town of Concord), 157–158 (Town of Acton).

[27] Francis D. Cogliano, *Revolutionary America, 1763–1815: A Political History*, 2nd ed. (New York: Routledge, 2009), 143.

[28] The rejected constitution can be found in Handlin and Handlin, *Popular Sources*, 190–201.

[29] Morison, *History of the Constitution*, 16. The voters for representatives were limited to free males at least twenty-one years of age who had resided in the town for one year and paid taxes, and specifically excluded "negroes, Indians and mulattoes." Handlin and Handlin, *Popular Sources*, 192–193. This expansion was balanced by higher thresholds to vote for senators and the governor (sixty pounds of personal estate—higher than required by the charter), and substantial estates to run for office: 200 pounds for representatives, 400 pounds for senators, and 1000 pounds for governor, with at least half of each amount being real estate. Gary B. Nash, *The Unknown American Revolution: The Unruly Birth of Democracy and the Struggle to Create America* (New York: Viking, 2005), 296. Nash has referred to the proposed constitution as "by far the most conservative in the North" and claims that only Maryland and South Carolina had more restrictive suffrage and candidate property qualifications. Ibid.

convene a body for the specific purpose of drafting a constitution aroused intense opposition, and the voters rejected the constitution by nearly a five-to-one margin.[30]

Constitutional Developments: 1780 Declaration and Constitution

Chastened by the rejection of the proposed constitution, the general court waited until February 1779 to ask the towns whether they wanted a new form of government and whether they wished to authorize representatives to call a state constitutional convention. Following affirmative answers to both questions, the general court issued a call for a constitutional convention to convene in September 1779. The final version of the constitution was to be transmitted to the towns for consideration at regular meetings of the male inhabitants, and would take effect if approved "by at least two thirds of those who are free and twenty one years of age, belonging to this State, and present in the several Meetings."[31] No property qualification would apply to votes for delegates or votes to ratify the constitution: "It derived all its authority from the people, in the widest contemporary political sense of that word; and to the people its work was submitted."[32]

A subcommittee consisting of Samuel Adams, John Adams, and James Bowdoin (the convention president) was charged with producing a draft constitution. The task fell entirely upon John Adams. Possessed of a deeply informed knowledge of constitutional law and history, and in possession of most of the previously adopted state constitutions, he was uniquely qualified for the role.[33] When the convention reconvened on

[30] Ronald M. Peters Jr., *The Massachusetts Constitution of 1780: A Social Compact* (Amherst: University of Massachusetts Press, 1978), 19. Had the 129 towns that did not report any returns done so, the defeat would have been even more pronounced.

[31] The Call for a Convention, June 1779, in Handlin and Handlin, *Popular Sources*, 403.

[32] Morison, *History of the Constitution*, 19.

[33] In drafting the document, Adams attempted to "balance interest groups by giving the generality of people and those of wealth and status each a place in government." Nash, *Unknown American Revolution*, 301.

October 28, 1779, it received the committee's report.[34] The period between October 28th and November 11th was spent debating the declaration of rights. Additional debate on the frame of government occurred in early 1780. On March 2nd of that year, the convention concluded its revisions and ordered the Massachusetts document printed and sent to the towns, along with an address recommending its acceptance.[35] The convention reconvened in June 1780, declared that the requisite two-thirds approval had been obtained, and set the date for inauguration as October 25, 1780.[36]

Having had one constitution rejected by the voters for want of a declaration of rights, the 1779-80 convention did not repeat that mistake. By the time the declaration was adopted, Massachusetts had six other state declarations from which to draw inspiration. Not surprisingly, many of the articles in the state's declaration of rights derived from provisions found in the Pennsylvania Constitution, which, in turn, drew on similar provisions in the Virginia Declaration of Rights.

The purposes of government were laid out in the preamble of the Massachusetts document in their order of importance: The community must secure the existence of the body politic, provide for its preservation and well-being, and protect and foster inalienable, natural, and civil rights. The sequencing indicated that the protection of the declared rights would take place in the context of the community's overarching commitment to preserving and fostering the health, safety, welfare, and moral character of the community. Following the example of other states, the preamble made

[34] The Report of a Constitution or Form of Government for the Commonwealth of Massachusetts, October 28, 1779, in *Journal of the Convention for Framing a Constitution of Government for the State of Massachusetts Bay...* (Boston: Dutton and Wentworth, 1832), 192–215. Adams's original draft has been lost.

[35] The address can be found in *Journal*, 216–221 and Handlin and Handlin, *Popular Sources*, 434–440.

[36] The method of determining approval was problematic. Voting was to be done on an article-by-article basis; proposed amendments by the towns would be addressed by the convention without resubmission to the people. In calculating its approval of each article, the convention added approvals, if amended, with unconditional approvals. Peters, *Massachusetts Constitution*, 22. Of 290 towns returning votes, only 42 accepted the document without amendment. Nash, *Unknown American Revolution*, 302. Nash credits the state for being a pioneer in utilizing popular ratification, but claims that through this manipulation of votes, "the results were overturned." Ibid., 303; see also Stephen E. Patterson, *Political Parties in Revolutionary Massachusetts* (Madison: University of Wisconsin Press, 1973), 245.

clear that the constitution included the declaration.[37] Along with other state constitutions adopted between 1776 and 1780, the Massachusetts Constitution made an explicit commitment to the doctrine of popular sovereignty: the source of all power was the people and all public servants were accountable to the people. In addition to language affording "the people" the right "to take measures necessary for their safety, prosperity and happiness" should the government fail to carry out its obligations (Const. 1780, preamble), the declaration conferred upon the people alone an "incontestible, unalienable, and indefeasible right to institute government; and to reform, alter, or totally change the same..." (Decl. 1780, Art. VII).[38] The constitution continued "[a]ll the laws which have heretofore been adopted, used, and approved in the Province, Colony, or State of Massachusetts Bay, and usually practised on in the courts of law" (Const. 1780, Ch. VI, Art. VI). Included within the scope of this provision would be the English common law.

Suffrage

The 1780 constitution granted the suffrage to males at least twenty-one years of age, and imposed a one-year town residency requirement to vote for representatives (Const. 1780, Ch. I, sec. II, Art. II; sec. III, Art. IV). Voters for any office had to have an annual income of three pounds or any estate of the value of sixty pounds, a contrast to the rejected constitution's absence of a property qualification for those voting for members of the house of representatives. The convention rejected motions to remove "male" from the voting qualifications for representatives and senators.[39] The apportionment for representatives was done not by the number of

[37] See, e.g., N.C. Const. 1776, Art. XLIV; Pa. Const. 1776, sec. 46; Vt. Const. 1777, sec. XLIII. Donald S. Lutz argues that these declarations were not considered part of the constitutions because they had their origin in colonial practice and English common law. *Popular Consent and Popular Control: Whig Political Theory in the Early State Constitutions* (Baton Rouge: Louisiana State University Press, 1980), 63–67.

[38] The Massachusetts Constitution has two parts: a declaration of rights (Part I) and a frame of government (Part II). Henceforth, references to Part I will be noted as "Decl." and references to Part II will be noted as "Const.".

[39] *Journal*, 92, 120–121, 136. All that is known about the size of the votes is the motions received a second. As qualifications to vote for governor were identical, the amendments would have conferred the right to vote for that office as well.

inhabitants but by the number of "rateable polls," defined by law as males sixteen years of age and older.[40]

Structural Provisions

Massachusetts included explicit separation of powers language in its constitution (Decl. 1780, Art. XXX), one of seven states to do so.[41] The legislative power was exercised jointly by a senate and a house of representatives. The governor possessed a veto power, but the legislature could override a veto on a two-thirds vote of both houses (Const. 1780, Ch. I, sec. I, Art. II). The constitution granted an executive council (rather than the legislature) the power to confirm executive appointments (ibid., Ch. II, sec. I, Art. IX). Granting tenure to most judicial officers "during good behavior" insured judicial independence (ibid., Ch. III, Art. I). The constitution also prohibited nearly all plural office-holding, a prohibition that applied to all three branches (ibid., Ch. VI, Art. II).

The structural provisions implementing the commitment to popular sovereignty lacked the rigor and specificity found in other state declarations. Although the people had the right to assemble and to address, petition, or remonstrate the legislature (Decl. 1780, Art. XIX), and the legislature was instructed to meet "frequently" (ibid., Art. XXII),[42] the constitution did not mandate that the doors of the general court remain open, require weekly printing of the proceedings of that body, or provide that the public had to have advance scrutiny of legislative bills.

In furtherance of the belief that short terms of office ensured accountability to the voters, senators, representatives, and the governor were each chosen for one-year terms (Const. 1780, Ch. I, sec. II, Art. I; sec. III, Art. I; Ch. II, sec. I, Art. II). The residency and property requirements for candidates seeking public office varied by office:

[40] Robert J. Taylor suggests Adams opted for this definition because he thought "polls" constituted a more accurate reflection of the people being represented. "Construction of the Massachusetts Constitution," *Proceedings of the American Antiquarian Society* 90, no. 2 (October 1981): 329.

[41] See Table 1, pp. 56–58.

[42] The frame required the legislature to meet annually (Const. 1780, Ch. I, sec. I, Art. I).

Office	Residency requirement	Property requirement
Governor	Inhabitant of commonwealth for 7 years	Freehold of 1000 pounds
Senator	Resident in commonwealth for 5 years; inhabitant of district at time of election	Freehold of 300 pounds at least, or possessed of personal estate of 600 pounds at least, or of both to same sum
Representative	Inhabitant of town for 1 year	Freehold of 100 pounds, or any rateable estate of 200 pounds

John Adams proposed that all of these officeholders be Christians, a requirement the convention dropped for all but the governor and lieutenant governor.[43]

To effectuate the people's right to "reform, alter, or totally change" the government (Decl. 1780, Art. VII), the 1780 constitution mandated that the general court in 1795 canvass the voters as to whether they believed the constitution needed to be revised. In the event two-thirds of the voters throughout the state believed amendment necessary, the general court would be required to issue precepts (authorizations) to elect delegates to a constitutional convention (Const. 1780, Ch. VI, Art. X).

Postscript: The Massachusetts Constitution of 1780, as amended, remains in force today. It is the oldest functioning constitution in the world. Of the thirty articles constituting the declaration of rights adopted by the convention, half have yet to be amended.

Constitution of Massachusetts [1780]

Part the First: A Declaration of the Rights of the Inhabitants of the Commonwealth of Massachusetts

I. All men are born free and equal, and have certain natural, essential, and unalienable rights; among which may be reckoned the right of enjoying and defending their lives and liberties; that of acquiring, possessing, and

[43] Taylor, "Construction of Massachusetts Constitution," 341. An oath of belief in the Christian religion was required for legislators, council members, and the governor and lieutenant-governor.

protecting property; in fine, that of seeking and obtaining their safety and happiness.[44]

II. It is the right as well as the duty of all men in society, publicly, and at stated seasons, to worship the SUPREME BEING, the great creator and preserver of the universe. And no subject shall be hurt, molested, or restrained, in his person, liberty, or estate, for worshipping GOD in the manner and season most agreeable to the dictates of his own conscience;

[44] The language of this provision, closely mirroring the Declaration of Independence's proclamation that all men are "created equal," was a modification of Adams's original language, which declared that all men "are born equally free and independent." Taylor, "Construction of Massachusetts Constitution," 334. Although Adams professed that "all men are born to equal rights," he believed the notion that all men were born with "equal powers and faculties, to equal influence in society, to equal property and advantages through life" to be a gross fraud. Letters to John Taylor of Caroline, Virginia, in Reply to His Strictures on Some Parts of the Defence of the American Constitutions, n.d., in John Adams, *The Works of John Adams, Second President of the United States* (Boston: Little, Brown and Co., 1851), 6:453–454.

This provision would be tested three years after adoption. In a case for criminal assault by Nathaniel Jennison against a former slave named Quock Walker, Chief Justice of the Supreme Judicial Court John D. Cushing instructed the jury as to the repugnance of slavery in light of the new article:

> ...whatever sentiments have formerly prevailed in this particular or slid in upon us by the example of others, a different idea has taken place with the people of America, more favorable to the natural rights of mankind, and to that natural, innate desire of Liberty, with which Heaven (without regard to color, complexion, or shape of noses) features) [sic] has inspired all the human race. And upon this ground our Constitution of Government, by which the people of this Commonwealth have solemnly bound themselves, sets out with declaring that all men are born free and equal -- and that every subject is entitled to liberty, and to have it guarded by the laws, as well as life and property -- and in short is totally repugnant to the idea of being born slaves. This being the case, I think the idea of slavery is inconsistent with our own conduct and Constitution; and there can be no such thing as perpetual servitude of a rational creature, unless his liberty is forfeited by some criminal conduct or given up by personal consent or contract.

[Charge of the Chief Justice] (1783), in *Proceedings of the Massachusetts Historical Society, 1873–1875* (Boston: The Society, 1875), 294. Emancipation was not immediate, but by the 1790 census, not one citizen in Massachusetts claimed to own a slave. Emily Blanck, "Seventeen Eighty-Three: The Turning Point in the Law of Slavery and Freedom in Massachusetts," *The New England Quarterly* 75, no. 1 (March 2002): 30. Blanck reports anecdotal evidence that a scattering of people lived as slaves into the 1790s. Ibid., 30–31.

or for his religious profession or sentiments; provided he doth not disturb the public peace, or obstruct others in their religious worship.[45]

III. As the happiness of a people, and the good order and preservation of civil government, essentially depend upon piety, religion and morality; and as these cannot be generally diffused through a community, but by the institution of the public worship of GOD, and of public instructions in piety, religion and morality: Therefore, to promote their happiness and to secure the good order and preservation of their government, the people of this Commonwealth have a right to invest their legislature with power to authorize and require, and the legislature shall, from time to time, authorize and require, the several towns, parishes, precincts, and other bodies-politic, or religious societies, to make suitable provision, at their own expense, for the institution of the public worship of GOD, and for the support and maintenance of public protestant teachers of piety, religion and morality, in all cases where such provision shall not be made voluntarily.

And the people of this Commonwealth have also a right to, and do, invest their legislature with authority to enjoin upon all the subjects an attendance upon the instructions of the public teachers aforesaid, at stated times and seasons, if there be any on whose instructions they can conscientiously and conveniently attend.

Provided notwithstanding, that the several towns, parishes, precincts, and other bodies-politic, or religious societies, shall, at all times, have the

[45] Similar to Md. Decl. 1776, Art. XXXIII. The original committee report made worship of the supreme being a DUTY, but not a right. Massachusetts did not expressly declare liberty of conscience a natural right. This article used the term "subject," one of several using that term (see Decl. 1780, Arts. III, XI, XII, and XIV). Such usage was rare in other early state constitutions. Of the constitutions adopted to that point, only Pennsylvania used that term in only one section (see Pa. Const. 1776, sec. 42). The Massachusetts Historical Society's annotations on the document note that the term survived the American Revolution and came to mean "a person subject to the laws as distinct from a citizen, who enjoyed political rights." "The Report of a Constitution or Form of Government for the Commonwealth of Massachusetts, 28 – 31 October 1779," *Founders Online*, National Archives, accessed September 29, 2019, https://founders.archives.gov/documents/Adams/06-08-02-0161-0002. [Original source: *The Adams Papers, Papers of John Adams*, ed. Gregg L. Lint, et al. (Cambridge, MA: Harvard University Press, 1989), 8:236–271]. Douglas Bradburn suggests that social hierarchies well-entrenched in the common law could not easily and immediately be effaced. Remnants of this tradition were reflected in the occasional use of the word "subjects" in state constitutions. *The Citizenship Revolution: Politics and the Creation of the American Union, 1774–1804* (Charlottesville: University of Virginia Press, 2009), 11–12.

exclusive right of electing their public teachers, and of contracting with them for their support and maintenance.

And all monies paid by the subject to the support of public worship, and of the public teachers aforesaid, shall, if he require it, be uniformly applied to the support of the public teacher or teachers of his own religious sect or denomination, provided there be any on whose instructions he attends: otherwise it may be paid towards the support of the teacher or teachers of the parish or precinct in which the said monies are raised.

And every denomination of christians, demeaning themselves peaceably, and as good subjects of the Commonwealth, shall be equally under the protection of the law: And no subordination of any one sect or denomination to another shall ever be established by law.[46]

IV. The people of this Commonwealth have the sole and exclusive right of governing themselves as a free, sovereign, and independent state; and do, and forever hereafter shall, exercise and enjoy every power, jurisdiction, and right, which is not, or may not hereafter, be by them expressly delegated to the United States of America, in Congress assembled.[47]

[46] Article III, the only article not written by Adams, was one of the most contentious articles in the constitution. Taylor, "Construction of Massachusetts Constitution," 331–332. In furtherance of the belief that religion was an indispensable agent for promoting and sustaining the morality of the people, this article mandated government support for "Protestant" teachers—an addition to the committee's report. The second section empowered the legislature to require compulsory church attendance. The third section provided that the towns, parishes, and religious societies had the right to elect their ministers. The fourth section created multiple establishments of Protestant churches; a citizen could decide to which Protestant church his contribution would go. Alternatively, the contribution could be paid towards the support of the teacher or teachers of the parish or precinct in which the said monies were raised. The convention also added the final paragraph, guaranteeing equal protection of the laws for Christians of all denominations who demeaned themselves peaceably.

For a thorough examination of this article, see John Witte Jr., "'A Most Mild and Equitable Establishment of Religion': John Adams and the Massachusetts Experiment," *Journal of Church and State* 41, no. 2 (Spring 1999): 213–252. Massachusetts ended government support for religion in 1833, the last state to do so.

[47] Similar to Pa. Decl. 1776, Art. III. The Massachusetts provision offered a more specific and far reaching claim than its Pennsylvania counterpart. What accounts for this difference? The Pennsylvania Constitution predated the drafting of the Articles of Confederation, which, by the time of the Massachusetts convention, had been adopted by all states except Maryland. The Articles provided: "Each state retains its sovereignty, freedom, and independence, and every power, jurisdiction, and right, which is not by this Confederation expressly delegated to the United States, in Congress assembled." Art. II. By asserting the power to do all but what was "expressly delegated" to the federal

V. All power residing originally in the people, and being derived from them, the several magistrates and officers of government, vested with authority, whether legislative, executive, or judicial, are their substitutes and agents, and are at all times accountable to them.[48]

VI. No man, nor corporation, or association of men, have any other title to obtain advantages, or particular and exclusive privileges, distinct from those of the community, than what arises from the consideration of services rendered to the public; and this title being in nature neither hereditary, nor transmissible to children, or descendants, or relations by blood, the idea of a man born a magistrate, lawgiver, or judge, is absurd and unnatural.[49]

VII. Government is instituted for the common good; for the protection, safety, prosperity and happiness of the people; and not for the profit, honor, or private interest of any one man, family, or class of men; Therefore the people alone have an incontestible, unalienable, and indefeasible right to institute government; and to reform, alter, or totally change the same, when their protection, safety, prosperity and happiness require it.[50]

VIII. In order to prevent those, who are vested with authority, from becoming oppressors, the people have a right, at such periods and in such manner as they shall establish by their frame of government, to cause their

government, Massachusetts reasserted its right as a sovereign entity to control its own affairs. The provision reflected the deep suspicion of a centralized government that could jeopardize its internal governance in ways similar to those imposed on the colony by the Crown. The Massachusetts ratifying convention for the U.S. Constitution proposed the following amendment: "That it be explicitly declared that all Powers not expressly delegated by the aforesaid Constitution are reserved to the several States to be by them exercised." *Documentary History of the Constitution of the United States of America, 1787–1870* (Washington: Department of State, 1894), 2:94. That proposal was rejected, and an alternative proposal without the word "expressly" became the Tenth Amendment. It came as no surprise that Massachusetts did not ratify the first ten amendments until nearly 150 years after they were proposed.

[48] Similar to Pa. Decl. 1776, Art. IV; Va. Decl. 1776, sec. 2.

[49] Similar to N.C. Decl. 1776, Arts. III, XXII; Va. Decl. 1776, sec. 4. The language of the Massachusetts Constitution is the most forceful, referring to hereditary privilege as "absurd and unnatural."

[50] Similar to Pa. Decl. 1776, Art. V; Va. Decl. 1776, sec. 3. The article also expressed an unalienable right to alter or abolish a tyrannical government. See p. 49, footnote 29 for other states having alter or abolish clauses.

public officers to return to private life; and to fill up vacant places by certain and regular elections and appointments.[51]

IX. All elections ought to be free; and all the inhabitants of this Commonwealth, having such qualifications as they shall establish by their frame of government, have an equal right to elect officers, and to be elected, for public employments.[52]

X. Each individual of the society has a right to be protected by it in the enjoyment of his life, liberty and property, according to standing laws. He is obliged, consequently, to contribute his share to the expense of this protection; to give his personal service, or an equivalent, when necessary: But no part of the property of any individual, can, with justice, be taken from him, or applied to public uses without his own consent, or that of the representative body of the people: In fine, the people of this Commonwealth are not controllable by any other laws, than those to which their constitutional representative body have given their consent. And whenever the public exigencies require, that the property of any individual should be appropriated to public uses, he shall receive a reasonable compensation therefor.[53]

XI. Every subject of the Commonwealth ought to find a certain remedy, by having recourse to the laws, for all injuries or wrongs which he may receive in his person, property, or character. He ought to obtain right and justice freely, and without being obliged to purchase it; completely, and without any denial; promptly, and without delay; conformably to the laws.[54]

[51] Similar to Pa. Decl. 1776, Art. VI. This article provided an example of a collective right exercised by and belonging to the community—the right to have vacancies filled through either regular elections or appointments, as prescribed in the frame of government.

[52] Similar to Pa. Decl. 1776, Art. VII; see also Va. Decl. 1776, sec. 6. The convention removed the word "male" from those inhabitants enjoying the suffrage, presumably to remove from an enduring declaration of principles any specific qualifications for the franchise, which were more appropriate for the frame of government. Taylor, "Construction of Massachusetts Constitution," 334–335.

[53] Similar to Pa. Decl. 1776, Art. VIII; Del. Decl. 1776, sec. 10; Vt. Decl. 1777, Art. IX. Unlike these three other states, this article did not include an exemption from compulsory service for conscientious objectors. The article also protected private property, though this protection was bounded by the community's power to take that property under specified conditions (i.e., for public purposes and upon payment of reasonable compensation).

[54] Similar to Md. Decl. 1776, Art. XVII; Del. Decl. 1776, sec. 12.

XII. No subject shall be held to answer for any crime or offence, until the same is fully and plainly, substantially and formally, described to him; or be compelled to accuse, or furnish evidence against himself. And every subject shall have a right to produce all proofs, that may be favorable to him; to meet the witnesses against him face to face, and to be fully heard in his defence by himself, or his council, at his election. And no subject shall be arrested, imprisoned, despoiled, or deprived of his property, immunities, or privileges, put out of the protection of the law, exiled, or deprived of his life, liberty, or estate; but by the judgment of his peers, or the law of the land.

And the legislature shall not make any law, that shall subject any person to a capital or infamous punishment, excepting for the government of the army and navy, without trial by jury.[55]

XIII. In criminal prosecutions, the verification of facts in the vicinity where they happen is one of the greatest securities of the life, liberty, and property of the citizen.[56]

XIV. Every subject has a right to be secure from all unreasonable searches, and seizures of his person, his houses, his papers, and all his possessions. All warrants, therefore, are contrary to this right, if the cause or foundation of them be not previously supported by oath or affirmation; and if the order in the warrant to a civil officer, to make search in suspected places, or to arrest one or more suspected persons, or to seize their property, be not accompanied with a special designation of the persons or objects of search, arrest, or seizure: and no warrant ought to be issued but in cases, and with the formalities, prescribed by the laws.[57]

XV. In all controversies concerning property, and in all suits between two or more persons, except in cases in which it has heretofore been

[55] Article XII preserved the fundamental right to a jury trial by providing that no person may be subjected to criminal punishment or loss of property without the judgment of his or her peers or "the law of the land," a phrase which dated back to Chapter 39 of Magna Carta. The article also included other rights, viz., the right to be free from self-incrimination, to confront witnesses, to produce proofs and to have counsel in support of his or her defense. Dropped by the convention, the right to a speedy trial has been found in Article XI. Commonwealth v. Hanley, 337 Mass. 384 (1958).

[56] Similar to Md. Decl. 1776, Art. XVIII; Del. Decl. 1776, sec. 13.

[57] Similar to Pa. Decl. 1776, Art. X. The inclusion of the word "unreasonable" was John Adams's contribution, his recognition of the need to balance the individual's liberty to be free from searches and seizures with the need of the body politic to properly enforce its laws and secure the safety of the citizens.

otherways used and practised, the parties have a right to a trial by jury; and this method of procedure shall be held sacred, unless, in causes arising on the high-seas, and such as relate to mariners wages, the legislature shall hereafter find it necessary to alter it.[58]

XVI. The liberty of the press is essential to the security of freedom in a state: it ought not, therefore, to be restrained in this Commonwealth.[59]

XVII. The people have a right to keep and to bear arms for the common defence. And as in time of peace armies are dangerous to liberty, they ought not to be maintained without the consent of the legislature; and the military power shall always be held in an exact subordination to the civil authority, and be governed by it.[60]

XVIII. A frequent recurrence to the fundamental principles of the constitution, and a constant adherence to those of piety, justice, moderation, temperance, industry, and frugality, are absolutely necessary to preserve the advantages of liberty, and to maintain a free government: The people

[58] Similar to Pa. Decl. 1776, Art. XI. The inclusion of the language "except in cases in which it has heretofore been otherways used and practised"—not present in Adams's original draft—clarified that the right would not extend beyond its use at the time of adoption. The article also allowed the legislature to alter this "sacred" right in narrowly specified cases.

[59] This provision, reflecting the delegates' acknowledgment that freedom of the press was an indispensable prerequisite of a free society, differed considerably from Adams's original draft:

> The people have a right to the freedom of speaking, writing and publishing their sentiments: The liberty of the press therefore ought not to be restrained.

Had the state retained the protection for freedom of speech, it would have joined Pennsylvania (Decl. 1776, Art. XII) and Vermont (Decl. 1777, Art. XIV). This omission was sharply criticized by the City of Boston. Returns from the Town of Boston, in Handlin and Handlin, *Popular Sources*, 761–762.

[60] This article declared the right to keep and bear arms "for the common defence." John Adams had previously defended the rights of citizens to smuggle arms into the country in response to attempts by military governor General Thomas Gage to seize firearms from the citizens of Boston and the provinces. Stephen P. Halbrook, "The Right to Bear Arms in the First State Bills of Rights: Pennsylvania, North Carolina, Vermont, and Massachusetts," *Vermont Law Review* 10 (1985): 300. Unlike Pennsylvania and Vermont, the article did not grant a specific right to bear arms for individual self-defense, although the individual's right to bear arms was essential if men were to perform their duty of militia service. See pp. 63-67 concerning the interplay between the militia and the right to bear arms. The hostility towards peacetime armies was manifest in other constitutions as well. See Table 2, pp. 65-66.

ought, consequently, to have a particular attention to all those principles, in the choice of their officers and representatives: And they have a right to require of their law-givers and magistrates, an exact and constant observance of them, in the formation and execution of the laws necessary for the good administration of the Commonwealth.[61]

XIX. The people have a right, in an orderly and peaceable manner, to assemble to consult upon the common good; give instructions to their representatives; and to request of the legislative body, by the way of addresses, petitions, or remonstrances, redress of the wrongs done them, and of the grievances they suffer.[62]

XX. The power of suspending the laws, or the execution of the laws, ought never to be exercised but by the legislature, or by authority derived from it, to be exercised in such particular cases only as the legislature shall expressly provide for.[63]

XXI. The freedom of deliberation, speech and debate, in either house of the legislature, is so essential to the rights of the people, that it cannot be the foundation of any accusation or prosecution, action or complaint, in any other court or place whatsoever.[64]

XXII. The legislature ought frequently to assemble for the redress of grievances, for correcting, strengthening, and confirming the laws, and for making new laws, as the common good may require.[65]

XXIII. No subsidy, charge, tax, impost, or duties, ought to be established, fixed, laid, or levied, under any pretext whatsoever, without the consent of the people, or their representatives in the legislature.[66]

[61] Similar to Pa. Decl. 1776, Art. XIV. Massachusetts joined the other states in adopting as a constitutional principle the idea that a republican government must be founded on the bedrock of virtue. The virtues listed reflected the close connection made between religion and the political realm that characterized Massachusetts from its inception.

[62] Similar to Pa. Decl. 1776, Art. XVI; N.C. Decl. 1776, Art. XVIII; Vt. Decl. 1777, Art. XVIII. The article also protected the right to "give instructions to [the] representatives," a practice rooted in the colony's history to 1640 in New England and one which played a meaningful part in the constitutional convention process.

[63] Similar to Del. Decl. 1776, sec. 7; Md. Decl. 1776, Art. VII; N.C. Decl. 1776, Art. V; Va. Decl. 1776, sec. 7.

[64] Similar to Md. Decl. 1776, Art. VIII.

[65] Similar to Md. Decl. 1776, Art. X. To implement this prescriptive, the frame mandated that the general court meet annually and designated the dates when this meeting would occur (Const. 1780, Ch. I, sec. I, Art. I).

[66] Similar to Md. Decl. 1776, Art. XII.

XXIV. Laws made to punish for actions done before the existence of such laws, and which have not been declared crimes by preceding laws, are unjust, oppressive, and inconsistent with the fundamental principles of a free government.[67]

XXV. No subject ought, in any case, or in any time, to be declared guilty of treason or felony by the legislature.[68]

XXVI. No magistrate or court of law shall demand excessive bail or sureties, impose excessive fines, or inflict cruel or unusual punishments.[69]

XXVII. In time of peace no soldier ought to be quartered in any house without the consent of the owner; and in time of war such quarters ought not to be made but by the civil magistrate, in a manner ordained by the legislature.[70]

XXVIII. No person can in any case be subjected to law-martial, or to any penalties or pains, by virtue of that law, except those employed in the army or navy and except the militia in actual service, but by authority of the legislature.[71]

XXIX. It is essential to the preservation of the rights of every individual, his life, liberty, property and character, that there be an impartial interpretation of the laws, and administration of justice. It is the right of every citizen to be tried by judges as free, impartial and independent as the lot of humanity will admit. It is therefore not only the best policy, but for the security of the rights of the people, and of every citizen, that the judges of the supreme judicial court should hold their offices as long as they behave themselves well; and that they should have honorable salaries ascertained and established by standing laws.[72]

[67] Similar to Md. Decl. 1776, Art. XV.

[68] Similar to Md. Decl. 1776, Art. XVI.

[69] Similar to Va. Decl. 1776, sec. 9, Md. Decl. 1776, Art. XXII, Del. Decl. 1776, sec. 16, N.C. Decl. 1776, Art. X. Massachusetts followed the lead of Delaware, Maryland, and North Carolina in using "cruel or unusual" punishment instead of Virginia's "cruel and unusual" language.

[70] Similar to Md. Decl. 1776, Art. XXXVIII, Del. Decl. 1776, sec. 21.

[71] Similar to Md. Decl. 1776, Art. XXIX. The requirement for legislative approval, unprecedented when added, reflected awareness on the part of the Massachusetts framers that martial law could be subject to abuse by a rogue executive.

[72] Similar to Md. Decl. 1776, Art. XXX. Previously, judges in Massachusetts were subject to competing masters: the 1691 charter gave the royal governor the authority to remove judges without cause, while the general court controlled the salaries of the governor and the judiciary. This tug of war led to a British attempt in 1772 to seize complete

XXX. In the government of this Commonwealth, the legislative department shall never exercise the executive and judicial powers, or either of them: The executive shall never exercise the legislative and judicial powers, or either of them: The judicial shall never exercise the legislative and executive powers, or either of them: to the end it may be a government of laws and not of men.[73]

Part the Second: The Frame of Government

* * *

Chapter I. ***The Legislative Power.***

Section II. ***Senate.***

[Art.] II. ... the senators shall be chosen in the following manner, viz.: There shall be a meeting on the first Monday in April, annually, forever, of the inhabitants of each town in the several counties of this Commonwealth ... and at such meetings every male inhabitant of twenty-one years of age and upwards, having a freehold estate within the Commonwealth, of the annual income of three pounds, or any estate of the value of sixty pounds, shall have a right to give in his vote for the senators for the district of which he is an inhabitant.

control of the judiciary by paying judicial salaries out of revenues drawn from unpopular taxes, leading to the formation of the Boston Committee of Correspondence. By securing tenure and salaries, this article addressed both sources of undue influence on judges.

Extensive debate took place as to whether judicial independence could be best achieved by giving judges lifetime tenure or by making them accountable to the people through elections and short terms of office. To that end, Massachusetts followed the lead of Virginia and Maryland and provided that supreme court judges would hold their offices during good behavior. It also included language, unique to the state, specifically affording the judiciary the right to "impartial[ly] interpet[]" the laws—which Lawrence Friedman and Lynnea Thody claim necessarily required the courts to exercise some form of judicial review. *The Massachusetts State Constitution* (New York: Oxford University Press, 2011), 97.

[73] Although not alone in inserting an explicit separation of powers provision in its constitution, see, e.g., Ga. Const. 1777, Art. I, Md. Decl. 1776, Art. VI, N.C. Decl. 1776, Art. IV, Va. Const. 1776, Massachusetts was the most emphatic in its language. The committee's version of this article applied only to the judiciary: "[t]he judicial department of the state ought to be separate from, and independent of, the legislative and executive powers."

Chapter I. ***The Legislative Power.***
Section III. ***House of Representatives.***

* * *

[Art.] IV. Every male person, being twenty-one years of age, and resident in any particular town in this Commonwealth for the space of one year next preceding, having a freehold estate within the said town of the annual income of three pounds, or any estate of the value of sixty pounds, shall have a right to vote in the choice of a Representative or Representatives for the said town.

Chapter II. ***Executive Power.***
Section I. ***Governor.***

* * *

III. Those persons who shall be qualified to vote for Senators and Representatives within the several towns of this Commonwealth shall, at a meeting to be called for that purpose, on the first Monday of April annually, give in their votes for a Governor, to the selectmen, who shall preside at such meetings …

Chapter V. ***The University at Cambridge and Encouragement of Literature,*** **etc.**
Section II. ***The Encouragement of Literature,*** **etc.**

Wisdom, and knowledge, as well as virtue, diffused generally among the body of the people, being necessary for the preservation of their rights and liberties; and as these depend on spreading the opportunities and advantages of education in the various parts of the country, and among the different orders of the people, it shall be the duty of legislators and magistrates, in all future periods of this Commonwealth, to cherish the interests of literature and the sciences, and all seminaries of them; especially the university at Cambridge, public schools, and grammar schools in the towns; to encourage private societies and public institutions, rewards and immunities, for the promotion of agriculture, arts, sciences, commerce, trades, manufactures, and a natural history of the country; to countenance and inculcate the principles of humanity and general benevolence, public and private charity, industry and frugality, honesty and punctuality in their dealings; sincerity, good humour, and all social affections, and generous sentiments among the people.[74]

Chapter VI. ***Oaths and Subscriptions; Incompatibility of and Exclusion from Offices; Pecuniary Qualifications; Commissions; Writs; Confirmation of Laws; Habeas Corpus; The Enacting Style; Continuance of Officers; Provision for a Future Revisal of the Constitutions,*** **etc.**

* * *

[Art.] VI. All the laws which have heretofore been adopted, used, and approved in the Province, Colony, or State of Massachusetts Bay, and usually practised on in the courts of law, shall still remain and be in full force, until altered or repealed by the legislature; such parts only excepted as are repugnant to the rights and liberties contained in this constitution.[75]

[Art.] VII. The privilege and benefit of the writ of *habeas corpus* shall be enjoyed in this Commonwealth in the most free, easy, cheap, expeditious and ample manner; and shall not be suspended by the Legislature, except upon the most urgent and pressing occasions, and for a limited time not exceeding twelve months.[76]

[74] The drafters of the Massachusetts Constitution, like most states, believed a knowledgeable citizenry to be critical for the success of republican government. They inserted a provision making it the duty of the legislature to "cherish the interests of literature and the sciences." The section remained mute as to the actions the legislature ought to take to cherish these interests. See the discussion of civic education and republican citizenship pp. 59-61.

[75] This section continued all of the previous laws of Massachusetts adopted during the state's colonial, provincial, and post-statehood periods. The term "laws" was later construed to include the common law. Commonwealth v. Churchill, 2 Met. 118, 123–124 (MA. 1840).

[76] Massachusetts was the second state to constitutionalize the writ of habeas corpus, allowing a prisoner to challenge confinement as being improper or illegal. See Ga. Const. 1777, Art. LXI. Long regarded as one of the most efficient and effective safeguards of individual liberty, the writ traces its origins back to the Assize of Clarendon (1166) and the English habeas corpus acts of 1640 and 1679. Conceding there may be conditions justifying its suspension, the framers took steps to ensure such suspensions would not be abused by requiring legislative consent, limiting its use to pressing and urgent situations, and placing a time limit of twelve months on any suspension.

New Hampshire

The area that would become New Hampshire was originally part of a land grant for the Province of Maine issued in 1622 to Sir Ferdinando Gorges and Captain John Mason from the Council for New England.[1] In 1629, the province was divided at the Piscataqua River, with Mason taking the portion between the Piscataqua and Merrimack rivers and renaming it New Hampshire, after the English county where he lived. Unlike other New England colonies settled by religious dissenters, New Hampshire began its existence as a proprietary colony.

The relationship between the settlers in New Hampshire and Massachusetts was controversial, tenuous, and complicated by land claims maintained by Mason's heirs. In 1641, New Hampshire became part of the Massachusetts Bay Colony and known as the Upper Province of Massachusetts. The agreement effecting this combination allowed New Hampshire settlers to retain local autonomy and did not condition civic privileges on membership in the Congregational (Puritan) Church.[2] On September 18, 1680, King Charles II issued a royal commission

[1] The grant included that land between the Merrimack and Sagadahock (later renamed Kennebec) rivers, see A Grant of the Province of Maine to Sir Ferdinando Gorges and John Mason, Esq., 10th of August, 1622, in Thorpe, *Constitutions*, 3:1622, roughly present-day New Hampshire and Western Maine.

[2] Anselm V. Hiester, "Religious Liberty in Pennsylvania and the Other American Colonies," *The Reformed Church Review* 9, no. 1 (January 1905): 95–96.

P. J. Galie et al., *Bills of Rights Before the Bill of Rights*,
https://doi.org/10.1007/978-3-030-44301-6_11

separating the Province of New Hampshire from the Colony of Massachusetts Bay, making it a royal province.

The new commission appointed a president (John Cutt) and a six-member council and mandated that a general assembly be chosen by voters of the province. Within a year the general assembly adopted the "General laws and Liberties." This code authorized civil and religious rulers to exert their authority over every sector of human experience, proscribed evil behavior, and maintained order "by upholding the power of family, church and town government."[3] Community cohesiveness and piety were believed to be the *sine qua non* of a well-ordered, decent community.

The focus on creating and sustaining a moral order in the colony did not preclude recognizing the liberties and rights of members of the community. Land titles were confirmed; an assembly was established[4]; liberty of conscience was granted to all Protestants[5]; trial by jury was guaranteed in civil and criminal cases[6]; and no person could be deprived of life or limb without consent of king and council.[7] The right to vote was provided to all freemen, defined as male Protestants, twenty-four years of age, possessed of twenty pounds taxable estate, and "not vitious[vicious] in life, but of honest & good conversation" who swore allegiance to the English Crown.[8] The first set of laws also provided a right to local self-government.[9]

From 1686 to 1689, New Hampshire was combined with several other colonies into the short-lived Dominion of New England. Following the demise of that entity, New Hampshire successfully petitioned the Massachusetts Bay Colony for annexation, a situation that lasted until

[3] David E. Van Deventer, *The Emergence of Provincial New Hampshire, 1623–1741* (Baltimore: Johns Hopkins University Press, 1976), 185.

[4] [Commission of John Cutt] (1680), in Thorpe, *Constitutions*, 4:2449.

[5] Ibid., 2448.

[6] The General Laws and Liberties of the Province of New Hampshire, March 16, 1679, in *Laws of New Hampshire Including Public and Private Acts and Resolves and the Royal Commissions and Instructions*, ed. Albert Stillman Batchellor, vol. 1, *Province Period* (Manchester, NH: The John B. Clarke Company, 1904), 23, 25.

[7] [Commission of John Cutt], 2448.

[8] General Laws, 25–26.

[9] Ibid., 26.

the Crown in 1691/1692 commissioned a new royal governor for New Hampshire, effectively separating the provinces.[10]

During the second half of the eighteenth century, dissatisfaction with British policies and practices—selective representation, nepotism, favoritism, and taxation without representation—gave rise to discontent, anger, and finally open resistance to British rule. The pro-British policies of Governor John Wentworth (1767–1775) made him a lightning rod for this discontent. He adjourned and then dissolved a recalcitrant legislature, but succeeded only in giving rise to a shadow legislature as colonists elected a provincial congress to represent them in sessions that began during July of 1774.

Unlike Massachusetts, New Hampshire did not have a governing charter; the colony had been governed by a royal commission, granted to all governors when they assumed office. When Wentworth abandoned the colony in August 1775, royal government ceased to exist and the provincial congress assumed the role of a colonial legislature.[11] Under the aegis of this extra-legal congress the transition from royal to Revolutionary government took place.

Constitutional Developments: 1776 Constitution

An October 18, 1775, petition from New Hampshire to the Continental Congress requesting authority to establish a new government elicited the following recommendation from the latter: "that the provincial Convention … call a full and free representation of the people, and that the representatives … establish such a form of government … [that] will best produce the happiness of the people, and most effectually secure peace and good order in the province…."[12] The Fifth Provincial Congress, meeting in Concord, quickly appointed a committee to draft a constitution. On January 5, 1776, the draft was presented to and passed by the congress, making New Hampshire the first colony to establish a state government.[13]

[10] Notwithstanding the formal separation of the provinces, they shared governors from 1699 to 1741, leading to numerous conflicts.

[11] Karen E. Andresen, "A Return to Legitimacy: New Hampshire's Constitution of 1776," *Historical New Hampshire* 31, no. 4 (Winter 1976): 159.

[12] *Journals of the Continental Congress, 1774–1789* (Washington, DC: Government Printing Office, 1905), 3:319.

[13] Andresen, "Return to Legitimacy," 155.

Absent a charter, the committee adopted a 911-word document—one-third of which was preamble—as a temporary measure to enable the state to claim a legitimate representative government. Modest though it was, that document became the first American state constitution. The language of the constitution reflected a desire for reconciliation with Great Britain:

> ...we conceive ourselves reduced to the necessity of establishing A FORM OF GOVERNMENT to continue during the present unhappy and unnatural contest with Great Britain; PROTESTING and DECLARING that we neaver sought to throw off our dependence upon Great Britain, but felt ourselves happy under her protection, while we could enjoy our constitutional rights and privileges. And that we shall rejoice if such a reconciliation between us and our parent State can be effected as shall be approved by the CONTINENTAL CONGRESS, in whose prudence and wisdom we confide.[14]

The constitution empowered the state legislature to make law but indicated such power was derived from the people and its very existence rested on the consent of the governed, both widespread notions throughout the colonies. It assumed that there existed a "people" with sufficient commitment to the principles and ideals represented in the document to form a separate political community.

The constitution accomplished its purpose as a stopgap measure despite having no provision for its amendment and, for all intents and purposes, no governor or independent judiciary. The document contained no declaration of rights and made no mention of any specific rights or liberties, but, as B. Thomas Schuman notes:

> The election of popular representatives implies majority rule, and apportionment of the council on the basis of population implies an egalitarian commitment. There is no direct reference to individual protections of rights, but by reference to the rights and privileges of Englishmen it suggests the protections of common law.[15]

[14] Constitution of New Hampshire (1776), in Thorpe, *Constitutions*, 4:2452.

[15] B. Thomas Schuman, "New Hampshire and the Constitutional Movement," in *The Constitutionalism of American States*, ed. George E. Connor and Christopher W. Hammons (Columbia: University of Missouri Press, 2008), 52.

Constitutional Developments: 1784 Declaration and Constitution

Though intended to last until the end of the Revolutionary War, defects in the 1776 constitution occasioned much discontent. Responding to that discontent, the legislature voted to hold a convention in June 1778. That convention gave New Hampshire the "distinction of being the first place in the world where a convention was elected and met for the sole purpose of drawing up a constitution, to be adopted when submitted to and approved by popular referendum."[16] Between 1779 and 1783, two separately elected conventions submitted a total of four constitutional drafts to be considered by voters in their respective town meetings. After the rejections of the first three submissions, a draft adopted by the convention in June 1783 obtained the required two-thirds majority and took effect in 1784.[17]

Ten other states had adopted constitutions prior to 1784, providing New Hampshire with a wealth of experience from which to draw. The 1780 Massachusetts Constitution headed the list of influences, a consequence of geographic propinquity and New Hampshire's former political union with that state. Much of the language about popular sovereignty, equality, and the communal rights and duties adopted by the 1784 convention came directly from its southern neighbor.

One salient difference between the Massachusetts and New Hampshire constitutions was the absence of a preamble in the latter. Rather than laying out the need for a governing charter and providing its underlying constitutional principles in a preamble, delegates opted to present the fundamental principles of the republic in the first four articles of the state's thirty-eight article "bill" of rights.[18] The bill contained one of the clearest explications of natural rights found in the early state constitutions: All

[16] Susan E. Marshall, *The New Hampshire State Constitution* (New York: Oxford University Press, 2011), 13.

[17] For a more detailed examination of this adoption process, and the sectionalism that made consensus difficult to achieve, see Lynn Warren Turner, *The Ninth State: New Hampshire's Formative Years* (Chapel Hill: University of North Carolina Press, 1983); Marshall, *New Hampshire State Constitution*, 9–12.

[18] The New Hampshire Constitution was the only constitution adopted between 1776 and 1790 that referred to a "bill," as opposed to a "declaration," of rights. See p. 8, footnote 18 for the use of "bills" and "declarations." Only Maryland's declaration, with forty-two articles, was longer than New Hampshire's.

men are born equally free and independent (Decl. 1784, Art. I); all men have "natural, essential and inherent rights," which include enjoying and defending life and liberty, acquiring, possessing, and protecting property, and seeking and obtaining happiness (ibid., Art. II); by entering into a state of society, men surrender some rights to ensure the protection of others, but the surrender is void absent an equivalent benefit (ibid., Art. III); and some rights by their very nature, such as "rights of conscience" are inalienable because no equivalent can be given for them (ibid., Art. IV).

Following the Massachusetts model of labeling the bill of rights "Part I" of the constitution and the form of government as "Part II," delegates foreclosed any claim that the bill was not part of the constitution, without saying so expressly.[19] The constitution included a section continuing all the laws which had "heretofore been adopted, used and approved, in the province, colony, or state of New-Hampshire, and usually practiced on in the courts of law," which kept the common law in force.[20]

The first article of the bill of rights set forth the core principle of popular sovereignty that all government of right originates from the people and is founded in consent (Decl. 1784, Art. I).[21] The people were exhorted that they "of right, ought, to reform the old, or establish a new government" in those situations where government's ends were perverted, public liberty was manifestly endangered, and other means of redress had proven ineffectual (ibid., Art. X). The declaration afforded the people the right to assemble and to instruct or request redress from the legislature by petition or remonstrance (ibid., Art. XXXII).

[19] References to Part I will be noted as "Decl." and references to Part II will be noted as "Const." Part II did not contain specific section numbers.

[20] *State v. Rollins*, 8 N.H. 550, 563 (1837). This provision constitutionalized a statute, adopted in April 1777, continuing the common law in force. An Act for the Re-establishing the General System of Laws Heretofore in Force in this State, April 9, 1777, in *Laws of New Hampshire Including Public and Private Acts and Resolves*, ed. Henry Harrison Metcalf, vol. 4, *Revolutionary Period, 1776–1784* (Bristol, NH: Musgrove Printing House, 1916), 87.

[21] This commitment to popular sovereignty was underscored in Article VIII of the declaration, in slightly different words.

Suffrage

Voters for both houses of the legislature and the governor were required to be males at least twenty-one years of age and had to pay a poll tax (a fixed tax assessed on every eligible individual). By 1784, several states had required payment of taxes instead of property ownership for voting but New Hampshire was the first to explicitly require a poll tax. The initial tax was ten shillings on all males over eighteen years of age.[22] When New Hampshire's requirement was adopted, it expanded the franchise as it was easier to satisfy than wealth requirements used in other states.

Structural Provisions

Delegates addressed the criticism leveled against the first constitution for inadequately separating the powers. Accepting as a truism the maxim "[w]hen the legislative and executive powers are united in the same person, or in the same body of magistrates, there can be no liberty,"[23] they inserted in the bill of rights language that the three branches "ought to be kept as separate from and independent of each other, as the nature of a free government will admit, or as is consistent with that chain of connection that binds the whole fabric of the constitution in one indissoluble bond of union and amity" (Decl. 1784, Art. XXXVII).

The constitution divided the state legislature into a two-house general court, composed of a senate and a house of representatives elected for one-year terms. The chief executive, titled the president of the state, was also elected by the people for a one-year term. The president did not have an executive veto, but, as president of the senate, was given both an equal vote as all other members in that body AND a casting vote in the event of a tie. The general court (legislature) was required to meet "frequently" (Decl. 1784, Art. XXXI), which the frame defined as annually. Concerning visibility of the general court, the constitution required a journal of

[22] An Act to Establish an Equitable Method of Making Rates and Taxes and Determining Who Shall be Legal Voters in Town and Parish Affairs and Also for Repealing Certain Acts Herein Aftermentioned, June 12, 1784, in *Laws of New Hampshire Including Public and Private Acts, Resolves, Votes, Etc.*, ed. Henry Harrison Metcalf, vol. 5, *First Constitutional Period, 1784–1792* (Concord, NH: Rumford Press, 1916), 9–10.

[23] Montesquieu, *The Spirit of the Laws*, trans. and ed. Anne M. Cohler, Basia C. Miller, and Harold S. Stone (Cambridge: Cambridge University Press, 1989 [1748]), Part II, Book 11, chap. 6.

its proceedings to be published immediately after every adjournment, and the yeas and nays to be entered on any question upon motion of any one member.

The form or frame of government placed restrictions on plural office-holding for officers in all branches of government. With the exception of justices of the peace, judicial officers held office during good behavior, providing a degree of judicial independence. The only term limits in the constitution were for delegates to Congress: No person could serve for more than three years in any span of six years.

Requirements for holding office were as follows:

Office	*Minimum Age*	*Estate*	*Residency*	*Religion*
President	30 years	500 pounds, half being freehold within state	Inhabitant of state at least 7 years	Protestant[a]
Senator	30 years	Freehold estate of 200 pounds within state	Inhabitant of state at least 7 years; inhabitant of the district	Protestant
Representative	No age specified	100 pounds, half being freehold within constituency	Inhabitant of state at least 2 years; inhabitant of the constituency	Protestant

[a]Non-Protestants would not be permitted to hold state office until 1877

Clergy members were not barred from holding office. In keeping with the assumption that the only legitimate source of political power resided in the people, money bills were required to originate in the house of representatives.

Delegates provided an institutional mechanism to make constitutional changes: Elections would be held seven years after the constitution took effect for delegates to be chosen for a convention to consider alterations. Any alterations were required to be approved by two-thirds of those voting on the question. No specific provisions were placed beyond the reach of the amendment process.

Postscript: In 1791, the state held a constitutional convention. The convention proposed seventy-two amendments to the existing constitution and submitted them to the voters in February 1792. Forty-six amendments were approved, creating inconsistencies within the existing document. Subsequently, the convention submitted an omnibus amendment addressing these inconsistencies, which the voters approved. The State of New Hampshire considers those changes a revision of the 1784 constitution. The 1792 amendments made only minor changes to the bill of rights. Although amended numerous times in the intervening 225-plus years, twenty-three of the thirty-eight articles in the 1784 declaration exist unchanged in the current constitution.

Constitution of New Hampshire [1784]

Part I: The Bill of Rights

ARTICLE I

All men are born equally free and independent; therefore, all government of right originates from the people, is founded in consent, and instituted for the general good.[24]

II. All men have certain natural, essential, and inherent rights; among which are—the enjoying and defending life and liberty—acquiring, possessing and protecting property—and in a word, of seeking and obtaining happiness.[25]

[24] By using the word "born," the New Hampshire provision more closely approximated the Massachusetts and Pennsylvania declarations than Virginia's. Wartime attrition and bounties offered by the state to slaveholders who manumitted black recruits brought a de facto end to slavery. Between 1773 and 1786, the number of slaves in New Hampshire plummeted from 674 to 46. Douglas Harper, "Slavery in New Hampshire," Slavery in the North, accessed February 16, 2020, http://slavenorth.com/newhampshire.htm.

Despite mimicking the language in the Massachusetts Constitution that led courts in that state to end slavery and the scholarly consensus that this provision ended the practice in New Hampshire, it is unclear whether the provision applied to all slaves or just to children of slaves born after 1783. The record seems to support the latter: The 1790 federal census counted 158 slaves; by 1800, it listed only eight. Harper, "Slavery in New Hampshire."

[25] New Hampshire joined the list of states setting forth the natural status of the rights to enjoy life and liberty, to acquire and possess property, and to pursue and obtain happiness. New Hampshire's declaration, unlike the declarations of Massachusetts, Pennsylvania, and Vermont, did not describe these rights as "inalienable" or "unalienable." Those states, along with Virginia, also included pursuing or obtaining safety as a natural right—a right absent from the New Hampshire declaration.

III. When men enter into a state of society, they surrender up some of their natural rights to that society, in order to insure the protection of others; and, without such an equivalent, the surrender is void.[26]

IV. Among the natural rights, some are in their very nature unalienable, because no equivalent can be given or received for them. Of this kind are the RIGHTS OF CONSCIENCE.[27]

V. Every individual has a natural and unalienable right to worship GOD according to the dictates of his own conscience, and reason; and no subject shall be hurt, molested, or restrained in his person, liberty or estate for worshipping GOD, in the manner and season most agreeable to the dictates of his own conscience, or for his religious profession, sentiments or persuasion; provided he doth not disturb the public peace, or disturb others, in their religious worship.[28]

VI. As morality and piety, rightly grounded on evangelical principles, will give the best and greatest security to government, and will lay in the hearts of men the strongest obligations to due subjection; and as the knowledge of these, is most likely to be propagated through a society by the institution of the public worship of the DEITY, and of public instruction in morality and religion; therefore, to promote those important purposes, the people of this state have a right to impower, and do hereby fully impower the legislature to authorize from time to time, the several towns, parishes, bodies-corporate, or religious societies within this state, to make adequate provision at their own expence, for the support and maintenance of public protestant teachers of piety, religion and morality:

[26] In language unique to New Hampshire, this article made clear that rights were not absolute: In agreeing to enter society, individuals surrendered some of these "natural rights," enabling the community to create the conditions under which its members could pursue happiness.

[27] Article IV made a distinction between natural and inalienable rights. The former were subject to limitations based on the consent of those who have agreed to enter the social contract; the latter were not—they could neither be given nor taken away. One clear example of an unalienable right was the sacred "right of conscience."

[28] Similar to Mass. Decl. 1780, Art. II. One important difference was that the Massachusetts provision referred to the "duty" as well as the right to "worship the Supreme Being." Article VI created multiple establishments, ostensibly of Protestant denominations, on a local option basis, requiring that all had equal status. For elaboration on the local option, see Leonard W. Levy, *The Establishment Clause: Religion and the First Amendment*, 2nd ed. (Chapel Hill: University of North Carolina Press, 1994), 42–45.

Provided notwithstanding, That the several towns, parishes, bodies-corporate, or religious societies, shall at all times have the exclusive right of electing their own public teachers, and of contracting with them for their support and maintenance. And no portion of any one particular religious sect or denomination, shall ever be compelled to pay towards the support of the teacher or teachers of another persuasion, sect or denomination.

And every denomination of christians demeaning themselves quietly, and as good subjects of the state, shall be equally under the protection of the law: and no subordination of any one sect or denomination to another, shall ever be established by law.

And nothing herein shall be understood to affect any former contracts made for the support of the ministry; but all such contracts shall remain, and be in the same state as if this constitution had not been made.[29]

VII. The people of this state, have the sole and exclusive right of governing themselves as a free, sovereign, and independent state, and do, and forever hereafter shall, exercise and enjoy every power, jurisdiction and right pertaining thereto, which is not, or may not hereafter be by them expressly delegated to the United States of America in Congress assembled.[30]

VIII. All power residing originally in, and being derived from the people, all the magistrates and officers of government, are their substitutes and agents, and at all times accountable to them.[31]

[29] Similar to Mass. Decl. 1780, Art. III. Although the provision prohibited one from being compelled to fund religious schools of a different denomination, the implementing statute allowed an individual to refuse to pay the tax for the Congregational Church only upon proof of belonging to another denomination. As religious diversity came to New Hampshire, the religious tax was repealed in 1819. An Act, in Amendment of an Act Entitled An Act, for Regulating Towns and the Choice of Town Officers, *Laws of New Hampshire Including Public and Private Acts, Resolves, Votes, Etc.*, vol. 8, *Second Constitutional Period, 1811–1820* (Concord, NH: Evans Printing Co., 1920), 821–822; See Richard Francis Upton, *Revolutionary New Hampshire: An Account of the Social and Political Forces Underlying the Transition from Royal Province to American Commonwealth* (Port Washington, NY: Kennikat Press, 1970 [1936]), 208–209.

[30] Similar to Mass. Decl. 1780, Art. IV.

[31] Similar to Mass. Decl. 1780, Art. V.

IX. No office or place whatsoever in government, shall be hereditary—the abilities and integrity requisite in all, not being transmissible to posterity or relations.[32]

X. Government being instituted for the common benefit, protection, and security of the whole community, and not for the private interest or emolument of any one man, family or class of men; therefore, whenever the ends of government are perverted, and public liberty manifestly endangered, and all other means of redress are ineffectual, the people may, and of right ought, to reform the old, or establish a new government. The doctrine of non-resistance against arbitrary power, and oppression, is absurd, slavish, and destructive of the good and happiness of mankind.[33]

XI. All elections ought to be free, and every inhabitant of the state having the proper qualifications, has equal right to elect, and be elected into office.[34]

XII. Every member of the community has a right to be protected by it in the enjoyment of his life, liberty and property; he is therefore bound to contribute his share in the expence of such protection, and to yield his personal service when necessary, or an equivalent. But no part of a man's property shall be taken from him, or applied to public uses, without his own consent, or that of the representative body of the people. Nor are the inhabitants of this state controllable by any other laws than those to which they or their representative body have given their consent.[35]

XIII. No person who is conscientiously scrupulous about the lawfulness of bearing arms, shall be compelled thereto, provided he will pay an equivalent.[36]

XIV. Every subject of this state is entitled to a certain remedy, by having recourse to the laws, for all injuries he may receive in his person, property or character, to obtain right and justice freely, without being

[32] Similar to Mass. Decl. 1780, Art. VI.

[33] First clause: similar to Pa. Decl. 1776, Art. V; Va. Decl. 1776, sec. 3. Second clause (right to reform the government): similar to Md. Decl. 1776, Art. IV.

[34] Similar to Mass. Decl. 1780, Art. IX.

[35] Similar to Mass. Decl. 1780, Art. X; Pa. Decl. 1776, Art. VIII; Del. Decl. 1776, sec. 10; Vt. Decl. 1777, Art. IX. It is noteworthy that, unlike the declarations of neighboring Massachusetts and Vermont, there was no requirement of just compensation for a taking. Cf. Penn. Decl. 1776, Art. VII.

[36] Similar to Del. Decl. 1776, sec. 10; Pa. Decl. 1776, Art. VIII; Vt. Decl. 1777, Art. IX.

obliged to purchase it; completely, and without any denial; promptly, and without delay, conformably to the laws.[37]

XV. No subject shall be held to answer for any crime, or offence, until the same is fully and plainly, substantially and formally, described to him; or be compelled to accuse or furnish evidence against himself. And every subject shall have a right to produce all proofs that may be favorable to himself; to meet the witnesses against him face to face, and to be fully heard in his defence by himself, and counsel. And no subject shall be arrested, imprisoned, despoiled, or deprived of his property, immunities, or privileges, put out of the protection of the law, exiled or deprived of his life, liberty, or estate, but by the judgment of his peers or the law of the land.[38]

XVI. No subject shall be liable to be tried, after an acquittal, for the same crime or offence.—Nor shall the legislature make any law that shall subject any person to a capital punishment, excepting for the government of the army and navy, and the militia in actual service, without trial by jury.[39]

XVII. In criminal prosecutions, the trial of facts in the vicinity where they happen, is so essential to the security of the life, liberty and estate of the citizen, that no crime or offence ought to be tried in any other county than that in which it is committed; except in cases of general insurrection in any particular county, when it shall appear to the Judges of the Superior Court, that an impartial trial cannot be had in the county where the offence may be committed, and upon their report, the assembly shall

[37] Similar to Mass. Decl. 1780, Art. XI.

[38] Similar to Mass. Decl. 1780, Art. XII. The importance of the jury to citizens of New Hampshire was underscored by the fact that four articles (Articles XV, XVI, XX, and XXI) in the declaration addressed this right.

[39] The sixteenth article barred double jeopardy, the trying of a person after acquittal for the same crime or offense. First appearing in America in the Massachusetts Body of Liberties (1641), sec. 42, the prohibition's placement in this article marked the first guarantee against the practice in an American constitution. It was almost certainly one of the sources for the Fifth Amendment of the U.S. Constitution. The second sentence, ensuring that jury trial would be available in situations where capital punishment was prescribed, derived from Mass. Decl. 1780, art. XII.

think proper to direct the trial in the nearest county in which an impartial trial can be obtained.[40]

XVIII. All penalties ought to be proportioned to the nature of the offence. No wise legislature will affix the same punishment to the crimes of theft, forgery and the like, which they do to those of murder and treason; where the same undistinguishing severity is exerted against all offences; the people are led to forget the real distinction in the crimes themselves, and to commit the most flagrant with as little compunction as they do those of the lightest dye: For the same reason a multitude of sanguinary laws is both impolitic and unjust. The true design of all punishments being to reform, not to exterminate, mankind.[41]

XIX. Every subject hath a right to be secure from all unreasonable searches and seizures of his person, his houses, his papers, and all his possessions. All warrants, therefore, are contrary to this right, if the cause or foundation of them be not previously supported by oath, or affirmation; and if the order in the warrant to a civil officer, to make search in suspected places, or to arrest one or more suspected persons, or to seize their property, be not accompanied with a special designation of the persons or objects of search, arrest, or seizure; and no warrant ought to be issued but in cases, and with the formalities prescribed by the laws.[42]

XX. In all controversies concerning property, and in all suits between two or more persons, except in cases in which it has been heretofore otherwise used and practiced, the parties have a right to a trial by jury; and this method of procedure shall be held sacred, unless in causes arising

[40] Similar to Mass. Decl. 1780, Art. XIII. The language in this provision was more forceful than its Massachusetts counterpart. The second clause allowed a defendant in an insurrection case to move the venue when an impartial trial seemed unlikely.

[41] Prior to the Revolution the penal code in New Hampshire, as in some other colonies, was severe—at least on the books. Death, brandings, and other forms of corporal punishment, such as the stocks and the pillory, were the stock-in-trade of punishment. Article XVIII presented a new view of punishment. This Enlightenment view—"reform not exterminate"—first appeared in an American state constitution in the 1776 Pennsylvania Constitution. See Pa. Const. 1776, sec. 39. No actual reforms pursuant to this article were made until 1791, when the death penalty was limited to eight crimes—down from the two hundred under colonial English law. Similar reductions were made in the use of sanguinary punishments such as whipping and branding. Upton, *Revolutionary New Hampshire*, 213–214.

[42] Similar to Mass. Decl. 1780, Art. XIV.

on the high seas, and such as relate to mariners wages, the legislature shall think it necessary hereafter to alter it.[43]

XXI. In order to reap the fullest advantage of the inestimable privilege of the trial by jury, great care ought to be taken that none but qualified persons should be appointed to serve; and such ought to be fully compensated for their travel, time and attendance.[44]

XXII. The Liberty of the Press is essential to the security of freedom in a state; it ought, therefore, to be inviolably preserved.[45]

XXIII. Retrospective laws are highly injurious, oppressive and unjust. No such laws, therefore, should be made, either for the decision of civil causes, or the punishment of offences.[46]

XXIV. A well regulated militia is the proper, natural, and sure defence of a state.[47]

XXV. Standing armies are dangerous to liberty, and ought not to be raised or kept up without the consent of the legislature.[48]

XXVI. In all cases, and at all times, the military ought to be under strict subordination to, and governed by the civil power.[49]

XXVII. No soldier in time of peace, shall be quartered in any house without the consent of the owner; and in time of war, such quarters ought not to be made but by the civil magistrate, in a manner ordained by the legislature.[50]

[43] One of four articles on the jury found in the New Hampshire declaration, this section guaranteed trial by jury in civil suits. It extended the right to a jury trial to all cases for which the right existed when the constitution was adopted in 1784, but not for certain proceedings unknown to the common law. Marshall, *New Hampshire Constitution*, 83.

[44] Article XXI was an aspirational right in the form of an admonitory directive to the legislature to provide a selection process that would enable it to realize its "sacred" purpose, i.e., ensuring that the rights to life, liberty, and property were guarded. The article also required that those serving on a jury were compensated for their time and expenses.

[45] Similar to Mass. Decl. 1780, Art, XVI. Like Massachusetts, this provision did not contain an explicit protection for freedom of speech.

[46] Similar to Del. Decl. 1776, sec. 11; Md. Decl. 1776, Art. XV; Mass. Decl. 1780, Art. XXIV; N.C. Decl. 1776, Art. XXIV. This article extended the prohibition against these laws to civil matters as well as criminal matters.

[47] Similar to Del. Decl. 1776, sec. 18.

[48] Similar to Del. Decl. 1776, sec. 19.

[49] Similar to Del. Decl. 1776, sec. 20.

[50] Similar to Mass. Decl. 1780, Art. XVII.

XXVIII. No subsidy, charge, tax, impost or duty shall be established, fixed, laid, or levied, under any pretext whatsoever, without the consent of the people or their representatives in the legislature, or authority derived from that body.[51]

XXIX. The power of suspending the laws, or the execution of them, ought never to be exercised but by the legislature, or by authority derived therefrom, to be exercised in such particular cases only as the legislature shall expressly provide for.[52]

XXX. The freedom of deliberation, speech, and debate, in either house of the legislature, is so essential to the rights of the people, that it cannot be the foundation of any action, complaint, or prosecution, in any other court or place whatsoever.[53]

XXXI. The legislature ought frequently to assemble for the redress of grievances, for correcting, strengthening and confirming the laws, and for making new ones, as the common good may require.[54]

XXXII. The people have a right in an orderly and peaceable manner, to assemble and consult upon the common good, give instructions to their representatives; and to request of the legislative body, by way of petition or remonstrance, redress of the wrongs done them, and of the grievances they suffer.[55]

XXXIII. No magistrate or court of law shall demand excessive bail or sureties, impose excessive fines, or inflict cruel or unusual punishments.[56]

XXXIV. No person can in any case be subjected to law martial, or to any pains, or penalties, by virtue of that law, except those employed in the

[51] Similar to Mass. Decl. 1780, Art. XXIII. Two differences: (1) the Massachusetts version used the term "ought," while New Hampshire used the word "shall;" and (2) the use of the clause "or authority derived from that body" was a New Hampshire addition.

[52] Similar to Mass. Decl. 1780, Art. XX. In this article, New Hampshire kept the use of the word "ought" used in the Massachusetts declaration.

[53] Similar to Mass. Decl. 1780, Art. XXI.

[54] Similar to Mass. Decl. 1780, Art. XXII. The long prorogation of the legislature by Governor Bennington Wentworth in the 1750s reinforced the need for a similar safeguard.

[55] Similar to Mass. Decl. 1780, Art. XIX. Where the Massachusetts declaration provided for "addresses, petitions or remonstrances," the New Hampshire document omitted "addresses."

[56] Similar to Mass. Decl. 1780, Art. XXVI.

army or navy, and except the militia in actual service, but by authority of the legislature.[57]

XXXV. It is essential to the preservation of the rights of every individual, his life, liberty, property and character, that there be an impartial interpretation of the laws, and administration of justice. It is the right of every citizen to be tried by judges as impartial as the lot of humanity will admit. It is therefore not only the best policy, but for the security of the rights of the people, that the judges of the supreme (or superior) judicial court should hold their offices so long as they behave well; and that they should have honorable salaries, ascertained and established by standing laws.[58]

XXXVI. Economy being a most essential virtue in all states, especially in a young one; no pension shall be granted, but in consideration of actual services, and such pensions ought to be granted with great caution, by the legislature, and never for more than one year at a time.[59]

XXXVII. In the government of this state, the three essential powers thereof, to wit, the legislative, executive and judicial, ought to be kept as separate from and independent of each other, as the nature of a free government will admit, or as is consistent with that chain of connection that binds the whole fabric of the constitution in one indissoluble bond of union and amity.[60]

XXXVIII. A frequent recurrence to the fundamental principles of the Constitution, and a constant adherence to justice, moderation, temperance, industry, frugality, and all the social virtues, are indispensably necessary to preserve the blessings of liberty and good government; the people ought, therefore, to have a particular regard to all those principles in the choice of their officers and representatives: and they have a right to

[57] Similar to Mass. Decl. 1780, Art. XXVIII.

[58] Similar to Mass. Decl. 1780, Art. XXIX. A major criticism of New Hampshire's 1776 constitution was its failure to provide judicial independence. This article connected "honorable salaries" and tenure during good behavior with the "preservation of... every individual ['s] life, liberty, property and character."

[59] Unique among early state constitutions, this limitation appears to have been a reaction to the practice by the royal government and the state government of granting pensions not based on service. Marshall, *New Hampshire Constitution*, 102.

[60] Similar to Mass. Decl. 1780, Art. XXX. Unlike the Massachusetts declaration, which made clear that each branch of government "shall never" exercise the powers of any other branch, this provision required only as much separation "as the nature of a free government will admit."

require of their law-givers and magistrates, an exact and constant observance of them in the formation and execution of the laws necessary for the good administration of government.[61]

Part II: The Form of Government

* * *

SENATE

THE senate shall be the first branch of the legislature: and the senators shall be chosen in the following manner, viz. Every male inhabitant of each town and parish with town privileges in the several counties in this state, of twenty-one years of age and upwards, paying for himself a poll tax, shall have a right at the annual or other meetings of the inhabitants of said towns and parishes, to be duly warned and holden annually forever in the month of March; to vote in the town or parish wherein he dwells, for the senators in the county or district whereof he is a member.

* * *

HOUSE OF REPRESENTATIVES

ALL persons qualified to vote in the election of senators shall be intitled to vote within the town, district, parish, or place where they dwell, in the choice of representatives.

* * *

EXECUTIVE POWER.—PRESIDENT

* * *

THOSE persons qualified to vote for senators and representatives, shall within the several towns, parishes or places, where they dwell, at a meeting to be called for that purpose, some day in the month of March annually, give in their votes for a president to the selectmen, who shall preside at such meeting …

[61] Similar to Mass. Decl. 1780, Art. XVIII.

* * *

ENCOURAGEMENT OF LITERATURE, &C

KNOWLEDGE, and learning, generally diffused through a community, being essential to the preservation of a free government; and spreading the opportunities and advantages of education through the various parts of the country, being highly conducive to promote this end; it shall be the duty of the legislators and the magistrates, in all future periods of this government to cherish the interest of literature and the sciences, and all seminaries and public schools, to encourage private and public institutions, rewards and immunities for the promotion of agriculture, arts, sciences, commerce, trades, manufactures and natural history of the country; to countenance and inculcate the principles of humanity and general benevolence, public and private charity, industry and economy, honesty and punctuality, sincerity, sobriety, and all social affections, and generous sentiments, among the people.[62]

* * *

OATH AND SUBSCRIPTIONS; EXCLUSION FROM OFFICES; COMMISSIONS; WRITS; CONFIRMATION OF LAWS; HABEAS CORPUS; THE ENACTING STILE; CONTINUANCE OF OFFICERS; PROVISION FOR A FUTURE REVISION OF THE CONSTITUTION, &C

* * *

THE estates of such persons as may destroy their own lives, shall not for that offence be forfeited, but descend or ascend in the same manner, as if such persons had died in a natural way. Nor shall any article which shall accidentally occasion the death of any person, be henceforth deemed a deodand, or in any wise forfeited on account of such misfortune.[63]

ALL the laws which have heretofore been adopted, used and approved, in the province, colony, or state of New-Hampshire, and usually practiced on in the courts of law, shall remain and be in full force, until altered and repealed by the legislature; such parts thereof only excepted, as are repugnant to the rights and liberties contained in this constitution: Provided

[62] Similar to Mass. Const. 1780, Ch. V, sec. II.

[63] Similar to N.J. Const. 1776, Art. XVII.

that nothing herein contained, when compared with the twenty-third article in the bill of rights, shall be construed to affect the laws already made respecting the persons or estates of absentees.[64]

THE privilege and benefit of the habeas corpus, shall be enjoyed in this state, in the most free, easy, cheap, expeditious, and ample manner, and shall not be suspended by the legislature, except upon the most urgent and pressing occasions, and for a time not exceeding three months.[65]

[64] Similar to Mass. Const. 1780, Ch. VI, Art. VI. This provision incorporated the common law.

[65] Similar to Mass. Const. 1780, Ch. VI, Art. VII. The Massachusetts provision was less restrictive, allowing habeas corpus to be suspended for up to twelve months.

States Adopting Constitutions Without Separate Declarations of Rights

South Carolina

Constitutional change in British America involved a gradual move away from proprietary colonies operated by private investors holding a charter to royal colonies under a governor appointed by the Crown. South Carolina, the more prosperous region of the proprietary Carolina colony with its slave plantations and merchant port in Charles Town (later Charleston), made this change in several steps. In 1712, it separated from North Carolina. In 1719, it was recognized as a royal colony.[1]

During its transition period, South Carolina adopted several rights protective statutes. In 1712, it became the first of the colonies to enact legislation recognizing a criminal defendant's right to call for evidence and witnesses in his favor.[2] That same year, the colony expanded access to the writ of habeas corpus, previously guaranteed by statute in 1692, by authorizing additional officials to grant the writ.[3] South Carolina also

[1] See pp. 181–184, for a discussion of Carolina's legal history pre-1712.

[2] A. E. Dick Howard, *Commentaries on the Constitution of Virginia* (Charlottesville: University Press of Virginia, 1974), 1:105; An Act for regulating of Trials in Cases of Treason and Misprision of Treason, 1712, in *The Statutes at Large of South Carolina*, ed. Thomas Cooper (Columbia, SC: A.S. Johnston, 1837), 2:539 (for the charge of treason).

[3] An Act to impower the Right Honorable the Governor of this Province, the Lords Deputies, the Chief Justice or the Justices of the Peace, and other Officers or Ministers within this Province, to execute and put in force in the same, an Act...commonly called the Habeas Corpus Act, December 12, 1712, in Cooper, *Statutes at Large*, 2:399. The preamble stated "no law or statute hath hitherto been made or enacted which better secures the liberty of the subject than [the Habeas Corpus Act]." Ibid. The act ensured

P. J. Galie et al., *Bills of Rights Before the Bill of Rights*,
https://doi.org/10.1007/978-3-030-44301-6_12

incorporated into its law the due process protections of Chapter 29 of Magna Carta (1225),[4] the Petition of Right (1628), and all of the common law not "inconsistent with the particular constitutions, customs and laws of this Province."[5] South Carolina's 1712 incorporation of the common law and statutes of England into its colonial law marked the first statutory enactment of Magna Carta in American history.[6]

A law guarding procedural rights was enacted in 1731, affirming the "ancient, known and fundamental" right to trial by a jury of one's peers, chosen through an "indifferent and impartial method."[7] This law also guaranteed that the criminally accused would have access to counsel, "a true copy of the whole indictment" three days before trial, and could call for witnesses to testify under oath and compel them to appear—all to ensure that the accused would have "proper assistance and all just and equal means allowed them to defend their innocencys."[8]

The popularly elected lower house of the colonial legislature, called the South Carolina Commons House of Assembly, however was less eager to protect the people's rights when those rights clashed with its own legislative privilege. In some cases, criticism of the Commons House resulted in a forced apology; in others, arrest and incarceration without the benefit of counsel, jury, or habeas corpus.[9] In 1733, the Commons House passed a bill suspending habeas corpus for any person taken into the custody of the

that "all and every person which now is or hereafter shall be within any part of this Province, shall have to all intents, constructions and purposes whatsoever, and in all things whatsoever, as large, ample and effectual right to and benefit of the said Act...as if he were personally in the said Kingdom of England." Ibid., 400.

[4] The 1225 charter, a confirmation of the 1215 charter, amplified Chapter 39 of the earlier document and renumbered it Chapter 29.

[5] An Act to put in force in this Province the several Statutes of the Kingdom of England or South Britain, therein particularly mentioned, December 12, 1712, in Cooper, *Statutes at Large*, 2:403, 413, 417, 513.

[6] Ibid., 401ff.

[7] An Act confirming and establishing the ancient and approved method of drawing Juries by ballot, in this Province, and for the better administration of justice in criminal causes..., August 20, 1731, in Cooper, *Statutes at Large*, 3:274.

[8] Ibid., 286.

[9] Michael E. Stevens, "'Their Liberties, Properties and Privileges': Civil Liberties in South Carolina, 1663–1791," in *The Bill of Rights and the States: The Colonial and Revolutionary Origins of American Liberties*, ed. Patrick T. Conley and John P. Kaminski (Madison, WI: Madison House, 1992), 406.

house and protecting judges who denied the writ; the Crown, however, disallowed the act.[10]

In the thirty years preceding the Revolution, social and political homogeneity characterized this "unusually well-governed colony."[11] Like its sister colonies, however, South Carolina bristled over mid-eighteenth century British measures threatening its right to internal taxation. The end of royal government in the colony was hastened by a dispute in 1769 over the Commons House's right to appropriate money free of executive approval—a long-standing practice contrary to royal instructions. Royal authorities learned of this practice when the house passed a resolution donating 1500 pounds from the colonial treasury to The Society of Gentlemen Supporters of the Bill of Rights—a London-based group organized to "defend and maintain the legal, constitutional Liberty of the subject" and to provide financial support to English radical John Wilkes.[12] The donation was a bold, symbolic gesture of South Carolina's commitment to American liberty.[13] London officials subsequently attempted to strip the Commons House of the appropriation powers, resulting in a firestorm that brought royal government in the colony to a halt. No annual tax bill was enacted for the last six years of the colony's existence, and after February 1771, law-making ceased altogether.[14] The Commons House refused to back down: Its claim that South Carolina's freeholders had the collective right through their representatives to decide how public funds would be used was a forceful assertion of popular sovereignty, namely, that all political power derived from the people.[15]

[10]Ibid., 406–407. The disallowance shows that protecting rights was not a one-way street.

[11]Robert M. Weir, *"The Last of American Freemen": Studies in the Political Culture of the Colonial and Revolutionary South* (Macon, GA: Mercer University Press, 1986), 26–27.

[12]Jack P. Greene, "Bridge to Revolution: The Wilkes Fund Controversy in South Carolina, 1769–1775," *The Journal of Southern History* 29, no. 1 (1963): 20–21; Robert M. Weir, *Colonial South Carolina: A History* (Millwood, NY: KTO Press, 1983), 305.

[13]Greene, "Bridge to Revolution," 21.

[14]Ibid., 52.

[15]Ibid., 32, 52.

The cessation of royal government in South Carolina gave rise to the creation of the second constitution in colonial America.[16] South Carolina's extra-legal provincial congress, elected on December 19, 1774, organized a council of safety to assume governance of the colony. The Second Provincial Congress began drafting a temporary constitution on February 3, 1776.[17] Some members objected that the congress lacked authority to draft a constitution as it had not been elected for that purpose and did not fairly represent the colony's population.[18] Others resisted any action that would make reconciliation with Britain less likely. Following the adoption of a March 21st act of Parliament proclaiming the colonies in open rebellion and authorizing severe retaliatory measures, the movement for a new frame of government accelerated.[19] South Carolina's first constitution was adopted five days later, on March 26, 1776.

Constitutional Developments: 1776 Constitution

As stated in its preamble, the 1776 constitution was meant to last only "until an accommodation of the unhappy differences between Great Britain and America can be obtained, (an event which, though traduced and treated as rebels, we still earnestly desire)." As a stopgap measure, South Carolina's first constitution was skeletal and contained no bill of rights. The preamble, however, declared that governments were created "by common consent" and identified "the people" as "the origin and end of all governments"—the popular sovereignty theory that would be a central component of all early state declarations of rights. The preamble also contained an implied right to trial by jury in the jurisdiction where the offense was committed,[20] a right made explicit by provisions in the

[16] New Hampshire's constitution, adopted January 5, 1776, and also temporary, was first.

[17] Paul A. Horne Jr., "The Evolution of a Constitution: South Carolina's 1778 Document," *South Carolina Historical Association* (1987): 7.

[18] Fletcher M. Green, *Constitutional Development in the South Atlantic States, 1776–1860: A Study in the Evolution of Democracy* (Chapel Hill: University of North Carolina Press, 1930), 61. The southeast coastal region (low-country) had 144 representatives, while the more populous western region (up-country) had just 40. Ibid.

[19] Horne, "Evolution of a Constitution," 7.

[20] Ibid.; Const. 1776, preamble: "...other unconstitutional and oppressive statutes have been since enacted by which the powers of admiralty courts in the colonies are extended

body of the constitution confining the jurisdiction of admiralty courts to maritime causes and requiring jury lists to be made and juries to be summoned (Const. 1776, Arts. XVII–XVIII). Additionally, Article XXIX guaranteed the continuation of current laws, which would include all the rights protected by statute. The constitution was silent on religious liberty, leaving the established Church of England in place.

Suffrage

South Carolina's first constitution based its suffrage requirements on the 1721 Election Act: free, white, Christian men at least twenty-one years old, who had resided in the province for a minimum of one year, and had either a freehold of fifty acres or property taxable at twenty shillings (even if not actually taxed),[21] were entitled to vote (Const. 1776, Art. XI). The corollary of the right to choose one's lawmakers was the right to be taxed only by one's representatives. Article VII required "all money-bills for the support of government" to originate in the general assembly (the only popularly elected body), with the legislative council confined to accepting or rejecting the bills.[22]

Structural Provisions

Although South Carolina's constitution contained no explicit commitment to the separation of powers, some dimensions of that doctrine were embodied in provisions limiting plural office-holding (Const. 1776, Arts.

beyond their ancient limits, and jurisdiction is given to such courts in cases similar to those which in Great Britain are triable by jury; persons are liable to be sent to and tried in Great Britain for an offence created and made capital by one of those statutes, though committed in the colonies...".

[21] In contrast, the 1721 Election Act required the property to actually have been taxed the preceding year or be liable for the amount in the election year. An Act to ascertain the manner and form of electing members to represent the inhabitants of this Province in the Commons House of Assembly, ... September 19, 1721, in Cooper, *Statutes at Large*, 3:136. The change allowed for the enlargement of the electorate, depending on the number of freemen who owned taxable property but for one reason or another were tax exempt.

[22] The first president under the new constitution, John Rutledge, asserted that the public should be told that the constitution guaranteed them the right of being taxed by their chosen representatives. Green, *Constitutional Development in the South Atlantic States*, 105.

IV, X), and giving certain judicial officers tenure during good behavior (ibid., Art. XX). The general assembly elected a legislative council from its own members, and those two bodies elected a president, vice-president, and a privy council. South Carolina was the first state to give its executive (the president) the power to veto legislation (ibid., Arts. VII, XXX).[23]

All officeholders were subject to the qualification requirements for service in the Commons House provided by the 1721 Election Act (Const. 1776, Arts. VI, XI). They had to be free men, at least twenty-one years old, who had resided in the state for a year, with a freehold of 500 acres and ten slaves, or other real property valued at 1000 pounds.[24] There was no religious requirement as there had been for electors, although officeholders had to swear an oath "on the holy evangelists" before taking their seats.[25]

Constitutional Developments: 1778 Constitution

The public reacted favorably to South Carolina's first constitution, but the Continental Congress's Declaration of Independence made clear a permanent frame of government was needed.[26] The second constitution, adopted on March 19, 1778, was more democratic and included additional rights. In addition to reaffirming the rights protections found in the 1776 constitution,[27] the new constitution contained a provision to reform the penal laws and make punishments more proportionate to the crimes (Const. 1778, Art. XL); a due process guarantee derived from Magna Carta (ibid., Art. XLI); a provision subordinating the military to the civil power (ibid., Art. XLII); and a provision protecting the liberty of the press (ibid., Art. XLIII).

The most notable change in South Carolina's second constitution was the disestablishment of the Anglican Church in favor of a general

[23] President Rutledge used this power to veto the bill enacting the 1778 constitution. He resigned his position and his second successor approved the new constitution. See Horne, "Evolution of a Constitution," 11–12.

[24] Act to ascertain the manner and form of electing members, 137.

[25] Ibid., sec. 9, 137.

[26] Horne, "Evolution of a Constitution," 9.

[27] Const. 1778, Arts. XXV, XXXIV retained the safeguard against the misuse of admiralty courts that protected the right to trial by jury, and the continued validity of the current laws governing the state, which included the common law and its privileges.

establishment of the Protestant religion, without tax support (ibid., Art. XXXVIII). Religious freedom, though expanded, was not universal. Non-Protestants who committed to the public worship of a monotheistic God and a future state of rewards and punishments would be "freely tolerated" and would enjoy civil liberties such as the right to vote; however, they could not hold public office or receive the legal benefits of incorporation for their place of worship. Article XXXVIII reflected the tension created by a commitment to liberty of conscience and the belief that "certain basic religious beliefs were essential for a civilized society."[28] Maintaining a religious commitment while expanding the range of acceptable religious beliefs was the accommodation all colonies would eventually make.

The 1778 constitution replaced the legislative council with a popularly elected senate (Const. 1778, Art. XII). Furthering the popular sovereignty principle of rotation in office, senators and representatives were subject to biennial elections (ibid., Arts. XII, XIII). The new constitution continued the prohibition on multiple office-holding (ibid., Arts. IV, VII, IX) and provided judicial officers (other than justices of the peace) tenure during good behavior (ibid., Art. XXVII). The president was renamed the governor and his veto power was removed, leaving the office vested with only executive authority (ibid., Art. XI).

Qualifications for suffrage remained largely as they were under the previous constitution, except that the religious requirement changed from "professing the Christian religion" to "acknowledg[ing] the existence of a God and believ[ing] in a future state of rewards and punishments," effectively including Jews. Requirements for holding office were as follows:

Office	*Minimum age*	*Estate*	*Residency*	*Religion*
Governor	No age specified	Settled plantation or freehold of 10,000 pounds	At least 10 years within state	Protestant

(continued)

[28] James Lowell Underwood, "The Dawn of Religious Freedom in South Carolina: The Journey from Limited Tolerance to Constitutional Right," in *The Dawn of Religious Freedom in South Carolina*, ed. James Lowell Underwood and W. Lewis Burke (Columbia: University of South Carolina Press, 2006), 32.

(continued)

Office	Minimum age	Estate	Residency	Religion
Senator	30 years	If resident of his parish or district: freehold estate of 2000 pounds in his parish or district If nonresident of his parish or district: freehold estate of 7000 pounds in his parish or district	At least 5 years within state	Protestant
Representative	21 years	If resident of his parish or district: freehold estate of 500 acres and ten slaves, or other real property valued at 1000 pounds If nonresident of his parish or district: freehold estate of 3500 pounds in his parish or district	At least 3 years within state	Protestant

The new requirement that legislators own property in the parish or district in which they served would ensure the interests of the representatives and their constituents were aligned. The use of slaves to satisfy property requirements, carried over from the previous constitution, cemented the institution of slavery in the state. South Carolina barred clergy from holding public office, in language tracking Article XXXIX of the 1777 New York Constitution: ministers and preachers "are by their profession dedicated to the service of God and the cure of souls, and ought not to be diverted from the great duties of their function" (Const. 1778, Art. XXI).

The 1778 constitution contained a straightforward method for constitutional revision: a ninety-day notice and the consent of a majority of both houses of the general assembly (ibid., Art. XLIV). It would soon be made clear that intention alone did not raise a constitution to the status of fundamental law. The state supreme court ruled that the constitutions of 1776 and 1778 were ordinary legislative acts subject to amendment or repeal like any other.[29]

Constitutional Developments: 1790 Constitution

Following the successful end of the Revolutionary War, popular discontent with the 1778 document emerged. Calls for a new constitution, as well as a bill of rights, intensified.[30] Notwithstanding such popular support, all legislative efforts for a state convention to draft a new constitution and bill of rights between 1784 and 1788 failed.[31]

On one occasion in 1787, the state's house of representatives struck out a recommendation of its committee for a bill of rights before forwarding a report for a new constitution to the senate.[32] What accounts for this hostility to a separate bill of rights? Although no direct evidence exists, some inferences can be drawn from the arguments made in opposition to a bill of rights in the federal Constitution that same year. Several delegates asserted that a bill of rights was not necessary, but agreed certain rights such as trial by jury and liberty of the press ought to be included in the Constitution.[33] Charles Cotesworth Pinckney, a delegate to the federal convention and a longtime member of South Carolina's house of representatives, noted that "such bills generally begin with declaring, that all men are by nature born free, now we should make that declaration with a very bad grace, when a large part of our property consists in men who are actually born slaves."[34] By eschewing a formal declaration of rights and placing rights provisions in the body of its constitution, South Carolina avoided dealing with the difficult subject of slavery.

One month after ratifying the federal Bill of Rights, the general assembly agreed to constituents' demands for a new state constitution. Unlike the previous two constitutions, the constitution of 1790 was drafted by

[29] Green, *Constitutional Development in the South Atlantic States*, 118.

[30] Horne, "Evolution of a Constitution," 12–13; Stevens, "'Their Liberties, Properties and Privileges'," 418.

[31] Stevens, "'Their Liberties, Properties and Privileges'," 418.

[32] Ibid.

[33] Ibid., 418–419. South Carolina's ratifying convention rejected a motion to draft a bill of rights and ratified the federal Constitution without one.

[34] Ibid., 419.

a special convention, to which delegates were elected specifically for that purpose.[35] The final product reflected an understanding of rights and liberties more focused on individual liberty. The pendulum was gradually swinging from the idea prominent in the first state constitutions "that private interests ought not to be set in competition with public good,"[36] to the view that permitting greater latitude for individual liberty was not inconsistent with maintaining a safe, prosperous, and decent community. In that vein, all religious requirements for voting and office-holding were removed. The tax-paying alternative to the freehold requirement for voters and the property qualifications for officeholders were reduced. Additional rights, collected in Article IX, included trial by jury and prohibitions against bills of attainder, ex post facto laws, excessive bail or fines, and cruel punishments. Nowhere is the evolution of rights in South Carolina's constitutions more apparent than in its religious liberty provisions. The state had moved in successive stages from the financial and ideological establishment of the Church of England left in place by the 1776 constitution, to the nonfinancial Protestant establishment in the 1778 constitution, to complete disestablishment and free exercise of religion in the 1790 constitution.

A more refined version of its predecessor, South Carolina's third constitution adopted many of the structural requirements necessary for republican government, including frequent elections and rotation in office (Const. 1790, Art. I, secs. 2, 7, 9, 10), prohibitions on plural office-holding (ibid., Art. I, sec. 21, Art. II, sec. 2, Art. III, sec. 1), and lifetime appointments for judges during good behavior, with fixed compensation (ibid., Art III, sec. 1). Article VII reiterated the assurances found in the constitutions of 1776 and 1778 that the protections of liberties found in existing statutory and common law were to remain in force.

The constitution's concluding article set forth the procedure for constitutional revision. A "convention of the people" could be called by the concurrence of two-thirds of both branches of the general assembly. Any alterations to the constitution required the agreement of two-thirds of both the house and the senate, then had to be published three months before the next house election and agreed to by two-thirds of

[35] James Lowell Underwood, *The Constitution of South Carolina*, vol. 3, *Church and State, Morality and Free Expression* (Columbia, SC: University of South Carolina Press, 1992), 77.

[36] Weir, *Colonial South Carolina*, 134.

both branches of the legislature in their first session after the election (ibid., Art. XI).

Postscript: The 1790 South Carolina Constitution remained in effect until 1861, when a constitutional convention adopted the state's fourth constitution (it has adopted seven to date). The rights article, Article IX, remained unchanged in the 1861 constitution except for the addition of a provision prohibiting the reestablishment of primogeniture and requiring legislation for the equitable distribution of intestate estates.

Constitution of South Carolina [1776]

* * *

XI. ... The qualifications of electors shall be the same as required by law, but persons having property, which, according to the rate of the last preceding tax, is taxable at the sums mentioned in the election act, shall be entitled to vote, though it was no actually taxed, having the other qualifications mentioned in that act; electors shall take an oath of qualification, if required by the returning-officer. The qualification of the elected to be the same as mentioned in the election act, and construed to mean clear of debt.[37]

* * *

XVII. That the jurisdiction of the court of admiralty be confined to maritime causes.[38]

XVIII. That all suits and process depending in any court of law or equity may, if either party shall be so inclined, be proceeded in and continued to a final ending, without being obliged to commence de novo. And the judges of the courts of law shall cause jury-lists to be made, and

[37] This article stipulated that the franchise requirements would remain as they had been under the 1721 Election Act. See footnote 21, above.

[38] This article was meant to remedy a perceived due process violation that had been perpetrated by the British. The royal authority's use of admiralty courts to prosecute Americans without the benefit of a jury and in some cases to try the accused overseas was a major grievance, as specified in the constitution's preamble. This article guaranteed that no such breach of due process rights would be allowed in South Carolina.

juries to be summoned, as near as may be, according to the directions of the acts of the general assembly in such cases provided.[39]

* * *

XXIX. That the resolutions of this or any former congress of this colony, and all laws now of force here, (and not hereby altered,) shall so continue until altered or repealed by the legislature of this colony, unless where they are temporary, in which case they shall expire at the times respectively limited for their duration.[40]

Constitution of South Carolina [1778]

* * *

XIII. ... The qualification of electors shall be that every free white man, and no other person, who acknowledges the being of a God, and believes in a future state of rewards and punishments, and who has attained to the age of one and twenty years, and hath been a resident and an inhabitant in this State for the space of one whole year before the day appointed for the election he offers to give his vote at, and hath a freehold at least of fifty acres of land, or a town lot, and hath been legally seized and possessed of the same at least six months previous to such election, or hath paid a tax the preceding year, or was taxable the present year, at least six months

[39] The courts had ceased functioning when royal government in the colony ended. The clear implication of this article was that the courts were to re-open and resume the practice of jury trials. President John Rutledge advised the members of the general assembly to let their constituents know that their new constitution guaranteed them the right of trial by jury. Green, *Constitutional Development in the South Atlantic States*, 105.

[40] This article proclaimed that the colony's current laws were to remain in force. As discussed earlier in this chapter, South Carolina's colonial assembly had passed a number of laws in furtherance of common law rights such as habeas corpus, trial by jury, and other procedural protections. Other legislative acts protected suffrage rights by imposing penalties for threatening or bribing a voter and exempting voters going to or from the polls from being served with civil process. Stevens, "'Their Liberties, Properties and Privileges'," 409. To promote free and fair elections, South Carolina mandated the use of the secret ballot—the first colony to do so. Weir, *Colonial South Carolina*, 72. Article XXIX made it clear that these rights were still recognized as the law of the land. Similar provisions, not reproduced here, were included in the 1778 and 1790 constitutions (Const. 1778, Art. XXXIV; Const. 1790, Art. VII).

previous to the said election, in a sum equal to the tax on fifty acres of land, to the support of this government, shall be deemed a person qualified to vote for, and shall be capable of electing, a representative or representatives, to serve as a member or members in the senate and house of representatives, for the parish or district where he actually is a resident, or in any other parish or district in this State where he hath the like freehold.

* * *

XXV. That the jurisdiction of the court of admiralty be confined to maritime causes.

* * *

XXXVIII. That all persons and religious societies who acknowledge that there is one God, and a future state of rewards and punishments, and that God is publicly to be worshipped, shall be freely tolerated. The Christian Protestant religion shall be deemed, and is hereby constituted and declared to be, the established religion of this State. That all denominations of Christian Protestants in this State, demeaning themselves peaceably and faithfully, shall enjoy equal religious and civil privileges. To accomplish this desirable purpose without injury to the religious property of those societies of Christians which are by law already incorporated for the purpose of religious worship, and to put it fully into the power of every other society of Christian Protestants, either already formed or hereafter to be formed, to obtain the like incorporation, it is hereby constituted, appointed, and declared that the respective societies of the Church of England that are already formed in this State for the purpose of religious worship shall still continue incorporate and hold the religious property now in their possession. And that whenever fifteen or more male persons, not under twenty-one years of age, professing the Christian Protestant religion, and agreeing to unite themselves In a society for the purposes of religious worship, they shall, (on complying with the terms hereinafter mentioned,) be, and be constituted a church, and be esteemed and regarded in law as of the established religion of the State, and on a petition to the legislature shall be entitled to be incorporated and to enjoy equal privileges. That every society of Christians so formed shall give themselves a name or denomination by which they shall be called and known in law, and all that associate with them for the purposes of worship shall be esteemed as belonging to the society so called. But that previous to the establishment and incorporation of the respective societies of every denomination as aforesaid, and in order to entitle them thereto, each society so petitioning shall have agreed to and subscribed in a book the following five articles, without which no agreement for union of men upon pretence of religion shall entitle them to be incorporated and esteemed as a church of the established religion of this State:

> 1st. That there is one eternal God, and a future state of rewards and punishments.
> 2d. That God is publicly to be worshipped.
> 3d. That the Christian religion is the true religion
> 4th. That the holy scriptures of the Old and New Testaments are of divine inspiration, and are the rule of faith and practice.
> 5th. That it is lawful and the duty of every man being thereunto called by those that govern, to bear witness to the truth.

And that every inhabitant of this State, when called to make an appeal to God as a witness to truth, shall be permitted to do it in that way which is most agreeable to the dictates of his own conscience. And that the people of this State may forever enjoy the right of electing their own pastors or clergy, and at the same time that the State may have sufficient security for the due discharge of the pastoral office, by those who shall be admitted to be clergymen, no person shall officiate as minister of any established church who shall not have been chosen by a majority of the society to which he shall minister, or by persons appointed by the said majority, to choose and procure a minister for them; nor until the minister so chosen and appointed shall have made and subscribed to the following declaration, over and above the aforesaid five articles, viz: "That he is determined by God's grace out of the holy scriptures, to instruct the people committed to his charge, and to teach nothing as required of necessity to eternal salvation but that which he shall be persuaded may be concluded and proved from the scripture; that he will use both public and private admonitions, as well to the sick as to the whole within his cure, as need shall require and occasion shall be given, and that he will be diligent in prayers, and in reading of the same; that he will be diligent to frame and fashion his own self and his family according to the doctrine of Christ, and to make both himself and them, as much as in him lieth, wholesome examples and patterns to the flock of Christ; that he will maintain and set forwards, as much as he can, quietness, peace, and love among all people, and especially among those that are or shall be committed to his charge. No person shall disturb or molest any religious assembly; nor shall use any reproachful, reviling, or abusive language against any church, that being the certain way of disturbing the peace, and of hindering the conversion of any to the truth, by engaging them in quarrels and animosities, to the hatred of the professors, and that profession which otherwise they might be brought to assent to. No person whatsoever shall speak anything in their religious assembly irreverently or seditiously of the government of this State. No person shall, by law, be obliged to pay towards the maintenance and support of a religious worship that he does not freely join in, or has not voluntarily engaged to support. But the churches, chapels, parsonages, globes, and all other property now belonging to any societies of the Church of England, or any other religious societies, shall remain and be secured to them forever. The poor shall be supported, and elections managed in the accustomed manner, until laws shall be provided to adjust those matters in the most equitable way.[41]

* * *

[41] Protestant Dissenters effectively pushed for equal treatment with a petition to the general assembly in January 1777. Presbyterian clergyman and assembly member Rev. William Tennent III presented the petition, along with a rousing speech against establishment as a violation of civil liberty and the right of conscience. Article XXXVIII embodied the main concessions dissenters were demanding—to be on an equal footing with Anglicans and to be freed from supporting a church they had not joined. See Edward McCrady, *The History of South Carolina in the Revolution 1775–1780* (New York: Russell & Russell, 1969), 209–213. This provision introduced and explicitly endorsed the idea of a general establishment. Protestant Christianity became the established religion of the state. Significantly, the only use of the word "right" in this article referred to a collective right: "that the people of this State may forever enjoy the right of electing their own pastors or clergy." The declaration required of ministers by this article--"That he is determined...committed to his charge"—was derived from The Ordering [Ordaining] of Priests found in *The Book of Common Prayer* (1662), https://justus.anglican.org/resources/bcp/1662/Orig_manuscript/ordinal.htm.

XL. That the penal laws, as heretofore used, shall be reformed, and punishments made in some cases less sanguinary, and in general more proportionate to the crime.[42]

XLI. That no freeman of this State be taken or imprisoned, or disseized of his freehold, liberties, or privileges, or outlawed, exiled or in any manner destroyed or deprived of his life, liberty, or property, but by the judgment of his peers or by the law of the land.[43]

XLII. That the military be subordinate to the civil power of the State.[44]

XLIII. That the liberty of the press be inviolably preserved.[45]

[42] Similar to Pa. Const. 1776, sec. 38. There is no record of the debate on the provisions that made up the 1778 constitution as the legislative journals were not preserved. Cole Blease Graham Jr., *The South Carolina State Constitution: A Reference Guide* (Westport, CT: Praeger, 2007), 11. A successful criminal sentencing appeal to the South Carolina legislature in 1786 cited the English Bill of Rights prohibition against cruel or unusual punishments but failed to mention this constitutional provision, suggesting the unsettled status of constitutional rights. Stevens, "'Their Liberties, Properties and Privileges'," 413; "Journals of the House of Representatives 1785–1786," in *The State Records of South Carolina*, ed. Lark Emerson Adams and Rosa Stoney Lumpkin (Columbia: University of South Carolina Press, 1979), 455–458, 696. The records do not indicate whether the legislature found the petitioner's reliance on the English Bill of Rights persuasive, but perhaps they considered it applicable given the incorporation clause (Article XXXIV) that preserved all the laws currently in force. The common law of England was declared to be in force in South Carolina by an act of the assembly in 1712, with its continued validity assured by the 1776 constitution. Act to put in force in this Province the several Statutes, 413–414; Const. 1776, Art. XXIX.

[43] This article proclaimed the due process guarantee that originated in Chapter 39 of Magna Carta (1215). The 1225 iteration of Magna Carta had already been adopted into South Carolina's statutes in 1712, making it likely the drafters viewed it as a fundamental right that ought to be given prominence in a constitution. This article was identical to the 1776 Maryland declaration's Article XXI, except for the deletion of the words "ought to" after "That no freeman of this state," opening the door to judicial enforcement.

[44] This article asserted civilian control over the military, a corollary of the principle that all political power was derived from the people. It ensured that the people would not be subject to a military dictatorship, a collective right protected in many of the early state declarations of rights.

[45] The language of this article offered a more strongly worded version of the 1776 Maryland declaration's Article XXXVIII. Freedom of the press in South Carolina had been subject to infringement by both the royal executive and the colonial legislature, but as the Revolution drew to a close, printers were becoming bolder in asserting their liberty and the assembly seemed less inclined to prosecute them for breach of legislative privilege. Stevens, "'Their Liberties, Properties and Privileges'," 407, 414–418.

Constitution of South Carolina [1790]

* * *

Article I

* * *

Sec. 4. Every free white man, of the age of twenty-one years, being a citizen of this State, and having resided therein two years previous to the day of election, and who hath a freehold of fifty acres of land or a town lot, of which he hath been legally seized and possessed at least six months before such election, or, not having such freehold or town lot, hath been a resident in the election district in which he offers to give his vote six months before the said election, and hath paid a tax the preceding year of three shillings sterling[46] towards the support of this government, shall have a right to vote for a member or members to serve in either branch of the legislature for the election district in which he holds such property or is so resident.[47]

* * *

Article VIII

Section 1. The free exercise and enjoyment of religious profession and worship, without discrimination or preference, shall forever hereafter be allowed within this State to all mankind: *Provided*, That the liberty of conscience thereby declared shall not be so construed as to excuse acts of licentiousness, or justify practices inconsistent with the peace or safety of this State.[48]

[46] Three shillings was the cost of a prayer book in the mid-eighteenth century, or the estimated equivalent of $13.40 in twenty-first century dollars. Ed Crews, "How Much Is That in Today's Money: One of Colonial Williamsburg's Most-Asked Questions Is among the Toughest," *Colonial Williamsburg Journal*, Summer 2002, 22–25.

[47] This article broadened the suffrage by removing all religious requirements for voting and by providing a reduced tax alternative to the freehold requirement. While the previous two constitutions spoke of persons "entitled to vote" (1776) and "qualified to vote" (1778), the new constitution stated unequivocally that qualified voters had a "right to vote."

[48] This section replaced the language of tolerance from the 1778 constitution with free exercise, ended the Protestant establishment, and proclaimed religious freedom for all. It

SEC. 2. The rights, privileges, immunities, and estates of both civil and religious societies, and of corporate bodies, shall remain as if the constitution of this State had not been altered or amended.

Article IX

SECTION 1. All power is originally vested in the people; and all free governments are founded on their authority, and are instituted for their peace, safety, and happiness.[49]

SEC. 2. No freemen of this State shall be taken, or imprisoned, or disseized of his freehold, liberties, or privileges, or outlawed, or exiled, or in any manner destroyed, or deprived of his life, liberty or property, but by the judgment of his peers, or by the law of the land; nor shall any bill of attainder, ex-post facto law, or law impairing the obligation of contracts, ever be passed by the legislature of this State.[50]

SEC. 3. The military shall be subordinate to the civil power.

SEC. 4. Excessive bail shall not be required, nor excessive fines imposed, nor cruel punishments inflicted.[51]

was taken nearly verbatim from the New York Constitution of 1777, Article XXXVIII, with one significant alteration. South Carolina's drafters changed "the liberty of conscience *hereby granted*" to "the liberty of conscience *thereby declared*"—a recognition that liberty of conscience was an inalienable right, not one that could be bestowed (or rescinded) by any earthly power. Communitarian norms of civic virtue and the subordination of individual interests to the public good were giving way to the realities of growing diversity, although the framers continued to insist on the overriding importance of the community by stipulating that religious freedom did not extend to immoral acts or threats to the peace and safety of the state.

Section 2 of this article assured Protestant churches that they would retain their "rights, privileges, immunities, and estates."

[49] The drafters of the 1790 constitution grouped a litany of rights provisions under Article IX. The Pennsylvania Constitution of 1790 had done the same. Since Pennsylvania's constitution had been printed in South Carolina newspapers in the months leading up to that state's convention, it seems likely to have influenced the drafters. The first section, declaring the principle of popular sovereignty, was borrowed from Article IX, section 2 of Pennsylvania's 1790 constitution. Given their thoughts on the subject (see p. 277, above), it is no surprise that South Carolina's political leaders bypassed Pennsylvania's first section declaring "that all men are born equally free and independent."

[50] Section 2 restated the due process clause present in the state's previous constitution, as well as the federal Constitution's prohibitions in Article I, section 10 against states passing bills of attainder, ex post facto laws, and laws impairing the obligation of contracts.

[51] Identical to Pa. Const. 1790, Art. IX, sec. 13. This guarantee, derived from the English Bill of Rights, had already been recognized in the state (see Const. 1778, Art. XL).

SEC. 5. The legislature shall not grant any title of nobility, or hereditary distinction, nor create any office the appointment to which shall be for any longer time than during good behavior.[52]

SEC. 6. The trial by jury, as heretofore used in this State, and the liberty of the press, shall be forever inviolably preserved.[53]

Article X

* * *

SEC. 5. The legislature shall, as soon as may be convenient, pass laws for the abolition of the rights of primogeniture, and for giving an equitable distribution of the real estate of intestates.[54]

[52] Similar to Pa. Const. 1790, Art. IX, sec. 24. Section 5 protected the collective right to a democratic government by prohibiting titles of nobility and ensuring public offices were held during good behavior only. The legislative prohibition on granting titles of nobility also echoed one of the federal Constitution's limits on the states (Art. I, sec. 10).

[53] Both of South Carolina's previous constitutions had implicitly protected trial by jury. The framers of the 1790 document made it explicit, although they also made it clear that trial by jury was already common practice in the state. The liberty of the press provision was given added weight by another constitutional provision limiting legislative privilege. Unlike the previous constitutions which declared that the legislature "shall enjoy all other privileges which have at any time been claimed or exercised," Article I, section 13 of the 1790 constitution closed the open-ended character of the protection by spelling out the specific circumstances in which the legislature could imprison a non-member:

> Each house may punish, by imprisonment, during sitting, any person not a member, who shall be guilty of disrespect to the house, by any disorderly or contemptuous behavior in its presence, or who, during the time of its sitting, shall threaten harm to the body or estate of any member, for anything said or done in either house, or who shall assault any of them therefor, or who shall assault or arrest any witness, or other person, ordered to attend the house, in his going to or returning therefrom, or who shall rescue any person arrested by order of the house.

[54] Primogeniture, by which a single male heir inherited all his family's real estate, was a vestige of aristocracy not consistent with the principles of a republic. A 1791 statute ended the practice. An Act for the Abolition of the Rights of Primogeniture, and for Giving an Equitable Distribution of the Real Estates of Intestates; and for Other Purposes Therein Mentioned, February 19, 1791, in Cooper, *Statutes at Large*, 5:162.

New Jersey

New Jersey began its life as part of the Dutch colony New Netherland in 1609, when English explorer Henry Hudson, under Dutch color, sailed through Newark Bay.[1] England had long asserted a claim to New Netherland based on the 1497 discoveries of John Cabot, and in March 1664, King Charles II granted his brother, James, Duke of York, a patent to the colony. Three months later, the duke granted the portion of the territory between the Hudson River and the Delaware River to Lord John Berkeley and Sir George Carteret, naming the territory New Jersey. A fleet sent by James sailed into what is now New York Harbor in August 1664, and obtained a bloodless surrender of New Netherland.

If the geographic history of the colony began in 1609, its constitutional history started across the Atlantic in medieval England.[2] According to one commentator, "[f]rom that time and place New Jersey inherited the two great branches of English law, known respectively as common

[1] The colony of New Netherland extended from Albany, New York to Delaware in the south, and included portions of what are now New York, New Jersey, Pennsylvania, Maryland, Connecticut, and Delaware. New Netherland Research Center, "What Was New Netherland?" http://www.nysl.nysed.gov/newnetherland/what.htm, accessed December 22, 2018.

[2] John Bebout, "Introduction," *Proceedings of the New Jersey State Constitutional Convention of 1844* (Compiled by the New Jersey Writers Project WPA: New Jersey State House Commission, 1942), xii.

P. J. Galie et al., *Bills of Rights Before the Bill of Rights*,
https://doi.org/10.1007/978-3-030-44301-6_13

law and equity, together with the basic principle of constitutionalism, that government should be *under*, not *above*, the law."[3]

In 1664/1665, Berkeley and Carteret promulgated a constitution or charter of governance. The *Concession and Agreement*, as it was called,[4] offered settlers and prospective settlers land, a degree of self-government, and basic rights such as freedom from taxation without the consent of elected representatives and full freedom to "judgments and consciences in matters of religion."[5] Under a three-part structure–governor, council, and elected deputies chosen by the towns–self-government began in New Jersey.

Following a series of disputes over land grants and titles, coupled with a short-lived revolt that temporarily overthrew the proprietary governor, in 1672, Berkeley and Carteret modified the concession, restricting suffrage and the ability to hold office to those "actually hold[ing] his or their lands by patent from us, the Lords proprietors,"[6] and strengthening the executive at the expense of the legislature.

In 1674, following the Dutch recapture and the subsequent return to the English of the former New Netherland area, Berkeley sold his interest in New Jersey to members of the Society of Friends (Quakers). From that point, New Jersey became two separate colonies, with the conveyed tract known thereafter as West Jersey.[7] In 1676/1677, the Quaker proprietors of West Jersey issued one of the more remarkable documents in American

[3] Ibid.

[4] The full title of the document was "The Concession and Agreement of the Lords Proprietors of the Province of New Caesarea, or New Jersey, to and With All and Every the Adventurers and All Such as Shall Settle or Plant There" (1664/1665) and its full text is found in Thorpe, *Constitutions*, 5:2535–2544.

[5] Ibid., 2537. The religious liberty granted by the concession was in stark contrast to the practice across the Atlantic, where a series of acts known as the Clarendon Code required all local government officials to take an oath and to conform to Anglican worship, prescribed the form of public prayer, punished those who attended nonconforming worship, and barred defrocked ministers from nearing their former places of ministry. Paul A. Hughes, "Politics and Religious Liberty in 17th-Century England," https://ekballo.wordpress.com/2010/05/28/politics-and-religious-liberty-in-17th-century-england/, accessed December 22, 2018.

[6] A Declaration of the True Intent and Meaning of Us the Lords Proprietors, and Explanation of There Concessions Made to the Adventurers and Planters of New Caesarea or New Jersey (1672), in Thorpe, *Constitutions*, 5:2545.

[7] Although the formal name of the colony was West New Jersey, most literature refers to it simply as West Jersey. That form is used here except in titles.

history, "The Charter or Fundamental Laws, of West New Jersey, Agreed Upon."[8] It was the "common law or fundamental rights and priviledges ... agreed upon ... to be the foundation of the government...."[9]

Among the rights included in the charter and accompanying concessions were religious liberty,[10] trial by jury,[11] the right to vote in annual elections,[12] open courts,[13] and freedom from imprisonment for debt.[14] A unicameral legislature meeting annually, along with a provision authorizing the people to instruct their representatives, ensured that the will of the colony's freemen would be mirrored in the decisions of the assembly. The most striking and forward-looking article of the document provided that the charter was "not to be altered by the legislative authority, or free assembly" and that the legislative body was "to make no laws that in the least contradict, differ or vary from the said fundamentals, under what pretence or allegation soever."[15] Any members of the free assembly who violated these restrictions would be "proceded against as traitors to the said government."[16] These chapters constituted an early recognition of a difference between statutory and fundamental (constitutional) law and an acknowledgment that the government must conform its actions to the requirements of the latter. These propositions, nascent in 1677 though now accepted as fundamental principles of our constitutional order, would

[8] In Thorpe, *Constitutions*, 5:2548–2551. The charter was part of a larger document, "The Concessions and Agreements of the Proprietors, Freeholders and Inhabitants of the Province of West New-Jersey, in America" (1676/1677), that can be found in Samuel Smith, *The Colonial History of New Jersey: A Reprint, with Maps* (Trenton, NJ: William S. Sharp, 1890), 521–539.

[9] Charter, or Fundamental Laws (1676/1677), Ch. XIII, 2548. Eugene R. Sheridan calls it "one of the most radical political documents in colonial American history." "A Study in Paradox: New Jersey and the Bill of Rights," in *The Bill of Rights and the States: The Colonial and Revolutionary Origins of American Liberties*, ed. Patrick T. Conley and John P. Kaminski (Madison, WI: Madison House, 1992), 258.

[10] Charter, or Fundamental Laws, Ch. XVI, 2549.

[11] Ibid., Ch. XVII, 2549.

[12] Concessions and Agreements (1676/1677), Ch. XXXII, 535.

[13] Charter, or Fundamental Laws, Ch. XXIII, 2551.

[14] Ibid., Ch. XVIII, 2549–2550.

[15] Ibid., Ch. XIII, 2548.

[16] Ibid., Ch. XIV, 2548.

be the vehicle by which the role of protector of rights would shift from the legislature to the judiciary.

In 1682, Carteret's trustees sold East Jersey to a group led by William Penn who, along with his partners, became known as the Twenty-Four Proprietors. The following year, these proprietors promulgated a new constitution for the colony.[17] That document guaranteed liberty of conscience for all who accepted belief in "the one Almighty and Eternal God" and who would agree to "live peaceably and quietly in a civil society."[18] That freedom, however, did not extend to "atheism," "irreligiousness," or the practicing of certain forms of licentious behavior, including "cursing, swearing, drunkenness, prophaness, whoring, adultery, murdering or any kind of violence, or indulging themselves in stage plays, masks, revells or such like abuses."[19] The constitution limited office-holding to those who believed in the divinity of Christ.[20] Conscientious objectors were exempted from the duty to bear arms in defense of the province.[21] The right to trial by jury was preserved.[22] Plural office-holding was prohibited, an indication of the colonists' belief in the importance of separating personnel for the preservation of liberty.[23]

The 1683 constitution never took effect, rejected by both the proprietor-appointed council and the provincial assembly. However, in 1699, the assembly passed–and the council and the proprietary governor approved–an Act Declaring the Rights and Privileges of English Subjects in East Jersey.[24] In contrast to the simple form of government embodied in the West Jersey concessions, the statute provided for a mixed or balanced regime—governor, council, and assembly—with the latter chosen by freeholders. It guaranteed members of the assembly speech and

[17] The Fundamental Constitutions for the Province of East New Jersey in America, Anno Domini 1683, in Thorpe, *Constitutions*, 5: 2574–2582.

[18] Ibid., Ch. XVI, 2579.

[19] Ibid., 2580.

[20] Ibid.

[21] Ibid., Ch. VII, 2576–2577.

[22] Ibid., Ch. XIX, 2580–2581.

[23] Ibid., Ch. XVII, 2580.

[24] Aaron Leaming and Jacob Spicer, eds., *The Grants, Concessions, and Original Constitutions of the Province of New Jersey: The Acts Passed During the Propriety Governments, and Other Material Transactions Before the Surrender Thereof to Queen Anne*, 2nd ed. (Somerville, NJ: Honeyman & Co, 1881), 368–372.

debate protections and provided for trial by a jury of twelve members, grand jury indictment, and due process of law.[25] Freedom of religious conscience was granted to those who professed "faith in God, by Jesus as Christ, his only son" and "d[id] not under that pretence, disturb the civil peace of this Province, or use this liberty to licentiousness," excepting those of the "Romish [Roman Catholic] religion." [26]

In 1702, in the wake of a series of land disputes, conflicts with New York, and threats from the Crown to consolidate the northern colonies under a single head, the proprietors of the two New Jerseys surrendered their government powers to Queen Anne. Following this union, the queen issued instructions to the new governor, Lord Cornbury, that included a due process of law clause echoing Chapter 39 of Magna Carta;[27] permitted liberty of conscience for all persons except papists;[28] allowed Quakers to affirm rather than swear an oath;[29] and mandated that he endeavor to get a law passed outlawing unhuman treatment by masters toward "their Christian servants, and their slaves...."[30] The instructions included a directive that judges and other officers could not be removed from office by the governor absent good cause, providing a measure of judicial independence.[31]

The combination of enticing land grants and religious freedom had the effect of attracting diverse groups of settlers to an already diverse colony. By the opening of the eighteenth century, "New Jersey was the most

[25] Ibid., 371–372. A later court decision, *Holmes v. Walton* (1780), held that the requirement of a twelve-member jury found in this concession and the common law was incorporated into the first state constitution. Wayne D. Moore, "Written and Unwritten Constitutional Law in the Founding Period: The Early New Jersey Cases," *Constitutional Commentary* 7, no. 2 (Summer 1990): 341–359. See commentary to Article XXII, below for additional treatment of *Holmes*.

[26] Leaming and Spicer, *Grants, Concessions*, 372.

[27] *Instructions for Our Right Trusty and Well Beloved Edward Lord Cornbury*, November 16, 1702, sec. 49, in Leaming and Spicer, *Grants, Concessions*, 633. Section 49 read: "You are to take care that no man's life, member, freehold, or goods be taken away or harmed in our said Province, otherwise than by established and known laws, not repugnant to, but as much as may be agreeable to the laws of England."

[28] Ibid., sec. 51, 633.

[29] Ibid., sec. 52, 633.

[30] Ibid., sec. 89, 642.

[31] Ibid., sec. 41, 630.

ethnically and religiously diverse" colony in America.[32] In addition to fostering–perhaps requiring–a strong commitment to religious liberty, the diversity helped shape the rights provisions later adopted in the state's first constitution. While the early declarations of rights found in states such as Virginia, Pennsylvania, Massachusetts, and Maryland exhibited communal and aspirational dimensions, these dimensions would be largely absent from the 1776 New Jersey Constitution.

Neither the consolidation of the two provinces nor the lofty words of the instructions to the governor resulted in stable, effective government for the colony. Provincial governors regularly exercised powers in support of Crown policies, creating division and deadlock between colonists and Crown. New Jersey joined the other colonies in disputing the claims of the Crown and in asserting rights based on the English Constitution, common law, and natural rights—the latter appearing with increasing regularity after 1760.[33]

By the middle of the 1770s, the colonial government's legitimacy came into question. Widespread public meetings to protest the king's policies and committees of correspondence filled the lacuna engendered by the lack of public support. On July 21, 1774, in response to British punitive measures against Massachusetts, including the closing of the port of Boston, seventy-two men from the various committees of correspondence gathered in New Brunswick to work toward grounding "the constitutional rights of America on a solid and permanent foundation."[34] At that meeting, prominent individuals were chosen to represent the interests of New Jersey at the First Continental Congress, to be held later that summer in Philadelphia. One historian has called the New Brunswick gathering an "illegal meeting…[and] a turning point in New Jersey Whig politics. The colony had come to the aid of a neighboring colony suffering

[32] Eugene Sheridan, "Study in Paradox," 249. One historian refers to this diversity as the colony's "defining characteristic." Quoted in David J. Fowler, "These Were Troublesome Times Indeed: Social and Economic Conditions in Revolutionary New Jersey," in *New Jersey in the American Revolution*, ed. Barbara J. Mitnick (New Brunswick, NJ: Rutgers University Press, 2005), 17.

[33] This period is ably covered in John E. Pomfret, *Colonial New Jersey: A History* (New York: Charles Scribner's Sons, 1973), chapters 6–9.

[34] *Minutes of the Provincial Congress and the Council of Safety of the State of New Jersey* (Trenton: Naar, Day & Naar, Printer, 1879), 26.

under British tyranny and, in the process, had been drawn into the revolutionary movement."[35]

The spontaneous outpouring of activism gave birth to the extra-constitutional assemblage at New Brunswick. It would be the first of four provincial congresses that would be the de facto governing bodies for the state. These congresses would direct the movement toward independence and write the state's first constitution.[36] The transfer of power from the established colonial political institutions to the provincial congress was accomplished with little violence or bloodshed.[37]

On July 2, 1776, two days before the Continental Congress officially declared American independence, New Jersey's Fourth Provincial Congress approved a state constitution. It did so in record time. A ten-man drafting committee appointed by the congress took only two days to produce a working draft; five days later, the constitution was adopted.[38] Producing a draft in two days suggests that one or more committee members likely arrived with a prepared text. This "makeshift" constitution, containing no amending procedure and providing that the document would become "null and void" should a reconciliation with Great Britain occur, would remain New Jersey's governing document for the next sixty-eight years.

Although not elected for the express purpose of creating a constitution, representatives to the Fourth Provincial Congress were chosen in the wake of a May 10, 1776, resolution by the Continental Congress recommending that colonies not having established governments "sufficient to the exigencies of their affairs ... adopt such government as shall, in the opinion of the representatives of the people, best conduce to the

[35] John Fea, "Revolution and Confederation Period: New Jersey at the Crossroads," in *New Jersey: A History of the Garden State*, ed. Maxine N. Lurie and Richard Veit (New Brunswick, NJ: Rutgers University Press, 2012), 70.

[36] Such spontaneous political action, celebrated by Hannah Arendt, *On Revolution* (New York: Viking Press, 1965[1963]), 238–247, and chapter six, is all the more remarkable when we consider that there were no newspapers in colonial New Jersey!

[37] A detailed account of this transfer is found in David A. Bernstein, "New Jersey in the American Revolution: The Establishment of a Government amid Civil and Military Disorder, 1770–1781" (PhD diss., Rutgers University, 1970), 65–169.

[38] *Journal of the Votes and Proceedings of the Convention of New Jersey, Begun at Burlington the Tenth of June 1776, and thence Continued by Adjournment at Trenton and New-Brunswick, to the Twenty-First of August Following* (Burlington NJ: Isaac Collins, 1776), 35–36.

happiness and safety of their constituents in particular, and America in general."[39] Moreover, there was an opportunity for debate, petitions, and discussion in anticipation of the election. Voters would have been aware that the resulting provincial congress might declare independence and undertake the task of writing a constitution.[40] Nonetheless, the actions of the congress in declaring itself to be the legitimate representative of the people, adopting a constitution without formal authorization, and implementing that constitution without obtaining the consent of the people through a ratification process were extraordinary. Exigent circumstances and subsequent support of the republican principles embodied in the document—not legality—would be the final arbiters of legitimacy.[41]

Constitutional Developments: 1776 Constitution

Though the preamble of the constitution proclaimed that "in congress assembled" they have agreed on "a set of charter rights and the form [frame] of a Constitution," there was no formal declaration of rights.[42] Assigning reasons for the omission is, perforce, inferential and speculative. The minutes of the provincial congress contain no record of discussions relative to any specific provisions of the constitution. What we do know is that two of the three states adopting constitutions before New Jersey–New Hampshire and South Carolina–ratified documents self-described as temporary that also lacked declarations of rights. With little guidance, drafters turned to the English Constitution and common law, the constitutional documents of the colony, and their experiences under English

[39] Worthington Chauncey Ford, et al., eds. *Journals of the Continental Congress, 1774–1789* (Washington: Government Printing Office, 1906), 4:342.

[40] For a description of the activities and publicity surrounding the election of the Fourth Provincial Congress, see Charles R. Erdman Jr., *The New Jersey Constitution of 1776* (Princeton, NJ: Princeton University Press, 1929), 22–26, and Bernstein, "New Jersey in the American Revolution," 161–165. Willi Paul Adams provides an account of the stream of petitions to the provincial congress that included specific suggestions for constitutional reform. *The First American Constitutions: Republican Ideology and the Making of the State Constitutions in the Revolutionary Era* (Lanham, MD: Rowman & Littlefield, 2001), 71–72.

[41] John Bebout suggests exigent circumstances as the reason. "Introduction," xv–xvii.

[42] The preamble mentioned no specific rights and none of the language of natural rights found in the Declaration of Independence appeared in that section.

rule.[43] Delegates may have thought that Article XXII of the new constitution, incorporating the common law of England and "so much of the statute law, as have been heretofore practised in this Colony, shall still remain in force...," provided citizens with ample protection for their rights.[44] When English sources did not provide sufficient protection, specific rights were placed in the document, as was the case with the guarantee of religious freedom, liberty of conscience (Const. 1776, Arts. XVIII, XIX), and suffrage requirements (ibid., Art. IV).

The Revolutionary War also may have played a role in the decision not to include a separate bill of rights. New Jersey was a "dangerous place."[45] More fighting took place in New Jersey than in any other state. While delegates debated the proposed constitution, a massive fleet of seventy British warships (roughly half of the Royal Navy), carrying a very large British Army—the largest force Britain had ever sent from its shores—approached the coast of Staten Island.[46] By midyear 1776, all of New Jersey and southern New York were either under the control of the British or were in danger of being so. Cecilia M. Kenyon dramatized the parlous situation: "[E]very member of the state assemblies or conventions that drafted constitutions was publicly committing himself to the Revolution and therefore placing his life in jeopardy should the Revolution fail."[47] Moreover, the colony was anything but united on the question of independence. As late as 1776 most people in New Jersey "still sought reform and reconciliation with Britain, not independence."[48] The constitution itself reflected this reluctance to join the common cause. It referred to

[43] Erdman, *New Jersey Constitution*, 44.

[44] Richard J. Connors, *The Constitution of 1776* (Trenton: New Jersey Historical Commission, 1975), 21. Erdman makes a similar surmise. *New Jersey Constitution*, 47.

[45] Mark Edward Lender, "The 'Cockpit' Reconsidered: Revolutionary New Jersey as a Military Theater," in Mitnick, *New Jersey in the American Revolution*, 45.

[46] Thomas Fleming, "Crossroads of the American Revolution," in Mitnick, *New Jersey in the American Revolution*, 2.

[47] "Constitutionalism in Revolutionary America," in *Constitutionalism: Nomos XX*, ed. J. Roland Pennock and John W. Chapman (New York: New York University Press, 1979), 91–92. Bernstein suggests that the delegates voting for the reconciliation clause may have been intimidated by the British invasion threat. "New Jersey in the American Revolution," 169–170.

[48] Fowler, "These Were Troublesome Times Indeed," 21.

New Jersey as a "colony" more than twenty times,[49] and concluded with the following statement:

> Provided always, and it is the true intent and meaning of this Congress, that if a reconciliation between Great-Britain and these Colonies should take place, and the latter be taken again under the protection and government of the crown of Britain, this Charter shall be null and void—otherwise to remain firm and inviolable.

After the constitution's adoption on July 2, several delegates, perhaps motivated by the Revolutionary fervor at the national level in neighboring Philadelphia, moved to have the reconciliation provision removed. The following day, delegates confirmed the original draft by a two-to-one margin.[50] The imminent danger of subjection facing New Jersey and the hesitancy and division in public opinion may have made extended deliberation about a declaration of rights seem premature.

New Jersey's constitution is notable for the absence of language found in the declarations of rights in most other states. No natural or inalienable rights were declared; no equality clause was present; no "alter or abolish" or right to revolution clauses were included. The preamble spoke of adopting a form of government that "shall best conduce to their own happiness and safety…." (Const. 1776, preamble).

The lack of a formal declaration of rights did not mean delegates were unconcerned about rights. For one, the preamble, though it mentioned no specific rights, spoke of the "cruel and unnatural manner" in which colonists had been treated for no other reason than "asserting their just rights." The constitution also incorporated the statutory law of the province (ibid., Art. XXI) as well as the common law and statute law of England (ibid., Art. XXII), which afforded colonists an extensive body of procedural and substantive protections such as Magna Carta, the English Petition of Right (1628), the Habeas Corpus Act (1679), and the English Bill of Rights (1689).

Of greater import are the rights the provincial congress did include. The three rights considered by colonists to be the anchors for all other rights—suffrage and self-government (Const. 1776, Art. IV), liberty of

[49] In September 1777, the legislature of New Jersey amended the constitution, substituting the words "state" and "states" for "colony" and "colonies."

[50] *Journal of the Votes and Proceedings*, 35–36.

conscience (ibid., Arts. XVIII, XIX), and trial by jury (ibid., Art. XXII)—were included in the constitution.

Suffrage

The New Jersey Constitution liberalized suffrage requirements, retaining a property qualification of fifty pounds of "proclamation money."[51] The latter qualification could be met by personal as well as real property. By eliminating any requirement of land ownership as a condition for voting,[52] New Jersey severed the historic connection between landed property and political rights.[53] The leading scholar of voting in New Jersey, Richard P. McCormick, concluded: "it was possible for a vast majority of adult white males to vote."[54] The state made the suffrage available to all "inhabitants," raising the question: Did they mean to include women, free African Americans, slaves, and Indians? Some scholars have concluded that use of the word "inhabitants" was an accident—an oversight due to the haste in drafting the document; that such a radical change would have occasioned some debate, at the very least, and that such an unprecedented and radical expansion of the electorate probably would not have garnered majority support.[55] Others suggest that it was a conscious decision.[56] Judith Apter Klinghoffer and Lois Elkis claim that the constitution writers, heady with Revolutionary radicalism, meant to include blacks

[51] "Proclamation money" was in currency rates established by a proclamation of Queen Anne in 1704. For an examination of how proclamation money worked in practice, see Ron Michener, "Money in the American Colonies," EH.net, https://eh.net/encyclopedia/money-in-the-american-colonies/, accessed November 18, 2018.

[52] The constitution also contained property qualifications for the holding of elected office. Members of the legislative council and assembly were required to be worth at least one thousand pounds and five hundred pounds of proclamation money, respectively (Const. 1776, Art. III).

[53] Richard P. McCormick, *Experiment in Independence: New Jersey in the Critical Period, 1781–1789* (New Brunswick, NJ: Rutgers University Press, 1950), 80.

[54] *New Jersey from Colony to State, 1609–1789* (Princeton, NJ: D. Van Nostrand Co., Inc., 1964), 123.

[55] Edward Raymond Turner, "Women's Suffrage in New Jersey, 1790–1807," *Smith College Studies in History* 1, no. 4 (July 1916): 176–178.

[56] Elizabeth Cady Stanton, Susan B. Anthony, and Matilda Joslyn Gage, *The History of Woman Suffrage* (Rochester: Charles Mann, 1881), 1:451–455.

and women.[57] McCormick is agnostic: "[w]hether the term 'inhabitants' included women, aliens, Negroes, and slaves was unclear, and was to be a source of confusion and controversy."[58] Not in dispute is the fact that the New Jersey provision was "an anomaly"[59] not found in any other early state constitution.

Slavery

The 1776 constitution did not address the question of slavery. New Jersey ranked second only to New York among northern colonies in the number of blacks and their percentage of the total population.[60] Deep-seated prejudices about the alleged depraved nature of blacks and the occasional insurrections that took place during the late seventeenth century produced black codes that sanctioned mutilation and other harsh punishments. The willingness of some slaves to entertain British offers of freedom during the Revolutionary War cemented the prejudice and hostility. According to Professor Clement Price, "support for the institution" of slavery "was stronger in New Jersey than in any other northern

[57] "'The Petticoat Electors': Women's Suffrage in New Jersey, 1776–1807," *Journal of the Early Republic* 12, no. 2 (Summer 1992): 166–169. Jan Ellen Lewis provides a recent articulation of the "they really meant to do it" position. "Rethinking Women's Suffrage in New Jersey, 1776–1807," *Rutgers Law Review* 63, no. 3 (Spring 2011): 1017–1035.

[58] Richard P. McCormick, *The History of Voting in New Jersey: A Study of the Development of Election Machinery, 1664–1911* (New Brunswick, NJ: Rutgers University Press, 1953), 69–70.

[59] Dorothy A. Mays, *Women in Early America: Struggle, Survival, and Freedom in a New World* (Santa Barbara, CA: ABC-CLIO, 2004), 383. Delight W. Dodyk, "'Troublesome Times A-Coming': The American Revolution and New Jersey Women," in Mitnick, *New Jersey in the American Revolution*, 150. Recent discoveries of poll lists show that women did vote in significant numbers before the right was taken away in 1807. Jennifer Schuessler, "On the Trail of America's First Women to Vote," *New York Times*, February 25, 2020, at C1.

[60] Giles R. Wright, "Moving Toward Breaking the Chains: Black New Jerseyans and the American Revolution," in Mitnick, *New Jersey and the American Revolution*, 116. The impact of independence, the Revolution, and the adoption of the New Jersey Constitution is captured by the title of Gregory Evans Dowd's article, "Declarations of Dependence: War and Inequality in Revolutionary New Jersey, 1776–1815," *New Jersey History* 103 (1985): 47–67.

colony."[61] In February 1804, the state passed a "gradual emancipation law" providing those female children of slaves born after July 4, 1804, would be freed when they reached twenty-one years of age, and male children would be freed at age twenty-five.[62] Complete abolition of slavery in the state did not occur, however, until ratification of the Thirteenth Amendment.[63]

Structural Provisions

Unlike a majority of early state constitutions, New Jersey's constitution contained no statement of the doctrine of separation of powers; nor were the institutions structured in such a way as to provide for such separation. The bicameral assembly and legislative council jointly elected the governor (Const. 1776, Art. VII). The judiciary was not mentioned in the vesting of government powers clause (ibid., Art. I); supreme court judges were selected by the legislature for seven-year terms (ibid., Art. XII); and the governor and legislative council served as the "Court of Appeals, in the last resort" (ibid., Art. IX). It was, in the words of one commentator, "a clearly dependent judiciary."[64] The only component of separation of powers found in the document was a restriction on plural office-holding (ibid., Art. XX).

The framers adopted various structural provisions designed to maintain popular sovereignty as an active principle, including annual terms for legislators (Const. 1776, Art. III), one of the most expansive suffrage provisions in the colonies (ibid., Art. IV), the direct election of members of the legislative council, sheriffs, and coroners (ibid., Arts. III, XIII), and term limits (three annual terms) for sheriffs and coroners (ibid., Art. XIII).[65]

[61] As quoted by Robert Hennelly "Secret History of a Northern Slave State: How Slavery Was Written into New Jersey's DNA," July 29, 2015, https://www.salon.com/2015/07/29/secret_history_of_a_northern_slave_state_how_slavery_was_written_into_new_jerseys_dna/, accessed March 6, 2020.

[62] An Act for the Gradual Abolition of Slavery, February 15, 1804, Acts 28th G.A. 2nd sitting, Ch. CIII, 251–254, http://njlegallib.rutgers.edu/slavery/acts/A78.html.

[63] New Jersey did not ratify the amendment until after it had already taken effect.

[64] Robert F. Williams, *The New Jersey State Constitution: A Reference Guide*, updated ed. (New Brunswick, NJ: Rutgers University Press, 1997), 5.

[65] After serving three one-year terms, a sheriff or coroner could be reelected only after a lapse of three years. Const. 1776, Art. XIII.

These provisions ensured that the government would remain close to the people and thus not likely to endanger their liberties. Article VI gave the assembly—the body most closely controlled by the citizens—exclusive power to originate or amend all money bills, providing further evidence of the state's commitment to popular sovereignty.

The Oath of Office required of all members of the legislature contained a remarkable passage relating to the protection of rights:

> I, *A. B.*, do solemnly declare, that, as a member of the Legislative Council, [*or Assembly, as the case may be,*] of the Colony of New-Jersey, I will not assent to any law, vote or proceeding, which shall appear to me injurious to the public welfare of said Colony, nor that shall annul or repeal that part of the third section in the Charter of this Colony, which establishes, that the elections of members of the Legislative Council and Assembly shall be annual; nor that part of the twenty-second section in said Charter, respecting the trial by jury, nor that shall annul, repeal, or alter any part or parts of the eighteenth or nineteenth sections of the same (Const. 1776, Art. XXIII).

The oath required all lawmakers to swear that they would not repeal three provisions of the constitution: annual terms for the legislature (representation),[66] religious liberty, and trial by jury.

The preamble declared that all constitutional authority ever possessed by the kings of Great Britain was "derived from the people," making the sovereignty of the people the foundation of the state. Article XXIII did provide, at least concerning certain specified protections, that legislative action would be *ultra vires*, suggesting that these provisions could only be altered with the direct consent of the people. If so, how would that popular consent be forthcoming? The document provided no mechanism for its revision. One inference to be drawn from the presence of the entrenchment clause is that all provisions not so limited by Article

[66] Between 1702 and 1776, colonial New Jersey had no stated requirement for periodic elections: only four assembly elections took place between 1754 and 1776. The Concession and Agreement of 1664/1665 and the Fundamental Agreements of the Freeholders, and Inhabitants of the Province of West Jersey (1681) provided for regular elections, but those provisions disappeared when New Jersey became a royal colony in 1702. Larry R. Gerlach, "Power to the People: Popular Sovereignty, Republicanism and the Legislature in Revolutionary New Jersey," in *The Development of the New Jersey Legislature from Colonial Times to the Present*, ed. William C. Wright (Trenton: New Jersey Historical Commission, 1976), 7ff.

XXIII were open to legislative amendment without the direct approval of the voters. This inference is consistent with the view that the Declaration of Independence resulted in the transfer of parliamentary powers to state governments possessing plenary powers to act absent specific constitutional prohibitions.

Postscript: The 1776 constitution remained in effect until 1844. In that year, a constitutional convention adopted and the people overwhelmingly ratified a new constitution. Article I of the new constitution, titled "Rights and Privileges," contained nineteen provisions that combined language of the declarations of rights found in the early state constitutions and the Bill of Rights of the U.S. Constitution.

Although the text of the 1776 constitution remained unchanged until 1844, its expansive suffrage provision suffered a much earlier demise. In 1807, the legislature enacted a statute formally excluding from the suffrage women, African Americans, and aliens.[67] The willingness of the legislature to de facto amend the constitution by legislative act points up the unsettled relationship in the early years of the republic between constitutional and legislative law. The 1844 constitution continued the suffrage restrictions adopted by the legislature in 1807.

Constitution of New Jersey [1776]

* * *

IV. That all inhabitants of this Colony, of full age, who are worth fifty pounds proclamation money, clear estate in the same, and have resided within the county in which they claim a vote for twelve months immediately preceding the election, shall be entitled to vote for Representatives in Council and Assembly; and also for all other public officers, that shall be elected by the people of the county at large.[68]

[67] Williams, *New Jersey State Constitution*, 82–87. Klinghoffer and Elkis argue that the move to reverse the diffusion of power unleashed by this radical broadening of the franchise on the part of "Republican elites" between 1776 and 1807 drew on the ideologies of gender, race, and nationality to justify reimposing the exclusions.

[68] The one-year residency requirement within the county in order to vote, lengthy by today's standards, was less demanding than the two years' residency required by Delaware, Pennsylvania (1790), and South Carolina (1790). See Table 3, pp. 70–71.

* * *

XVI. That all criminals shall be admitted to the same privileges of witnesses and counsel, as their prosecutors are or shall be entitled to.[69]

XVII. That the estates of such persons as shall destroy their own lives, shall not, for that offence, be forfeited; but shall descend in the same manner, as they would have done, had such persons died in the natural way; nor shall any article, which may occasion accidentally the death of any one, be henceforth deemed a deodand, or in anywise forfeited, on account of such misfortune.[70]

XVIII. That no person shall ever, within this Colony, be deprived of the inestimable privilege of worshipping Almighty God in a manner agreeable to the dictates of his own conscience; nor, under any pretence whatever, be compelled to attend any place of worship, contrary to his own faith and judgment; nor shall any person, within this Colony, ever be obliged to pay tithes, taxes, or any other rates, for the purpose of building or repairing any other church or churches, place or places of worship, or for the maintenance of any minister or ministry, contrary to what he believes to be right, or has deliberately or voluntarily engaged himself to perform.[71]

XIX. That there shall be no establishment of any one religious sect in this Province, in preference to another; and that no Protestant inhabitant

[69] This protection embodied an equality principle: defendants must have a meaningful opportunity, at least as advantageous as that possessed by the prosecution, to establish the essential elements of their case. Encompassed within the text were the rights to be represented by counsel, to call witnesses in one's defense, and to confront adverse witnesses. It had its origin in English statutes and colonial enactments. Indeed, most colonies permitted a more robust right to counsel than was available to Englishmen under the common law. George Dargo, *Roots of the Republic: A New Perspective on Early American Constitutionalism* (New York: Praeger, 1974), 67–68.

[70] Article XVII protected the property of individuals who committed suicide from escheating to the state. This provision, first found in Chapter XXX of the Concessions and Agreements of West Jersey (1676/1677), was a departure from the practice in Great Britain, where the forfeiture of a suicide's goods and chattels to the Crown was not abolished until the Forfeiture Act of 1870. David S. Markson, "The Punishment of Suicide - A Need for Change," *Villanova Law Review* 14, no. 3 (Spring 1969): 465. Another departure from English law terminated the practice that an article of property (e.g., a farm animal) causing the death of a person was forfeited to God ("deodand" literally means "given to God"), that is, transferred to the Crown to be sold and the proceeds used for charitable purposes.

[71] Articles XVIII and XIX were derived from the religious liberty tradition embodied in the various concessions, agreements, and constitutions adopted during the colonial period. See pp. 289–294, above. The liberty afforded by these provisions was not absolute: Office-holding and full enjoyment of civil rights were available only to Protestants.

of this Colony shall be denied the enjoyment of any civil right, merely on account of his religious principles; but that all persons, professing a belief in the faith of any Protestant sect, who shall demean themselves peaceably under the government, as hereby established, shall be capable of being elected into any office of profit or trust, or being a member of either branch of the Legislature, and shall fully and freely enjoy every privilege and immunity, enjoyed by others their fellow subjects.

* * *

XXI. That all the laws of this Province, contained in the edition lately published by Mr. Allinson, shall be and remain in full force, until altered by the Legislature of this Colony (such only excepted, as are incompatible with this Charter) and shall be, according as heretofore, regarded in all respects, by all civil officers, and others, the good people of this Province.

XXII. That the common law of England, as well as so much of the statute law, as have been heretofore practised in this Colony, shall still remain in force, until they shall be altered by a future law of the Legislature; such parts only excepted, as are repugnant to the rights and privileges contained in this Charter; and that the inestimable right of trial by jury shall remain confirmed as a part of the law of this Colony, without repeal, forever.[72]

[72] Article XXI provided continuity with the past by incorporating and preserving the laws of the colony judged to be consistent with the newly independent republic. Article XXII incorporated the common law and statute law that had been in effect prior to the Declaration of Independence. Like other colonies, New Jersey did not always follow English common law. This was particularly true when it came to religious liberty, where the legislature and the royal courts of New Jersey were more solicitous of religious interests and values. Divergences from the common law took place in other areas as well. The subordinate status of women in the common law was mitigated by colonial conditions giving women a "functional independence and importance not found in the British Isles." Dodyk, "Troublesome Times A-Coming," 140. As William E. Nelson notes, New Jersey officials found "a channel to navigate between the strict requirements of the law, on the one hand, and the cultural realities of their society on the other." *The Common Law in Colonial America*, vol. 2, *The Middle Colonies and the Carolinas, 1660–1730* (New York: Oxford University Press, 2013), 143.

The final clause, declaring the right to trial by jury part of the constitution "without repeal, forever," made this clause "unamendable." It raised the question of whether one constituent body could foreclose "forever" a subsequent constituent body's power to rewrite or amend the constitution. What is clear is that the legislature lacked the power to change the common law or statutory law in this area. Among the earliest known examples of judicial review in the American colonies, ***Holmes v. Walton*** (1780), declared unconstitutional a legislative attempt to change the common law and statutory requirement of a twelve-member jury. Moore, "Written and Unwritten Constitutional Law," 348–351.

Georgia

Conceived by General George Oglethorpe and associates as an asylum for persecuted Protestants and a fresh start for the debt-ridden facing prison, Georgia was founded in 1732, making it the youngest of the thirteen British-American colonies.[1] Advertised as "… the greatest social and Philanthropic experiment of the age,"[2] its founding had the added benefit of protecting the northern colonies from Spanish and French intruders. Shortly after its inception, the colony outlawed slavery, the first colony-wide ban on slavery in British North America.[3]

[1] Albert Berry Saye, *A Constitutional History of Georgia, 1732–1945* (Athens: University of Georgia Press, 1948), 13; see Reba Carolyn Strickland, *Religion and the State in Georgia in the Eighteenth Century* (1939; reprint, New York: AMS Press, Inc., 1967), 12–18. Oglethorpe originally intended to take settlers largely from debtors' prisons, creating a "debtor's colony" where they could learn trades and work off their debts—thus the misleading sobriquet "penal colony."

[2] Quoted in Walter A. McDougall, *Freedom Is Just Around the Corner: A New American History 1585–1828* (New York: HarperCollins, 2004), 129.

[3] Kenneth Coleman, "Frontier Haven: Georgia and the Bill of Rights," in *The Bill of Rights and the States: The Colonial and Revolutionary Origins of American Liberties*, ed. Patrick T. Conley and John P. Kaminski (Madison, WI: Madison House, 1992), 444. The prohibition was not always enforced and gradually fell into desuetude. Coleman provides a succinct summary of Georgia's response to slavery between 1730 and 1788. Ibid., 446–450.

P. J. Galie et al., *Bills of Rights Before the Bill of Rights*,
https://doi.org/10.1007/978-3-030-44301-6_14

Georgia's charter, issued by King George II (who named the colony after himself), vested complete governing authority in a board of twenty-one trustees.[4] The charter also designated fifteen of the trustees to be the common council of the corporation and instructed them to form "laws, statutes and ordinances" that were "not repugnant to the laws and statutes of England."[5] Although the early settlers of Georgia were not given political rights, the charter granted them liberty of conscience, free exercise of religion to all but "papists," and the rights and privileges of Englishmen:

> Also we do, for ourselves and successors, declare, by these presents, that all and every the persons which shall happen to be born within the said province, and every of their children and posterity, shall have and enjoy all liberties, franchises and immunities of free denizens and natural born subjects, within any of our dominions, to all intents and purposes, as if abiding and born within this our kingdom of Great-Britain, or any other of our dominions … there shall be a liberty of conscience allowed in the worship of God … and that all such persons, except papists, shall have a free exercise of their religion, so they be contented with the quiet and peaceable enjoyment of the same, not giving offence or scandal to the government.[6]

The charter also permitted Quakers to substitute an affirmation for an oath.[7] The liberal policies contained in Georgia's charter attracted numerous Protestant dissenters to the province.[8]

[4] Of the original trustees, only one (Oglethorpe) ever set foot in the colony. Scott D. Gerber, "The Origins of the Georgia Judiciary," *The Georgia Historical Quarterly* 93, no. 1 (Spring 2009): 58.

[5] Charter of Georgia (1732), in Thorpe, *Constitutions*, 2:772. There were only three laws passed by the trustees during their twenty years of authority; they governed mostly through suggestions and resolutions. Gerber, "Origins of the Georgia Judiciary," 58–59.

[6] Charter of Georgia, 773. Liberty of conscience was the right to hold beliefs unmolested, while free exercise was the right to publicly act on one's beliefs. Joel A. Nichols, "Religious Liberty in the Thirteenth Colony: Church-State Relations in Colonial and Early National Georgia," *New York University Law Review* 80, no. 6 (December 2005): 1695 n. 2.

[7] Charter of Georgia, 774.

[8] Marjorie Daniel, "Anglicans and Dissenters in Georgia, 1758–1777," *Church History* 7, no. 3 (September 1938): 247.

A decade into the trusteeship, growing numbers of Georgians pressed to have the same rights of self-government long enjoyed by inhabitants of other colonies.[9] On March 19, 1749/1750, the common council authorized the election of a unicameral representative assembly.[10] This assembly acted merely as an advisory board and met only once before Georgia became a royal colony two years later.[11] Under royal government, a popularly elected Commons House of Assembly exercised actual legislative authority. The Church of England became the established church in 1758, but it was a weak establishment that did not affect the status of dissenting churches.[12] The assembly ensured broad religious toleration by mandating that no Anglican minister "exercise any Eclesiastical Law or Jurisdiction whatsoever."[13]

Georgia's population and economy grew significantly during the royal period, although it was still financially dependent on Britain; it had a popular and respected royal governor, James Wright, and could rely heavily on the British Indian Department for protection from potentially hostile neighbors. These reasons, inter alia, served to dampen the colony's interest in joining the Revolutionary movement.[14] Georgia did follow the lead of the other American colonies in opposing the Sugar and Stamp Acts, the Townshend Acts, and the Intolerable Acts, although its

[9] Kenneth Coleman, *Colonial Georgia: A History* (Millwood, NY: KTO Press, 1989), 109.

[10] Gerber, "Origins of the Georgia Judiciary," 62; Saye, *Constitutional History of Georgia*, 42–43.

[11] Gerber, "Origins of the Georgia Judiciary," 62; Saye, *Constitutional History of Georgia*, 43, 58. Royal government was not actually instituted until 1754. Coleman, *Colonial Georgia*, 175.

[12] Coleman, *Colonial Georgia*, 231; Nichols, "Religious Liberty in the Thirteenth Colony," 1718. For a detailed account of the history of dissenting sects in colonial Georgia, see Nichols, "Religious Liberty in the Thirteenth Colony," 1702–1712, 1734–1765.

[13] An Act for Constituting and Dividing the Several Districts and Divisions of this Province into Parishes, and for Establishing of Religious Worship therein According to the Rites and Ceremonies of the Church of England; and also for Impowering the Church Wardens and Vestrymen of the Respective Parishes to Assess Rates for the Repair of Churches, the Relief of the Poor, and Other Parochial Services, March 15, 1758, *The Colonial Records of the State of Georgia*, ed. Allen D. Candler (Atlanta: Chas P. Byrd, 1910), 18:271–272.

[14] Kenneth Coleman, *The American Revolution in Georgia, 1763–1789* (Athens: University of Georgia Press, 1958), 72; Coleman, "Frontier Haven," 453.

responses were tepid in comparison.[15] Ultimately, Georgia's sympathies and interests lay with its sister colonies in declaring independence from Britain.[16]

In 1775, Georgians began electing an extra-legal provincial congress to exercise legislative power over the colony. On April 15, 1776, that provincial congress adopted a temporary governing document titled "Rules and Regulations"—considered by some to be the state's first constitution.[17] The document grounded political authority on the consent of the governed, stating that all power originated with the people and all government was intended for their benefit.[18] It provided a rough outline of three branches of government and declared that previously recognized statutes and common law would remain in force, to the extent they did not interfere with the laws of the Continental Congress or the provincial congress.[19]

After the Continental Congress issued the Declaration of Independence, Georgia held a special election to select delegates for a constitutional convention authorized to establish a permanent constitution.[20] In anticipation of the election, President Archibald Bulloch, chief executive under the Rules and Regulations, exhorted voters to choose their delegates wisely for the task ahead:

> America must stand or fall by the virtue of her inhabitants; consequently, the utmost caution must necessarily be used by the people of this State, in

[15] Coleman, *American Revolution in Georgia*, 16, 18, 24, see generally 16–38. In response to the Stamp Act of 1765, the Commons House agreed to back any actions taken by the Stamp Act Congress and endorsed that body's memorial and petitions. However, Georgia angered the other colonies by being the only one from which revenue was collected under the act.

[16] Coleman, "Frontier Haven," 453; Saye, *Constitutional History of Georgia*, 78; Ethel K. Ware, *A Constitutional History of Georgia* (New York: Columbia University Press, 1947), 16.

[17] Coleman, *American Revolution in Georgia*, 76; Ware, *Constitutional History of Georgia*, 24–25.

[18] 1776 Rules and Regulations of the Colony of Georgia, accessed December 18, 2018, https://georgiainfo.galileo.usg.edu/topics/government/related_article/constitutions/rules-and-regulations-of-the-colony-of-georgia-1776.

[19] Ibid.

[20] Fletcher M. Green, *Constitutional Development in the South Atlantic States, 1776–1860: A Study in the Evolution of Democracy* (Chapel Hill: University of North Carolina Press, 1930), 60.

> choosing men of unsuspected characters, men whose actions had proved their friendship to the cause of freedom, and men whose depth of political judgment qualified them to frame a constitution for the future government of the country.[21]

After meeting on and off between October 1776 and February 1777, the delegates adopted a new constitution on February 5, 1777.[22] Although not submitted to the people for ratification, five hundred copies of the constitution were ordered to be printed for their perusal, with the Act of Distribution (an act governing the distribution of intestate estates) and the Habeas Corpus Act appended.[23]

Constitutional Developments: 1777 Constitution

The constitution's preamble appealed to natural rights, denouncing Parliament's conduct as "repugnant to the common rights of mankind," forcing the American people "to assert the rights and privileges they are entitled to by the laws of nature and reason." Although the constitution contained no separate declaration of rights,[24] it did include several rights.[25] Among the rights explicitly protected were the fundamental rights of suffrage (Const. 1777, Art. IX), liberty of conscience (ibid., Art. LVI), and trial by jury (ibid., Art. LXI); also included were the right to represent one's self in court (ibid., Art. LVIII), freedom from excessive fines or bail (ibid., Art. LIX), the writ of habeas corpus (ibid., Art. LX), and freedom of the press (ibid., Art. LXI).

[21] Quoted in Hugh M'Call, *The History of Georgia: Containing Brief Sketches of the Most Remarkable Events Up to the Present Day (1784)* (Atlanta: A. B. Caldwell, 1909 [1816]), 2:322.

[22] Saye, *Constitutional History of Georgia*, 99.

[23] Ware, *Constitutional History of Georgia*, 32. The Act of Distribution and Habeas Corpus Act were incorporated in Articles LI and LX of the new constitution, respectively.

[24] There is little, if any, documentation of the convention's work. Concerning a declaration of rights, Willi Paul Adams writes laconically: "The congress decided against a declaration of rights." Willi Paul Adams, *The First American Constitutions: Republican Ideology and the Making of the State Constitutions in the Revolutionary Era*, expanded ed. (Lanham, MD: Rowman & Littlefield, 2001), 81.

[25] One historian has generously described the catalogue of rights in the Georgia Constitution as "fairly comprehensive." Saye, *Constitutional History of Georgia*, 101.

Like other early state constitutions lacking a separate declaration of rights, Georgia's constitution did not contain aspirational language touting civic virtue or equality. However, these principles were implicit in several provisions. The widespread belief among colonists that religion and education fostered civic-minded citizens was given constitutional status in provisions allowing people to be taxed for the support of their religion (ibid., Art. LVI) and authorizing the legislature to erect public schools (ibid., Art. LIV).[26] Articles XI and LI, requiring that titles of nobility be renounced before a person could vote or hold office and prohibiting entail (the practice of leaving all of a family's wealth to a single male heir), reflected the egalitarian principle that a citizen's status is achieved, not ascribed by birth.

Suffrage

The preamble lifted the expression of popular sovereignty from the Rules and Regulations, declaring that authority to create the new frame of government came from "the people, from whom all power originates, and for whose benefit all government is intended." Central to the implementation of the principle of popular sovereignty is the question of suffrage. The right to vote was restricted to white males over the age of 21 who had resided in the state for six months.[27] The state's modest property qualifications—ownership of property worth ten pounds and taxpayer status, or engagement in a mechanical trade—meant that all those who met the other qualifications would be eligible to vote.[28] Georgia's egalitarian character is apparent in its exemption of mechanics (tradesmen and skilled craftsmen) from the property requirement.[29] The latter severed voting

[26] See *infra* note 53.

[27] Six months was the shortest residency requirement for suffrage in the state constitutions adopted between 1776 and 1790. New York was the only other state to adopt a six-month residency requirement. See N.Y. Const. 1777, Art. VII; Table 3, pp. 70–71.

[28] Coleman, *American Revolution in Georgia*, 84. The property requirements were less stringent than those required under royal government—a freehold of 50 acres or other property worth 50 pounds—but more restrictive than the resolution of Georgia's Second Provincial Congress on July 14, 1775, granting the right to vote to all taxpayers. Ware, *Constitutional History of Georgia*, 15; Coleman, "Frontier Haven," 450; Saye, *Constitutional History of Georgia*, 92.

[29] Samuel Johnson's *Dictionary of the English Language* (1755), defined "mechanick" as "a manufacturer; a low workman." "Page View, Page 1277," *A Dictionary of the English*

eligibility from ownership of real property, jettisoning the Whig theory of suffrage wherein the ownership of land demonstrated a person's permanent attachment to the community. There were no religious qualifications for voting, and the constitution allowed voters to substitute an affirmation in place of the oath of allegiance to the state, permitting Quakers to vote. Voting was considered both a right and a civic duty—Georgia emphasized the duty aspect by authorizing a fine for those eligible to vote who failed to do so without a reasonable excuse.[30] To implement the constitutional protection of free and open elections, voters were not to be hindered from voting by process servers, and military men were to appear at elections as regular citizens, presumably to prevent intimidation.[31]

Structural Provisions

The institutions established by the constitution reflected the state's commitment to keeping popular sovereignty active. The legislature, the branch most accountable to the people, was dominant—unchecked by an executive veto. Annual elections (Const. 1777, Art. II), restrictions against multiple office-holding (ibid., Art. XVII), and the "unalterable rule that the house of assembly shall expire and be at an end, yearly and every year, on the day preceding the day of election" (ibid., Art. III) kept this branch responsive to its constituents. Considered a key defense against tyranny, rotation in office was also required of governors, who could only serve one out of every three years (ibid., Art. XXIII).

Language: A Digital Edition of the 1755 Classic by Samuel Johnson, ed. Brandi Besalke, last modified: December 6, 2012, https://johnsonsdictionaryonline.com/page-view/?i=1277. This extension of the suffrage was a notable departure from the sentiments among property holders that such men had "lesser abilities" and "ought by nature to acquiesce in the judgment of their social betters." Howard B. Rock, "The American Revolution and the Mechanics of New York City: One Generation Later," *New York History* 57, no. 3 (July 1976): 371.

[30] Const. 1777, Art. XII: "Every person absenting himself from an election, and shall neglect to give in his or their ballot at such election, shall be subject to a penalty not exceeding five pounds; the mode of recovery, and also the appropriation thereof, to be pointed out and directed by act of the legislature: *Provided, nevertheless*, That a reasonable excuse shall be admitted." No evidence has been found that this provision was ever enforced. Coleman, "Frontier Haven," 454.

[31] A similar law had been enacted in 1761 that prohibited and penalized voter intimidation and provided that voters should be free from arrest and service of process while going to and from the polls. Candler, *Colonial Records*, 18:469–471.

Representatives in the unicameral legislature ("house of assembly") were required to be at least twenty-one years old, Protestant, residents of the state for at least twelve months and the county they represented for at least three months prior to an election, with a freehold or other property worth 250 pounds (ibid., Art. VI). The house of assembly chose the governor and executive council from among its ranks (ibid., Art. II).

Article I gave formal recognition of the separation of powers: "the legislative, executive, and judiciary departments shall be separate and distinct, so that neither exercise the powers properly belonging to the other." This intended check on governmental power was furthered by prohibitions against plural office-holding (ibid., Arts. XVII–XVIII). Article VII prohibited the legislature from passing laws contrary to the constitution. Who would enforce this supremacy provision against legislative overreach? Judicial review had yet to be established and the executive branch had no check on the legislature. Constitution makers in Georgia, like other states, relied on an informed, vigilant citizenry to exercise this key function. Georgia's judicial system provided an additional opportunity for citizen participation. In contrast to the bifurcated practice of judges deciding the legal rules and principles that applied to a given case and juries determining the facts, juries in Georgia (as in five other states) were judges of both fact and law (ibid., Art. XLI).[32] Authorizing juries to decide the law and the facts, along with the annual election of most judicial officers (ibid., Art. LIII), placed the judicial power in the hands of the people. If either party in a suit was dissatisfied with the jury's verdict, they could appeal within three days and have a new trial by a special jury (ibid., Art. XL). The special jury was sworn to bring in a verdict not repugnant to the constitution, "of which they shall Judge" (ibid., Art. XLIII). This additional language "seems to be the earliest official recognition of a review of the grounds of cases in the light of their constitutionality."[33] Although not meant to suggest judicial review of legislative acts,[34] granting the jury this authority enabled the people to nullify or blunt what they believed were unconstitutional laws or an unconstitutional application of the law.

[32] See William E. Nelson, *The Common Law in Colonial America*, vol. 4, *Law and the Constitution on the Eve of Independence, 1735–1776* (New York: Oxford University Press, 2018), 23–44. Juries could refer to the bench for clarification on a point of law and were sworn to bring in a verdict according to law and the constitution. Const. 1777, Art. XLII.

[33] Ware, *Constitutional History of Georgia*, 43 n. 18.

[34] Ibid.

Consistent with the state's commitment to popular sovereignty, the method of revision outlined in the constitution of 1777 required petitions from a majority of counties signed by a majority of the voters of each county, upon receipt of which the assembly would order a convention to consider the proposed alterations (ibid., Art. LXIII). Georgia was the first state to establish a procedure that placed the impetus for constitutional revision directly in the hands of the people.[35]

Four months after the constitution was adopted, the Georgia Assembly passed a statute continuing in force the common law, formerly recognized English statutes, and previously enacted laws of the colonial assembly, so long as they were compatible with Continental Congress and state resolves and regulations, and "in particular" with the constitution.[36] This enactment extended the rights of Georgians beyond those delineated in the constitution: the rights found in common law and English statutes would also be recognized.

Constitutional Developments: 1789 Constitution

The British occupation of Georgia from 1778 to 1782 offered the new constitutional regime little opportunity to function properly. Six years after the expulsion of the British, Georgia took steps to form a second constitution.[37] Three conventions were held between November 1788 and May 1789.[38] The first convention, comprised of three members from each county chosen by the assembly,[39] drafted and published a constitution for consideration by the public. Rather than holding a referendum, the state elected delegates to a second convention tasked

[35] Ibid., 46.

[36] Candler, *Colonial Records*, 19, pt. 2:58–60. Similar acts passed in 1783 and 1784. Ibid., 243–248, 290–292.

[37] Conflicting opinions exist concerning whether the convoluted procedure that was used did in fact comply with the constitutional revision process set forth in the constitution of 1777. Historians Coleman, Saye, and Ware conclude that the constitutional amending process was not followed (Coleman, *American Revolution in Georgia*, 271; Saye, *Constitutional History of Georgia*, 113, 136; Ware, *Constitutional History of Georgia*, 46), but John N. Shaeffer disagrees, arguing that the revision generally complied with the process. See "Georgia's 1789 Constitution: Was it Adopted in Defiance of the Constitutional Amending Process?" *The Georgia Historical Quarterly* 61, no. 4 (Winter 1977): 329–341.

[38] See Saye, *Constitutional History of Georgia*, 137–142.

[39] Coleman, *American Revolution in Georgia*, 271.

with adopting or rejecting the new constitution.[40] Exceeding its limited authority, the second convention amended the proposed constitution, most notably by eliminating property qualifications for voting and lowering the freehold requirement for eligibility to serve as a representative.[41] The amended constitution was once again published before the election of a third convention that, in a matter of days, adopted the constitution with only minor alterations.[42] Although not submitted directly to the voters, the approval of the 1789 constitution by a convention elected for that purpose represented an acknowledgment that constitutional change requires an extraordinary adoption process.

Like its predecessor, the constitution of 1789 did not contain a separate bill of rights.[43] It preserved the rights to trial by jury, freedom of the press, and habeas corpus contained in the first constitution, but eliminated the prohibition against excessive fines and bail.[44] Article IV, section 1 broadened the suffrage by removing the property qualification for voting, and religious liberty was expanded through the removal of religious qualifications for office-holding. The free exercise provision shed its "peace and safety" limitation—the reasons for and practical impact of this change are not clear. It was unlikely to have created religious exemptions from laws of general applicability.[45]

The new constitution contained a stronger version of the separation of powers. In addition to retaining the prohibition against multiple office-holding (Const. 1789, Art. I, sec. 10), it created a bicameral legislature (ibid., Art. I, sec. 1); a governor with more authority, including the veto power (ibid., Art. II, sec. 10)[46]; and the establishment of a "competent salary" for superior court judges that could not be altered during their three-year terms, a measure that would promote judicial independence

[40] Saye, *Constitutional History of Georgia*, 139.

[41] Ibid., 140.

[42] Ibid., 140–142.

[43] Walter McElreath surmises that a bill of rights was omitted to avoid the question of slavery. *A Treatise on the Constitution of Georgia* (Atlanta: The Harrison Company, 1912), 84, 88.

[44] It is not clear why this provision was left out of the new constitution. No records of convention proceedings have been found. Coleman, *American Revolution in Georgia*, 272.

[45] See Vincent Philip Munoz, "Church and State in the Founding-Era State Constitutions," *American Political Thought* 4, no. 1 (Winter 2015): 15–17.

[46] The governor was still elected by the legislature.

(ibid., Art. III, sec. 5). Recognizing the constitution as a higher law, not to be altered through the normal legislative process, the drafters included a specific provision for the election of members in 1794 to a constitutional convention and a process to be followed for making amendments.[47]

Postscript: An amendment adopted by the 1795 convention provided for the election of delegates two years later to another constitutional convention. That convention created and adopted the constitution of 1798, which would remain in effect for the next sixty-three years. Notably, the 1798 constitution more carefully defined legislative power, made the governorship a popularly elected office, and prohibited ex post facto laws and the further importation of slaves. It would not be until the constitution of 1861, after the state seceded from the Union, that Georgia would have a formal bill of rights (called a "Declaration of Fundamental Principles").

Constitution of Georgia [1777]

Article I. The legislative, executive, and judiciary departments shall be separate and distinct, so that neither exercise the powers properly belonging to the other.[48]

* * *

Art. IX. All male white inhabitants, of the age of twenty-one years, and possessed in his own right of ten pounds value, and liable to pay tax in this State, or being of any mechanic trade, and shall have been resident six months in this State, shall have a right to vote at all elections for representatives, or any other officers, herein agreed to be chosen by the people at large; and every person having a right to vote at any election shall vote by ballot personally.

[47] Const. 1789, Art. IV, sec. 7: "At the general election for members of assembly, in the year one thousand seven hundred and ninety-four, the electors in each county shall elect three persons to represent them in a convention, for the purpose of taking into consideration the alterations necessary to be made in this constitution, who shall meet at such time and place as the General Assembly may appoint; and if two-thirds of the whole number shall meet and concur, they shall proceed to agree on such alterations and amendments as they think proper, Provided, That after two-thirds shall have concurred to proceed to alterations and amendments, a majority shall determine on the particulars of such alterations and amendments."

[48] Similar to Va. Const. 1776.

* * *

Art. XI. No person shall be entitled to more than one vote, which shall be given in the county where such person resides, except as before excepted; nor shall any person who holds any title of nobility be entitled to a vote, or be capable of serving as a representative, or hold any post of honor, profit, or trust in this State, whilst such person claims his title of nobility; but if the person shall give up such distinction, in the manner as may be directed by any future legislation, then, and in such case, he shall be entitled to a vote, and represent, as before directed, and enjoy all the other benefits of a free citizen.[49]

* * *

Art. XXXVII. All causes and matters of dispute, between any parties residing in the same county, to be tried within the county.[50]

Art. XXXVIII. All matters in dispute between contending parties residing in different counties shall be tried in the county where the defendant resides, except in cases of real estate, which shall be tried in the county where such real estate lies.

Art. XXXIX. All matters of breach of the peace, felony, murder, and treason against the State to be tried in the county where the same was committed. All matters of dispute, both civil and criminal, in any county where there is not a sufficient number of inhabitants to form a court, shall be tried in the next adjacent county where a court is held.

[49] The one person, one vote rule was an anti-corruption measure, and the requirement that those claiming titles of nobility give up their title in order to vote or hold office reflected the state's commitment to the proposition that all men were born equally free—the keystone of the Declaration of Independence.

[50] Articles XXXVII–XXXIX contained procedural protections necessary to ensure fair trials: cases between residents of the same county were to be tried in that county, and when the parties lived in different counties, the trial would take place in the defendant's county of residence (except in cases involving real estate). Criminal cases involving breach of the peace, felony, murder, or treason were to be tried where the offense was committed. This was likely inspired by the Crown's claim of having the authority to transport colonists accused of treason to England to stand trial, loudly condemned by colonial legislatures as a violation of the right to be tried by a jury of one's peers. As an additional protection for the criminally accused, a grand jury of at least eighteen would consider whether criminal charges should be brought, and an affirmative decision would require the concurrence of at least twelve. Const. 1777, Art. XLV.

* * *

ART. LI. Estates shall not be entailed; and when a person dies intestate, his or her estate shall be divided equally among their children; the widow shall have a child's share, or her dower, at her option; all other intestates' estates to be divided according to the act of distribution, made in the reign of Charles the Second, unless otherwise altered by any future act of the legislature.[51]

* * *

ART. LIV. Schools shall be erected in each county, and supported at the general expense of the State, as the legislature shall hereafter point out.[52]

* * *

ART. LVI. All persons whatever shall have the free exercise of their religion; provided it be not repugnant to the peace and safety of the State;

[51] Ending the practice of entail, whereby a family's wealth was concentrated in a single male heir, promoted equality and discouraged the growth of an aristocracy.

[52] The establishment of schools at state expense was deemed necessary to form civic-minded citizens. The exigencies of war delayed implementation of this provision until after the British were ousted from Savannah in 1782. Keith Whitescarver, "Creating Citizens for the Republic: Education in Georgia, 1776–1810," *Journal of the Early Republic* 13, no. 4 (Winter 1993): 457; Coleman, *American Revolution in Georgia*, 225. In 1783, the legislature, responding to the governor's call for legislation to promote good character by encouraging religion and education, created an academy in Augusta and authorized the building of a church. Coleman, *American Revolution in Georgia*, 222; Whitescarver, "Creating Citizens," 458. The act also authorized the grant of 1000 acres of vacant land in each county to be used to erect free schools. Candler, *Colonial Records*, 19, pt. 2:255; Coleman, *American Revolution in Georgia*, 225.

In 1785, Georgia became the first state to charter a university. The act to charter the University of Georgia began with an explanation of the basis for state education:

> ...It should therefore be among the first objects of those who wish well to the National prosperity to encourage and support the principles of Religion and Morality, and early to place the Youth under the forming hand of security that by Instruction they may be moulded to the love of Virtue and good order...

Candler, *Colonial Records*, 19, pt. 2:363–364.

and shall not, unless by consent, support any teacher or teachers[53] except those of their own profession.[54]

* * *

ART. LVIII. No person shall be allowed to plead in the courts of law in this State, except those who are authorized so to do by the house of assembly; and if any person so authorized shall be found guilty of malpractice before the house of assembly, they shall have power to suspend them. This is not intended to exclude any person from that inherent privilege of every *freeman*, the liberty to plead his own cause.[55]

[53] "Teachers" referred to in Article LVI meant ministers—public teachers of piety and religion.

[54] The language of this article was closer to the language in Georgia's 1732 charter than the constitutions of other states. The charter provided: "all such persons, except papists, shall have a free exercise of their religion, so they be contented with the quiet and peaceable enjoyment of the same, not giving offence or scandal to the government."

With its historical foundation of largely harmonious religious pluralism, Georgia broadened the religious liberty guaranteed in the charter by extending free exercise to Catholics and allowing taxation only for the support of one's own religion—effectively disestablishing the Church of England. Nichols, "Religious Liberty in the Thirteenth Colony," 1735; Coleman, *American Revolution in Georgia*, 83. Contrariwise, Article VI required legislators to be Protestant. The measure reflected Georgia's long-held distrust of Catholics, originating in English policy and intensified by fears of military conflict with the Catholic French and Spanish. Nichols, "Religious Liberty in the Thirteenth Colony," 1749. The religious requirement was not, however, enforced against a Catholic member from Chatham County elected under the new constitution. Strickland, *Religion and the State in Georgia*, 164. Unlike the provision allowing an affirmation in place of an oath for voting, officeholders were required to swear an oath, effectively barring Quakers from holding office. The religious qualifications for office-holding were seen as necessary conditions for a well-ordered community in which collective rights were protected; they ensured that those in power did not hold beliefs perceived by the community to be dangerous to liberty. The disqualifying belief of Catholics was their purported allegiance to a foreign power (the Pope), and, in the case of Quakers, their pacifism. Under Article LXII, clergymen "of any denomination" were prohibited from serving in the legislature, as the office of religious leader, the sacred realm, and the office of political leader, the secular realm, were viewed by many as separate and incompatible.

Georgia's leaders tempered their free exercise guarantee with the qualifier that it not be repugnant to the peace and safety of the state. This limit on free exercise was applied a year later when Georgia levied double taxation on those who had religious objections to serving in the military. Strickland, *Religion and the State in Georgia*, 175.

[55] In granting the legislature the power to regulate the practice of law, the drafters made it clear that this was not meant to abrogate a freeman's natural right to represent himself. The right of self-representation had a long history in English common law and was

ART. LIX. Excessive fines shall not be levied, nor excessive bail demanded.[56]

ART. LX. The principles of the *habeas-corpus* act shall be a part of this constitution.[57]

ART. LXI. Freedom of the press and trial by jury to remain inviolate forever.[58]

perhaps even more fervently adhered to in colonial America due to anti-lawyer sentiment, the result of "cringing Attorneys-General and Solicitors-General of the Crown and the arbitrary Justices of the King's Court, all bent on the conviction of those who opposed the King's prerogatives, and twisting the law to secure convictions." *Faretta v. California*, 422 U.S. 806, 826 (1975), quoting Charles Warren, *A History of the American Bar* (Boston: Little, Brown, and Co., 1911), 7. (The Court's extensive treatment of the legal history of the right of self-representation can be found at 422 U.S. at 821–832). In fact, the right to counsel was considered subordinate to the "primary right of the accused to defend himself." *Faretta*, 422 U.S. at 829–830. Georgia's 1777 constitution was one of three state constitutions to explicitly protect the right of self-representation. See Pa. Decl. 1776, Art. IX; Vt. Decl. 1777, Art. X.

[56] This substantive protection against excessive bail and fines had its origin in the English Bill of Rights of 1689: "That excessive bail ought not to be required, nor excessive fines imposed..." Bernard Schwartz, *The Bill of Rights: A Documentary History* (New York: Chelsea House Publishers, 1971), 1:43. Similar to Pa. Const. 1776, sec. 29 ("Excessive bail shall not be exacted for bailable offences: And all fines shall be moderate.").

[57] Georgians would continue to have the benefit of habeas corpus protection against unlawful imprisonment. Both common law habeas corpus and the English Habeas Corpus Act (1679) were in effect in Georgia during the entire colonial period and remained in effect until abrogated and supplanted by the habeas corpus provisions of the Georgia Code of 1861. Donald E. Wilkes Jr., "From Oglethorpe to the Overthrow of the Confederacy: Habeas Corpus in Georgia, 1733–1865," *Georgia Law Review* 45, no. 4 (Summer 2011): 1020, 1033–1034, 1034 n. 74. Delegates attached the 1679 act to the first printed copies of the constitution so the public would be fully aware of the protections it afforded. Georgia's was the first state constitution to expressly mention the writ of habeas corpus in its constitution, although Article XIII of North Carolina's declaration provided that "every freeman, restrained of his liberty, is entitled to a remedy, to inquire into the lawfulness thereof, and to remove the same, if unlawful." Other states incorporated habeas corpus protection implicitly by declaring the continuation of laws currently in force. See text accompanying footnotes 119–121, at p. 86.

[58] Freedom of the press and trial by jury were vital rights to the American colonists and were included in all but one of the seven state constitutions that had been adopted before Georgia's. The only state that did not include both these rights was New Jersey, which did not include a free press provision. A free press kept the public informed of the government's actions, a necessary prerequisite to self-government and the activation of popular sovereignty. Trial by a jury of one's peers was a fundamental protection of one's life, liberty, and property. Along with representation, it was the guardian of all other rights. Recent threats by Parliament to the great alarm and consternation of the colonists likely provoked the "inviolate forever" ending.

Constitution of Georgia [1789]

* * *

Article III

* * *

Section 4. All causes shall be tried in the county where the defendant resides except in cases of real estate, which shall be tried in the county where such estate lies, and in criminal cases, which shall be tried in the county where the crime shall be committed.

* * *

Article IV

Section 1. The electors of the members of both branches of the general assembly shall be citizens and inhabitants of this State, and shall have attained to the age of twenty-one years, and have paid tax for the year preceding the election, and shall have resided six months within the county.[59]

* * *

Sec. 3. Freedom of the press and trial by jury shall remain inviolate.

Sec. 4. All persons shall be entitled to the benefit of the writ of *habeas corpus.*

Sec. 5. All persons shall have the free exercise of religion, without being obliged to contribute to the support of any religious profession but their own.[60]

[59] The new constitution removed the property qualification for voting, extending the right to all adult taxpayers who met the residency requirement. With no race or gender qualifications, on its face this article seemed to allow free blacks and women to vote, but that was neither the intent nor the practice. Stephen B. Weeks, "The History of Negro Suffrage in the South," *Political Science Quarterly* 9, no. 4 (December 1894): 674; Saye, *Constitutional History of Georgia*, 143. The penalty for not exercising one's duty to vote was removed.

[60] Georgia ostensibly strengthened its religious freedom provision by eliminating the qualifying phrase that such free exercise "be not repugnant to the peace and safety of the State." The belief that the state had a role in promoting religion, thus encouraging virtuous citizens, was still apparent in the clause allowing people to be taxed in support

SEC. 6. Estates shall not be entailed; and when a person dies intestate, leaving a wife and children, the wife shall have a child's share, or her dower, at her option; if there be no wife, the estate shall be equally divided among the children and their legal representatives of the first degree. The distribution of all other intestate estates may be regulated by law.

of their own religion, thus permitting multiple establishments. Distrust of non-Protestant religions and their compatibility with republican principles was fading, as evidenced by the removal of religious qualifications for office-holding. Candidates for office were allowed to substitute an affirmation for an oath (Const. 1789, Art. I, sec. 15), thus enabling Quakers to serve as representatives. All clergymen were still ineligible for political office (Const. 1789, Art. I, sec. 18).

New York

New York began its existence as part of the Dutch colony of New Netherland. In 1626, Peter Minuit purchased Manhattan Island from a local Native American tribe. The colony remained in Dutch hands until 1664 when the English established control and renamed it New York.[1] Dutch merchants established the colony as a commercial republic. From the beginning New Netherland, and in particular its capital, New Amsterdam (modern-day New York City), had a diverse population—only 50% were actually Dutch. The commercial beginnings, along with its religious and ethnic diversity, would leave an indelible stamp on New York and be reflected in the character of its first constitution. The first influence on New York's constitutional tradition of rights was the Dutch Republic's introduction of a jurisprudence of religious tolerance to the Western Hemisphere.[2]

Despite strong opposition from the Calvinist clergy, the Dutch West India Company reluctantly permitted most heterodox believers to remain in North America. Unlike seventeenth-century Puritan New England

[1] For more information about the founding of New Netherland and its eventual takeover by the English, see pp. 165–167.

[2] Joep de Koning, "Governor's Island and the Origins of Religious Tolerance," in *Opening Statements: Law, Jurisprudence, and the Legacy of the Dutch in New York*, ed. Albert M. Rosenblatt and Julia C. Rosenblatt (Albany: State University of New York Press, 2013), 163; Evan Haefeli, *New Netherland and the Dutch Origins of American Religious Liberty* (Philadelphia: University of Pennsylvania Press, 2012), passim.

P. J. Galie et al., *Bills of Rights Before the Bill of Rights*,
https://doi.org/10.1007/978-3-030-44301-6_15

and Anglican Virginia, which shut out Lutherans, Anabaptists, 'Independents,' Quakers, Catholics, and Jews, these groups established a permanent presence in New Netherland:

> ...this countenancing of 'erring spirits' reflected pragmatic calculation on the part of the [West India Company], desperate for settlers on their American frontier, as well as the peculiarly urban nature of New Amsterdam as a commercial crossroads for refugees. But it also reflected the role of liberty of conscience at the core of Reformed [Dutch Calvinist] self-understanding, arguably a contribution of lasting importance in America as well as in the Netherlands.[3]

By the time of the English takeover in 1664, the Dutch colony had become the first multi-ethnic, upwardly mobile society on America's shores.[4]

What began as a guarantee of freedom of conscience and connivance at surreptitious worship for religions other than Calvinism continued when the English assumed control. English authorities extended the policy of religious toleration to all who professed Christianity. Additionally, they promised protection of life and property to all residents.

English governors of New York were confronted with two legal traditions: Dutch customary law centered in and around Manhattan Island and the Hudson Valley and a "rude, untechnical variant of the common law carried from Puritan New England and practiced without the intercession of lawyers" in Westchester, Long Island, and Staten Island.[5] Governor Richard Nicolls chose to allow a degree of autonomy for Dutch law when he promulgated the Duke's Laws in 1665, which closely resembled the Massachusetts Laws and Liberties of 1648, a code with which residents would have been familiar and would have found unobjectionable.[6]

[3] Steven Jaffe, review of Haefeli, *New Netherland and the Dutch Origins*, in Reviews in History, January 2013, http://www.history.ac.uk/reviews/review/1363, accessed February 28, 2020.

[4] Russell Shorto, *The Island at the Center of the World: The Epic Story of Dutch Manhattan and the Forgotten Colony That Shaped America* (New York: Doubleday, 2004), 3.

[5] William E. Nelson, *The Common Law in Colonial America*, vol. 2, *The Middle Colonies and the Carolinas, 1660–1730* (New York: Oxford University Press, 2013), 30.

[6] By the second decade of the eighteenth century, English common law had replaced the Dutch legal system in New York. The procedural apparatus of the English common law

Levying taxes without giving into demands for representative government opened the possibility of an exodus of colonists to New Jersey, so the Duke of York agreed to establish an assembly.

The first general assembly approved a Charter of Liberties and Privileges in 1683.[7] The charter codified the religious liberty policies of the colony, guaranteeing freedom of public worship to all who "professe[d] faith in God by Jesus Christ."[8] The charter did not separate church and state; rather, it permitted government support for all Christian churches (multiple establishments).[9] It included a due process clause derived from articles 39 and 40 of Magna Carta,[10] trial by jury,[11] a right to bail,[12] grand jury indictment for felonies,[13] and a provision forbidding the quartering of soldiers.[14] The charter, a landmark in the development of constitutional government and liberty in New York, was never approved. James, Duke of York, originally signed the charter, but had second thoughts after becoming King James II and refused to confirm it. Nevertheless, tolerance and the principles enunciated in the English Constitution and common law had taken root and would not be expunged by the stroke of a kingly pen.

The 1688 Glorious Revolution forced the abdication of James II and established parliamentary supremacy. After an unsettling power struggle in the colony, a new assembly was called under the authority of the

provided the protections first proclaimed in the "due process" or "law of the land" clause of Magna Carta. Intrusive regulations of everyday life and economic regulation connected with Dutch practice disappeared. In contrast to Dutch legal practice, the common law "restricted the power of government in general and central government in particular. The common law authorized use of government's prosecutorial and regulatory powers only when precedent justified that use...." Nelson, *Middle Colonies and the Carolinas*, 59.

[7] [New York] Charter of Liberties and Privileges (1683), in *Colonial Origins of the American Constitution: A Documentary History*, ed. Donald S. Lutz (Indianapolis: Liberty Fund, 1998) [hereinafter "Charter of Liberties and Privileges"], 256–262.

[8] Charter of Liberties and Privileges, 260.

[9] Ibid., 261–262.

[10] Ibid., 258.

[11] Ibid., 259.

[12] Ibid.

[13] Ibid.

[14] Ibid.

restored English monarchy of William and Mary. In 1691, the assembly reasserted the principles and liberties found in the original charter, while excluding "persons of the romish [Catholic] religion" from the religious liberty provision.[15] Several anti-Catholic policies were enacted in the colony, including a religious test for holding office and a ban on Roman Catholicism as a form of worship.[16] Although the 1691 act did not receive royal assent, it remained in effect for six years. As Charles Z. Lincoln noted in his magisterial work on the New York Constitution the lack of royal assent "probably…did not materially affect any principle declared in it."[17]

The Movement Towards Independence 1765–1776

Beginning with the Stamp Act (1765) and ending with the Intolerable Acts of 1774, New Yorkers actively protested what they viewed as oppressive parliamentary statutes. Claiming the right to self-taxation, the resistance went beyond petitions and included demonstrations, boycotts, mob actions, beatings, and threats to those thought to be British sympathizers. Organizations like the Sons of Liberty and the society of "Mechanics" began to issue and enforce orders. The Sons of Liberty published an announcement, *The Association of the Sons of Liberty of New York*, in which it threatened that anyone who assisted in support of the Tea Act (1773) would be an "enemy to the liberties of America."[18] As a result,

[15] An Act Declaring What Are the Rights and Privileges of their Majesties' Subjects Inhabiting with the Province of New York, May 13, 1691, in *Foundations of Colonial America: A Documentary History*, ed. W. Keith Kavenagh (New York: Chelsea House, 1973), 2:897.

[16] John Webb Pratt, *Religion, Politics, and Diversity: The Church-State Theme in New York History* (Ithaca, NY: Cornell University Press, 1967), 37; Jason K. Duncan, *Citizens or Papists? The Politics of Anti-Catholicism in New York, 1685–1821* (New York: Fordham University Press, 2005).

[17] *The Constitutional History of New York: From the Beginning of the Colonial Period to the Year 1905; Showing the Origin, Development, and Judicial Construction of the Constitution* (Rochester: Lawyer's Cooperative Publishing Co., 1906), 1:441.

[18] See Benjamin H. Irvin, "Tar, Feathers, and the Enemies of American Liberties," *The New England Quarterly* 76, no. 2 (June 2003): 197; see also Carl L. Becker, *The History of Political Parties in the Province of New York, 1760–1776* (Madison: University of Wisconsin Press, 1968 [1909]), 105–106.

the New York East India agents resigned. The New York Assembly took no action.[19]

By 1774 revolutionary committees began to appear and became de facto governing bodies. Governor Tryon dissolved the assembly in April 1775. By the end of that year, the provincial government possessed neither power nor consent.[20] When British General Howe placed New York under martial law in August 1776, Tryon retained his nominal title as governor, but with little power. A series of extra-constitutional provincial congresses would act as the governing body for the colony until the adoption of the 1777 constitution.

The Third Provincial Congress reported on May 27, 1776, that "the old form of Government is becoming, ipso facto, dissolved," and recommended a new election be called as "the right of framing, creating or remodeling Civil Government is and ought to be in the People."[21] By insisting on an active role for the people in forming a government, the Mechanics and Sons of Liberty, among others, helped ensure that popular sovereignty would be the source for the creation and operation of the new governing order.

On July 9, 1776, the delegates selected at this special election convened as the Fourth Provincial Congress. They began with a statement of their purpose: "to institute and establish such a government as they shall deem best calculated to secure the rights, liberties, and happiness of the good people of this colony…"[22] On August 1st, the convention selected a committee to "report a plan for instituting and framing a form of Government [and] report…a Bill of Rights ascertaining and declaring the essential rights and privileges of the good people of this State as

[19] The story of this "revolution from below" has been well told by Pauline Maier, *From Resistance to Revolution: Colonial Radicals and the Development of American Opposition to Britain, 1765–1776* (New York: W. W. Norton, 1992) and Gary B. Nash *The Unknown American Revolution: The Unruly Birth of Democracy and the Struggle to Create America* (New York: Viking Press, 2005), passim.

[20] Edward Countryman, *A People in Revolution: The American Revolution and Political Society in New York, 1760–1790* (New York: W. W. Norton, 1989), 96, 124.

[21] Peter Force, ed., *American Archives, Consisting of a Collection of Authentick Records, State Papers, Debates and Letters and Other Notices of Public Affairs, the Whole Forming a Documentary History of the Origin and Progress of the North American Colonies … in Six Series* (Washington, DC: M. St. Clair Clark, 1837–1853), 4th Series, 6:1338.

[22] Ibid., 1391.

the foundation for such form of Government."[23] The committee never reported a draft of a bill of rights, and it was not until April 20, 1777, that a constitution was proclaimed.

Constitutional Developments: 1777 Constitution

New York's first constitution did not contain a formal declaration of rights, though it did contain several rights' protecting provisions. In this respect, New York followed New Jersey and not the other mid-Atlantic states of Delaware, Maryland, and Pennsylvania. Records of the convention proceedings do not provide a direct answer as to why the committee failed to report a bill of rights. What we know from the official records is that a committee was directed to produce a bill of rights and never did, and that there were no objections or questions about this failure recorded during the convention's debate on the draft constitution.[24] Charles Lincoln, the dean of New York constitutional historians, is silent on the absence of a bill of rights or the committee's failure to report one.

The provincial congress was tasked with conducting the war effort, running the government, and writing a constitution—all carried out under wartime conditions. Forced to move four times throughout its deliberations, it was literally a convention on the run. Key members of the convention, also members of a council of safety, were charged with overseeing secret military operations that sometimes required them to choose between attending meetings of the committee drafting the constitution and carrying out clandestine operations. We know that work on the constitution was delayed because of these conflicting obligations and the difficulty in achieving quorums. Some members thought it foolish to be debating a constitution while the state's very existence as an independent entity was in question. The southern part of the state was under British control, putting the entire state in danger. With good reason, Christopher Tappen and Gilbert Livingston thought it would be well "first to endeavor to secure a State to govern, before we established a form to

[23] Ibid., 1466.

[24] *Journals of the Provincial Congress, Provincial Convention, Committee of Safety and Council of Safety of the State of New York, 1775–1777* (Albany: Thurlow Weed, 1842), 1:887ff.

govern it."[25] Bernard Mason suggests that delegates, alarmed at the seriousness of the threat, may have believed that a definition of rights would inhibit the government's flexibility in suppressing counterrevolutionary activity.[26]

Further evidence for this explanation was the failure of the convention to add a prohibition against ex post facto laws while simultaneously including a clause prohibiting attainders but excepting acts committed before the termination of the war (Const. 1777, Art. XLI).[27] New York was *the* stronghold of Toryism in America with three or four times more Loyalists than any other colony.[28] Moreover, the British maintained control of New York City and the surrounding territory until the end of the war. A large number of Loyalists engendered fear of a fifth column that would engage in enlisting personnel and supplying food and intelligence to the British.

A Committee for Detecting Conspiracies[29] was formed by the convention to combat the dangers. Its charge: "do **every act and thing whatsoever**, which may be necessary to enable them" to "detect[] and defeat[] all conspiracies ... against the liberties of America."[30] In short, the committee would operate unconstrained by any due process requirements. When it received complaints about deportations carried out without due process, the complainants were told to wait until proper courts were established to receive fair, impartial trials. In the interim, the committee mandated "no greater Liberty be allow'd them than what

[25] Christopher Tappen and Gilbert Livingston to the Convention, August 24, 1776, *American Archives*, 5th Series, 1:1542. Lincoln provides more detail on these difficulties. *Constitutional History*, 1:491–495.

[26] Bernard Mason, "New York State's First Constitution," in *New York and The Union*, ed. Stephen L. Schechter and Richard B. Bernstein (Albany: New York State Commission on the Bicentennial of the United States Constitution, 1990), 181. Agreeing with Mason are William A. Polf, Robert Emery, and Patricia Bonomi.

[27] Lincoln, *Constitutional History*, 1:547.

[28] Claude Halstead Van Tyne, *The Loyalists in the American Revolution* (New York: Macmillan Co., 1902), 103; Wallace Brown, *The Good Americans: The Loyalists in the American Revolution* (New York: William Morrow and Co., 1969), 226.

[29] The convention subsequently dissolved the committee and formed a successor body, the Commission for Detecting and Defeating Conspiracies.

[30] *Journals of the Provincial Congress*, 1:638 (emphasis added).

humanity may require."[31] Deportations and the expropriation and redistribution of Loyalists' property began in 1776 and continued after the adoption of the constitution in April of 1777.

All the more remarkable, then, is the fact that these considerations did not inhibit the convention from including some rights protections in the document itself. Milton M. Klein concluded: "No reasonable explanation for the random inclusion of some rights and the omission of others seems evident."[32] The evidence currently available does not provide a definitive answer, but the necessities of war and the exigent circumstances under which the convention operated make its decision not to include a full-blown declaration of rights understandable. Although Pennsylvania, Delaware, Maryland, and Virginia also operated under wartime conditions and included declarations of rights, these states adopted their constitutions earlier than New York, before the war and its concomitant dangers had intensified.

Robert Yates, a delegate to the 1777 convention, writing while ratification of the national Constitution was under consideration, added another dimension to the wartime conditions explanation:

> …it was urged by those in favor of a bill of rights that the power of the rulers ought to be circumscribed, the better to protect the people at large from the oppression and usurpation of their rulers. The English petition of rights, in the reign of Charles the First, and the bill of rights in the reign of king William, were mentioned as examples to support their opinions. Those in opposition admitted that in establishing governments, which had an implied constitution, a declaration of rights might be necessary to prevent the usurpation of ambitious men, but that was not our situation, for upon the declaration of independence it had become necessary that the exercise of every kind of authority 'under the former government should be totally suppressed, and all the power of government exerted under the authority of the people of the colonies;' that we could not suppose that

[31] As quoted by Howard Pashman, *Building a Revolutionary State: The Legal Transformation of New York, 1776–1783* (Chicago: University of Chicago Press, 2018), 53.

[32] "Liberty as Nature's Gift: The Colonial Origins of the Bill of Rights in New York," in *The Bill of Rights and the States: The Colonial and Revolutionary Origins of American Liberties*, ed. Patrick T. Conley and John P. Kaminski (Madison, WI: Madison House, 1992), 216.

> we had an existing constitution or form of government, express or implied, and therefore our situation resembled a people in a state of nature, who are preparing 'to institute a government, laying its foundation on such principles, and organizing its powers in such form as to them shall seem most likely to effect their safety and happiness,' and as such, the constitution to be formed would operate as a bill of rights.
>
> These and the like considerations operated to induce the convention of New York to dismiss the idea of a bill of rights, and the more especially as the legislative state officers being elected by the people at short periods, and thereby rendered from time to time liable to be displaced in case of mal-conduct.[33]

In contrast to the states that adopted declarations of rights, New York's rights provisions contained no use of the word "ought," no lofty aspirations, and none of the admonitions or exhortations that characterized the declarations of earlier constitutions. The absence of a formal declaration of rights, however, cannot be taken as an indication of indifference to rights. The state did adopt as its preamble the Declaration of Independence, which contained the fundamental principles on which natural rights republics were founded.

The document opened with a commitment to popular sovereignty as the foundation of republican government (Const. 1777, Art. I). Article XXXVIII provided as strong a statement of liberty of conscience and freedom of religion found in any of the early constitutions. Of equal significance, and unique among the state provisions proclaiming the liberty of conscience, delegates derived that right from "the benevolent principles of rational liberty." New York would recognize liberty of conscience, but that liberty would not be derived from nor be dependent on religion or theology. Having described the source of danger to religious liberty—"spiritual oppression and intolerance wherewith the bigotry and ambition of weak and wicked priests and princes have scourged mankind…," John Jay, the likely author of the article, grounded the source of that right in reason or natural rights. Article XXXV incorporated the common law,

[33]The Letters of Sydney, Written by Robert Yates, and Printed in the New York Journal, June 1788, in *Essays on the Constitution of the United States, Published During Its Discussion by the People, 1787–1788*, ed. Paul Leicester Ford (Brooklyn: Historical Printing Club, 1892), 299–300.

providing New Yorkers with an extensive array of procedural and substantive rights.[34]

Among other rights included were provisions for suffrage, elections, and representative institutions. Along with these collective or communal rights were provisions that ensured the safety and independence of the members of the community, due process of law, the right to trial by jury, and the right to counsel. The rights included were not randomly chosen; they were the rights colonists believed to be fundamental as they provided security for all other rights.[35]

Two additional rights clauses protected Indian land rights from fraudulent contracts (Const. 1777, Art. XXXVII) and provided the right of conscientious objection for Quakers (ibid., Art. XL). Like other state constitutions without a formal declaration of rights, most of the rights provisions were placed near the end of the document.

"Mad with Politics"

The nature of rights provisions, and the language used therein, shifted the focus away from a communitarian context and concern for the conditions and prerequisites for ordered liberty to a focus on individual rights. The explanation for this shift may be found in the character of the state. Michael G. Kammen has noted that New York was "less English and more diverse than that of any other British possession."[36] Patricia U. Bonomi has spoken of a "divided" and "contentious" people and a "mixture of nations...," and suggested that the "early appearance and growing legitimacy of self-interest as a public concept may well have been the sharpest single innovation of colonial politics."[37] Popular disorder in New York was part of a long history of regional, religious, and group conflicts such

[34] For the "Anglicization" of colonial New York law, see William E. Nelson's description of the "Triumph of the Common Law in New York," in *Middle Colonies and the Carolinas*, 43–60.

[35] See pp. 67–87 for greater detail on this point.

[36] *Colonial New York: A History* (New York: Oxford University Press, 1996), 75.

[37] *A Factious People: Politics and Society in Colonial New York* (New York: Columbia University Press, 1971), 10, 18, 282.

that New York seemed to observers to be "mad with politics."[38] Diversity and contentiousness cut into the heart of the republican ideal of public-spiritedness, defined as the belief that in a republic the citizens collectively were the most reliable protectors of liberty. That commitment, proclaimed in the declarations of rights adopted by other states, was noticeably absent from New York's constitution.

Suffrage

Eligibility for electing assembly members was restricted to male inhabitants of "full age" who had personally resided within the county for six months before the election and possessed a freehold of the value of twenty pounds within the county, or have rented a tenement therein of the yearly value of forty shillings, and been rated and paid taxes to the state (Const. 1777, Art. VII). The freehold requirement to vote for senators and the governor was one hundred pounds over and above all debts charged thereon (ibid., Arts. X, XVII). Freemen in the cities of Albany and New York were grandfathered the right to vote. An oath or affirmation of loyalty to the state was required (ibid., Art. VIII).

This toleration and acceptance of diversity did not extend to Catholics. Although the first constitution removed the disenfranchisement of Catholics and bans against public worship, the document required anyone wishing to become a citizen to renounce all allegiance to any and all foreign powers "in all matters, ecclesiastical as well as civil" (Const. 1777, Art. XLII). This naturalization oath was voided by the national Constitution, but a similar oath was required by statute a year following that document's adoption for all wishing to hold public office in the state.[39]

In a departure from existing practice, the constitution required the implementation of voting by secret ballot for legislators, but the legislature was given the power to terminate this "experiment" if it proved less conducive to the safety and interest of the state (Const. 1777, Art. VI).

[38] Milton M. Klein, "Shaping the American Tradition: The Microcosm of Colonial New York," *New York History* 59, no. 2 (April 1978): 197.

[39] An Act Requiring All Persons Holding Offices or Places under the Government of the State to Take the Oaths Therein Mentioned, February 8, 1788, *Laws of the State of New York Passed at the Sessions of the Legislature Held in the Years 1785, 1786, 1787, and 1788, Inclusive* (Albany: Weed, Parsons and Company, 1886), 1:637.

The argument was made that the secret ballot would "preserve the liberty and equal freedom of the people" (ibid.), presumably because voice voting invited intimidation and coercion of employees by employers, of the weak by the powerful, and of individuals by groups. The constitution provided voting by ballot would not occur for legislators until after the war, and an act implementing that practice was passed in 1787. The state did adopt a statute in 1778 providing elections by ballot for governor and lieutenant-governor.

Slavery

During its colonial period, New York adopted one of the most severe black codes in the northern colonies, going so far as to prohibit African Americans from owning property.[40] Little was done during the Revolutionary War to end slavery, although in 1781 the legislature voted to manumit slaves serving in the armed forces. In 1788, New York banned the slave trade outright, and a gradual abolition law achieved passage in 1799. A successor law in 1817 went further: it provided for the uncompensated emancipation of approximately 10,000 enslaved blacks who were born before the date of the gradual abolition law, effective July 4, 1827. That date would mark the end of slavery in New York. Sean Wilentz calls it the first general emancipation law in the United States.[41]

Structural Provisions

The constitution established a bicameral legislature consisting of an annually elected assembly and a senate elected for four-year terms. The governor was chosen by the people and given a three-year term, long by the standards of the day (Const. 1777, Art. XVII). Judicial independence was assured by the fact that the chancellor, the judges of the supreme court, and the first judge of the county court in each county were entitled to hold their offices during good behavior or until they reached 60 years of age (ibid., Art. XXIV). Sheriffs and coroners, appointed annually by a council of appointment, were incapable of holding office more than four

[40] Arthur Zilversmit, *The First Emancipation: The Abolition of Slavery in the North* (Chicago: University of Chicago Press, 1967), 13–24.

[41] *Property in No Man: Slavery and Antislavery at the Nation's Founding* (Cambridge, MA: Harvard University Press, 2018), 41.

years successively (ibid., Art. XXVI). The constitution contained restrictions on plural office-holding, although it did allow county court judges to serve as senators (ibid., Art. XXV). Ministers were barred from holding any civil or military office within the state (ibid., Art. XXXIX). The constitution provided for legislative transparency, requiring the doors to be kept open except when required by the welfare of the state and mandating that journals of the proceedings be kept "in the manner heretofore accustomed..." (ibid., Art. XV).

New York's constitution, alone among the constitutions adopted by the states during the period under study, contained a council of revision to veto bills "inconsistent with the spirit of th[e] constitution, or with the public good" (Const. 1777, Art. III). The council consisted of the governor, the chancellor, and the judges of the supreme court. This early form of judicial review arose out of fears that the legislature might act to trench on rights and citizens might be unwilling or unable to rebuke them. The political culture that emerged from New York's history of political factionalism rendered untenable assumptions about the polity and the community that undergirded other early state constitutions. In a pluralistic—not to say contentious—society, judicial protection may well have appeared to be the only option available to a polity committed to the protection of rights.

Postscript: Although New York did not have a constitutional bill of rights until it adopted a second constitution in 1821, the state did adopt a statutory bill of rights in 1787. Blending provisions taken from the 1777 constitution, the 1683 Charter of Liberties and Privileges, and parts of English common law and statute law, New Yorkers established a panoply of rights more extensive and complete than those found in the national Bill of Rights adopted five years later. Robert Emery puts the law in its historical context:

> ...rights declared by the constitution and by the Act concerning the rights of citizens formed the corpus of fundamental rights inherited by New York State citizens from their Anglo-colonial legal heritage. In other words, they indicated the extent to which the principles declared by Magna Carta, the Petition of Right, and the 1689 Bill of Rights were still valid and enforceable in the new jurisdiction.[42]

That statutory bill of rights is reprinted below.

[42] Robert Emery, "New York's Statutory Bill of Rights: A Constitutional Coelacanth," *Touro Law Review* 19, no. 2 (Winter/Spring 2003): 372.

Constitution of New York [1777]

I. This convention, therefore, in the name and by the authority of the good people of this State, doth ordain, determine, and declare that no authority shall, on any presence whatever, be exercised over the people or members of this State but such as shall be derived from and granted by them.

* * *

VII. That every male inhabitant of full age, who shall have personally resided within one of the counties of this State for six months immediately preceding the day of election, shall, at such election, be entitled to vote for representatives of the said county in assembly; if, during the time aforesaid, he shall have been a freeholder, possessing a freehold of the value of twenty pounds, within the said county, or have rented a tenement therein of the yearly value of forty shillings, and been rated and actually paid taxes to this State: *Provided always*, That every person who now is a freeman of the city of Albany, or who was made a freeman of the city of New York on or before the fourteenth day of October, in the year of our Lord one thousand seven hundred and seventy-five, and shall be actually and usually resident in the said cities, respectively, shall be entitled to vote for representatives in assembly within his said place of residence.[43]

* * *

XIII. And this convention doth further, in the name and by the authority of the good people of this State, ordain, determine, and declare, that no member of this State shall be disfranchised, or deprived of any the rights

[43] Some controversy exists as to the number of adult white males who were eligible to vote under these restrictions. Early studies claimed that over half the adult male population was disenfranchised. Becker, *History of Political Parties*, 11. A more recent study offers a different picture, concluding that 100 percent of the adult white males in New York City qualified under these requirements. Robert E. Brown, *Charles Beard and the Constitution: A Critical Analysis of "An Economic Interpretation of the Constitution"* (Princeton, NJ: Princeton University Press, 1956). Milton M. Klein concludes that the qualified electorate in the rural areas of New York "may quite possibly, then, have been as large as that of New York City and Albany." "Democracy and Politics in Colonial New York," *New York History* 40, no. 3 (July 1959): 237. Although free blacks were eligible to vote, the property requirement that disenfranchised poor males, black and white, fell disproportionately on African Americans.

or privileges secured to the subjects of this State by this constitution, unless by the law of the land, or the judgment of his peers.[44]

* * *

XXXIV. *And it is further ordained*, That in every trial on impeachment, or indictment for crimes or misdemeanors, the party impeached or indicted shall be allowed counsel, as in civil actions.[45]

XXXV. And this convention doth further, in the name and by the authority of the good people of this State, ordain, determine, and declare that such parts of the common law of England, and of the statute law of England and Great Britain, and of the acts of the legislature of the colony of New York, as together did form the law of the said colony on the 19th day of April, in the year of our Lord one thousand seven hundred and seventy-five, shall be and continue the law of this State, subject to such alterations and provisions as the legislature of this State shall, from time to time, make concerning the same. That such of the said acts, as are temporary, shall expire at the times limited for their duration, respectively. That all such parts of the said common law, and all such of the said statutes and acts aforesaid, or parts thereof, as may be construed to establish or maintain any particular denomination of Christians or their ministers, or concern the allegiance heretofore yielded to, and the supremacy, sovereignty, government, or prerogatives claimed or exercised by, the King of Great Britain and his predecessors, over the colony of New York and its inhabitants, or are repugnant to this constitution, be, and they hereby are, abrogated and rejected. And this convention doth further ordain, that the resolves or resolutions of the congresses of the colony of New York, and of the convention of the State of New York, now in force, and not repugnant to the government established by this

[44] The language of this article came directly from Chapter 39 of Magna Carta. Bernard Schwartz, *The Bill of Rights: A Documentary History* (New York: Chelsea House Publishers, 1971), 1:12, and the Charter of Liberties and Privileges. Charter of Liberties and Privileges, 258.

[45] The right to counsel in the early American states was broader than under English common law, which did not allow counsel in felony cases until well into the nineteenth century. John Peter Zenger had counsel in his seditious libel trial in 1735, indicating that New York no longer followed the English common law practice. Felix Rackow, "The Right to Counsel: English and American Precedents," *The William and Mary Quarterly* 11, no. 1 (January 1954): 16–17. This article constitutionalized the right to counsel, making it clear that the right attached to all criminal prosecutions as well as to civil cases.

constitution, shall be considered as making part of the laws of this State; subject, nevertheless, to such alterations and provisions as the legislature of this State may, from time to time, make concerning the same.[46]

* * *

XXXVII. And whereas it is of great importance to the safety of this State that peace and amity with the Indians within the same be at all times supported and maintained; and whereas the frauds too often practiced towards the said Indians, in contracts made for their lands, have, in divers instances, been productive of dangerous discontents and animosities: Be it ordained, that no purchases or contracts for the sale of lands, made since the fourteenth day of October, in the year of our Lord one thousand seven hundred and seventy-five, or which may hereafter be made with or of the said Indians, within the limits of this State, shall be binding on the said Indians, or deemed valid, unless made under the authority and with the consent of the legislature of this State.[47]

XXXVIII. And whereas we are required, by the benevolent principles of rational liberty, not only to expel civil tyranny, but also to guard against that spiritual oppression and intolerance wherewith the bigotry and ambition of weak and wicked priests and princes have scourged mankind, this convention doth further, in the name and by the authority of the good people of this State, ordain, determine, and declare, that the free exercise

[46] Article XXXV was meant to ease the transition from colony to independent state by settling questions about the status of the common law and colonial statutes. The incorporation of the common law was significant. Given the history of the common law in the colony, see supra note 6 and accompanying text, it is not surprising New Yorkers saw the common law as a repository of liberty and the primary guarantor of English liberties. Daniel J. Hulsebosch, *Constituting Empire: New York and the Transformation of Constitutionalism in the Atlantic World, 1664–1830* (Chapel Hill: University of North Carolina Press, 2005), 35, 42.

For most of the colony's history, the Church of England insisted that it was the only legally established church, but New York City and three adjoining counties had multiple establishments. This article wiped the slate clean by prohibiting any establishment of religion. See Leonard W. Levy, *The Establishment Clause: Religion and the First Amendment*, 2nd ed. (Chapel Hill: University of North Carolina Press, 1994), 28.

[47] By the opening of the eighteenth century, speculators had persuaded Indians to part with millions of acres of land. J. Hampden Dougherty, *Constitutional History of the State of New York*, 2nd ed. (New York: Neale Publishing Company, 1915), 177. This article voided those contracts.

and enjoyment of religious profession and worship, without discrimination or preference, shall forever hereafter be allowed, within this State, to all mankind: ***Provided***, That the liberty of conscience, hereby granted, shall not be so construed as to excuse acts of licentiousness, or justify practices inconsistent with the peace or safety of this State.[48]

* * *

XL. And whereas it is of the utmost importance to the safety of every State that it should always be in a condition of defence; and it is the duty of every man who enjoys the protection of society to be prepared and willing to defend it; this convention therefore, in the name and by the authority of the good people of this State, doth ordain, determine, and declare that the militia of this State, at all times hereafter, as well in peace as in war, shall be armed and disciplined, and in readiness for service. That all such of the inhabitants of this State being of the people called Quakers as, from scruples of conscience, may be averse to the bearing of arms, be therefrom excused by the legislature; and do pay to the State such sums of money, in lieu of their personal service, as the same; may, in the judgment of the legislature, be worth. And that a proper magazine of warlike stores, proportionate to the number of inhabitants, be, forever hereafter,

[48] John Jay's polemical, preamble-like language may have reflected the persecution suffered by his Huguenot ancestor, Pierre Jay. One of John Jay's unsuccessful amendments would have prohibited Catholics from holding citizenship. Jay took the position that Catholics were papists and therefore could not be citizens and that Catholicism was at heart a conspiracy against Protestantism, and, as such, subversive, or at least politically dangerous. John Webb Pratt, ***Religion, Politics, and Diversity: The Church-State Theme in New York History*** (Ithaca, NY: Cornell University Press, 1967), 85. The history of anti-Catholicism in colonial and Revolutionary New York, along with Jay's role in crafting the religious provisions of the 1777 constitution, are given extensive treatment by Jason K. Duncan, *Citizens or Papists? The Politics of Anti-Catholicism in New York, 1685–1821* (New York: Fordham University Press, 2005), 20–44.

The convention rejected or softened most of Jay's amendments but left some harsh, thinly veiled references to Catholicism. On the other hand, New York was the only state that did not require a religious test for holding office and, along with New Jersey, came closest to establishing complete religious freedom. The last sentence of this article was a clear acknowledgment that the community could determine the extent and limits of that right.

at the expense of this State, and by acts of the legislature, established, maintained, and continued in every county in this State.[49]

XLI. And this convention doth further ordain, determine, and declare, in the name and by the authority of the good people of this State, that trial by jury, in all cases in which it hath heretofore been used in the colony of New York, shall be established and remain inviolate forever. And that no acts of attainder shall be passed by the legislature of this State for crimes, other than those committed before the termination of the present war; and that such acts shall not work a corruption of blood.[50] And further, that the legislature of this State shall, at no time hereafter, institute any new court or courts, but such as shall proceed according to the course of the common law.

The New York Statutory Bill of Rights [1787]

Be it enacted by the People of the State of New York represented in Senate and Assembly and it is hereby enacted and declared by the authority of the same.

First That no authority shall, on any pretense whatsoever be exercised over the citizens of this State but such as is or shall be derived from and granted by the people of this State.[51]

Second That no citizen of this State shall be taken or imprisoned or be disseised of his or her freehold or liberties of free customs or outlawed or

[49] Along with most every other state, New York constitutionalized the duty of citizens to serve in the militia in defense of the community—a duty owed by all citizens who enjoy the protection of society and the rights it guaranteed. The constitution said nothing about the danger of standing armies, civilian control of the military, or the quartering of soldiers, although the statutory bill of rights contained a detailed provision limiting the latter practice. See Bill of Rights, sec. 13 below.

The exemption fee was fixed at ten pounds per annum. Solicitous concern for the protection of Quakers reflected in this clause can be traced to the Flushing Remonstrance (December 25, 1657), a protest by English freeholders of Flushing and Jamaica to Dutch Governor Peter Stuyvesant because he had forbidden Quakers from holding religious meetings. It is considered a landmark in the struggle for religious freedom. http://www.nycourts.gov/history/legal-history-new-york/legal-history-eras-03/history-era-03-flushing-remonstrance.html.

[50] By an act of October 23, 1779, fifty-eight persons, of whom three were females, were attainted and banished from the state for adherence to the enemy. This was the only act passed by this clause.

[51] Similar to 1777 Const., Art. I.

exiled or condemned or otherwise destroyed, but by lawful judgment of his or her peers or by due process of law.[52]

Third That no citizen of this State shall be taken or imprisoned for any offence upon petition or suggestion unless it be by indictment or presentment of good and lawful men of the same neighbourhood where such deeds be done, in due manner or by due process of law.[53]

Fourth That no person shall be put to answer without presentment before justices, or matter of record, or due process of law according to the law of the land and if anything be done to the contrary it shall be void in law and holden for error.[54]

Fifth That no person, of what estate or condition soever shall be taken or imprisoned, or disinherited or put to death without being brought to answer by due process of law, and that no person shall be put out of his or her franchise or freehold or lose his or her life or limb, or goods and chattels, unless he or she be duly brought to answer and be forejudged of the same by due course of law and if anything be done contrary to the same it shall be void in law and holden for none.[55]

Sixth That neither justice, nor right shall be sold to any person, nor denied nor deferred; and that writs and process shall be granted freely and without delay to all persons requiring the same and nothing from. Henceforth shall be paid or taken for any writ or process but the accustomed fee for writing and for the seal of the same writ or process and all fines duties and impositions whatsoever heretofore taken or demanded under what name or description soever, for or upon granting any writs, inquests, commissions or process to suitors in their causes shall be and hereby are abolished.[56]

[52] Derived from Magna Carta, Ch. 39, in Schwartz, *Bill of Rights*, 112; Petition of Right (1628), [sec. III], in Schwartz, *Bill of Rights*, 1:20; Charter of Liberties and Privileges, in Lutz, *Colonial Origins*, 258.

[53] Derived from Magna Carta, Ch. 39, 12; Petition of Right, [sec. VII], 20; Charter of Liberties and Privileges, 259.

[54] Derived from Magna Carta, Ch. 39, 12.

[55] Derived from Magna Carta, Ch. 39, 12 Petition of Right, [sec. IV], 20; Charter of Liberties and Privileges, 258.

[56] Derived from Magna Carta, Ch. 40, 12; Charter of Liberties and Privileges, 258.

Seventh That no citizens of this State shall be fined or amerced without reasonable cause and such fine or amercement[57] shall always be according to the quantity of his or her trespass or offence and saving to him or her, his or her contentment; That is to say every freeholder saving his freehold, a merchant saving his merchandize and a mechanick saving the implements of his trade.[58]

Eighth That excessive bail ought not to be required, nor excessive fines imposed, nor cruel and unusual punishments inflicted.[59]

Ninth That all elections shall be free and that no person by force of arms nor by malice or menacing or otherwise presume to disturb or hinder any citizen of this State to make free election upon pain of fine and imprisonment and treble damages to the party grieved.[60]

Tenth That it is the right of the citizens of this State to Petition the person administering the government of this State for the time being, or either house of the legislature and all commitments and prosecutions for such petitioning are illegal.[61]

Eleventh That the freedom of speech and debates and proceedings in the senate and assembly shall not be impeached or questioned in any court or place out of the senate or assembly.[62]

Twelfth That no tax duty aid or imposition whatsoever shall be taken or levied within this State without the grant and assent of the people of this State by their representatives in senate and assembly and that no citizen of this State shall be by any means compelled to contribute to any gift loan tax or other like charge not set laid or imposed by the legislature of this State: And further, that no citizen of this State shall be constrained to arm himself or to go out of this State or to find soldiers or men of

[57] An amercement was a monetary penalty.

[58] Derived from Magna Carta, Chs. 20–22, 10–11; English Bill of Rights (1689), in Schwartz, *Bill of Rights*, 1:43; Charter of Liberties and Privileges, 258–259.

[59] Derived from English Bill of Rights, 43.

[60] Derived from English Bill of Rights, 43.

[61] Derived from English Bill of Rights, 42; Declaration and Resolves on Colonial Rights of the First Continental Congress (1774), Resolve No. 8, in Barry Alan Shain, ed., *The Declaration of Independence in Historical Context: American State Papers, Petitions, Proclamations, and Letters of the Delegates to the First National Congresses* (New Haven, CT: Yale University Press, 2014), 213.

[62] Derived from English Bill of Rights, 43.

arms either horsemen or footmen, if it be not by assent and grant of the people of this State by their representatives in senate and assembly.[63]

Thirteenth That by the laws and customs of this State the citizens and inhabitants thereof cannot be compelled against their wills to receive soldiers into their houses and to sojourn them there and therefore no officer military or civil nor any other person whatsoever shall from henceforth presume to place, quarter or billet any soldier or soldiers upon any citizen or inhabitant of this State of any degree or profession whatever without his or her consent and that it shall and may be lawful for every such citizen and inhabitant to refuse to sojourn or quarter any soldier or soldiers notwithstanding any command order warrant or billeting whatever.[64]

[63] Derived from Magna Carta, Ch. 12, 10; Petition of Right, [sec. X], 21; English Bill of Rights, 42; Charter of Liberties and Privileges, 258.

[64] Derived from Petition of Right, [sec. VI], 20; English Bill of Rights, 42; Charter of Liberties and Privileges, 259.

States Maintaining Their Colonial Charters

Connecticut

The colony of Connecticut began in 1633 when the Dutch established the first trading post on the Connecticut River Valley in what is now the town of Hartford. The Dutch presence was soon overtaken by a large influx of settlers into the valley from the Massachusetts Bay Colony, an emigration that formed three towns, Hartford, Wethersfield, and Windsor. A provisional government was authorized and instituted under a commission (the March Commission) issued in 1636 by the General Court of Massachusetts to eight persons who "had resolved to transplant themselves and their estates unto the River of Connecticut."[1]

When the March Commission expired in 1637, the three towns created a general court of magistrates, beginning the process of establishing a government for the commonwealth. Among the early settlers was Thomas Hooker, a prominent theologian and inspirational leader now considered the "Father of Connecticut." Hooker preached the opening sermon on May 31st of that year, marking the founding of a new political order.[2]

In his sermon, Hooker listed three doctrines derived from Deuteronomy 1:13: that "the choice of public magistrates belongs unto the people by Gods own allowance"; that "the privilege of election which belongs to

[1] J. Hammond Trumbull, *Historical Notes on the Constitutions of Connecticut, 1639–1818* (Hartford: Brown & Gross, 1873), 7.

[2] There is no verbatim record of the sermon. We have shorthand notes taken by members in attendance.

P. J. Galie et al., *Bills of Rights Before the Bill of Rights*,
https://doi.org/10.1007/978-3-030-44301-6_16

the people it must not be exercised according to their humors but according to the blessed will and law of God"; and "[those] who have power to appoint officers and magistrates it is in their power also to set the bounds and limits of the power and places unto which they call them."[3]

Hooker's advocacy of popular sovereignty and popular control of civil government earned him, in the eyes of subsequent generations, a reputation as a harbinger of democracy.[4] Recently, Michael Besso has argued, however, that Hooker's sermon was not as much a political theory as an instruction to his congregation and audience about their religious duties as persons living under a government God had ordained for them.[5] Besso's conclusion is telling:

> These doctrines can be considered as advocacy for a political theory only by stripping them of the context within which Hooker had embedded them. To do this, the existing assessments treated these doctrines as ends in themselves... **they failed to consider existing biblical authority for these doctrines and instead treated them as expressions of newly developing political theory.**[6]

Colonial historian Charles M. Andrews described the colony as more representative of the Puritan ideal of a Heavenly City of God than the Massachusetts Bay Colony:

> ...she possessed but one church, one prevailing habit of religious thought, one dominating religious purpose in the hearts of her people, one controlling policy that directed her government towards religious ends and proclaimed her for what she was, a religious Puritan state, set apart from the rest of the world as a home and refuge for the people chosen of God and sanctified to his glory.[7]

[3] As quoted in Michael Besso, "Thomas Hooker and His May 1638 Sermon," *Early American Studies* 10, no. 1 (Winter 2012): 200.

[4] See, e.g., Vernon Louis Parrington, *Main Currents in American Thought*, vol. 1, *The Colonial Mind, 1620–1800* (New York: Harcourt, Brace, 1927), 58–62.

[5] Besso notes that Hooker's sermon followed Calvin's preaching on the same passage. Besso, "Thomas Hooker," 208–215.

[6] Ibid., 215 (emphasis added).

[7] *Our Earliest Colonial Settlements: Their Diversities of Origin and Later Characteristics* (1933; reprint, Ithaca, NY: Cornell University Press, 2009), 118–119.

The Fundamental Orders (Constitution of 1638)

In January 1638/1639, the Connecticut General Court adopted the Fundamental Orders—the colony's design for self-government. A civil covenant, the orders created a religious colony for Puritans only.[8] The preamble began, "[f]orasmuch as it hath pleased the Allmighty God...," and continued: "well knowing where a people are gathered togather the word of God [the Bible] requires that to mayntayne the peace and vnion of such a people there should be an orderly and decent Gouerment established according to God...."[9] The Fundamental Orders consisted of eleven numbered paragraphs that established election procedures, created officers and prescribed their duties, and authorized the legislature to enact regulations to order civil affairs for the towns and all the people. The overriding purpose of the civil compact was "to mayntayne and p^{r}searue the liberty and purity of the gospell of our Lord Jesus wch we now p^{r}fesse...[and] the disciplyne of the Churches, wch according to the truth of the said gospell is now practised amongst vs...."[10]

Fundamental rights were recognized in the orders, though narrowly defined. They included rights to elect officials; in the event the leaders refused to call the standing courts as required in the orders, the freemen were authorized to instruct the constables to order the election of deputies who would constitute a body authorized to "do any Acte of power, wch any other Generall Courte may."[11] There was no formal bill of rights.[12]

[8] David A. Weir provides a detailed analysis of the differences between civil and church covenants, as well as the interplay between the two in colonial New England. *Early New England: A Covenanted Society* (Grand Rapids, MI: Wm. B. Eerdmans, 2005), 2–14. Christopher Collier, the leading student of Connecticut's constitutional history, emphasizes the secular dimensions of the Fundamental Orders, claiming that Hooker called "for the constitution of a *civil* body politic, just as he and his followers had already constituted themselves an *ecclesiastical* body politic." "The Fundamental Orders of Connecticut and American Constitutionalism," *Connecticut Law Review* 21 (1989): 865.

[9] Fundamental Orders of Connecticut (1638/1639), in Thorpe, *Constitutions*, 1:519.

[10] Ibid.

[11] Ibid., 521.

[12] Much ink has been expended on the question of whether the Fundamental Orders was America's first constitution. Colonial officials and public figures treated the document as fundamental. The charter was placed at the beginning of various codes of law, along with other founding documents, and early commentators on Connecticut law considered it a constitution. George Brinley, in his prefatory note to *The Laws of Connecticut: An*

The Fundamental Orders prefaced Connecticut's Code of 1650, with the former designated in that document as "the Constitution of 1638."[13] The 1650 code maintained the eleven provisions of the 1638/1639 orders, adding a twelfth section and a preamble to that section:

> Preamble
>
> Fforasmuch as the free fruition of such libberties, immunities, priviledges, as humanity, civility and Christianity call for, as due to every man in his place and proportion, without impeachment and infringement, hath ever beene and ever will bee the tranquillity and stabillity of Churches and Commonwealths; and the denyall or deprivall thereof, the disturbance, if not ruine of both.
>
> 12. *It is thereof ordered by this Courte, and authority thereof*, That no man's life shall bee taken away; no man's honor or good name shall be stained; no man's person shall bee arrested, restreined, bannished, dismembred, nor any way punnished; no man shall bee deprived of his wife or children; no man's goods or estate shall bee taken away from him nor any ways indammaged, under colour of law, or countenance of authority;

Exact Reprint of the Edition of 1673 (Hartford: n.p., 1865) called it "the first written Constitution originating in the new world, and the model for all succeeding ones." Ibid., v. Trumbull echoed that judgment in his *Historical Notes*, 6, as did nineteenth-century American historian John Fiske. John Fiske, *The Beginnings of New England or the Puritan Theocracy in Its Relation to Civil and Religious Liberty* (Boston: Houghton Mifflin, 1899), 127. Christopher Collier defended Connecticut's designation as the "Constitution State:" "If the Fundamental Orders do not fulfill the requirements of a modern constitution...there is...another dimension to the significance of the Orders.... For the first time ever, that historians have been able to discover, the people had created a government for themselves and had begun to live their lives by it." Collier, "Fundamental Orders," 866, 868–869. Collier takes the position that the Fundamental Orders, though not a "fully developed written constitution," possessed the "essential elements of constitutionalism," i.e., a document that defined and limited the government. Ibid., 867–869. Wesley W. Horton finesses the question, calling the orders "the first written framework of a government in the history of mankind." *The Connecticut State Constitution* (New York: Oxford University Press, 2011), 7.

[13] *The Code of 1650, Being a Compilation of the Earliest Laws and Orders of the General Court of Connecticut: Also, the Constitution, or Civil Compact, Entered into and Adopted by the Towns of Windsor, Hartford and Wethersfield in 1638–9* (Hartford: Andrus & Judd, 1833), 11–18. See also Christopher Collier, "The Common Law and Individual Rights in Connecticut before the Federal Bill of Rights," *Connecticut Bar Journal* 76 (2002): 8–9. Collier's article is a thorough and exemplary essay on the rights tradition in Connecticut prior to the adoption of the national Bill of Rights. Although our comparative approach and theoretical framework lead us, on occasion, to alternative readings, Professor Collier's work has been invaluable and we have relied on his findings at various points.

> unless it bee by the vertue or equity of some express law of the Country warranting the same, established by a Generall Courte and sufficiently published, or in case of the defect of a law, in any perticular case, by the word of God.[14]

The preamble began with the assertion that the recognition of "such libberties, immunities, priviledges, as humanity, civility and Christianity call for" are the indispensable prerequisites for a peaceful and stable social order. Section 12 repeated Chapter 39 of Magna Carta in extended colonial garb. The provision that no person's life, liberty, reputation, or property could be taken except by and according to the law of the land was *the* fundamental protection against arbitrary government.[15] The colony was a communitarian order, governed by the Bible—one that subjected nearly all aspects of human behavior to regulation. The rights recognized—self-government and consent of the governed—were communal. The protection of life, liberty, and estate were guaranteed only insofar as the standing laws of the colony permitted, and those standing laws were pervasive and intrusive: witchcraft, blasphemy, heresy, neglect of public worship, contemnors of God's holy ordinances, cursing of parents, stubborn children, idleness, lascivious carriage (wantonness), adultery, fornication, and homosexuality were among the activities punished.[16] Due process was not substantive: public officials were bound by the requirements of the law, but due process was not viewed as grounds to challenge a duly enacted law. In Connecticut's first fifty years, even the liberty of conscience was restricted, with heretical publications such as "Quakers bookes or manuscripts containing their errors..." banned.[17]

[14] *Code of 1650*, 18–19.

[15] Collier suggests that the phrase "express law" introduced the distinction between civil rights and natural rights, the former being those rights implied by the presence of government. Thus individuals have a natural right to possess and enjoy their property, but the conditions and terms of that possession and enjoyment would be matters for the community to decide. The right to property is natural; its protection is civil.

[16] See *Code of 1650*, 28–30, 44–45, 48.

[17] J. Hammond Trumbull, *The Public Records of the Colony of Connecticut Prior to the Union with the New Haven Colony, May, 1665* (Hartford: Brown & Parsons, 1850), 1:308.

The Connecticut Charter of 1662

The Restoration of the English monarchy in 1660 put the colony in jeopardy: it had never been officially sanctioned by the Crown. Two years later, King Charles II approved a charter that was subsequently ratified by the Connecticut General Court. The charter was not a grant of new powers; rather, it was a recognition by the king of the colony as a self-governing polity already established by the people and a confirmation of the rights and privileges "against the aggression of neighboring governments and the possible encroachment of the Crown..."[18] The charter also expanded the boundaries of the colony to include New Haven, which, until that time, was a separate, self-governing entity.

The 1662 charter did not contain a declaration of rights and offered only modest rights protections. Beyond reaffirming the right to home rule and representative government,[19] the charter extended the common law protections of England to all residents:

> ...That all, and every the Subjects of Us, Our Heirs, or Successors, which shall go to inhabit within the said Colony, and every of their Children, which shall happen to be born there, or on the Seas in going thither, or returning from thence, shall have and enjoy all Liberties and Immunities of free and natural Subjects within any the Dominions of Us, Our Heirs or Successors, to all Intents, Constructions and Purposes whatsoever, as if they and every of them were born within the realm of *England*.[20]

Property rights were explicitly recognized, with colonists granted the same rights as any person in the realm of England to "have, take, possess, acquire, and purchase Lands, Tenements ...or any Goods or Chattels, and ... to lease, ... sell, and dispose of ..." such property.[21]

The charter could be altered by a simple majority vote of the general assembly (the body created by the charter to take the place of the general court). This was a remarkable provision: although the charter had been granted by the king, the few times it was altered, e.g., the assembly's vote

[18] Trumbull, *Historical Notes*, 10.

[19] Charter of Connecticut (1662), in Thorpe, *Constitutions*, 1:531–533.

[20] Ibid., 533.

[21] Ibid., 530.

in 1698 to divide itself into a bicameral body, London was never consulted. Instead, Connecticut managed "to combine royal approval with all the privileges of self-government... able ...to exist as an autonomous state."[22] Believing it needed legitimacy, Connecticut sought authorization for self-government from the king, but did not want—nor did it expect—England to supervise the operations of its government.

1776 Declaration of Rights and Privileges

As tensions between the colonies and the Crown increased in the latter half of the eighteenth century, Connecticut was one of a few states that did not resort to a provincial congress. In 1776, while other colonies were beginning the task of writing constitutions commensurate with their status as newly independent states, Connecticut adopted "An Act Containing an Abstract and Declaration of the Rights and Privileges of the People of this State, and Securing the Same."[23] It continued in force the charter of 1662 as the organic law of the state.[24]

The preamble to the 1776 statute adopted the preamble to the twelfth paragraph of the 1650 code. The 1776 act formally recognized the state's independence from the Crown, and decreed that the 1662 charter "shall ... remain the Civil Constitution of this State, under the sole Authority of the People thereof, independent of any King or Prince whatever"[25]—a formal declaration of popular sovereignty. The second paragraph of the statute repeated the rights protections found in the 1650 document but eliminated the "word of God" (The Bible) as a basis for punishment. This removal reflected the diminished legal status of religion in Connecticut and a movement to limit the discretion of magistrates by providing more well-defined codes of law.[26] The 1776 act extended equal justice to free

[22] Charles M. Andrews, "On Some Early Aspects of Connecticut History," *The New England Quarterly* 17, no. 1 (March 1944): 14. Among the colonies, only Connecticut and Rhode Island could make this claim.

[23] *Acts and Laws of the State of Connecticut in America* (Hartford: Hudson & Goodwin, 1805), 21–22.

[24] Ibid., 21.

[25] Ibid.

[26] The wide discretion magistrates exercised when deciding cases based on the "word of God" engendered complaints of arbitrariness. Between the Code of 1650 and the 1776 act, Connecticut had periodically codified its statutes to define crimes, delineate

inhabitants of other friendly American states and foreigners, announcing Connecticut's newly acquired status as an equal sovereign entity. The final paragraph guaranteed bail to those charged with all but capital crimes, contempt in open court, and other exceptions provided by law.

Despite having the phrase "Declaration of Rights" in its title, the 1776 statute did not resemble the declarations of rights adopted by other states between 1776 and 1790. Rights having a colorable claim to constitutional status in Connecticut included only the right to self-government, the broad due process clause added to the 1650 code, the 1776 proclamation of popular sovereignty, recognition of equal justice for all inhabitants of the states and friendly foreign powers, and the guarantee of bail.[27] The absence of a full-blown declaration of rights, with explicit constitutional status immunizing it from change by ordinary legislative action, raised questions as to the efficacy of these protections—susceptible as they were to legislative override or disregard.

The Common Law and the Protection of Rights in Connecticut

The 1662 charter guaranteed citizens of Connecticut the protections of the common law of England. Although all states had adopted some version of the common law by the time of the Revolution, Connecticut applied this law with special force:

> ...not only by the vague wording of many statutes and the discretion allowed magistrates but also by the frequent practice of many of these magistrates to depart in significant respects from the letter of the

procedures, and specify punishments, taking steps to realize the promise of Chapter 39 of Magna Carta as embodied in the 1650 code.

[27] There were other rights recognized in Connecticut, but those rights were to be found in the statutes of the colony and in what one commentator has aptly labeled "common-law constitutionalism." Collier, "Common Law," 1. See also Christopher Collier, "Liberty, Justice, and No Bill of Rights: Protecting Natural Rights in a Common-Law Commonwealth," in *The Bill of Rights and the States: The Colonial and Revolutionary Origins of American Liberties*, ed. Patrick T. Conley and John P. Kaminski (Madison, WI: Madison House, 1992), 105, where he refers to this tradition as "Magisterial Discretion and the Common Law."

law.…magistrates …described their function as enforcement of 'the principles of reason and justice' where no statute prevailed; … and bringing about outcomes 'agreeable to the law of nature and reason.'[28]

Connecticut's interpretation of the common law reflected a degree of independence unrivaled by other colonies. Collier describes the local nature of the law:

…when cases arose for which magistrates could find no relevant statute, or when statutes provided for magisterial discretion, the Bible, with its potential for varied interpretations, became the authority for decisions. Ultimately, these decisions came to constitute a local common law, distinct from that of England. Further, Connecticut was unique among the British-American colonies in rejecting any element of English common law that was not adopted locally.[29]

Wesley Horton goes further: "Since Connecticut basically has a common law constitution, its constitutional history starts with the founding of the colony in 1636."[30] Zephaniah Swift, former Chief Justice of the Connecticut Supreme Court and author of the first legal treatise published in America, wrote extensively on the active role courts played in applying common law principles when the statutes were silent or ambiguous.[31] Due process of law in Connecticut was largely judge-made. A remarkable example of Connecticut's commitment to due process was the judicially fashioned rule of statutory construction that laws "against the general rights and liberties of the citizens … must, therefore, be cautiously and strictly pursued"[32]—a precursor of judicial review.[33]

Connecticut judges also zealously protected the right to counsel. The colony had no statute guaranteeing counsel, but as early as 1750 the

[28] Collier, "Liberty, Justice," 106. Collier offers examples of rights protected on natural law or common law grounds. "Common Law," 31.

[29] Collier, "Common Law," 22–23.

[30] Horton, *Connecticut State Constitution*, 4.

[31] *A System of the Laws of the State of Connecticut* (Windham, CT: John Byrne, 1795), 1:45–47.

[32] *Johnson v. Stanley*, 1 Root 245, 246 (Conn. 1791).

[33] A judicial consensus on this strict construction had emerged by 1773. Collier, "Common Law," 35.

judicial practice was to appoint counsel in all cases where the defendant requested it, making the guarantee more extensive than in most other colonies:

> We have never admitted that cruel and illiberal principle of the common law of England, that when a man is on trial for his life, he shall be refused counsel, and denied those means of defence, which are allowed, when the most trifling pittance of property is in question.[34]

Other common law rights afforded Connecticut residents were the right to unprejudiced jurors and a degree of freedom from unreasonable search and seizure.[35] Although Connecticut, along with the other colonies, restricted the rights of assembly and free association during the Revolution,[36] in post-Revolution years these rights were understood to exist.[37]

The Connecticut Constitutional Order

Although some texts have labeled Connecticut's 1776 statute a "constitution,"[38] the state deemed its charter (continued by the 1776 statute) the fundamental law of the state, even though it had not been ratified by the people, did not provide a declaration of rights, and was susceptible to being altered by ordinary legislation. In doing so, Connecticut's constitutional order followed the English constitutional tradition: it lacked a single, written document and contained an amorphous mixture of natural law, statutory law, and common law. By the time Connecticut adopted its Fundamental Orders, the English understanding of a constitution rested on the assumption that the manners, culture, and traditions of the people

[34] Swift, *System of the Laws*, 2:398.

[35] Collier, "Liberty, Justice," 106.

[36] See Broadus Mitchell, *The Price of Independence: A Realistic View of the American Revolution* (New York: Oxford University Press 1974), passim; and Howard Pashman, *Building a Revolutionary State: The Legal Transformation of New York, 1776–1783* (Chicago: University of Chicago Press, 2018).

[37] Collier, "Liberty, Justice," 106.

[38] James Bradley Thayer, *Cases on Constitutional Law, with Notes* (Cambridge: Charles W. Sever, 1894), 1:434.

form the real constitution.[39] Connecticut's political culture, even after the Revolution, reflected that understanding, rather than the view that would come to dominate constitution-making in America.

The opposition of Oliver Ellsworth and Roger Sherman to a national Bill of Rights at the 1787 Constitutional Convention reflected Connecticut's understanding of the character and role of a constitution. Christopher Collier encapsulated that understanding:

> ...limited government was taken for granted. Calvinist theory limited civil government, the Fundamental Orders of 1639 proclaimed it, the Charter of 1662 established it, common law enforced it, tradition demanded it, and frequent elections guaranteed it.[40]

Limits on government reflected a deep-seated commitment to the liberties of the citizens, a commitment derived from their understanding of God's word. Oliver Ellsworth could argue there was no need to outlaw ex post facto laws, as lawyers and ordinary citizens in Connecticut would say "that ex post facto laws were void of themselves."[41] Roger Sherman, reflecting the English understanding of a constitution, wrote that frequent elections, along with the common law, were "a much greater security than a declaration of rights, or restraining clauses upon paper."[42] In "Letters of a Countryman, II," Sherman laid out the basis for his assertion:

> The only real security that you can have for all your important rights must be in the nature of your government. If you suffer any man to govern you who is not strongly interested in supporting your privileges, you will certainly lose them. If you are about to trust your liberties with people whom it is necessary to bind by stipulation, ... your stipulation is not worth even the trouble of writing. No bill of rights ever yet bound the supreme

[39] See Martin Loughlin, *The British Constitution: A Very Short Introduc*tion (Oxford: Oxford University Press, 2013), 12.

[40] Christopher Collier, *All Politics Is Local: Family, Friends, and Provincial Interests in the Creation of the Constitution* (Hanover, NH: University Press of New England, 2003), 50.

[41] *Debates on the Adoption of the Federal Constitution in the Convention Held at Philadelphia, in 1787*, ed. Jonathan Elliott (Philadelphia: n.p., 1836), 5:462.

[42] Roger Sherman, Letter Dated December 8, 1787, in *Supplement to Max Farrand's The Records of the Federal Convention of 1787*, ed. James H. Hutson (New Haven, CT: Yale University Press, 1987), 286.

> power longer than the *honey moon* of a new married couple, unless the *rulers were interested* in preserving the rights....[43]

The character and political culture of the Connecticut colony provided the conditions that supported their understanding. For most of its history, Connecticut was a small, self-governing, homogeneous, Puritan commonwealth. A bicameral legislature elected by an alert, active citizenry was the dominant branch of the government. Such conditions made gaps between constituent sentiment and legislative action unlikely. Some portion of the adult men, or their elected representatives, chose those who governed or guided them in religion, politics, and the military; and the gaps between the well-to-do and the less well-off were "uncommonly small."[44]

Legislation and adoptions of the English common law to colonial conditions enabled rights to flourish in Connecticut as well as any of the colonies, without the formal constitutional declarations of rights adopted by the other newly independent states.[45] The sections below outline the way certain rights were treated in pre- and post-Revolutionary Connecticut.

Suffrage

All adult inhabitants of towns could vote for town officials, but only freemen could vote for colony-wide officers. The process of selecting freemen changed throughout the colonial period, ranging from admission by the general court (1662–1689), to admission by certain officers (1689–1729), and subsequently to admission by town clerks in open town meetings of the freemen.[46] Inhabitants had to take an oath of fidelity; freemen had to take a Freeman's Oath.[47] Qualifications for freeman status in mid-seventeenth century Connecticut consisted of being twenty-one years of age, a person of "an honest and peaceable conversation,"

[43] November 22, 1787, in *Collected Works of Roger Sherman*, ed. Mark David Hall (Indianapolis: Liberty Fund, 2015), 484.

[44] Collier, *All Politics Is Local*, 13.

[45] See Jackson Turner Main, *Society and Economy in Colonial Connecticut* (Princeton, NJ: Princeton University Press, 1985).

[46] Albert Edward McKinley, *The Suffrage Franchise in the Thirteen English Colonies in America* (Philadelphia: University of Pennsylvania, 1905), 415.

[47] The oaths are found in Brinley, *Laws of Connecticut*, 53.

and possessing an estate of thirty pounds or service in some office in the commonwealth.[48] The property requirements changed over time, but as early as 1702 consisted of either real estate with an annual income of forty shillings or personal property assessed at forty pounds.[49] Property ownership was widespread, and by 1776, between sixty-five and eighty percent of inhabitants were eligible for freeman status.[50] African Americans were legally eligible to vote until 1814, but that was a mere formality. As in many other places in the North, there is no evidence they ever attempted to vote, in colonial times or after the Revolution.

From the colony's beginnings, African Americans, free or enslaved, enjoyed few social, economic, and political freedoms. Despite the paucity of blacks in seventeenth-century Connecticut, a black code was enacted to control and restrict their movement. That code was not limited to slaves: Free blacks without passes had to pay costs if stopped and brought before a magistrate.[51] On the eve of the Revolution, Connecticut had the largest number of slaves (6464) in New England. The importation of slaves was banned in 1776; abolition of the institution itself occurred in stages. A 1784 statute provided that black and mulatto children born after March 1, 1784 would become free at age twenty-five.[52] In 1797, that age was reduced to twenty-one.[53]

Women were not eligible to vote or run for office. Indians were not freemen and were not part of the public life of the community. They were

[48]Trumbull, *Public Records*, 1:331.

[49]McKinley, *Suffrage Franchise*, 415.

[50]No more than sixty percent of adult males likely took the freeman's oath in the 1780s. Collier, *All Politics Is Local*, 14 and the studies cited therein; Robert J. Dinkin, *Voting in Revolutionary America: A Study of Elections in the Original Thirteen States, 1776–1789* (Westport, CT: Greenwood Press, 1982), 39; Chilton Williamson, *From Property to Democracy 1760–1860* (Princeton, NJ: Princeton University Press, 1960), 165–166.

[51]See Bernard C. Steiner, *History of Slavery in Connecticut* (Baltimore: Johns Hopkins University Press, 1893), 12–13, for a summary of these restrictions. Unlike whites, African Americans were relieved from compulsory military duty after 1660. David O. White, *Connecticut's Black Soldiers, 1775–1783* (Chester, CT: Pequot Press, 1973), 11.

[52]An Act Concerning Indian, Mulatto, and Negro Servants and Slaves, sec. 13, *Acts and Laws of the State of Connecticut*, 399.

[53]An Act in Addition to An Act, Entitled "An Act Concerning Indian Mulatto and Negro Servants and Slaves," May 1797, *The Public Records of the State of Connecticut*, comp. Albert E. Van Dusen (Hartford: Connecticut State Library, 1953), 9:38–39.

forbidden to pass through the colony during the night,[54] and English colonists were forbidden to live among them "in a prophane course of life"—such as adopting their religion and customs.[55] Restrictions on private land transactions and trading in certain goods between colonists and Indians were imposed. In short, the rights and liberties laid out in this chapter were largely confined to white Europeans.

Religious Liberty

Connecticut was a religious colony, with Congregationalism its only faith. Theoretically, church and state were separated; practically, these institutions were "so interwoven that separation would have meant the severance of soul and body."[56] The colony supported the Congregational Church, gave it monopoly status, and required taxes for its support. In turn, the church supported the political leaders: only members of approved congregations were eligible for the magistracy; the cooperative arrangement created an elite ruling class referred to as the "Standing Order." The oath of fidelity, required of all who wished to live in the colony, in effect excluded Quakers, Jews, Ranters, Adamites, atheists, and later, Catholics.[57] Few, if any, such individuals resided in the colony.

As religious diversity increased, so did the pressure to relax these restrictions. In 1675, the colony exempted Quakers from attending public worship. A 1708 statute, subsequently referred to as The Act of Toleration, freed those who "soberly dissent from the way of worship and ministrie [the Congregational Church] established by the ancient laws of this government,"[58] affording colonists freedoms similar to those found in the English Toleration Act of 1689. However, the colony's toleration

[54] Trumbull, *Public Records*, 1:408.

[55] Ibid., 530.

[56] Charles M. Andrews, *The River Towns of Connecticut: A Study of Wethersfield, Hartford, and Windsor*, in the Johns Hopkins University Studies in Historical and Political Science, 7th ser., nos. 7–9 (Baltimore, 1889), 22.

[57] The Oath of Fidelity (1640) is found in Brinley, *Laws of Connecticut*, 53. Ranters were an anarchic, quasi-religious movement that emerged in 1648 to the horror of orthodox Puritans. Adamites were a seventeenth-century sect whose members believed that they existed in a state of grace, claiming to have regained the innocence that Adam and Eve possessed before the Fall.

[58] Trumbull, *Public Records*, 5:50.

law did not exempt nonconformists from paying taxes for the Congregational minister.

Members of the Church of England (Anglicans) were granted an exemption from taxes used to support Congregational churches in 1727.[59] In 1729, similar exemptions followed for Quakers and Baptists.[60] To qualify for the exemption, individuals had to certify that they were attending services and present at the regular meetings of the church, but compliance with the conditions was not rigorously enforced.[61] Connecticut moved closer to the position adopted by Evangelicals, viz., that the state and church should be separate, but that the state should accommodate and even promote a variety of religious beliefs and denominations. In 1777, the law permitted Quakers to affirm rather than to swear an oath.[62]

The 1708 Toleration Act had certain limitations. It allowed churches of other faiths to form, but did not permit Congregationalists wishing to withdraw from the establishment to form their own churches. Connecticut removed this limitation in the revised code of 1784. A short-lived 1791 act requiring dissenters who wished to be exempt from supporting the established church to obtain exemptions from civil officials who themselves were members of that church was replaced by "An Act securing equal Rights and Privileges to Christians of every denomination in this State."[63]

The extension of privileges did not go far enough for some. Critics noted that the extension did not apply to heathens, deists, and Jews. John Leland, a well-known outspoken Baptist elder, fulminated unsparing criticism of the laws.[64] The force of this objection is blunted somewhat

[59] Trumbull, *Public Records*, 7:106–107.

[60] Ibid., 237, 257.

[61] After 1773, most New England towns ceased to collect religious taxes from those who conscientiously refused to pay them. William G. McLoughlin, "The Role of Religion in the Revolution: Liberty of Conscience and Cultural Cohesion in the New Nation," in *Essays on the American Revolution*, ed. Stephen G. Kurtz and James H. Hutson (New York: W. W. Norton, 1973), 205.

[62] An Act Relative to the People Commonly Called Quakers, *Acts and Laws of the State of Connecticut*, 348.

[63] *Acts and Laws of the State of Connecticut*, 360.

[64] Leland's polemics are summarized by Trumbull, *Historical Notes*, 32.

by the fact that there were few, if any, such individuals inhabiting Connecticut during this period. By the end of the eighteenth century, every church was granted a right to govern itself and to tax its members for congregational purposes; all religious bodies were allowed the right of free incorporation; and no one in Connecticut was compelled to attend Sabbath services, even though compulsory attendance laws remained on the books. M. Louise Greene describes the Hobson's choice facing the colonists, and the resulting compromise it produced:

> It was a concession by the community to a very few among their number, who were divergent in church polity and practice, but who were united in a Protestant creed and in the conviction, held then by every respectable citizen, that every man should be made to attend and support some accepted and organized form of Christian worship.[65]

Protection of Life, Liberty, and Property

Zephaniah Swift described the jury as "coeval with our government, ...one of the most valuable privileges that can be enjoyed in civil society, and essential to the preservation of civil liberty."[66] Extensive statutory attention was given to trial and grand juries,[67] including the rights to choose a jury or a bench trial, challenge jurors, and appeal.[68] The colony's 1672 statutory revision did away with six-person juries, and the right to a jury trial was extended to both criminal and civil cases.[69] Jurors were selected from the freemen of the town, contrary to the English procedure where the sheriff returned the panel.[70] In a foretaste of modern practice, jury trials were frequently waived by the parties, making them

[65] *The Development of Religious Liberty in Connecticut* (Boston: Houghton, Mifflin, and Company, 1905), 218–219. Greene's understanding parallels the civic republicanism that was a growing part of the political culture of America in the eighteenth century. See pp. 72–80 for a discussion of the interplay between religion and the promotion of civic virtue in the early state constitutions.

[66] Swift, *System of the Laws*, 1:230.

[67] Brinley, *Laws of Connecticut*, 37.

[68] Ibid., 3–4, 27, 67.

[69] Twelve was the default position in English law.

[70] Bradley Chapin, *Criminal Justice in Colonial America, 1606–1660* (Athens: University of Georgia Press, 1983), 34.

more a promise than a practice. John M. Murrin claims that juries were not normally used in noncapital cases in seventeenth-century Connecticut, though they were used in civil proceedings.[71]

Justice was to be granted without partiality or delay. A statute of limitations prevented indictments sought after one year from the offense.[72] Defendants had a right to bail in most cases.[73] Statutes prohibited double jeopardy, cruel and unusual punishment, and coerced confessions.[74] Protection against self-incrimination was provided: "no person required to give testimony aforesaid shall be punished for what he doth confesse against himselfe when under oath."[75] Punishments that were "Inhumane, Barbarous or Cruel" were prohibited.[76]

Statutory rights extended to the economic and social realm. The liberty to trade and emigrate were guaranteed,[77] and monopolies were limited on the grounds that competition would be profitable for the colony.[78] The colony provided social and positive rights, requiring towns to care for the poor and to provide an education for every child.[79] A review of the panoply of rights that Connecticut residents enjoyed through their 1662 charter, the various statutes, and common law protections demonstrates that they were comparable to the rights afforded in most of the early state constitutions.

Postscript: Connecticut continued to operate under its existing charter until 1818 when the state adopted its first state constitution. That constitution continued to embrace the civic republican view of religion's

[71] "Magistrates, Sinners, and a Precarious Liberty: Trial by Jury in Seventeenth-Century New England," in *Saints and Revolutionaries: Essays on Early American History*, ed. David Hall, John M. Murrin, and Thad W. Tate (New York: W. W. Norton & Co., 1984), 152–206.

[72] Brinley, *Laws of Connecticut*, 34.

[73] Ibid., 32.

[74] Ibid., 58, 65.

[75] Trumbull, *Public Records*, 4:236.

[76] Brinley, *Laws of Connecticut*, 58.

[77] Ibid., 66.

[78] Ibid., 52.

[79] Ibid., 63.

role in promoting civic virtue.[80] The 1818 constitution remained in effect for 147 years, replaced in December 1965 by the current constitution.

Act Containing an Abstract and Declaration of the Rights and Privileges of the People of This State, and Securing the Same [1776]

PREAMBLE:
The People of this State, being by the Providence of God, free and independent, have the sole and exclusive Right of governing themselves as a free, sovereign, and independent State; and having from their Ancestors derived a free and excellent Constitution of Government whereby the Legislature depends on the free and annual Election of the People, they have the best Security for the Preservation of their civil and religious Rights and Liberties. And forasmuch as the free Fruition of such Liberties and Privileges as Humanity, Civility and Christianity call for, as is due to every Man in his Place and Proportion, without Impeachment and Infringement, hath ever been, and will be the Tranquility and Stability of Churches and Commonwealths; and the Denial thereof, the Disturbance, if not the Ruin of both.[81]

Paragraph 1. Be it enacted and declared by the Governor, and Council, and House of Representatives, in General Court assembled, That the ancient Form of Civil Government, contained in the Charter from Charles the Second, King of England, and adopted by the People of this State, shall be and remain the civil Constitution of this State, under the sole authority of the People thereof, independent of any King or Prince whatever. And that this Republic is, and shall forever be and remain, a free, sovereign and independent State, by the name of the STATE OF CONNECTICUT.[82]

2. And be it further enacted and declared, That no Man's Life shall be taken away: No Man's Honor or good Name shall be stained: No Man's

[80] See Conn. Const. of 1818, Art. VII, secs. 1–2.

[81] The preamble contained the constitutional principles and fundamental rights that would constitute the republic.

[82] This paragraph formally adopted the charter as the civil constitution of the state, while asserting its status as a sovereign entity with final authority to exercise the police power in accord with the sovereign will of the people.

Person shall be arrested, restrained, banished, dismembered, nor any Ways punished: No Man shall be deprived of his Wife or Children: No Man's Goods or Estate shall be taken away from him, nor any Ways indamaged under the Colour of Law, or Countenance of Authority; unless clearly warranted by the Laws of this State.[83]

3. That all the free Inhabitants of this or any other of the United States of America, and Foreigners in Amity with this State, shall enjoy the same justice and Law within this State, which is general for the State, in all Cases proper for the Cognizance of the Civil Authority and Court of Judicature within the same, and that without Partiality or Delay.[84]

4. And that no Man's Person shall be restrained, or imprisoned, by any authority whatsoever, before the Law hath sentenced him thereunto, if he can and will give sufficient Security, Bail, or Mainprize[85] for his Appearance and good Behaviour in the mean Time, unless it be for Capital Crimes, Contempt in open Court, or in such Cases wherein some express Law doth allow of, or order the same.[86]

[83] Paragraph 2 was taken from the *1655 New Haven's Settling in New England and Some Lawes for Government* (London: Livewell Chapman, 1656), 15–16, which was likely derived from the Massachusetts Body of Liberties (1641), sec. 1. Both were derived from English constitutional history, in particular Magna Carta and its progeny.

[84] Connecticut became the only state to adopt a constitutional provision defining the rights of non-residents. North Carolina (Const. 1776, sec. XL), Pennsylvania (Const., 1776, sec. 42), and Vermont (Const. 1777, sec. XXXVIII) provided that foreigners, after taking an oath of allegiance, might acquire real estate, and after one year's residence, be deemed free citizens. See also Pa. Decl. 1776, Art. XV.

[85] Mainprize was the action of procuring the release of a prisoner on someone's undertaking to stand surety—a 'mainpernor'—for his or her appearance in court at a specified time.

[86] This paragraph originally appeared in a 1672 Connecticut revision of the laws, but was probably derived from section 18 of the Massachusetts Body of Liberties (1641). *The Public Statute Laws of the State of Connecticut*, Book 1 (Hartford: Hudson & Goodwin, 1808), 24.

Rhode Island

Roger Williams was to Rhode Island what William Penn was to Pennsylvania: a visionary founder of a refuge for persecuted religious dissidents. Banished from the Massachusetts Bay Colony in 1635 for religious heterodoxy, Williams purchased land from the Narragansett Indians and established a colony he named Providence. A brief "agreement" executed by "masters of families" in 1637 vested government authority in a majority of these householders with the all-important limitation that such control was to be exercised "only in civil things"[1]—a recognition of the separation of church and state and, by implication, religious toleration and liberty of conscience.[2]

In *The Bloody Tenent, of Persecution, for Cause of Conscience* (1644), Williams, quoting Martin Luther, gave full expression to this idea:

> …the *Lawes* of the *Civill Magistrates* government extends no further then over the *body* or *goods,* and to that which is *externall:* for over the *soule God* will not suffer any man to *rule:* onely he *himselfe* will rule there. Wherefore whosoever doth undertake to give *Lawes* unto the *Soules* and *Consciences*

[1] Providence Agreement (1637), in *Colonial Origins of the American Constitution: A Documentary History*, ed. Donald S. Lutz (Indianapolis: Liberty Fund, 1998), 161–162.

[2] The Providence Agreement foreshadowed fundamental principles that would provide the foundations for the republican constitutions adopted by former colonies in the wake of the Declaration of Independence.

P. J. Galie et al., *Bills of Rights Before the Bill of Rights*,
https://doi.org/10.1007/978-3-030-44301-6_17

> of Men, he usurpeth that *government* himselfe which appertaineth unto *God*, &c.[3]

Williams epitomized these beliefs in his phrase "soul liberty."

From its beginning, the colony attracted strong-willed, independent, individuals. Town independence preceded colonial unity. The original towns—Providence, Portsmouth, Newport, and Warwick—were founded, as historian Sydney V. James put it, "so that their inhabitants would not have to live with other people."[4] James aptly describes the precariousness of the founding:

> The establishment of Rhode Island was a process, including the formation of a cluster of towns, not just one, and gathering them into a colony with a character of its own. Nobody set out to do that in 1636 and nobody could be sure it had been done until about seventy years later.[5]

Local self-government and the fact that the colony covered a mere thirty square miles contributed to the democratic character of the settlements. Combined, they enabled freemen to exercise a high degree of control over government officials. That control took the form of instructions on specific issues and the use of the initiative and referendum.[6]

Initial attempts to provide a general government for the towns floundered on this independence, but a growing population necessitated the representative institutions that grew up alongside the direct democracy of the first agreement.[7] In March 1640/1641, the towns of Portsmouth and Newport joined in a federation, and the following year, the General Court of Election issued a founding document providing for representative government. The document also provided that "none bee accounted a Delinquent for *Doctrine*: Provided, it be not directly repugnant to ye

[3] *The American Republic: Primary Sources*, ed. Bruce Frohnen (Indianapolis: Liberty Fund, 2002), 46.

[4] *Colonial Rhode Island: A History* (New York: Charles Scribner's Sons, 1975), 13.

[5] James, *Colonial Rhode Island*, 1.

[6] John P. Kaminski, "Democracy Run Rampant: Rhode Island in the Confederation," in *The Human Dimensions of Nation Making: Essays on Colonial and Revolutionary America*, ed. James Kirby Martin (Madison: State Historical Society of Wisconsin, 1976), 244–246.

[7] A more detailed examination of the evolution of government structures in Rhode Island is provided by Sydney V. James, "Rhode Island: From Classical Democracy to British Province," *Rhode Island History* 43, no. 4 (November 1984): 119–127.

Government or Lawes established."[8] The same general court also passed an act protecting property rights:

> It is ordered, Established and Decreed, unanimouslie, that all men's Proprieties in their Lands of the Island, and the Jurisdiction thereof, shall be such, and soe free, that neyther the State nor any Person or Persons shall intrude into it, molest him in itt, to deprive him of anything whatsoever that is, or shall be within that, or any of the bounds thereof; and that this Tenure and Propriety of his therein shall be continued to him, or his, or to whomsoever he shall assign it for Ever.[9]

In 1643, Williams traveled to London to secure a charter he hoped would unite the mainland and island communities for the first time in a single body politic. The patent for the "Incorporation of Providence Plantations, in the Narraganset-Bay, in New England" granted by Parliament on March 14, 1643/1644, was the first legal recognition of the Rhode Island towns by the mother country.[10] It granted the inhabitants "full Power and Authority to rule themselves…by such a Form of Civil Government, as by voluntary consent of all, or the greater Part of them, they shall find most suitable to their Estate and Condition…."[11] The patent acted as a catalyst for the original towns and their inhabitants to create a systematized federal commonwealth.

The "Acts and Orders of 1647," drawn up pursuant to the 1643 patent, is considered Rhode Island's first constitution. It contained a bill of rights and provided for a "Democraticall" government, that is, a government "held by ye free and voluntarie consent of all, or the greater parte of the free Inhabitants."[12] Elaborate initiative and referendum procedures

[8] [Organization of the Government of Rhode Island] (1642), in Lutz, *Colonial Origins*, 173.

[9] Samuel Greene Arnold, *History of the State of Rhode Island and Providence Plantations*, 4th ed. (Providence: Preston & Rounds, 1899), 1:148.

[10] It was a patent granted by Parliament rather than a royal charter because Charles I had been forced to flee London.

[11] Patent for Providence Plantations (1643), in Thorpe, *Constitutions*, 6:3210.

[12] Acts and Orders of 1647, in Lutz, *Colonial Origins*, 185.

helped maintain that control.[13] The document contained a law of the land, or due process clause, derived from Magna Carta,[14] and provided for grand jury indictment and trial by jury, among other criminal procedure rights.[15] More generally, it incorporated the common law of England "so farr, as the nature and constitution of our place will admit."[16] The Acts and Orders concluded with a guarantee of religious liberty:

> …and otherwise than thus what is herein forbidden, all men may walk as their consciences perswade them, every one in the name of his God. And lett the Saints of the Most High walk in this Colonie without Molestation in the name of Jehovah, their God for Ever and Ever, &c., &c.[17]

The 1644 parliamentary patent and the 1647 Acts and Orders reflected principles set forth in Williams's *Bloody Tenent.* The government would:

- obey God's ordinance to "conserve the civil peace;"
- embody the principle that the "sovereign, original, and foundation of civil power lies in the people" who may erect a government that in their view will accomplish God's ordinance; and
- exercise "no more power, nor for no longer time, than the civil power, or people consenting and agreeing, shall betrust them with."[18]

Rhode Island displayed more compassion in its criminal justice than surrounding colonies. The 1647 acts exempted poor persons who stole

[13] John Russell Bartlett, ed., *Records of the Colony of Rhode Island and Providence Plantations, in New England* (Providence: A. Crawford Greene and Brother, 1856), 1:148–149. These procedures were repealed in 1650 and 1664. Ibid., 228–229; see also page 27 of volume two of that work.

[14] Bartlett, *Records of the Colony*, 1:157.

[15] Ibid., 198–200. In March 1668/1669, a law was enacted allowing indictees aid of an attorney "to plead any poynt of law that may make for the clearing of his innocencye." Bartlett, *Records of the Colony*, 2:239.

[16] Bartlett, *Records of the Colony*, 1:158.

[17] Ibid., 190. The same laws also allowed those of "different consciences" to affirm rather than swear an oath. Ibid., 181.

[18] Roger Williams, *Bloudy Tenent of Persecution for Cause of Conscience* (Macon, GA: Mercer University Press, 2001 [1644]), 154–155.

out of hunger from felony burglary prosecution[19] and prohibited imprisonment for debt.[20] A statute adopted three years later prohibited banishment as a punishment for any offense.[21]

Internally, centrifugal forces continued to threaten the colony; externally, the restoration of the monarchy under Charles II in 1660 put the colony's governing charter in jeopardy. The same Parliament that had been the source of the colony's legitimacy had also been responsible for deposing and executing Charles's father. These dangers prompted colony leaders to secure a royal charter in 1663. A landmark in Rhode Island's history, it would remain the constitution of Rhode Island for 180 years, surviving the colony's declaration of independence and ratification of the national Constitution.

The 1663 charter laid the foundations for "virtual self-government."[22] It established a self-governing colony wherein officials from the governor and assemblymen to most local public officials would be chosen directly in town meetings by the freemen or appointed annually by elected representatives. The charter also granted Rhode Islanders the rights found in the common law and English Constitution, providing that all subjects "shall have and enjoye all libertyes and immunityes of ffree and naturall subjects ... as if they, and every of them, were borne within the realme of England."[23] Such rights would have included the right to a trial by jury and the procedural protections afforded by the common law.

The capstone of liberties in the charter was the "full libertie in religious concernements."[24] The charter commanded: "noe person within the sayd colonye, at any tyme hereafter, shall bee any wise molested, punished, disquieted, or called in question, for any differences in opinione in matters of religion...."[25] Religious liberty was not new to the colony; it had been

[19] Bartlett, *Records of the Colony*, 1:167.

[20] Ibid., 181.

[21] Ibid., 229.

[22] David S. Lovejoy, *Rhode Island Politics and the American Revolution, 1760–1776* (Providence: Brown University Press, 1958), 69.

[23] Charter of Rhode Island and Providence Plantations (1663), in Thorpe, *Constitutions*, 6:3220.

[24] Ibid., 3212.

[25] Ibid., 3213.

an uncontested principle from the colony's inception. Noteworthy, however, was a rationale the Crown accepted in granting this freedom not available in England:

> *And whereas*, in theire humble addresse, they have ffreely declared, that it is much on their hearts (if they may be permitted), to hold forth a livlie experiment, that a most flourishing civill state may stand and best bee maintained...with a full libertie in religious concernements; and that true pietye rightly grounded upon gospell principles, will give the best and greatest security to sovereignetye, and will lay in the hearts of men the strongest obligations to true loyaltye....[26]

The charter vindicated Williams's commitment to the separation of church and state and absolute liberty of conscience. However, it did make a distinction between belief and action—a distinction all colonial communities embraced. The latter would be subject to the conditions that the subjects behave "peaceablie and quietlie, and not useing this libertie to lycentiousnesse and profanenesse nor to the civill injurye or outward disturbeance of others..."[27]

The "livlie experiment" referenced in the charter challenged or modified what had been an article of faith in the colonies, namely that well-ordered communities required the direct involvement of the state in religious matters. The founding would enable inhabitants to pursue "sober, serious and religious intentions, of godlie edifieing themselves, and one another, in the holie Christian ffaith and worship...."[28] The charter's claim that "true pietye rightly grounded upon gospell principles" would provide the greatest security to sovereignty and foster the strongest obligations in men indicated that even separatists like Williams considered a religious sensibility necessary for a well-ordered community.

After 1663, the colony became a haven for religious believers of all stripes: Baptists, Separatists, Antinomians (followers of Anne Hutchinson),[29] Quakers, Sephardic Jews, and Huguenots. However, in 1719, a

[26] Ibid., 3212.

[27] Ibid., 3213.

[28] Ibid., 3211.

[29] Antinomians held the moral law "not binding upon Christians, who are under the law of grace." David D. Hall, ed., *The Antinomian Controversy, 1636–1638: A Documentary History*, 2d ed. (Durham, NC: Duke University Press, 1990), 3.

religious test denied Catholics and non-Christians freeman status, suggesting even Rhode Island could not escape completely the pervasive and intense anti-Catholic sentiment widespread in the colonies.[30]

Along with its stirring commitment to religious liberty, the charter provided explicit and detailed protection for private property, granting colonists the freedom:

> to have, take, possesse, acquire and purchase lands, tenements...or any goods or chattels, and ...to lease, graunt...sell and dispose of, at their owne will and pleasure, as other... people of this our realme of England...[31]

Provisions permitting fishing off the coast of New England and other adjoining bodies of waters traditionally trawled by the colonists and affording the right to travel throughout the rest of the English colonies were also included in the charter.[32] The charter provided for an elected assembly with members serving annual terms and seats apportioned by towns,[33] affirming the precedence of these historically important entities over equality of representation.

The Right to Vote and the Charter

The charter did not establish suffrage requirements; rather, it authorized the assembly to "choose, nominate, and apoynt" the freemen of the colony.[34] Having the status of a freeman meant more than having the right to vote. Only freemen could hold office, sit on a jury, or initiate lawsuits. Rhode Island made a distinction between a freeman of a town and a freeman of the colony. Freemen of the towns could not vote to elect deputies to the colonial assembly.[35] Each town separately determined

[30] This animus toward Catholics derived from the religious divisions unleashed by the Reformation. Protestant reformers identified Catholicism with support of monarchical government, allegiance to a foreign power (papacy), and the Inquisition. For reformed Protestants—Congregationalists and Presbyterians—there would be no Lords—spiritual or temporal. By 1798, the religious test was completely removed.

[31] Charter of Rhode Island and Providence Plantations, 3213.

[32] Ibid., 3219, 3221.

[33] Ibid., 3216.

[34] Ibid., 3215.

[35] Bartlett, *Records of the Colony*, 2:113.

town freemanship; the general assembly conferred colony-wide freemanship to persons recommended by town officials. In 1723, the assembly adopted a freehold specification for town freemanship, and made all town freemen eligible to vote for deputies to the assembly.[36] Holding public office—a right reserved for freemen—was also a duty. Freemen in Rhode Island could lose their freeman status if they refused to serve in office,[37] further evidence of the correlative nature of rights and duties in early America.

In 1666, the colony adopted a bicameral legislature,[38] effectively balancing the strong commitment to the independence of the towns with pursuit of a colony-wide common good. By the first two decades of the eighteenth century, the towns had lost much of their autonomy and had accepted the duties and regulations given to them by the central government.[39]

Recognizing and Realizing Rights

The colony's practice did not always match its principles. As the leading student of Rhode Island's political and constitutional history, Patrick T. Conley, notes, "for nearly two centuries the spirit of Rhode Island's famed guarantee was violated because both colony and state imposed various civil disabilities and discriminatory policies upon religious minorities, especially Roman Catholics."[40] A religious test, added in 1719, denied

[36] Patrick T. Conley, "Rhode Island: Laboratory for the 'Lively Experiment'," in *The Bill of Rights and the States: The Colonial and Revolutionary Origins of American Liberties*, ed. Patrick T. Conley and John P. Kaminski (Madison, WI: Madison House, 1992), 144. Although scholarly assessments differ on the percentage of individuals meeting the eligibility requirement, one statistic showed that by 1760, upwards of 75 percent of male inhabitants were eligible to vote. See the detailed analysis and studies cited by Patrick T. Conley, *Democracy in Decline: Rhode Island's Constitutional Development, 1776–1841* (Providence: Rhode Island Historical Society, 1977), 49.

[37] Bartlett, *Records of the Colony*, 2:112–113.

[38] Ibid., 144.

[39] Sydney V. James, "Colonial Rhode Island and the Beginnings of the Liberal Rationalized State," in *Essays in Theory and History: An Approach to the Social Sciences*, ed. Melvin Richter (Cambridge, MA: Harvard University Press, 1970), 170.

[40] Conley, "Rhode Island: Laboratory for the 'Lively Experiment'," 131.

freeman status to Catholics and non-Christians-an act contrary to the protections of the 1663 charter.[41] In 1756, the colony demanded an oath of allegiance and abjuration, and administered these requirements to suspicious persons. Refusal to take the oath resulted in designation as a "Popish recusant" and confiscation of property. Rhode Island refused to naturalize Jews until 1798, and no Jew attained the status of a freeman of the colony during that time.[42]

During the first fifty years of the colony's existence, the towns adopted measures banning the enslavement of African Americans and Indians. Colonial historian Charles McLean Andrews called one of these laws "the first legislative act of emancipation in the history of the colonies."[43] Native Americans received similar protection, only to lose it following King Philip's War (1675–1678).[44] Slavery also reappeared after that war, with Rhode Island playing a major role in the slave trade.[45] In 1784, an Emancipation Act gave freedom to all children born to slave mothers after March 1, 1784. During the last quarter of the eighteenth century, most of the other newly independent states adopted similar laws.

[41] Ibid., 144. Conley chronicles the confused provenance of this provision:

> The statute was allegedly passed in the March 1663 session of the General Assembly. Its enactment then or at any time prior to 1719 is possible but highly improbable. No such statute appears in the original proceedings of the General Assembly for 1663, nor is it found in the preserved proceedings of any subsequent session.

"The Digest of 1798-The State's First Code of Law," Law Day Address delivered to Rhode Island Supreme Court, May 1998 (copy provided by Professor Conley). Nonetheless, as Conley concedes, the statute was reaffirmed three times between 1730 and 1767. Similar measures aimed at limiting full civil rights or limiting the right to hold office to Protestants appeared in numerous state constitutions adopted between 1776 and 1790. See Table 4, pp. 76–78.

[42] Conley, "Rhode Island: Laboratory for the 'Lively Experiment'," 131.

[43] As quoted in Conley, "Rhode Island: Laboratory for the 'Lively Experiment'," 146.

[44] Conley describes these measures in more detail. Ibid., 147–150.

[45] Jay Coughtry, *The Notorious Triangle: Rhode Island and the African Slave Trade, 1700–1807* (Philadelphia: Temple University Press, 1981).

Constitutional Revision, Courts, and the Protection of Rights

The charter of 1663 made no provision for its revision, giving rise to a fundamental constitutional issue after the colony declared its independence from Great Britain: Who possessed the power to alter the charter? The charter authorized the legislature to establish the structures of government—the right of self-governance—but did not include the right or power to amend the charter, nor did it make any assertions of popular sovereignty. Nonetheless, the assembly, without specifically amending or purporting to void the charter, approved the Declaration of Independence, a document proclaiming a commitment to popular sovereignty, and agreed to join the Articles of Confederation. On what authority were these decisions made? There was no referendum, convention, or special election by the freemen: The general assembly, on its own authority, altered the source of sovereign power in the charter.

A second related question also remained unanswered: Who was responsible for enforcing the charter's provisions against violators? One answer arose in the context of Rhode Island's response to the financial collapse and depression of the 1780s. That crisis sparked debtor relief measures, including the issuance of paper money—with nothing of value to back it up—that could be used to pay taxes and debts. This measure met with resistance from merchants and creditors. The assembly passed laws punishing those who refused to accept the paper currency and establishing special non-jury courts to try violators, from which there was no appeal. In the case of *Trevett v. Weeden* (1786), the state's highest court heard a challenge to the provision of the law permitting non-jury trials on the ground that, among others, the law violated the fundamental right to a trial by jury. The defendant argued that it was the duty of judges to declare such an action void (judicial review). By implication, the argument was a critique of the charter, which gave the legislature power to select and retain judges—powers that clashed with the goal of an independent judiciary. The judges, though receptive to the defendant's claims (a few expressed the view that the law was unconstitutional), refused to decide the constitutional issue and dismissed the suit on jurisdictional grounds.[46]

[46] Patrick T. Conley provides insightful analysis of the case in "Rhode Island's Paper Money Issue and Trevett v. Weeden (1786)," *Rhode Island History* 30, no. 2 (Summer 1971): 95–108. Other courts would soon take that step. By the end of the eighteenth

A Constitutional Declaration of Rights?

Rhode Island's decision not to call a convention to create a new state constitution meant that if the state wished to add a declaration of rights similar to those found in other states, statute law would be its only option. The opportunity to take that step arose when the national Constitution proposed by the 1787 Constitutional Convention came before the states for ratification. Congress had requested the states to call conventions to consider ratification of the proposed Constitution. The Anti-Federalists who controlled the state legislature in Rhode Island repeatedly refused to do so, at one point submitting the Constitution to a referendum (where it was handily defeated).[47] Facing the prospect of exclusion from the Union, the general assembly, on January 17, 1790, agreed to convene a convention–the first in the state's history.

When the convention opened on March 1, 1790, the U.S. Constitution had been in effect for 20 months.[48] The convention took action on three separate questions, recorded in its "Form of Ratification and Amendments 29 May 1790."[49]

The convention recommended that "previous to the adoption of the federal Constitution, there be a Declaration, or Bill of Rights, asserting and securing from encroachments the essential and inalienable rights of the people of this state."[50] That declaration consisted of eighteen articles that were nearly identical in substance and numbering to the amendments proposed to the U.S Constitution by the Virginia Ratifying Convention

century, state courts were asserting the power to judge the constitutionality of government actions. See Scott Douglas Gerber's monograph, *A Distinct Judicial Power: The Origins of an Independent Judiciary, 1606–1787* (New York: Oxford University Press, 2011), wherein he argues that assertions of the power of judicial review were more likely to be made in states with the strongest commitment to judicial independence.

[47] Center for the Study of the American Constitution, University of Wisconsin-Madison, "The Rhode Island State Referendum on the Constitution," https://csac.history.wisc.edu/states-and-ratification/rhode-island/referendum/, accessed December 13, 2019.

[48] The Constitution became effective on June 21, 1788, upon ratification by the ninth state, New Hampshire.

[49] John P. Kaminski, et al., eds., *The Documentary History of the Ratification of the Constitution*, vol. 26, *Ratification of the Constitution by the States: Rhode Island (3)* (Madison: Wisconsin Historical Society Press, 2013), 996.

[50] Preamble to Drafting Committee's Report, quoted in Kevin D. Leitao, "Rhode Island's Forgotten Bill of Rights," *Roger Williams Law Review* 1, no. 1 (Spring 1996): 44.

in 1788.[51] The delegates' rationale appeared to be: Before we ratify the Constitution, we should proclaim the rights of Rhode Islanders. Delegates claimed the rights in their declaration were "consistent with the Constitution" and could not "be abridged or violated." For these reasons, no action on the part of the national government was required and delegates requested none.[52]

The second order of business involved the twelve amendments to the Constitution that Congress had submitted to the states for ratification. The convention recommended ratification of all "except the second article…."[53] There is no evidence that Rhode Island considered the amendments adopted by Congress a "Bill of Rights."[54] Finally, the convention recommended twenty-one amendments to various articles of the U.S. Constitution, nearly all of which focused on protecting the state's sovereignty by limiting the powers of the national government.[55] This latter recommendation took the form of exhorting Rhode Island's future senators and representatives to work assiduously toward their adoption.

If delegates intended the eighteen-article declaration to be a statement of the rights of the citizens of Rhode Island, what was its legal status? After declaring independence, Rhode Island did not adopt a constitution—content to retain its "unamendable" colonial charter. For that reason, the status of the declaration was problematic. Kevin Leitao contends that although the convention did not have a mandate to adopt a declaration, approval by the convention and ratification by the town freemen constituted an explicit, formal assertion of popular sovereignty that conferred the stamp of legitimacy on the declaration.[56]

[51] Kaminski, *Ratification of the Constitution by the States: Rhode Island (3)*, 997–1000.

[52] Ibid., 999.

[53] The rejected amendment concerned congressional pay. It became the Twenty-Seventh Amendment in 1992. Rhode Island ratified the remaining eleven amendments, ten of which were ratified by the requisite number of states in 1791, and subsequently became known as the "Bill of Rights."

[54] Some state ratifying bodies did not even consider the twelve amendments as a package. Pauline Maier, *Ratification: The People Debate the Constitution, 1787–1788* (New York: Simon & Schuster, 2010), 460–461.

[55] These amendments are available in Kaminski, *Ratification of the Constitution by the States: Rhode Island (3)*, 1000–1002.

[56] Leitao, "Rhode Island's Forgotten Bill of Rights," 34–35. The leading student of Rhode Island's constitutional history, Patrick T. Conley, calls Leitao's conclusion "faulty." Patrick T. Conley and Robert G. Flanders Jr, *The Rhode Island State Constitution* (New

Whatever the merits of the case for a "forgotten Bill of Rights,—forgotten it was—by the courts and the legislature. No record of the declaration exists in the state's statutes or digests of the law. Leitao summed up its curious history:

> [E]xisting accounts of the 1790 convention reveal that the State of Rhode Island has a forgotten bill of rights enacted by the people in the constitutional convention which ratified the United States Constitution. This Declaration of Rights was the first constitutional document created by the sovereign people of Rhode Island. Once ratified, the Declaration of Rights of the People of Rhode Island fell into virtual total obscurity. There is no record of any enforcement of rights under it.[57]

Postscript: In 1798, the Rhode Island assembly authorized the creation of a digest of state laws.[58] It did not contain the declaration of rights adopted by the state convention in 1790 but did contain Rhode Island's first statutory bill of rights—"An Act Declaratory of Certain Rights of the People of this State"[59] containing ten sections that defined the criminal procedure rights available to Rhode Islanders. The digest also consisted of a declaration that the common law was "to continue to be in force"

York: Oxford University Press, 2011), 309. Conley interprets the convention's action as follows:

> This declaration was clearly an expression of concern by the ratifying convention's Antifederal majority to the United States Congress regarding the threat to liberty posed by the new government of the United States. A textual and contextual analysis of the document can yield no other conclusion. No one at that time or since considered it otherwise, and the General Assembly (which never ratified the 1790 declaration) neither included it in the public laws nor based its 1798 statutory bill of rights upon it. The Declaration of Rights did indeed apply to the "people of the state," but it was intended to protect them not from their local officials but from the novel and distant central government whose potential appetite for power was then unknown.

Conley, "Digest of 1798." How the declaration would accomplish this is not clear. If Professor Conley is correct, the declaration was a *cri di coeur* from a colony facing draconian retribution from the national government if it failed to ratify the Constitution.

57 Leitao, "Rhode Island's Forgotten Bill of Rights," 32.

58 *The Public Laws of the State of Rhode-Island and Providence Plantations* (Providence: Carter & Wilkinson, 1798), 75.

59 Ibid., 79–81.

where not modified or abolished.[60] Also adopted was "An Act Relative to Religious Freedom, and the Maintenance of Ministers," which included the statement that "our civil rights have no dependence on our religious opinions,"[61] in effect prohibiting religious requirements as a condition for office-holding or voting in the state.

In 1843, Rhode Island adopted its first indigenous constitution. Article I of that constitution, a "Declaration of Certain Constitutional Rights and Principles," gave constitutional status to rights, a fitting capstone to the state's long tradition of liberty and independence.

Declaration of Rights Adopted by Constitutional Convention [1790][62]

1. That there are certain natural rights, of which men, when they form a social compact, cannot deprive or divest their posterity,— among which are the enjoyment of life and liberty, with the means of acquiring, possessing and protecting property, and pursuing and obtaining happiness and safety.[63]
2. That all power is naturally vested in and consequently derived from the people: That magistrates, therefore, are their trustees and agents, and at all times amenable to them.[64]
3. That the powers of government may be reassumed by the people, whensoever it shall become necessary to their happiness:— That the rights of the States respectively to nominate and appoint

[60] Ibid., 78.

[61] Ibid., 82.

[62] This declaration of rights, the last one proposed by a state government prior to ratification of the national Bill of Rights, epitomized the rights tradition found in the declarations of rights adopted by the states between 1776 and 1790. It is available in Kaminski, *Ratification of the Constitution by the States: Rhode Island (3)*, 997. Taken almost entirely from amendments proposed to the U.S. Constitution by the Virginia Ratifying Convention, the Rhode Island declaration does not include any rights that had not previously appeared in earlier state declarations.

[63] Similar to Amendment 1 proposed to the U.S. Constitution by the Virginia Ratifying Convention, June 27, 1788 (Va. Ratifying Conv.). The amendments proposed by the Virginia ratifying convention can be found online at: http://www.let.rug.nl/usa/documents/1786-1800/the-anti-federalist-papers/amendments-proposed-by-the-virginia-convention-(june-27-1788)-.php.

[64] Similar to Va. Ratifying Conv., amend. 2.

all State officers, and every other power, jurisdiction and right, which is not by the said Constitution clearly delegated to the Congress of the United States, or to the departments of government thereof, remain to the people of the several States, or their respective State governments, to whom they may have granted the same;—and that those clauses in the said Constitution which declare that Congress shall not have or exercise certain powers, do not imply, that Congress is entitled to any powers not given by the said Constitution;—but such clauses are to be construed, as exceptions to certain specified powers, or as inserted merely for greater caution.[65]

4. That religion, or the duty which we owe to our Creator, and the manner of discharging it, can be directed only by reason and conviction, not by force or violence-and therefore all men have an equal, natural, and unalienable right to the free exercise of religion, according to the dictates of conscience;—and that no particular religious sect, or society, ought to be favoured or established by law, in preference to others.[66]
5. That the legislative, executive and judiciary powers of government, should be separate and distinct;—and that the members of the two first may be restrained from oppression, by feeling and participating the public burdens, they should at fixed periods be reduced to a private station, return into the mass of the people, and the vacancies be supplied by certain and regular elections-in which all or any part of the vacancies be supplied by certain and regular elections, in which all or any part of the former members to be eligible or

[65] Similar to Ratification of the Constitution by the State of New York; July 26, 1788. The detailed limits on any congressional power and the assertion of states' rights targeted the enumerated powers of the national Constitution. Prohibiting the federal government from taking certain action did not imply that it would be able to take other actions not so limited. Since the national government was a government of enumerated powers, powers not enumerated would be beyond its legal authority. States did not think this limitation, standing alone, would suffice, thus Article 3. If it were meant to be part of the state law, as Leitao argues, its effect would have been largely symbolic, as the Supremacy Clause would take precedence.

[66] Similar to Va. Ratifying Conv., amend. 20.

ineligible, as the rules of the Constitution of government and the laws shall direct.[67]

6. That elections of Representatives in Legislature ought to be free and frequent-and all men, having sufficient evidence of permanent common interest with and attachment to the community, ought to have the right of suffrage: And no aid, charge, tax or fee, can be set, rated or levied upon the people, without their own consent, or that of their Representatives, so elected;—nor can they be bound by any law, to which they have not, in like manner, assented for the public good.[68]
7. That all power of suspending laws, or the execution of laws, by any authority, without the consent of the Representatives of the people in the Legislature, is injurious to their rights, and ought not be exercised.[69]
8. That in all capital and criminal prosecutions, a man hath a right to demand the cause and nature of his accusation—to be confronted with the accusers and witnesses—to call for evidence, and be allowed counsel in his favour—and to a fair and speedy trial by an impartial jury of his vicinage, without whose unanimous consent he cannot be found guilty (except in the government of the land and naval forces) nor can he be compelled to give evidence against himself.[70]
9. That no freeman ought to be taken, imprisoned, or disseized of his freehold, liberties, privileges or franchises, our outlawed, or exiled, or in any manner destroyed, or deprived of his life, liberty or property, but by the trial by jury, or by the law of the land.[71]
10. That every freeman restrained of his liberty is entitled to a remedy, to enquire into the lawfulness thereof, and to remove the same,

[67] Verbatim from Va. Ratifying Conv., amend. 5. Article 5 tracked provisions mandating separation of powers and term limits found in other state constitutions.

[68] Verbatim from Va. Ratifying Conv., amend. 6. Articles 6 and 7 institutionalized the state's commitment to popular sovereignty and defined the requirements for membership in the body politic.

[69] Similar to Va. Ratifying Conv., amend. 7.

[70] Similar to Va. Ratifying Conv., amend. 8.

[71] Similar to Va. Ratifying Conv., amend. 9.

if unlawful;—and that such remedy ought not to be denied or delayed.[72]

11. That in controversies respecting property, and in suits between man and man, the ancient trial by jury, as hath been exercised by us and our ancestors, from the time whereof the memory of man is not to the contrary, is one of the greatest securities to the rights of the people, and ought to remain sacred and inviolate.[73]
12. That every freeman ought to obtain right and justice freely, and without sale-completely, and without denial,—promptly, and without delay—and that all establishments or regulations, contravening these rights, are oppressive and unjust.[74]
13. That excessive bail ought not to be required, nor excessive fines imposed, nor cruel or unusual punishments inflicted.[75]
14. That the people have a right peaceably to assemble together, to consult for their common good, or to instruct their Representatives;—and that every person has a right to petition, or apply to the Legislature, for redress of grievances.[76]
15. That every person has a right to be secure from all unreasonable searches and seizures of his person, his papers, or his property;—and therefore that all warrants to search suspected places, or seize any person, his papers, or his property, without information upon oath, or affirmation of sufficient cause, are grievous and oppressive;—and that all general warrants (or such in which the place or person suspected are not particularly designated) are dangerous, and ought not to be granted.[77]
16. That the people have a right to freedom of speech, and of writing and publishing their sentiments:—That freedom of the press is one of the greatest bulwarks of liberty, and ought not be violated.[78]

[72] Similar to Va. Ratifying Conv., amend. 10.

[73] Similar to Va. Ratifying Conv., amend. 11.

[74] Similar to Va. Ratifying Conv., amend. 12.

[75] In using "cruel or unusual punishment" rather than "cruel and unusual punishment," Rhode Island followed North Carolina (Decl. 1776, Art. X) and Maryland (Decl. 1776, Art. XXII), deviating from Va. Ratifying Conv., amend. 13.

[76] Similar to Va. Ratifying Conv., amend. 15.

[77] Similar to Va. Ratifying Conv., amend. 14.

[78] Similar to Va. Ratifying Conv., amend. 16.

17. That the people have a right to keep and bear arms:—That a well-regulated militia, including the body of the people capable of bearing arms, is the proper, natural, and safe defence of a free State:—that the militia shall not be subject to martial law, except in time of war, rebellion, or insurrection:—That standing armies in time of peace are dangerous to liberty, and ought not to be kept up, except in cases of necessity;—and that at all times the military should be under strict subordination to the civil power:—That in time of peace no soldier ought to be quartered in any house without the consent of the owner-and in time of war, only by the civil magistrate, in such manner as the law directs.[79]
18. That any person religiously scrupulous of bearing arms ought to be exempted, upon payment of an equivalent to employ another to bear arms in his stead.[80]

[79] Similar to Va. Ratifying Conv., amends. 17 and 18.

[80] Similar to Va. Ratifying Conv., amend. 19.

Epilogue

Rights Without Rebellion

During the mid-1780s, the country experienced widespread recession. Discontent over government economic policies that fell unequally on small farmers and debtors gave rise to petitions for relief. In response, seven states issued paper money (which depreciated the currency and made it easier for debtors to repay obligations), and several provided debt relief.[1]

In states where the petitions went largely unanswered and the economic crisis deepened, community-wide meetings were organized to air the grievances. When those efforts proved futile, in some cases protest took the form of mobilizing armed resistance, with self-styled "regulators" attempting to reignite the connection with the resistance and the extra-legal conventions called during the Revolutionary period. Rebel leaders understood their protests as a form of popular constitutionalism appealing to "alter or abolish" clauses in their constitutions. Government supporters responded: We have a constitutional republic deriving its authority from the will of the people. The dispute was not over popular sovereignty. It turned on the question: Who had legitimate claim to

[1] An examination of the states' responses to the fiscal crisis is provided in George William Van Cleve, *We Have Not a Government: The Articles of Confederation and the Road to the Constitution* (Chicago: University of Chicago Press, 2017), chapter 7.

P. J. Galie et al., *Bills of Rights Before the Bill of Rights*,
https://doi.org/10.1007/978-3-030-44301-6_18

pronounce the will of the people? Could there be multiple expressions of the sovereign will?[2]

The most well-known of these movements, Shays's Rebellion in 1786–1787, was an extension of the protests and resistance that had been plaguing Massachusetts since the adoption of its state constitution in 1780. During that rebellion, regulators stopped the Springfield courts from functioning, justifying the action as a remonstrance and pointing to Article VII of the Massachusetts Constitution (the alter or abolish clause). They demanded redress of grievances, not revolution. If the regulators were a majority of voters in 1786, arguably they were entitled to invoke the sovereignty of the people under Article VII. Pauline Maier asserts the resistance followed "the tradition of the early American crowds who defended the urgent interests of their communities when the lawful authorities failed to act ...only after the normal channels of redress had proven inadequate."[3]

With elements of the militia sympathetic to the protesters, the governor raised a private army and put down Shays's Rebellion. Upon ending the rebellion, the government's response was anything but draconian. Key leaders were prosecuted, two were hung, and Shays fled to Vermont, later to be pardoned; nearly all, however, were pardoned, and policies were adopted to alleviate their grievances.[4]

The discontent manifest in Shays's Rebellion was not confined to Massachusetts. In 1786, farmers in New Hampshire, responding to similar hard money policies, surrounded the legislature and demanded relief. The ensuing "Exeter Riots" ended the following day with no casualties and militant leaders receiving light sentences. The legislature called for a referendum on paper money that was soundly defeated by a three-to-one margin. Suffering under similar economic policies, citizens in Rhode Island obtained relief at the ballot box, with the legislature adopting the

[2] Christian G. Fritz, *American Sovereigns: The People and America's Constitutional Tradition Before the Civil War* (Cambridge: Cambridge University Press, 2008), 95. Fritz examines rebellion as an early attempt "by the people" to express its collective will. Ibid., 108–116.

[3] *From Resistance to Revolution: Colonial Radicals and the Development of American Opposition to Britain, 1765–1776* (New York: Alfred A. Knopf, 1972), 22.

[4] William Pencak, "'The Fine Theoretic Government of Massachusetts Is Prostrated to the Earth': The Response to Shays's Rebellion Reconsidered," in *In Debt to Shays: The Bicentennial of an Agrarian Rebellion*, ed. Robert A. Gross (Charlottesville: University Press of Virginia, 1993), 121.

most radical monetary policy in the confederation.[5] Seeking to broker the competing interests and sharp divisions, legislators in other states adopted compromises between the contending parties.[6]

By the 1780s, the homogeneous community, assumed by republican/Whig thinkers and Reformed Protestants to be the foundation of ordered liberty and republican government, had disappeared, replaced by a heterogeneous population fractured by religious, economic, and geographic interests. Summarizing the research on these developments, Robert Gross concluded: New England was experiencing revolution in every aspect of its life. This discontent extended to other states.[7]

Under such conditions, recognizing expressions of popular sovereignty would be no easy task. How could one differentiate between a protest that reflected the will of the community from a faction, a mob, or a dangerous insurrection? Under the condition of heterogeneity, how likely was it that a consensus would form on the judgment that the government had acted in violation of its fiduciary power to promote the commonweal and that resistance was the proper recourse?

Rights Without Rebellion: The New Order

Michael Lienesch's pronouncement on the impact of Shays's and other forms of unrest that "[t]he Constitution was secure, but rebellion had lost its legitimacy and had been relegated to the preconstitutional past"[8] captures the transition from our first tradition of rights to the "new order of the ages." Richard L. Bushman explored the loss of community as a consequence of an increasingly complex, expanding economy and demographic diversity.[9] Bruce H. Mann examined the shift in the handling

[5] One key means for enforcing these paper money policies imposed limitations on the right to a jury trial. These limitations were challenged in the Rhode Island case of *Trevett v. Weeden* (1786). See p. 378, above for discussion of this case.

[6] See Van Cleve, *We Have Not a Government*, 212.

[7] See Jack D. Marietta and G. S. Rowe, *Troubled Experiment: Crime and Justice in Pennsylvania, 1682–1800* (Philadelphia: University of Pennsylvania Press, 2006), 263–265.

[8] "Reinterpreting Rebellion: The Influence of Shays's Rebellion on American Political Thought," in Gross, *In Debt to Shays*, 182.

[9] *From Puritan to Yankee: Character and the Social Order in Connecticut, 1690–1765* (Cambridge, MA: Harvard University Press, 1967).

of arbitration from a voluntary communal process to "the pale imitation of legal adjudication."[10] Norma Basch found that notions of consent and social contract embedded in Revolutionary ideas made legal dissolution of marriage and divorce more acceptable, loosening community bonds and allowing for, if not encouraging, voluntary dissolution outside the law.[11] Thomas M. Doerflinger concludes that a vigorous spirit of enterprise and social mobility under conditions of adversities provided fertile soil for rapid economic development without establishing a cohesive business elite.[12] Nathan O. Hatch, following on his description of *The Democratization of American Christianity*,[13] demonstrates that, like the increased opportunities and choices in a dynamic and expanding economy, the Second Great Awakening created a "marketplace of religious choices," offering the possibility for Protestants to follow their consciences in choosing among a growing number of denominations.[14]

Of equal and lasting significance, the debate over paper money and debt relief gave rise to "new concerns about potential majority tyranny and interstate harms."[15] The treatment of Loyalists by Revolutionary governments provided further impetus for judicial intervention.[16] Those

[10] *Neighbors and Strangers: Law and Community in Early Connecticut* (Chapel Hill: University of North Carolina Press, 1987), 136.

[11] "From the Bonds of Empire to the Bonds of Matrimony," in *Devising Liberty: Preserving and Creating Freedom in the New American Republic*, ed. David Thomas Konig (Stanford: Stanford University Press, 1995), 223–229.

[12] *A Vigorous Spirit of Enterprise: Merchants and Economic Development in Revolutionary Philadelphia* (Chapel Hill: University of North Carolina Press, 1986).

[13] *The Democratization of American Christianity* (New Haven, CT: Yale University Press, 1989).

[14] "The Second Great Awakening and the Market Revolution," in Konig, *Devising Liberty*, 243.

[15] Van Cleve, *We Have Not a Government*, 212–213.

[16] Daniel J. Hulsebosch claims that the treatment of Loyalists during the Revolution provided the occasion and "inspired the justifications for the earliest examples in American courts of what is now called judicial review of legislation." "A Discrete and Cosmopolitan Minority: The Loyalists, the Atlantic World, and the Origins of Judicial Review," *Chicago-Kent Law Review* 81, no. 3 (2006): 826. James E. Pfander explores the role of state legislatures in fostering judicial intervention. States that seized Loyalists' property during the Revolution authorized judicial determinations of claims to post-forfeiture assets held by the state. "Sovereign Immunity and the Right to Petition: Towards a First Amendment Right to Pursue Judicial Claims Against the Government," *Northwestern University Law Review* 91, no. 3 (Spring 1997): 939.

concerns would provide new justifications for a more active judiciary as a safeguard against majority tyranny.[17]

The adoption of the national Constitution and Bill of Rights marked the end of America's experiment in Revolutionary constitution-making. A federal Union had been achieved, providing national security and the framework for a national economy. That establishment was not without its costs. The compromises on slavery proved too much for the Union to bear. The increasing number of states, along with their diversity and dynamism, undercut the communitarianism that was the *sine qua non* of active popular sovereignty.

The most dramatic of the devices offering citizens an opportunity to assert their will outside normal institutional channels were the "alter or abolish clauses" of the state constitutions. By the 1790s, the inspiration for and activation of these provisions had faded. Two states that rewrote their constitutions—Vermont in 1786 and Delaware in 1792—muted these clauses. Delaware relegated its clause to the preamble. Vermont confined the right to remove officials in "a constitutional manner by regular elections" (Decl. 1786, Art. VIII) and eliminated the word "abolish" from its declaration. Pennsylvania's 1790 constitution moved away from the hortatory and admonitory language of its 1776 constitution and closer to the national Constitution, both in form and substance.[18] Thermidor had set in.

By the end of the nineteenth century, state constitutions had incorporated additional and more accessible procedures for involving the public in constitutional revisions, chief among them a requirement that all constitutional changes must be approved by the people at popular referenda.[19] Revolutionaries, Anti-Federalists, abolitionists, suffragists, civil rights activists, feminists, gay rights advocates, and Black Lives Matter protestors enlarged the sense of constitutional possibility and moved the country towards expanded understandings of liberty, equality, and citizenship.

[17] Scott Douglas Gerber, *A Distinct Judicial Power: The Origins of an Independent Judiciary, 1606–1787* (New York: Oxford University Press, 2011).

[18] See pp. 124–125, 136–141.

[19] John J. Dinan, *The American State Constitutional Tradition* (Lawrence: University Press of Kansas, 2006), 29. See also his *Keeping the People's Liberties: Legislators, Citizens, and Judges as Guardians of Rights* (Lawrence: University Press of Kansas, 1998).

The apotheosis of popular sovereignty, evident in the first constitutions, proved a chimera. Its replacement, judicial review exercised by an independent judiciary and a tradition of civic participation—active citizens motivated by the constitutional principles and ideas found in the declarations—offered an alternative.[20] Far from perfect, it became our way of finding "proximate solutions to insoluble problems."[21]

[20] Elizabeth Beaumont chronicles the history of these movements in *The Civic Constitution: Civic Visions and Struggles in the Path Toward Constitutional Democracy* (New York: Oxford University Press, 2014), iv.

[21] Reinhold Niebuhr, *The Children of Light and the Children of Darkness: A Vindication of Democracy and a Critique of Its Traditional Defense* (New York: Charles Scribner's Sons, 1960), 118.

The manufacturer's authorised representative in the EU is Springer Nature Customer Service Centre GmbH, Europaplatz 3, 69115 Heidelberg, Germany. If you have any concerns regarding our products, please contact ProductSafety@springernature.com

Printed and bound by CPI Group (UK) Ltd, Croydon, CR0 4YY

22/09/2026

02220984-0009